University Teaching in Focus provides a foundational springboard for early career academics preparing to teach in universities. Focusing on four critical areas – teaching, curriculum, students, and quality/leadership – this succinct resource offers university teachers a straightforward approach to facilitating effective student learning. The book empowers university teachers and contributes to their career success by developing teaching skills, strategies, and knowledge, as well as linking theory to practice. Written in a clear and accessible style by internationally acclaimed experts, including international contributions from Sally Brown and Paul Blackmore, topics include:

- learning theories;
- assessment;
- discipline-based teaching;
- curriculum design;
- problem-based and work-integrated learning;
- effective classroom teaching; and
- flexible modes of delivery.

   The needs of diverse student groups are explored and the scholarship of teaching and learning is addressed within a quality and leadership framework. The book also makes reference to seminal works and current resources. Real-world cases illuminate the theoretical content and 'Your Thoughts' sections encourage reflection and adaptation to local contexts. *University Teaching in Focus* explores ways that teachers can effectively engage students in life-long learning, extending their capacity to solve problems, to enter the workforce, to understand their discipline, and to interact positively with others in a global community throughout their professional lives.

Lynne Hunt is Emeritus Professor, University of Southern Queensland and Adjunct Professor, University of Western Australia.

Denise Chalmers is Winthrop Professor and Director of the Centre for the Advancement of Teaching and Learning at the University of Western Australia.

University Teaching in Focus

A learning-centred approach

Edited by Lynne Hunt and Denise Chalmers

LONDON AND NEW YORK

Published in Australia and New Zealand by ACER Press, an imprint of
Australian Council for Educational Research Ltd
19 Prospect Hill Road, Camberwell
Victoria, 3124, Australia

This edition published 2013 by Routledge
2 Park Square, Milton Park, Abingdon, Oxon OX14 4RN

Simultaneously published in the USA and Canada
by Routledge
711 Third Avenue, New York, NY 10017

Routledge is an imprint of the Taylor & Francis Group, an informa business

British Library Cataloguing in Publication Data
A catalogue record for this book is available from the British Library

Library of Congress Cataloging in Publication Data
A catalog record for this book has been requested

ISBN: 978-0-415-64405-1 (hbk)
ISBN: 978-0-415-64406-8 (pbk)
ISBN: 978-0-203-07969-0 (e-bk)

Typeset in Baskerville and Frutiger-Light
by ACER Project Publishing

Printed and bound by CPI Group (UK) Ltd, Croydon, CR0 4YY

FOREWORD

Mantz Yorke

University Teaching in Focus draws on a number of theoretical propositions about teaching and learning as well as evidence for the effectiveness of teaching practices. What we have here is a 'thinking person's guide' – useful, because teaching is not a simple matter that can be expressed in a set of rules applicable to all circumstances. Rather, it has to be approached in terms of a set of principles to be applied in a manner appropriate to circumstances. Some approaches are more likely to meet with success than others, but none guarantees universal success. As Hunt, Chalmers and Macdonald indicate in Chapter 2, 'Effective teaching is the outcome of decision-making based on evidence arising from research, experience of teaching students in different contexts and responses to students' feedback. Good … teaching takes place when teachers create positive and effective learning experiences for their students.' Hence this book is much more than a set of prescriptions, as is evident from the invitations throughout its chapters to consider your own responses to the evidence.

Academics must have the double capability of discipline and teaching expertise. Whilst they possess the former as a matter of course, many will need to develop the latter and this book will help them. Of course, all academics who made their way through the educational system to get to their current positions have gained an appreciation of good and bad aspects of teaching. This can, however, lead to experience being mistaken for expertise. This book bridges the gap in ways that will help students to benefit from their programs of study. New teachers are not the only potential beneficiaries of the knowledge and expertise within the pages of this book – those who have been teaching for some time are also likely to find ideas for the development of their pedagogic practice. I can truthfully say that I have.

Higher education has broadened the demands on students in that the possession of a first degree is not the passport to a career that it once was. Looking at a list of expectations produced by the Confederation of British Industry (2011), I reflected that I left university having obtained a degree but with little of the 'extra' that employers currently demand from today's graduates. My time at university coincided with a participation rate of less than 10 per cent of the cohort of school-leavers, and the demand for graduates exceeded the supply. It was generally sufficient to pass the exams in order to gain graduate-level employment, and there was no pressure on teachers in respect of retention and completion – indeed, a high failure rate was often taken as evidence of an insistence on high academic standards. If students failed their assessments, then it must have been a reflection of their personal failings and nothing to do with the teaching that they had received. Things are very different today, and governments around the world are concerned to assure the standards of teaching in higher education. This book addresses such matters of quality assurance by focusing on the knowledge and skills that higher education teachers need to facilitate student learning.

I once used the phrase 'quality as moral purpose' (Yorke 2000, p. 21) in an unavailing attempt to turn the discourse relating to 'quality' away from procedures and technicalities associated with assurance and towards a focus on student development. After all, if student development is 'got right', then the assurance activities ought to pick up the achievement. Or, put another way, the key is for the institution and its organisational units to insist on a culture of learning, and to create and sustain the conditions for this to take place. The pressure on students, teachers and institutions to achieve rapid results (for example, as represented respectively in terms of grades, progression or completion and position in ranking tables) makes sustaining a commitment to 'learning goals' in preference to 'performance goals' (Dweck 1999) a considerable challenge.

The challenges for today's teachers in higher education are multidimensional. In addition to teaching their academic subjects, they are expected to facilitate the development in students of a broad slew of graduate attributes (or 'employability'). They also have to engage with a student body that is diverse in demographic background (for example, age, gender, ethnicity and disability) and mode of engagement (full-time, part-time or at a distance). The pressures are readily apparent. Resources, such as this book, that support teachers in their teaching roles have an important part to play in mitigating the pressures as well as contributing to the development of a satisfying level of expertise as a teacher.

However, teachers of today have an advantage over their predecessors, in that there is an ever-growing accumulation of evidence – well represented in the chapters of this book – regarding approaches that are likely to lead to success in their students. The style of this book emulates the student-centred approach espoused by providing theoretical, practical and memorable discussion to facilitate teaching and curriculum development. Angelo, for example, exhorts you to apply the parrot test: 'is there any way that a student could pass your subject simply through rote memorisation – or by plagiarising or cheating – and without demonstrating deep learning? If the answer is yes, then the subject fails the parrot test'.

The chapters in this book accord with the best of contemporary thinking about higher education, such as, for example, the conclusions reached by Pascarella and Terenzini (2005) regarding the value of active learning:

> With striking consistency, studies show that innovative, active, collaborative, and constructivist instructional approaches shape learning more powerfully, in some forms by substantial margins, than do conventional lecture-discussion and text-based approaches.
>
> (Pascarella & Terenzini 2005, p. 646)

Converting a conclusion of this sort back into teaching sessions suited to the specific educational context is the challenge addressed in *University Teaching in Focus*. It involves consideration of how to maximise student engagement in learning and the extent to which the proposed approach fits with other components of the curriculum, including assessment. Tales, not entirely apocryphal, of multiple demands across a program for student presentations and assessments based solely on the writing of essays illustrate a need to focus on a diverse range of assessment to enhance students' skill development.

Students often take time to 'get it' as regards the demands that higher education makes of them. The first year is particularly important in constructing a shared appreciation of expectations which include independence (and at times collaboration) in studying; a preparedness to engage actively with the subject matter; a willingness to go beyond mere regurgitation of received materials; the avoidance of plagiarism; and a commitment to learn from formative assessments. In a diverse student cohort none of these can be taken for granted. Newly enrolled students may have to unlearn some of their existing assumptions and practices. All this adds to the intriguing challenges for teachers in higher education which they will be able to face in an informed and considered manner after reading the overview of key issues provided in the chapters of this book.

Whilst teaching may, for some teachers, be an individual activity, the curriculum as a whole involves a collection of teachers. If that collection is a cohesive group, or perhaps a set of coherent sub-groups, then pedagogic advantages can accrue. Gibbs (2010) points to the benefit to teaching and learning that can arise from group discussion:

> Studies at Oxford Brookes University concerning why some subjects regularly produced better student performance than others found no differences in any quantitative measure of presage variables [i.e., funding, staff to student ratios, the quality of teaching staff and the quality of students]. However, a qualitative follow-up study found that the high performing subjects were characterised by healthy 'communities of practice' involving much discussion of how to solve

teaching problems so as to make the entire programme work well for students. In contrast, subjects with consistently low average marks were characterised by a corresponding lack of talking about teaching, and a fragmented focus on individual courses ...

(Gibbs 2010a, pp. 47–48)

The considerate institution, via its academic organisational units, does not leave its teachers to wrestle alone with the challenges of teaching and assessing. Indeed, most now offer foundation courses in teaching, for which this book has been written.

Whilst writing this foreword, I recalled the first single-handed transatlantic race that took place in 1960. The rules were simple – to cross the starting and finishing lines, but with an open choice of route. The sailors had to judge how to make best use of weather and wave, given the rig of their yacht and their own physical capabilities. What would be best for one would not necessarily be best for another. Of course, some actions would necessarily be determined by general principles of sailing. In regard to teaching, this story illustrates the importance of doing things in a way that combines the teacher's individuality with principles of teaching for charting a path to quality student learning. So, too, does an anecdote involving the celebrated psychologist Robert Sternberg:

Once, while listening to a lecture ... Sternberg marveled at how well the teacher was able to establish rapport and communicate with the audience. He commented to the person sitting next to him that he wished that he could deliver a lecture so effectively. She looked at him for a moment and then commented, 'He does it his way; you do it your way.' Her point was right on target. Each person has to find his or her own path. There is no one path that works for everyone.

(Sternberg & Grigorenko 2000, p. 9)

May all who read this book find a personal path that gives a sense of achievement through the successes of their students, together with the satisfaction of a job well done.

CONTENTS

FIGURES

TABLES

CASES

Lynne Hunt is Emeritus Professor, University of Southern Queensland and Adjunct Professor, University of Western Australia. She has taught at all levels from transition to university to doctoral supervision in social science, education and health science departments and worked as Associate Dean (Teaching and Learning) at Edith Cowan University, Leader of the Teaching and Learning Development Group at Charles Darwin University and Pro Vice-Chancellor (Learning and Teaching) at the University of Southern Queensland.

She received an Australian Executive Endeavour Award in 2009 and won the 2002 Australian Award for University Teaching in the Social Science category and the 2002 Prime Minister's Award for Australian University Teacher of the Year. She was a member of the Board of the Australian Learning and Teaching Council and two of its subcommittees from its inception in August 2004 until March 2008.

Denise Chalmers is Winthrop Professor and Director of the Centre for the Advancement of Teaching and Learning at the University of Western Australia with responsibility for academic and professional development related to teaching and learning, including postgraduate teaching, curriculum development, e-learning and evaluation of teaching. Prior to this she was a foundation Director at the Carrick Institute for Learning and Teaching in Higher Education (renamed the Australian Learning and Teaching Council) and Director of the Teaching and Educational Development Institute at the University of Queensland. She is President of the Council of Australian Directors for Academic Development.

She has been a leader or team member of several projects on identification and implementation of indicators and measures of impact on teaching preparation programs in higher education, rewarding and recognising quality teaching in higher education through systemic implementation of indicators and metrics on teaching and teachers' effectiveness, teaching large classes, training, support and management of sessional teaching staff, and strategies for effective dissemination of project outcomes.

ABOUT THE CONTRIBUTORS

(listed alphabetically)

Tom Angelo is Professor of Higher Education, Founding Director of the Curriculum, Teaching and Learning Centre, and Pro Vice-Chancellor (Curriculum and Academic Planning) at La Trobe University. He also directs the Design for Learning Project, an ambitious revision and redesign of La Trobe's entire undergraduate curriculum. He has served as university teacher, academic developer, academic manager and researcher in the United States of America, New Zealand and Australia and has consulted on teaching, assessment, and learning improvement in 18 countries and all 50 of the United States. His primary interests are in design and evaluation of curriculum and formative assessment of learning.

Christine Asmar is Senior Lecturer in Indigenous Higher Education at Murrup Barak, the Melbourne Institute for Indigenous Development, at the University of Melbourne. Her research has long focused on Indigenous issues in higher education, and her Teaching Fellowship from the Australian Learning and Teaching Council enabled her to develop new web resources for Indigenous teaching. She coordinates Melbourne's Summer School for Indigenous Postgraduate Students from around Australia, and continues to work collaboratively to advance Indigenous teaching and research, within and beyond her institution.

Michelle Barker is Professor of International Business and Asian Studies, Griffith Business School, and Senior Fellow, Griffith Institute for Higher Education. Her professional and academic career has centred on intercultural capacity building of university students, teachers and professional staff. She leads research on internationalisation of the curriculum and the ExcelL (Excellence in Cultural Experiential Learning and Leadership) Intercultural Skills Program. Michelle won the 2003 Australian Award for University Teaching for the ExcelL Program, the 2005 Individual Teacher Award (Law, Economics, Business) and an Australian Endeavour Executive Award in 2011. She is International Fellow, Leeds Metropolitan University, and International Fellow, Centre for Applied Cross-Cultural Research, University of Victoria, Wellington.

Paul Blackmore is Professor of Higher Education and Director of King's Learning Institute at King's College London, where he has been since 2007. Before this he was Professor of Higher Education and Director of the Centre for the Study of Higher Education at Coventry University. In 1995, he established the Centre for Academic Practice at the University of Warwick, which he directed for more than 10 years. In 1996, he established the national Standing Conference on Academic Practice, a group with a shared interest in a holistic view of academic expertise. His research interests are in the conceptualisation and exploration of professional expertise, including its social dimensions, particularly leadership roles in academic settings. Paul has published about 60 articles and book chapters. He co-edited *Towards Strategic Staff Development in Higher Education* in 2003. His most recent book, *Strategic Curriculum Change in Universities: Global trends,* draws from a major international study of curriculum change in research-intensive institutions. Paul is a member of the Society for Research into Higher Education's Governing Council and a co-convenor of its Academic Practice Network.

Lyn Brodie is Associate Professor in the Faculty of Engineering and Surveying, University of Southern Queensland, where she has implemented major curriculum change by designing problem-based learning (PBL) for a large, diverse and online cohort of students. She has also developed training programs to introduce teaching staff to the use of PBL in online learning environments. Her innovative work has been recognised through two Australasian Association for Engineering Education Excellence awards, an Australian Carrick Citation and a National Carrick Award for Programs that Enhance Learning.

Christine Broughan is Head of Applied Research within the department of Student Services at Coventry University. She teaches Psychology for the University of Oxford and the Open University. She has a key role in exploring the progression and achievement of minority student groups, and works with international partners to develop an inclusive approach to teaching, learning and assessment to improve the student learning experience in higher education.

Sally Brown is Emeritus Professor at Leeds Metropolitan University and was Pro Vice Chancellor (Academic) until July 2010. She is also Adjunct Professor at the University of the Sunshine Coast, Queensland, Visiting Professor at the University of Plymouth and an independent consultant. She is Senior Fellow of the Higher Education Academy, Fellow of the Staff and Educational Development Association, and a United Kingdom National Teaching Fellow. She is widely published in the field of teaching, learning and assessment and a frequent workshop facilitator and keynote speaker at conferences and events in the UK and internationally.

Michael Christie is Professor of Education at Charles Darwin University where he works on collaborative research and consultancies which involve and examine interactions between western and Australian Aboriginal knowledge practices. The Yolngu (north east Arnhemland Aboriginal) studies program, which he developed in collaboration with Yolngu elders, won the Australian Prime Minister's award for the best tertiary teaching program in Australia in 2005. He was a National Fellow of the Australian Learning and Teaching Council in 2009, during which time he developed and implemented a program for Aboriginal elders on traditional land in very remote places to teach their languages and culture to tertiary students around the world, using new information and communication technologies.

Jonathan Garnett is Dean of the Institute for Work Based Learning and Professor of Work Based Knowledge at Middlesex University, London. Jonathan has over 19 years experience at the leading edge of the development and operation of work-integrated learning at higher education level (certificate to doctorate) with public and private sector organisations in the UK and internationally. Current research interests include the development and use of university-level work-integrated learning to enhance the intellectual capital of organisations.

Mick Healey is a higher education consultant and researcher and Emeritus Professor at the University of Gloucestershire. He is an Honorary Professor at the University of Queensland and a Visiting Professor at Edinburgh Napier University and the University of Wales Newport. He was one of the first people in the United Kingdom to be awarded a National Teaching Fellowship and be made a Senior Fellow of the Higher Education Academy. He has published more than 150 articles and presented more than 350 workshops and keynotes in Australasia, Europe and North America. He is co-editor for the *International Journal for Academic Development*.

Alan Jenkins has long taught and researched geography and contemporary China studies in higher education in the UK and North America. He was a founding editor of the international *Journal of Geography in Higher Education*. He is now an educational developer and researcher on higher education and Emeritus Professor at Oxford Brookes University, UK. His current main area of expertise is on the relations between teaching and discipline-based research and on adapting and mainstreaming US-style undergraduate research programs to other national systems. He has done a range of research studies in this area and many consultancies and workshops internationally.

Kerri-Lee Krause is Pro Vice-Chancellor (Education), University of Western Sydney. She is internationally recognised for her research on the contemporary undergraduate student experience and implications for quality and standards in institutional settings, and the evolving nature of academic work. Her leadership role connects the quality of the student experience and outcomes with capacity-building for academic staff responsible for curriculum enhancement.

Ray Land is Professor of Higher Education and Director of the Centre for Learning, Teaching and Research in Higher Education at Durham University. He previously held similar roles at the Universities of Edinburgh, Coventry and Strathclyde. He is a Fellow of the Royal Society of Arts, the Staff and Educational Development Association, and the Higher Education Academy. His research interests include educational development, threshold concepts and troublesome knowledge, research-teaching linkages, and theoretical aspects of digital learning. Recent books include *Threshold Concepts within the Disciplines* and *Threshold Concepts and Transformational Learning*.

Ranald Macdonald is Emeritus Professor in Academic Development at Sheffield Hallam University, UK, following early retirement in 2009 and works as a freelance higher education consultant. He is a UK Staff and Educational Development Association Senior Fellow and UK National Teaching Fellow. His current work includes support for early career academics, promoting variety in academic development practices, challenging approaches to assessment and plagiarism, and supporting educational change at all levels. He has run workshops, given keynotes and acted as an advisor in many countries.

Lee Partridge is Assistant Professor and academic developer at the Centre for the Advancement of Teaching and Learning at the University of Western Australia. With a background in science and education, she now works primarily with early career academics. She has been recognised by her institution and in national awards for her contribution to teaching, learning and the student experience. Her research interests encompass diverse aspects of the student experience including educational development, academic integrity and undergraduate research.

Phil Race started as a scientist, before becoming an educational developer working at the University of Glamorgan, University of Leeds then Leeds Metropolitan University, where he remains Emeritus Professor, as well as Visiting Professor at the University of Plymouth and at University Campus Suffolk at Bury St Edmunds. In 2007, the UK Higher Education Academy awarded him a National Teaching Fellowship, and the status of Senior Fellow. In 2010 he was awarded the honour of European Educator of the Year by EuroChrie. His best-known books include *Making Learning Happen*, *The Lecturer's Toolkit* and *How to Get a Good Degree*.

Patricia M Reeves is Associate Professor of Social Work at the University of Georgia. Her research interests include psychosocial development during adolescence and adulthood, particularly the coping issues and processes of individuals living with HIV/AIDS and the protective and risk factors associated with violence and academic failure in adolescence. Her research is currently funded by the US Centers for Disease Control and Prevention. Winner of several teaching awards, she was inducted into the University of Georgia Teaching Academy in 2010.

Thomas C Reeves is Professor Emeritus of Learning, Design, and Technology at The University of Georgia. His research interests include evaluation, educational design research, authentic learning tasks, and education in developing countries. He works as an e-learning design and evaluation consultant for the World Health Organization and others. He is a Fellow of the Association for the Advancement of Computing in Education and the Australasian Society for Computers in Learning in Tertiary Education.

Martyn Stewart is an educational developer at Liverpool John Moores University and Fellow of the Higher Education Academy. He specialises in developing an evidence-based approach to tertiary teaching that utilises published research and institutional datasets to inform curriculum design. He started as a scientist and continues to teach geology alongside his educational development work. As well as geology research, he has published studies on student engagement and teaching complex knowledge. He is currently working on a major project examining the second-year student experience.

Keith Trigwell is Professor of Higher Education in the Institute for Teaching and Learning at the University of Sydney. He was previously Director of the Centre for Excellence in Preparing for Academic Practice and Reader in Higher Education at the University of Oxford. His research interests include investigating qualitative differences in university teaching and students' learning experiences, including development of the Approaches to Teaching Inventory, teaching–research relations and the scholarship of teaching. He is a former co-president of the International Society for the Scholarship of Teaching and Learning, and in 2010 received a Lifetime Achievement Award (Leadership) from the Society. He was coordinating editor of the international journal *Higher Education* from 2005 to 2011.

Mantz Yorke had a varied career in education before becoming a senior manager at the then Liverpool Polytechnic. He spent two years on secondment as Director of Quality Enhancement at the Higher Education Quality Council before returning to his institution as Director of the Centre for Higher Education Development, where he researched various aspects of the student experience. He has published widely on higher education, the bulk of his work encompassing the interlinked themes of student success, employability, assessment and retention. He is currently Visiting Professor in the Department of Educational Research, Lancaster University, UK.

INTRODUCTION

*Lynne Hunt and
Denise Chalmers*

Universities and governments throughout the world increasingly require university teachers to undertake qualifications and professional development programs to prepare them for their teaching roles. In some countries, such as the United Kingdom, Sweden and Norway, participation in teaching development programs is mandated. This textbook is designed to support foundational teaching development programs of this nature.

The book focuses on the key areas of teaching, curriculum, students, quality and leadership. It provides university teachers with a straightforward approach to facilitating effective undergraduate learning. It aims to empower university teachers by developing teaching skills, strategies and knowledge, and it seeks to contribute to the career success of university teachers. It achieves this by linking theories with practice and by providing easily accessible information and resources. The book provides succinct analyses of foundational knowledge and skills associated with core aspects of university teaching, looking at what university teachers need to know about students and what they need to know about teaching, curriculum, quality and leadership. Each chapter refers to influential works on the topic and provides good practice examples and strategies that have been used successfully by other university teachers. While this is a book for teachers, its focus is clearly on students, exploring ways that teachers can engage students effectively in lifelong learning, extending their capacity to solve problems, enter the workforce, understand their discipline and work positively with others in a diverse community.

The book acknowledges contemporary critiques of higher education that draw attention to the corporatisation of academia and the neo-conservatism inherent in discussion of matters such as regulation, standards, benchmarking and auditing. However, this book adopts a practical approach with the aim of supporting those involved with university teaching and learning in their current contexts. In so doing, it seeks to empower academics to lever corporate and quality assurance agendas to enhance university teaching. This does not imply an uncritical acceptance of agendas in higher education. Rather, the focus is sharply on university teaching and on providing the best possible learning experience for students.

An international perspective has been taken because university teachers and students work and study in a global context. This acknowledges that universities around the world have a shared commitment and responsibility to facilitate the learning of university students while operating in diverse cultural, political and economic environments. Accordingly, this book explores the broad principles and practice of university teaching so that readers can critically adapt them to their local higher education settings. The 'Your thoughts' sections and 'Cases' describe practices and applications, and provide opportunities to reflect on what might work with your students, in your subject, your university and your cultural and regional context.

PART 1
FOCUS ON TEACHING

University expectations about teaching have changed over the last quarter of a century. The traditional lecture and tutorial modes of teaching at universities have been challenged by student-centred pedagogies. In popular parlance, the so-called 'sage on the stage' has been replaced by the 'guide on the side', but this risks a marginalised role for university teachers who have considerable discipline and practice-based expertise to offer. Accordingly, Part 1 of this book recognises the centrality of the processes and practices of teaching. It is an approach that draws on McWilliam's (2008) description of teachers as 'meddlers in the middle' and Cousin's 'transactional curriculum inquiry', which is 'neither student-centred nor teacher-centred but something more active, dynamic and in-between' (2009, p. 270).

Students agree that university teachers do matter. Scott (2005) reported that students want capable and responsive staff, drawing from his analysis of comments from some 95 000 students who had recently completed their university studies. Yet there is no single approach or method of teaching that will work well in every context. Effective teaching involves a thoughtful approach that addresses questions about what works best for a particular student cohort, a particular discipline and specified learning purposes.

Part 1 provides a focus on teaching, starting with Martyn Stewart's succinct overview of learning theories. Chapter 1 explores groups of theories that describe different aspects of learning. It introduces the language and core principles of learning theory and provides a framework for university teachers to analyse why they choose to teach as they do and how they might enhance their practice.

In Chapter 2, Lynne Hunt, Denise Chalmers and Ranald Macdonald establish the theme – continued throughout the book – that the point of teaching is to facilitate students' learning. They focus on face-to-face classroom teaching while acknowledging that the qualities of good teaching prevail no matter the mode of delivery. Drawing on an international evidence base, they identify what

1

makes teachers effective and how to design effective learning environments with particular reference to small and large group teaching.

University teachers and their students are bound by a passion for the discipline they study, and the associated research. In Chapter 3, Ray Land builds on this idea to explore 'signature ways of thinking and practising', noting that all disciplines have key 'threshold' concepts that must be understood to transform students' thinking. Successful negotiation of the thresholds opens conceptual terrain and provides access to new academic discourses.

In Chapter 4, Denise Chalmers and Lee Partridge move beyond discipline-based teaching to a focus on students' graduate attributes, which are the 'discipline specific knowledge and skills, broader professional and attitudinal dispositions related to the discipline, and the academic skills that underpin effective learning and inquiry'. They outline stand-alone and embedded approaches to teaching them and offer a range of teaching strategies that will enable students to demonstrate that they have acquired their university's specified graduate qualities.

Assessment is integral to students' learning and to student retention in their degree programs. In their discussion of fit-for-purpose, effective assessment, in Chapter 5, Sally Brown and Phil Race identify a range of tactics that attune assessment and feedback to student's learning. The chapter covers the qualities and purpose of assessment and it explores what and how to assess students' work, with particular reference to authentic assessment.

Together, the five chapters provide a focus on the importance of engaging students actively in their own learning.

CHAPTER 1

UNDERSTANDING LEARNING: THEORIES AND CRITIQUE

Martyn Stewart

Keywords
learning theories, behaviourism, constructivism, cognitive development, social learning, self concept

Theories of learning arise from multiple disciplines: philosophy of education, psychology, pedagogic studies, sociology and, more recently, neuroscience. This variety of feeder disciplines provides a rich understanding of learning. It also presents us with a complex evidence base and mix of interpretations with contrasting vocabularies and epistemologies that lead to debate and controversy. This chapter introduces the main groups of learning theories and key debates. It introduces terms such as 'constructivism' and 'behaviourism' that you may encounter in teaching and learning literature and it explores practical applications arising from the theories. The purpose of the chapter is to empower you to participate in conversations about pedagogy and to analyse the implications of learning theories for your discipline, your teaching and your students. An understanding of learning theories, their applications, limitations and their continuing refinement provides you with a powerful vocabulary and framework for organising thinking and making sense of the challenging demands of university teaching.

Towards contemporary theories of learning

Prior to the early 20th century, most educational thinking focused on philosophical debates about the nature of learning (see Palmer 2001). A key thinker was the progressive educationalist John Dewey, who railed against the authoritarian, rote learning, drilling approach that characterised teaching of the age that prioritised facts over understanding. He argued that this model did nothing for children's sense of exploration or growth. Students should be active in the learning process, and education should engage and enlarge experience. He made an incalculable impact on education systems, and his ideas reverberate in our current understanding about how students of all ages learn.

Learning by association: behaviourist perspectives

From the early 20th century the advancement of science brought a new empirical approach to the study of learning. Characterised by experimentation, much involved the investigation of animal learning behaviour: you will probably be familiar with Pavlov's famous 1903 experiments with dogs and bells (Pavlov 1927). Initially studying digestion, he observed that the dogs were changing behaviour over time, learning to anticipate the arrival of food on sight of an associated stimulus, such as a bowl. Further experiments paired unrelated stimuli, such as sounds, with the food, and the dogs quickly learnt this association too. Pavlov referred to this process of changing behaviour by repeatedly pairing stimuli as conditioning, and so began a huge step forward in our understanding of learning by association.

Pavlovian conditioning, also known as classical conditioning, forms part of everyday learning and the shaping of perceptions. Students are not born, for example, with a fear of exams, but test anxiety can develop from association with previous negative experiences. Similar experimental work blossomed in the United States, deepening our understanding of learning through association, reinforcement and incremental growth (Thorndike 1898). Where Pavlov demonstrated how learning occurred through the simple pairing of stimuli, Skinner (1938) developed experiments that required pigeons and rats to perform tasks that would then be rewarded. By modifying tasks and using series of positive rewards and negative reinforcers he demonstrated how behaviours could be *shaped* and *reinforced* towards target outcomes. These experiments established another major principle of learning referred to as instrumental or operant conditioning.

The influence of behaviourist theory

These studies influenced a school of research known as 'behaviourist' because of its focus on learning as observable changes in behaviour. Results demonstrated how learning occurs by environmental conditioning, connecting actions with outcomes, reacting to feedback and strengthening through repeated action. They also demonstrated the importance of specifying clear learning targets and structuring learning tasks to achieve these. The recognition that behaviour could be shaped and directed through a teacher's intervention left a great legacy: Power to the teacher!

Associative learning represents a core learning process and task design principles are applied particularly in relation to the attainment of competencies, developing skills and to design of staged online learning units. The language arising out of behaviourist principles – learning outcomes, specifications, levels, standards, targets, competencies – is found throughout the literature and policies governing course design.

Practical applications: behaviourist perspectives

Principles and associated pedagogies arising from behaviourist research highlight the role of the teacher in designing and controlling the learning environment. These principles and pedagogies include:

- the use of practice and repetition to reinforce skills and memory associations
- an emphasis on systematic routine and organised activities
- an emphasis on the teacher specifying the structure, content and delivery of learning activities
- a focus on clear and assessable learning objectives and target outcomes
- the use of instructional designs that facilitate step-by-step attainment of increasingly complex competencies and skills
- an emphasis on feedback to direct learners' behaviour towards target outcomes
- use of incentives, rewards, penalties and disciplining strategies
- individualised programs that allow students to work at their own pace.

Criticisms of teaching based on early behaviourist principles

While leading to enormous leaps forward in our understanding of learning as a process, the rigidity of the empirical methodologies proved a limitation. The researcher, as a distant observer of behavioural change, was encouraged to view the mind as a blank canvas.

Behaviourist research was often over-interpreted, giving rise to an authoritarian, teacher-centred and outcome-based view of learning (Figure 1.1). The teacher came to be seen as the owner of knowledge, controller of the learning environment, with students as passive recipients; empty vessels to be filled with knowledge. Free will was considered an illusion. Emphasis on the short-term attainment of learning outcomes led to an assumption that the education program had been a success once targets had been met, irrespective of the teaching method. Rote learning is certainly effective at achieving results in the short term, but its long-term effectiveness remains questionable.

FIGURE 1.1   Behaviourist teaching methods could be authoritarian, transmissive and downplay the role of the learner. Cartoon © Claudio Furnier, used under licence from www.CartoonStock.com

Some saw the methods of these studies, their 'input–output' analyses, and the generalisation of findings from animal experiments to an understanding of human learning as limited and naïve (Chomsky 1959; Piaget 1952; Vygotsky 1978). Dealing only with observable sense data meant that internal mental processing and more fuzzy concepts like 'thinking' were not considered since they could not be measured objectively. Only the external, behavioural manifestation of thinking could accurately be measured. How could we study learning without reference to thinking? Surely we are more than the sum of our behaviours?

Thinking and understanding: cognitivist and constructivist perspectives

In reaction to behaviourism, Gestalt psychologists such as Köhler (1925) and Wertheimer (1959) took a more holistic view of behaviour and the mind. We don't simply learn what is in front of us, they argued; rather, the mind seeks patterns and relationships and elaborates to interpret the information as a whole. They suggested that the mind's sophistication in pattern-seeking and cognitive restructuring ultimately can lead to the formation of insight.

Cognitive constructivism

Cognitivist researchers explored how we come to store, retrieve and process information, how our thinking strategies develop and how we assimilate new experiences to make sense of the world. They argued for more emphasis on key questions not answered through behavioural experiments. Why does a five-year-old think differently from a fifty-five-year-old? What of higher-order thinking, such as moral and ethical reasoning? What about the different strategies that individuals adopt to solve problems? How do we go from memorising or associating facts to the generation of new ideas?

At the forefront of early cognitivist thinking in the 1920s and 1930s, Piaget noted that children's thinking appeared illogical to adults, so he studied how thinking patterns matured. Piaget (1952) proposed that children developed different ways of perceiving, interpreting and gaining meaning at different stages of growth. Through observations, analysis of dialogue and simple perception and memory tests, he identified a sequence of cognitive levels through which children progressed. The implication of this for teaching in schools was profound because there was little point in teaching certain levels of complexity, reasoning or abstraction until children's minds had developed an appropriate level of sophistication. These ideas led Einstein to comment that Piaget's discovery 'was so simple, only a genius could have thought of it' (cited in Papert 1999). Piaget's work was rediscovered by educationalists in the 1960s (Duckworth 1964) and school teaching responded accordingly.

Of wider significance was Piaget's notion that the maturing brain develops concepts: flexible frameworks into which we assimilate knowledge and experience. Piaget referred to these conceptual networks as 'schemas'. Understanding becomes increasingly sophisticated as schemata grow and restructure during the process of assimilating new information. By adulthood, a person has developed countless schemata for everything from peeling an orange to sophisticated concepts like love and anger.

Piaget's criticism of behaviourist research was that we can only understand how to improve education once we understand how we deal with information mentally: 'To present an adequate notion of learning one must first explain how the individual manages to construct and invent, not merely how he repeats and copies' (Piaget 1970). When we do so, we realise that the process of learning involves active construction and, accordingly, learning should itself be active: 'Children have real understanding only of that which they invent themselves, and each time that we try to teach them something too quickly, we keep them from reinventing it themselves' (Piaget, quoted in Papert 1999, p. 105).

This thinking reinvigorated a philosophy of learning known as 'constructivism', essentially a theory that knowledge can be constructed only in the mind of the learner. This reflected much of Dewey's thinking and was now given a stronger foundation through Piaget's work. The onus was clearly shifting to the learner as the creator of understanding.

7

Since the 1960s research has mushroomed to provide insight into thinking development. Bloom and Krathwohl (1956) developed a taxonomy of educational objectives of great practical value to teachers in understanding the structure of cognitive skill development and in formulating learning objectives in course design. Within their classification, cognitive skills are arranged in a hierarchy of increasing demand, from recall and manipulation to synthesis and evaluation.

Cognitive preferences

Research has also focused on individual differences in cognition. For example, Gardner (1983) argued that there are multiple intelligences which individuals possess to varying degrees. These include linguistic, musical, logical–mathematical, spatial and interpersonal intelligences. In contrast, Sternberg (1996) conceived intelligence as the success with which an individual selects, adapts to and shapes the real-world environment by integrating various practical, analytical and creative skills.

Individuals process information differently. Riding and Cheema (1991) reviewed studies into cognitive style and learning preference, concluding that findings could be grouped into two dimensions. An analyst–holist continuum describes ways in which a person may deal with information. An 'analyst' would break information into constituent parts, dealing with these separately while a 'holist' deals with a concept as a complete entity. A visualist–verbaliser continuum describes how a person thinks through either processing images or through text and language. Most learners will be multi-modal rather than fall into the extreme ends of these categories. This research is valuable in that it informs teachers about the nature of differences and encourages reflection about teaching.

Information processing and memory

Understanding how the brain encodes information and transfers this to and from memory has significance for teaching. Learning and retrieval is made easier if existing schemata are activated prior to presenting new information through, say, reminders, revision or reading (Jensen 1998). Externalising memory, for example using concept maps, representations or lists, can help with 'computational offloading', freeing the brain from recalling the information to examine its content and relationships (Zhang & Norman 1994).

We have also learnt from studies of working memory and cognition that the order in which information is encoded is significant, as is the method. Where information is learnt and retrieved using a variety of methods it is more likely to be recalled (Baddeley 2000; Baddeley & Hitch 1974; Healy et al. 2000). Retrieval is also stronger when information is associated with meaning. Inspiring teachers are memorable because they use surprise, novelty, emotion or attach relevance and meaning to the information (Jensen 1998). Analogies, storytelling and metaphors are useful strategies to attach meaning to new learning.

Studies into cognitive loading highlight the limitations of working memory which, at any one time, is thought to hold only a small number (seven chunks) of information during processing. Awareness of this for teachers is important as there are real limits to what the brain can absorb while simultaneously processing information (Sweller 1988). This explains why students look drained as you approach slide 50 in your one-hour lecture. This has practical implications for how learning episodes are sequenced, showing a need for chunking of information and provision of space to limit overload and to allow information to be worked. Dempster (1988) highlighted the importance of spacing effects, and revealed how material distributed across several sessions is better remembered than when concentrated within a single session.

Neuroscience

Neuroscientists provide a direct look at the brain's functioning through imaging. This field is exploding some influential ideas and 'edumyths' about how people learn. For instance, the brain's hemispheres are known to specialise but there is no evidence to support the popular idea of the intuitive 'right brain' or rational 'left brain' (OECD 2007). Similarly discredited is the idea that the brain's structure is defined by infancy or by adolescence. While there are sensitive periods for limited aspects of language development in infants, evidence suggests that the brain retains plasticity over its lifetime (Koizumi 2004; OECD 2007).

Neuroeducational research offers fresh insight into motivation through examination of the brain's reward system. Howard-Jones (2010), for example, questions why some students drift off in a well-planned lesson, then go home and get captivated for hours in computer games. Experimental studies showed that release of dopamine, a reward chemical, is triggered when there is greater unpredictability and uncertainty associated with learning, which has implications for the design of learning activities and games (Howard-Jones & Demetriou 2009). This effect was shown to be more significant for male students.

Advances in neuroscience support cognitive studies into working memory and its influence on attention (Fukuda & Vogel 2009) and highlight the importance of learning space in instructional design. Taylor et al. (2007), for example, describe how the brain has the neural machinery to learn from errors, which has implications for how university teachers create an environment for learning, implying a need for practice space to ensure error-making, a natural part of the learning process. Finally, neuroscience illuminates the fundamental role of emotion in learning, with Immordiano-Yang and Damasio (2007) suggesting that emotional processes are particularly important in transferring learning to the outside world (Howard-Jones 2010).

The influence of cognitive and constructivist theory

A major contribution of these theories is the view that learners are not passive, uniform, empty vessels into which we can pour second-hand knowledge. Effective learning occurs when the learner is actively involved in the primary construction of knowledge. Constructivists don't reject behaviourist theories but argue that association is only an isolated part of a more general process of learning. Piaget (1970) argued that the simple conditioned association between bell and food for Pavlov's drooling dogs would quickly fade when the ring of the bell failed to be rewarded; it is a temporary link. For the association to *persist* it must be assimilated with other concepts as part of an active process of schemata building and modification.

Evidence is growing that learning has more durable retention when taught using active, constructivist methods. Dochy et al. (2003) conducted a meta-analysis of more than 40 empirical studies on the effects of problem-based learning. They found that the method had a positive effect on development of skills, and that while students gained slightly less knowledge compared to conventional teaching, they remembered more of it. This was reinforced by Doğru and Kalander (2007) in a comparative study of teacher- and student-centred methods in science classes. After teaching, immediate tests revealed no significant difference between the methods. However, students taught by constructivist methods demonstrated better retention of knowledge in a follow-up assessment 15 days later.

For more didactic teaching and lecturing formats, cognitive research signals the importance of not overloading students' brains.

Practical applications:
cognitivist and constructivist perspectives

Pedagogies arising from cognitivist research focus on schemata development, catering for individual differences in cognitive style and teaching that supports how the brain processes information. They include:

- emphasising not just new knowledge but assimilation with prior understanding, building on previous learning and exploring relationships
- activities that prevent cognitive loading by creating space for note-taking or discussion and by breaking teaching sessions into manageable chunks
- activating prior learning through use of summaries, reading prompts or questioning
- strategies such as discussion, note-building and questioning, which relate new information to existing information to aid assimilation, encoding and memorisation
- using variety and mixed media in teaching to accommodate sensory preferences
- presenting concepts in varied ways, for example in constituent parts and holistically, to cater for different cognitive styles

- 'externalising' thinking, for example through the use of lists, concept maps or flow diagrams to explore relationships between concepts
- using analogies or metaphors to help attach meaning and assimilate new learning
- using novelty, surprise and emotional engagement to capture the mind's attention and help memorisation.

Pedagogies arising from constructivist studies emphasise student-centred, active learning and the role of the teacher as facilitator. They include:
- an emphasis on students being active in constructing their understanding of knowledge
- a focus on discovery, exploration, experimentation and developing and testing hypotheses
- project work, research-based learning, problem- and enquiry-based learning methods (see Brodie 2012; Jenkins & Healey 2012)
- awareness of the learning process through use of reflective learning activities, self assessment and evaluation
- the role of the teacher as a guide, providing 'scaffolding' to learning – that is, to ensure the student has the requisite knowledge, skills and support to negotiate a new piece of learning – and prompting the student through questioning or modelling.

Criticisms of teaching based on cognitivist and constructivist principles

Kirschner et al. (2006) describe student-centred constructivist teaching as 'unguided methods of instruction' and argue the need for greater structure to learning activities, particularly for those students with limited prior knowledge. Noting that strategies like problem-based learning are intended to simulate professional scenarios, they argue that a distinction needs to be made between how an expert operates in their profession and how students learn that profession. The systematic nature of scientific enquiry, they say, does not lend itself well to the self-instructional techniques required of, say, problem-based learning. They argue that activities involving free exploration of a complex environment can be cognitively detrimental to learning. In response, Schmidt et al. (2007) argue that the underlying principles of problem-based learning are entirely compatible with our cognitive structures and point to the flexibility in guidance within these teaching methods.

Behaviourist and much cognitivist research have also received criticism from social psychologists and sociologists for their emphasis on how individuals learn, as if this occurs in isolation. This is almost never the case, they argue, and we must therefore focus on the effects and influences of social and cultural interaction.

Learning from others: social and situated learning perspectives

Since the 1950s, research has demonstrated the power of social influence on people's attitudes and behaviours. Conformity and obedience appear to be strongly influenced by our confidence in our own judgements. We appear more likely to conform to a group norm when we are unsure, or to bow to peer pressure to gain social approval (Asch 1955; Milgram 1963). Further, we can mimic others unconsciously. Termed the 'chameleon effect' by Chartrand and Bargh (1999), this is thought to be linked to empathy since the most empathetic people appear to mimic most.

A phenomenon that you will encounter with group learning is that of social loafing – the reduced effort that individuals make, often unintentionally, when working in a team (Latané 1981). Relevant also to the classroom is an effect termed social facilitation, whereby an individual's performance is strengthened or inhibited by the pressure of performing before an audience. The positive or negative direction relates to how easy or difficult the task is perceived to be (Guerin 1986; Towler 1986).

In classroom debate or online communities, it is possible that the strength of students' viewpoints can be amplified as a result of siding with others of similar opinion, an effect called group polarisation (Wilson et al. 1975). Another powerful effect, 'group-think', describes poor decision-making arising from a desire to maintain harmony within the group (Janis 1972).

Social constructivism

Vygotsky was an originator of social constructivism. He highlighted the social origins of thinking, through the influence of language, culture and the interventions of others as we construct understanding (Vygotsky 1978). In particular, he emphasised the critical role of teachers in extending the potential of individual learning. He demonstrated that left to his or her own devices, a child could get so far with problem-solving, but with 'scaffolding' support from a teacher could achieve far more. This extended zone of potential he termed the 'zone of proximal development' (ZPD, Figure 1.2) and argued that it was towards the top of this zone that a teacher needed to target activities and support strategies such as modelling (demonstrating examples) and bridging (helping make connections). Scaffolding activities could include the use of step-by-step instructions, question prompting, demonstrations, peer collaboration, cues to students, analogies, directed study and graphic organisers. Teachers can break down tasks for students and make explicit the purpose and context of tasks.

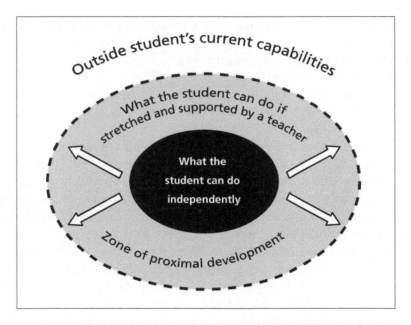

FIGURE 1.2   Vygotsky's zone of proximal development

Social learning theory

Bandura drew attention to the influence of observing people around us. His social learning theory notes that 'Learning would be exceedingly laborious, not to mention hazardous, if people had to rely solely on the effects of their own actions to inform them what they do' (Bandura 1977a). He demonstrated that much learning occurs by observing and imitating the behaviours of people around us, and assimilating their experiences into our own developing understandings. Termed vicarious or observational learning, modelling is central to this process. It is particularly influential in the formation of expectations, in the adoption of new behaviours ('watch and learn') and for developing students' self-efficacy.

Situated learning

Lave and Wenger (1991) argued that learning should be regarded not so much in terms of being educated as part of a formal program, but as a social act that occurs in everyday life. They suggest it involves the process of engaging with 'communities of practice', which refers to differing situated contexts in which individuals experience learning. For example, a student will likely be a member of multiple communities: a project group within a course unit, the wider course cohort, a student residence community, a sports club and perhaps an employee in a part-time job. Lave and Wenger suggest that learning is situated in distinct contexts and that success in any one is a function of how well individuals fit in and

13

learn to become competent in that setting. Characteristic features of communities of practice include:

- shared interest, passion and commitment
- an identity defined by this common interest
- active engagement and interaction between members
- a structure through which advancement is possible
- use of technical language
- shared competence that distinguishes members from others.

Lave and Wenger explain how individuals enter communities at the periphery, initially involved in activities that are less important, then gradually move towards the centre becoming established members as competency, identity and involvement in key community processes develops.

Their key point is that, rather than acquiring structures or constructing models to understand the world, we participate within and adapt to frameworks that already possess structure. The implication is that we should refocus emphasis on social engagements to consider how learners become active participants in these communities, how barriers to entry are overcome and how identities develop within these social groups: 'the purpose is not to learn *from* talk but to learn *to* talk to legitimise one's position in a community' (Lave & Wenger 1991).

Social and situated learning theories have particular significance to tertiary teaching because they broaden appreciation of the complex contexts in which learning takes place.

Practical applications: social and situated learning

Pedagogies arising from social and situated learning emphasise the value of social interaction in expanding understandings and transferring learning across contexts. They include:

- identifying what students can already do and supporting learning in the 'zone of proximal development'
- an emphasis on community formation and collaborative learning, actively constructing shared understandings
- classroom debate to explore and value alternative viewpoints
- developing awareness of social learning processes
- providing opportunity to apply learning from the closed world of the campus to the real world
- developing organisational awareness by providing opportunities for peripheral forms of engagement in professional communities
- use of collaborative knowledge building tools such as wikis and online discussion boards
- an emphasis on role models.

Criticisms of social and situated learning

The main criticisms of social learning theories concern the extent to which social interactions influence behaviour. Critics argue that these theories tend to reject genetic factors as significant determinants of behaviour: the classic nature versus nurture debate (Bouchard et al. 1990).

The principles of situated learning theory are often applied to the workplace as a learning environment. Hughes et al. (2007) argue that the original empirical work was carried out in atypical communities not easily equated to modern professional workplaces. Another criticism is that the theory presumes that communities of practice are reasonably stable and that the learner adapts to a structured, self-contained environment. Instead, we live in a world of change where such communities are unstable, evolve rapidly, and within which membership is highly mobile. The process of crossing boundaries between these situated communities in itself provides a stimulus for learning (Engestrom et al. 1995).

Being human: self-theories and humanistic perspectives

The final group of theories discussed in this chapter considers the role of experiential learning and personal growth. Proponents of these theories reject the notion that humans are simply biological objects about whom everything can be explained by networks of causes. They ask: what about being human and phenomena such as choice and free will? What motivates a person to succeed? How do our self-perceptions determine how we learn?

Maslow (1970) was at the forefront in directing attention to the growth potential of people. His theory stated that humans are motivated towards self-actualisation – realising their potential – but that a hierarchy of lower-order needs require satisfaction before the learner can reach this level. These start with survival and belonging needs and progress towards higher-order needs of esteem, desire to learn and, ultimately, fulfilling potential. The implication of this theory is that students need a supportive context in which to learn: if students feel that they belong, they will be motivated to fulfil their potential and learn for learning's sake.

Rogers (1983) also believed in this natural propensity to learn. He stressed the primary role of the teacher as creating the environment, climate and conditions for this development to occur.

Reflection and transformative learning

The transformative learning theory developed by Mezirow (1991) centres on the thinking processes that occur when a person examines existing understandings and a change in perspective results. Mezirow emphasised the central role of critical reflection in working through existing beliefs, assumptions and attitudes, and stressed the role of the teacher in creating a 'safe' learning environment to nurture reflective expression.

Reflective learning was developed further by Schön (1983). He argued that contemporary methods of teaching in professional courses were inappropriate for dealing with real-world problems that are 'messy', often unique, multifaceted and shaped by factors that are highly situational. The professional may often be required to make difficult judgements in the face of ethical, political, economic or moral concerns. Schön argued for a step beyond simply matching classroom problems to textbook theories; the practitioner is required to call heavily on professional experience to construct solutions on-demand to unique situations. He developed the notion of the professional as a 'reflective practitioner', placing great value on reflective analysis of experience and on highly developed and sophisticated expert or 'tacit' knowledge.

Experiential learning theories that examine how experience fits into a cycle of learning are popular in teacher and management education. The most famous, that of Kolb (1984), involves a four stage cycle of 'experience–reflection–conceptualisation–experimentation'. These theories are valuable in guiding the sequencing of learning activities.

Self-theories

Rotter (1966) developed a scale to assess a person's 'locus of control'. This related to a person's belief about their ability to control events. To illustrate, a student with a high *internal* locus of control would believe that achievement of a task is dependent on their own behaviours and actions: 'I know if I put the work in I'll be able to conquer algebra.' In contrast, a student with an *external* locus of control might believe that success or failure is beyond their control and the responsibility of others: 'I was never taught to do algebra properly.' Recent evidence suggests locus of control may be a function of stages in the life-span, with an increase towards a more internal locus developing up until middle age (Heckhausan & Schulz 1995).

Attribution theory (Weiner 1974) extends the notion of control further by examining explanations that people use to justify successes and failures. In addition to the internal or external dimension, this considers whether causes of success or failure are stable and controllable. For example, the difficulty of a task is stable and remains outside of a learner's control. In contrast, effort is not stable: a student has a great deal of control. Students who believe success is attributable to effort will be more likely to work harder.

Self-theories feed into the concept of self-efficacy, which is seen increasingly as central to student success. Self-efficacy refers to a person's belief in their capabilities to make a difference and succeed (Bandura 1977b, 1995). This belief has an influence on how goals are defined and how tasks are approached. Students with low self-efficacy are likely to believe that certain tasks are outside their capability and will tend to avoid such challenges. Bandura explained how self-efficacy could be developed through positive experiences where tasks are mastered and through witnessing others successfully meet challenges. Positive feedback, persuasion and encouragement play a central role. There is strong empirical evidence for the positive link between self-efficacy, academic achievement and other mediating effects, such as motivation and self-regulation (Pajares 1996).

Dweck (1999) examined belief systems surrounding implicit theories of intelligence. She proposed that students sit somewhere along a continuum of mindset between a fixed view of intelligence, where success is believed to be a function of innate ability, and a malleable, incremental view of intelligence, where success is believed to be a function of hard work and study. Knight and Yorke (2004) considered the implications of this for developing students' self-efficacy in university teaching by exploring the belief systems of both students and academic staff and the dynamics of their interaction. They concluded that the ideal scenario is when both teacher and student hold malleable views of intelligence with the teacher providing supportive developmental feedback on which students can act to improve. The worst scenario is when both teacher and student hold fixed views of intelligence leading to a shared belief that 'not a lot can be done'.

Conceptions of learning and discipline understandings

Swedish educationalists Marton and Säljö (1976) developed a qualitative research methodology, called phenomenography, which explored the subjectively different ways that people experience the same phenomenon. They applied this study to the ways that students read books, and distinguished between 'surface' approaches where students read simply to memorise facts to gain sufficient knowledge to pass a test, and 'deep' approaches, where the reader is concerned with understanding the meanings of texts. This approach has been applied in higher education to understand and compare variations in students' and teachers' conceptions of learning. For example, Prosser, Trigwell and Taylor (1994) identified different ways that academics' understand and experience science teaching, ranging from simple conceptions of transmitting information to more sophisticated intentions to facilitate conceptual change in learning. This phenomenographic approach has also been applied across academic disciplines to understand variation in students' understanding of subject learning, for example in music learning (Reid 2001) and of fieldwork in geography (Stokes et al. 2011).

Also related to subject learning and discipline understandings is the theory of threshold concepts (Chapter 3, Land 2012; Meyer & Land 2006a). This describes powerful but troublesome concepts within disciplines that students need to cross in order to progress in their understanding of that subject. Crossing these thresholds leads to transformed ways of thinking about the subject.

Influences of humanistic and self-theories

One of the curiosities in university teaching is the professed abhorrence of spoon-feeding students by many academics, who then choose to teach in largely didactic ways. Humanistic and self-theories have demonstrated that if we wish to encourage self-directed learning we should create the supportive climate. This requires the teacher to step back and focus on students' personal growth.

The phenomenographic studies have contributed to our understanding of the ways teachers and students conceptualise learning, or concepts within their discipline. This arms the teacher with a crucial insight of the differing ways that students understand subject concepts which can inform approaches to teaching.

Practical applications: Humanistic and self-theories and other studies of student learning

Pedagogies arising out of humanistic philosophy, self-theories and variation in understanding highlight the role of personal growth and transforming mindsets. Teaching may be characterised by:

- an emphasis on attitudes over techniques
- identifying individual learning goals and effective learning strategies
- letting go and passing responsibility and choice for learning to the student, for example using negotiated learning contracts
- an emphasis on student support and integrated personal development planning in the curriculum
- a focus on developing skills in meta-cognition, reflection on belief systems, self-awareness of study approaches
- breaking down fixed and negative belief systems
- creating a positive environment conducive to self-directed learning
- positive role models
- an awareness of the multiple ways learners experience course concepts.

Criticisms of teaching arising out of principles of humanistic and self-theory research

Humanistic psychology as advocated by Maslow and Rogers has been criticised for lacking a cumulative empirical base, for encouraging self-centredness (Seligman & Csiksczentmihalyi 2000), and for an over-optimistic view, assuming that all students are capable of self-actualisation. Critics argue that individuals often choose to ignore the positive choices in front of them and follow a negative path. Taken to its extreme, a humanistic education would be more like an open, educational retreat rather than the form of education with which we are familiar. While of great influence in personal development models, the movement has never fully materialised across formal education.

Experiential learning cycles like that of Kolb (1984) are also dogged by criticism that they are underdeveloped and lack scientific validity. Seaman (2008) suggests such models are best thought of as ideologies rather than theories with scientific foundation.

The assumption that self-theories are universal, while based on western studies, has been questioned. Gould (1999) suggests Heckhausen and Schulz's (1995) life-span theory of locus of control breaks down when seen from diverse cultural contexts. Others suggest different factors that may be more significant to student success than self-theories, for example the importance of intrinsic interest in the subject, and career orientation (Kember et al. 2010; Schiefele & Winteler 1992).

Making sense of theory in practice

So, is it necessary to understand learning theory to teach in universities? Think about your own subject: why is theory necessary to any practice or profession? It helps to provide a framework and structure to organise thinking. It suggests other ways of seeing the world and assists in locating problems and identifying solutions.

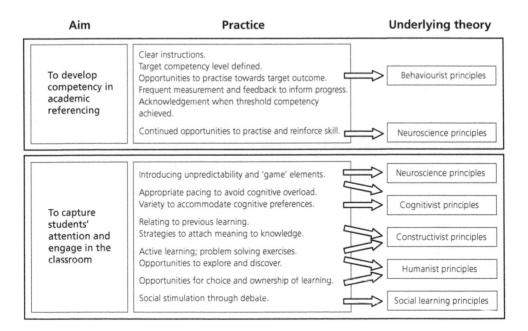

FIGURE 1.3 Examples of how a specific learning outcome or more general teaching and learning aims can draw from theoretical principles to inform teaching designs

19

Figure 1.3 illustrates how a teacher might draw on theoretical principles to strengthen the design of teaching activities. A useful exercise for the reader would be to reflect on your own teaching aims – as either specified intended learning outcomes or more general aims – and to relate these to the different theories outlined in this chapter. For more detailed reviews of learning theories, their evolution and applications see Jarvis et al. (2003), Brown (2004) and Haggis (2009).

A good teacher will make an impact. Teaching and curriculum design that is informed by an understanding of how students learn optimises effective learning. Awareness of different learning processes allows teachers to make sense of the spectrum of teaching methods available and guide selection of the most appropriate tools to secure learning outcomes.

CHAPTER 2

EFFECTIVE CLASSROOM TEACHING

*Lynne Hunt, Denise Chalmers
and Ranald Macdonald*

Keywords
learning environments, large group teaching, lecture method, small group teaching,
curriculum

> The teacher's fundamental task is to get students to engage in learning activities
> that are likely to result in achieving [the desired learning] outcomes. It is
> helpful to remember that what the student does is actually more important in
> determining what is learned than what the teacher does.
>
> (Schuell 1986, p. 429)

> The new teacher who has techniques for breaking the ice, for encouraging class
> participation, and for getting the course organised is more likely to get off to a
> good start. Once you find that teaching can be fun, you will enjoy devoting time
> to it, you will think about it, and you will develop into a competent teacher.
>
> (Svinicki & McKeachie 2011, p. 3)

Perspectives on teaching

What is the purpose of classroom teaching? Some teachers want to cover the
content of the subject. Others argue that time spent with students is too limited
and valuable to be spent delivering content that can be gleaned from independent
study (Biggs & Tang 2007). The ready availability of information and resources
such as textbooks, online study resources and recorded lectures has challenged
university teachers to reconsider the best use of the time spent with students. The
perspective taken in this chapter is that time taken talking 'at' students should be
minimised while the time for students to be involved actively in the development

of their understanding and skills should be maximised and extended beyond the formally scheduled class time into personal and group study.

'The aim of teaching is simple: it is to make student learning possible.' In his oft-quoted phrase, Ramsden (2003, p. 7) prompts the question: 'How can we make student learning possible?' The answer involves being interested in and knowing your students, having a comprehensive grasp of your subject and professional knowledge, understanding how learning happens, developing a wide repertoire of approaches to teaching, engaging with your colleagues and continually reflecting on, evaluating and developing your practice.

Effective university teaching is a holistic endeavour that embraces not only the practice of teaching but an understanding of how students learn (Chapter 1, Stewart 2012) in an inclusive and supportive learning environment (Chapter 11, Broughan & Hunt 2012; Chapter 12, Barker 2012; Chapter 13, Christie & Asmar 2012); curriculum development (Chapter 6, Angelo 2012); assessment and feedback to students (Chapter 5, Brown & Race 2012); scholarship and reflective practice (Chapter 15, Trigwell 2012); and continuous quality improvement (Chapter 14, Krause 2012). University teaching may take place online (Chapter 7, Reeves & Reeves 2012), through one-to-one supervision, lectures, workshops, tutorials, practica or fieldwork, and in laboratories and studios. Effective teaching is an outcome of decision-making that arises from knowing why you are doing what you are doing. Such decision-making starts and finishes with students. What is the entering behaviour of your students? What do they already know and what can they already do? What do you want to achieve with and for your students and what do you want your students to achieve? How will your students be transformed (Cranton 2006) by studying the subjects that you teach and how will you help them to get to a new point in their understanding?

This chapter draws attention to teaching practices that support students' learning with a particular focus on classroom teaching. It seeks to encourage university teachers to create effective learning environments for their students by exploring how to distil and present content and organise learning activities for large and small groups of students (Fink 2003). A key assumption is that while good university teaching is informed by discipline-specific considerations (Berthiaume 2009; Chapter 3, Land 2012), it is not limited by disciplinary habits of practice that can masquerade as 'traditions'.

Our understanding and beliefs about teaching and learning affect what we do as teachers and what we expect from our students (Entwistle et al. 2000; Kember 1997; Prosser & Trigwell 1999). Some common beliefs held by university teachers are that teaching ensures that students:
• know a lot – these teachers will focus on giving lectures that cover the content of the subject that students are expected to study away from the classroom
• understand and can apply the information they have learnt – teachers who believe this are more likely to provide students with pre-readings so that

class time can be used to clarify information and identify applications and limitations, and

- are transformed by their learning and come to understand things in different ways – teachers who believe this challenge their students to consider different viewpoints and present conflicting information from different sources and perspectives.

YOUR THOUGHTS

- What do you believe is your role as a teacher?
- What do you think is most important for your students to do in tutorials or laboratory sessions?
- What is the role of students in your classes? What do you expect of them?

What makes a teacher effective?

Teaching is an important part of the iterative cycle of students' learning. Structuring content in a logical manner, helping students to understand its relevance and application through asking questions that challenge them, directing them towards alternative resources and guiding them in their development of independent study skills, demonstrating empathy to the needs of individuals and the groups or teams in which they are working, providing them feedback on their learning – all require the very active involvement of the teacher (Cowan 2006).

Studies in a number of countries, such as those by Bain (2004) in the United States, Ballantyne et al. (1997) in Australia, and Kember and McNaught (2007) in Australia and Hong Kong, have identified characteristics of outstanding university teachers. Bain concluded that, 'without exception, outstanding teachers know their subjects extremely well' (2004, p. 15). While this is important, it is not sufficient, as Bain explains: 'exceptional teachers treat their lectures, discussion and problem-based sessions, and other elements of teaching as serious intellectual endeavours as intellectually demanding and important as their research and scholarship' (p. 17). They create a 'natural critical learning environment' in which 'people learn by confronting intriguing, beautiful, or important problems, authentic tasks that will challenge them to grapple with ideas, rethink their assumptions, and examine their mental models of reality' (p. 18). These highly effective teachers also 'reflect a strong trust in students ... believe that students want to learn, and they assume, until proven otherwise, that they can' (p. 18). Finally, the research has confirmed that all outstanding teachers are reflective and 'assess their own efforts ... to make appropriate changes' (p. 19).

Ballantyne et al. (1997) identified three dominant themes associated with effective teaching: 'a love for one's discipline (and the desire to share it with others), valuing students and their perspectives, and making learning possible'. Using the same data set with a further group of teachers from Hong Kong, Kember and McNaught (2007) identified some principles of good university teaching. These included ensuring 'that students have a thorough understanding of fundamental concepts, if necessary at the expense of covering excessive content' (p. 158), establishing the relevance of what is being taught, challenging beliefs and engaging students in a variety of learning tasks. To summarise, effective teachers care about their subject and their students and understand how effective learning happens. The challenge for each university teacher is to combine these laudable aims into effective practices.

YOUR THOUGHTS

- How will I teach?
- How will I present my excitement and knowledge of my discipline to students?
- What can I find out about my students?
  - ◊ How will I find out what they already know about the subject?
  - ◊ How do I find out why they are studying the subject?
  - ◊ How do I take account of how students learn when I plan my teaching?

Designing effective learning environments

This section explores how to design effective learning environments through: the selection and organisation of content; use of a variety of learning and teaching strategies; ideas about how to work with large and small groups of students; and discussion about the importance of consolidation.

Selecting content

In selecting content, take note of subjects that students have previously studied and those that follow. This will indicate the required breadth and depth of content. One simple question guides the content selection process: 'What do I want my students to be able to know and do by the end of this learning episode?' Normally this question is answered in the learning outcomes identified in the approved subject outline – this is the contract between your university and its students. It is what students are expecting to learn. Generally speaking, subject objectives are sufficiently broad to allow some creativity in the selection of content. Indeed, Bain (2004) found that outstanding teachers 'avoid objectives that are arbitrarily tied to the specific topics of the course and favour those that embody the kind of thinking and acting expected for life' (p. 17).

There is a difference between 'must-know' and 'nice-to-know' content. In professional courses the 'must-know' can predominate. Must-know knowledge can be made explicit to students through formal teaching and resources such as class notes and online resources so that students may be directed to this information through in-class activities, guided private study and assessment tasks. However, this need not be the limit of what is taught. There is scope to manage content imaginatively in a way that contributes to coherent learning experiences through which students learn content, skills and develop personal capacity (Chapter 4, Chalmers & Partridge 2012).

A common temptation is to 'overstuff' the curriculum with content. A useful metaphor to describe this is to think of packing a suitcase for a holiday. Initially, the suitcase is filled with items that are 'nice to have' or 'just in case'. However, when the suitcase becomes too heavy to carry, the next step is to discard all but the essential items. Think of selecting content in this manner. The task is to 'unpack the curriculum'. Teachers of subjects that are taken by students from many discipline areas become practised at this because they know that their students are not going to be discipline specialists. These subjects are referred to as 'service' subjects. For example, statistics may be studied by student nurses, psychologists, engineers and accountants. Teachers must ask themselves, 'What is it that these particular students need to know or be able to do? What is the essence of what students need to learn?' Case 2.1 is an extract from a teaching portfolio (Hunt 2002) which shows the process of thinking about the essence of what students need to learn.

CASE 2.1 TEACHING THE ESSENCE OF A SUBJECT
Lynne Hunt, Edith Cowan University

Biomedical science student: 'This is the 22nd out of 22 subjects that I need to do. Everything has been black and white so far and I didn't need your 40 shades of grey.'
Teacher: 'Didn't you like the subject?'
Student: 'Oh, it was awesome.'

What I thought was going to be a complaint was actually a compliment and appropriate to a social science lecturer committed to the development of critical thinking. Nonetheless, this student made me realise that my teaching needed to change: I was now teaching service social science subjects, required for 'hard science' students.

Teaching social sciences in the applied area of health required that I reflect on the essence of my discipline in order to teach its core elements. I did this by directing students' attention to the graduate skills that lie at the heart of the social sciences: social and political awareness; social research; critical thinking; and written and oral communication.

An alternative approach to the selection of content is to consider what professions the students will be entering. We may hope they will be professional, empathetic, questioning, ethical practitioners rather than graduates who just know a lot about their subjects. But what does this mean in a complex, uncertain world where people are likely to change jobs and careers a number of times? In learning for what Barnett (2007) calls 'an unknown future' in an 'age of uncertainty' it is students' ability to identify their own learning needs and to take responsibility for their own learning, often working collaboratively with others, that will see them judged as a success, rather than whether they are able to pass an examination requiring them to regurgitate facts and concepts.

Organising content

An old teaching and communications adage remains good advice for organising the presentation of selected material in lectures, tutorials and workshops: 'Tell them what you are going to do – do it – then tell them what you have done.' This captures the essence of a well-organised presentation. It has a clear introduction that outlines the presentation; then progresses through each point one at a time with examples and applications, concluding with a summary of the main points. A presentation should have no more than three to five key points. Any more is too much for the students to understand at one time. This may sound highly structured, indeed it may be argued that the advent of the internet creates opportunities for non-linear learning, but, when faced with lectures, students overwhelmingly report that they appreciate a well-organised presentation that has clear signposts flagging key points, with examples to make sense of what they mean or how they apply. Teachers know their subject so well that some points may seem obvious and self-evident, but for students grappling with new terminology and concepts, it can seem like a foreign language.

Structure scaffolds students' learning and examples help them to link new material with prior knowledge. This leads to the need to consider students' level of learning when organising content. Are you teaching a first-year, second-year or advanced-level subject? What do the students already know? What will they need to know for the subject that follows? Some things need to be learned before further learning is possible. These are referred to as threshold concepts (Chapter 3, Land 2012).

YOUR THOUGHTS

Critique a lecture that you have prepared, attend a lecture of a colleague or listen to a recorded lecture.

- Does the lecture have a clear introduction setting out the direction of the lecture?
- How many points are made in the lecture?
- Are these points illustrated with examples that link to prior learning or that demonstrates their application?

- Does the lecture appropriately reflect the students' level of learning and link forward to future learning requirements?
- Are students provided the opportunity to consolidate their learning through some in-lecture activities and a summary of key points?

Using a variety of learning and teaching activities

The shift in focus from didactic teaching, sometimes described as the 'sage on the stage' model to the 'guide on the side' model, has been challenged by McWilliam (2008) who argues that teachers should be 'meddlers in the middle'. These are teachers who challenge students to think and understand differently. To do this, university teachers need a repertoire of activities that will engage students actively in learning. Scott (2005) found in his study of nearly 95 000 graduates that students appreciate a range of interactive classroom learning strategies such as buzz groups, debates, lectures and small group work for peer learning, independent study and negotiated learning. These latter might include self-paced learning packages and online modules on some topics or for the whole subject. Students do not have to be on campus or in front of a teacher to learn effectively. They value opportunities for applying what they are learning through practice-oriented and problem-based learning (Chapter 9, Brodie 2012) that incorporates case studies and site visits as well as simulated environments, such as mock trials, and laboratory work.

There are many university and national websites that host a wealth of discipline-focused teaching and learning activities and resources, for example the Higher Education Academy in the United Kingdom, Carnegie Foundation in the United States of America, Ako Aotearoa in New Zealand and the Office of Learning and Teaching site in Australia. These are evidence based and can confidently be used to extend repertoires of learning and teaching activities.

Designing effective learning in large groups

Lectures are the most traditional form of university teaching. However, in the contemporary shift in pedagogy from didactic to student-engaged teaching and learning processes, lectures have lost their reputation as an effective means of student learning:

> The formal lecture is a refuge for the faint-hearted, both lecturer and students. It keeps channels of communication closed, freezes hierarchy between lecturer and students and removes any responsibility on the student to respond ... students remain as voyeurs; the lecture remains a comfort zone ... the students' unsettling is held at a distance.
>
> (Barnett 2000b, p. 159)

In contrast, it might be argued that a dazzling presentation of well-organised material from a lecturer who is passionate about the subject may be worth a multitude of small-group discussions between students who have yet to gain mastery of the subject matter. At the heart of the debate is the understanding of what lectures are. They can be didactic or interactive and engaging:

> But lectures from highly effective teachers nearly always have the same five features of natural critical learning ... They begin with a question (sometimes embedded in a story), continue with some attempt to help students understand the significance of the question (connecting it to larger questions, raising it in provocative ways, noting its implications), stimulate students to engage the question critically, making an argument about how to answer that question (complete with evidence, reasoning and conclusion) and end with conclusions. The only exception? Sometimes the best teachers leave out their own answers whereas less successful lecturers often only include that element, an answer to a question that no one has raised.
>
> (Bain 2004, p. 107)

All the essential qualities of good university teaching apply in successful lectures. These include providing opportunities for interaction and student participation and checking and consolidating learning. Strategies include maintaining good eye contact with the students, pausing regularly to provide students with opportunities to regain their concentration and consider the points that have been raised using techniques such as buzz group discussions. Good lectures are well structured. They set clear objectives and identify in advance the milestones of the lecture. They headline key learning points, establish the relevance to student assessment, link theory and practice by reference to tutorials or practical sessions and create opportunities for students to provide feedback about their learning.

Strategies to engage students with the teacher and each other in large classes include asking the students to write a half-page response at various points during the semester. For example, in the first week, students might be asked to write a brief biography to introduce themselves to the university teacher. They might then introduce themselves to each other. This gives students a chance to get to know at least one other person in the class early in semester. The brief biography can then be left with the teacher as students leave the class, or students can be asked to post it on the subject website. In Week 2, the roughly collated information from these can be reported to the student to provide them with general overview of their cohort. For example, international students could be welcomed, noting the range of countries represented in the lecture theatre. In Week 3, students might be asked to write a brief response on what they have been finding most difficult to understand so far. In Week 4, the teacher could include a brief revision of common problems or post further explanations and resources on the subject website. An alternative to the half-page response activity is to use Post-it® notes, asking students for one key idea or question. These can then be 'posted' on the walls as the students leave the lecture theatre and they can also read each other's responses.

The use of technology in lectures can increase student engagement and support student learning in large classes in a number of ways. For example, some teachers use clickers (classroom response systems) to gain immediate audience response during lectures. Clickers can be used to provide the teacher and the students with immediate feedback on in-class quizzes, to poll opinions and to gauge students' understanding of a topic in a non-threatening and engaging way. Clickers are specific-purpose instruments, but mobile phones can also be used in a similar way in conjunction with open-access software. To find out more about using clickers, two short videos on YouTube® provide a good introduction: 'Using clickers in the college classroom' (CIIA 2007) and 'How to use clickers effectively' (CU-SEI 2009).

Another technology increasingly used in lectures is the lecture capture system for uploading online for later use. The lecture capture system was primarily designed to assist students revise a lecture but it has the added benefit for international students and students with disabilities who appreciate the opportunity to repeat the lecture when language difficulties or speed of the presentation can make learning difficult. It also integrates learning activities for on-campus and distance education students. The additional provision of follow-up or take-home activities further enhances students' understanding of the lecture.

The design of a lecture is a decision-making process. What emerges will depend on the nature of the student body, the extent to which students study on or off campus, and the discipline. For example, maths, science and accounting teachers have found tablet computers to be very useful for conveying numerical information to students in lectures and online (Tront 2007).

Many university websites provide guidelines on lecturing, much of which was summarised in an Australian project on Teaching Large Classes (AUTC 2003). There is an extensive literature on how to lecture, including Svinicki and McKeachie (2011), Fry et al. (2009), Light et al. (2009), Race (2007), Jarvis (2006), Knight (2002a), MacGregor et al. (2000) and Davis et al. (1983). Some take a critical perspective and ask 'Why lecture?' – drawing on research on learning to support their case. Others seek to maximise student learning outcomes of lectures.

Designing effective learning in small groups

Small group teaching may include tutorials, workshops, fieldwork and laboratory settings, which provide opportunities for students to engage actively with learning, to enhance practical skills and to develop graduate attributes such as critical thinking and oral communication, including listening skills (Chapter 4, Chalmers & Partridge 2012; Jaques & Salmon 2007). Typically, the small class sessions draw on content that has been introduced in lectures or in directed personal study.

A common form of small group teaching is the tutorial where the focus is on students' active participation. Ground rules, in which staff and student roles and expectations are mutually established, will clarify expectations about student participation. This might be accomplished through individual or group contracts.

YOUR THOUGHTS

Students' personal contracts: Consider the following outline of a student's personal contract and tailor it to the learning needs of your students by adding and deleting question items.

My expectations of this subject are:

- ...
- ...
- ...

My expectations of my fellow students are:

- ...
- ...
- ...

My expectations of my teacher/tutor are:

- ...
- ...
- ...

I am prepared to make the following commitment to study in terms of:
- attendance…
- contribution to class discussion…
- reading…
- enhancing study skills…

My concerns as I begin this unit are:

- ...
- ...
- ...

What I intend to do about my concerns is:

- ...
- ...
- ...

An effective tutorial activity is the jigsaw method. This method ensures that each student can contribute something unique to small group discussion. It is so called because each student works on only one piece of a learning task, subsequently fitting it together, like a jigsaw piece, with information developed by other students to achieve the big picture of the issue. It is an effective method of learning because students must be able to explain to others. This has a powerful effect on the quality of learning. The jigsaw method is organised in the following way.

1. Assign each student an appropriate reading (or section of a reading) and ask them to summarise the main ideas.
2. Arrange students into small groups of those who have focused on the same reading or section to consolidate their understanding
3. Rearrange students into groups covering all the sections of the task. Each group will contain one student who studied section one, another who studied section two, and so on. Invite students to take turns explaining their section to the others.
4. Consolidate the activity by reviewing important ideas and attending to any questions that arose in the small groups.

The jigsaw approach avoids a problem often encountered in small groups: students working from a position of ignorance. The initial activities of independent study and consolidation of their piece of the jigsaw ensures that in the final activity each group comprises informed participants. Although readings are commonly used, they are not essential to the jigsaw method. For example, you might want students to examine an issue from a number of theoretical perspectives, and so each student is assigned a particular theoretical perspective to use in examining the issue (Chalmers & Fuller, 1996).

Planning is an important feature in designing all effective learning environments, including tutorials. Bertola and Murphy (1994, p. 8) recommended planning tutorials in terms of content and process and provide guidelines for tutors that include consideration of how to:

- discuss controversial issues
- consolidate knowledge
- clarify issues
- headline major themes
- solve problems
- outline alternative perspectives
- analyse arguments
- assess evidence
- encourage listening skills
- generate questions
- develop group skills

- practise presentation skills
- resolve conflict
- practise self-criticism, and
- develop interpersonal skills and positive attitudes.

YOUR THOUGHTS

- Select three items from Bertola and Murphy's guidelines that you would like to include in your teaching activities.

- Write one short paragraph on how you anticipate planning for each in your tutorials.

A common challenge in small group teaching is that students do not complete prescribed reading and, even if they do, they have insufficient analytical skills to interrogate the material. In the early years of university study, these are skills that may need to be taught rather than assumed. In subjects that have an examination, one way to focus students' attention on the importance of regular reading is to provide the exam questions early in the semester and discuss in tutorials how different readings might contribute to answers. This approach fosters timely reading and demonstrates how to question and use evidence.

The regular reading scheme also encourages students to engage in systematic reading. It is highly versatile and can be adapted to suit different class sizes, used for online learning environments and in different disciplines and university contexts. Students are given a colour-coded card on which to summarise each week's prescribed reading. The following week, the notes are discussed in class. The small size of the card forces distillation of key points and targeted note taking. After their notes have been reviewed in class discussion, students hand in their cards for storage. The card may be handed in *only* in the week following the prescribed reading. This is what promotes regular reading. On the day of the exam, the lecturer returns the collated cards to their owners for use during the exam. This is a voluntary incentive scheme but students learn quickly the benefits of participation. Students are enthusiastic about the system and report that they work harder because of regular reading schemes. The aim is continuous, independent learning, rather than continuous assessment.

Persuading students to develop opinions based on the evidence presented in readings and tutorials may be a challenge. This can be addressed using the 'stand and deliver' strategy, which forces a public stance and facilitates debate. Students are invited to cluster at fixed points in the room. One side of the room signifies agreement with a statement, the other disagreement and in the middle is neutral territory. When students have moved to their positions they must speak with like-minded classmates to justify their point of view. This empowers students with the skills and knowledge to articulate their opinions.

Developing the ability to question is an important learning skill. Case 2.2 describes a strategy to develop students' questioning skills.

CASE 2.2   STRATEGY TO DEVELOP STUDENTS' QUESTIONING SKILLS
(Hogan 1999, pp. 11–13; adapted from Beers 1986)

- Ask students to write one to two questions derived from class discussion, readings or their independent thinking.
1. Collect and collate these and in the following week distribute a handout containing the questions and a table of Bloom's taxonomy of six cognitive levels and two keywords for each category (Bloom & Krathwohl 1956).

Level	Keywords
knowledge	state, list
comprehension	explain, identify
application	apply, demonstrate
analysis	compare, differentiate
synthesis	create, hypothesise
evaluation	judge, revise

2. Ask students to classify questions from the collated list using the table.
3. Discuss with the group the advantages and disadvantages of using Bloom's taxonomy and the functions of various types of questions. For example, is it useful to have lower-order questions when material is new or difficult to understand? In contrast, higher-order questions tend to be more interesting and challenging.
4. Invite students to write their original questions one step higher.
5. Consider selecting some questions to include in the final exam.
6. Provide opportunities for students to choose their own assignment questions. Drafts of questions may be discussed in class or online and appraised by peers.

Designing effective learning in workshops

The traditional university model of teaching through lectures and tutorials can be modified by creative timetabling decisions. For example, lectures and tutorials for 150 students might be reorganised as three workshops with 50 students in each. The workshop model is facilitated by flat learning spaces but the design of interactive learning experiences is the defining feature. Workshops should utilise a variety of learning strategies. A single workshop might include discussion of the readings for that week, jigsaw group discussion, simulation games or watching a video while writing answers to prepared questions. The design of the workshop must accord with the objectives of the subject and should aim to facilitate the development of graduate qualities and skills and prepare students for successful completion of assignments. The role of the teacher is to 'meddle in the middle' to assist students to engage with other students and to develop and extend their own understanding and skills. Case 2.3 illustrates how a large class can be run as a workshop.

CASE 2.3   TEACHING IN LARGE GROUPS IN A WORKSHOP CLASS
Ranald Macdonald, Sheffield Hallam University

A large group class need not be a lecture. It could take the form of a workshop in a large, flat space. For example, in a first-year business studies course of 200, students were divided into groups of 50, and then into learning groups of four to six engaged in similar activities, using slightly different cases or data. They worked on tasks, presented their finding to other groups or to the whole class with the lecturer introducing and summing up the session, which was scheduled for three hours. Students were free to take a break when they thought it necessary. As the year progressed the groups increasingly identified cases for themselves and began to move outside the broadly presented learning outcomes for the course. They applied their acquired knowledge and skills to increasingly complex, ambiguous contexts with uncertain outcomes and collected the evidence for their learning in a portfolio which, because the institution required an examination, they took into the examination as the case studies they had developed themselves. Instead of individual students coming to the lecturer with their learning problems, they were encouraged to see their learning groups as a peer support mechanism. If the problem could not be resolved in their group, they could approach another group and, finally, the lecturer. The emphasis was on students taking responsibility for their own learning through collaboration.

Designing effective practical learning environments

Practical learning environments may include anything from small-scale practicum experience, for example, for the completion of one assignment, to fieldwork (JISC 2012), laboratory learning, clinical placements or work-integrated learning degree programs (Cooper et al. 2010; Chapter 10, Garnett 2012). The principles of designing effective classroom teaching apply in practical contexts as for any learning environments. These include the selection and organisation of materials, the alignment of the practical learning with learning objectives and assessment (Chapter 6, Angelo 2012), students' active engagement and the integration of discipline learning with development of graduate attributes. Ideally, practical learning involves the application of discipline-based learning, and it also involves the acquisition of skills.

Consolidation and self-reflection

Consolidation is an essential component in the design of effective learning environments. At its best, consolidation moves beyond asking students to 'Tell me how much you know' to 'Show me the evidence of what you have learned, how you learned it, how well you think you have learned it and what would have helped you learn it better. Tell me areas where you think you could improve your learning and how you could go about it.'

Consolidation can happen at any point, not just at the end of semester. For example, the use of frequent informal small quizzes embedded in lectures, tutorials and workshops, through to formal assessment that requires students to demonstrate understanding or skills, can all effectively contribute to consolidation of their understanding and provide them opportunities to reflect on the quality of their learning.

Marking assessments is also a key element in consolidation of students' learning, as Case 2.4 shows.

CASE 2.4   PROVISION OF FEEDBACK TO PROMOTE LEARNING

Lynne Hunt, Edith Cowan University

When I return marked assignments, I ask students to work in small study groups to combine learning points arising from my written comments on their individual assignments. The collated comments are used to stimulate reflective thinking about points needing improvement. In this exercise I use the snowball strategy so that each individual at first works alone, then in pairs and finally in groups of four, before noting in class discussion the most significant items of the written feedback on assignments. This means that students are rehearsing 'points for improvement' at least four times.

In the second assignment, I allocate marks to an appendix that requires students to demonstrate how they used the feedback from the first assignment to enhance the quality of their writing in their second assignment. I do this to reinforce the importance of a reflective approach to their own work and to encourage an understanding that feedback is provided as points for improvement, not just a justification for grades.

....

Conclusion

Effective teaching is the outcome of decision-making based on evidence arising from research, experience of teaching students in different contexts and responses to students' feedback.

Good classroom teaching takes place when teachers create positive and effective learning experiences for their students.

This chapter has outlined issues to consider when planning for teaching students in large and small group classroom settings, such as:

- What is your personal belief about what is effective teaching?
- How will you prepare your lectures and presentations?
- How will you facilitate your students' learning in classroom sessions?
- How will you provide your students with transformative learning experiences?
- What will you do to consolidate their learning?
- How will you respond to student feedback about your teaching?

The decisions are yours. Teaching is a journey. Your narrative will change and expand to accommodate the 'supercomplexity' (Barnett 2007) of teaching in contemporary universities as the concluding 'teacher's tale' in Case 2.5 shows.

CASE 2.5   A TEACHER'S TALE
Ranald Macdonald, Sheffield Hallam University

Making a mid-career change from being a research economist in a major bank to teaching in higher education, I gave up my job to undertake a teaching course. There, my unusually enlightened, and certainly radical, tutor suggested that, instead of going to all the lectures and seminars designed to condition me into a particular way of teaching, I should read two books – Carl Rogers' *Freedom to Learn for the 80s* (1983) and Paulo Freire's *Pedagogy of the Oppressed* (1970). This was a transformational experience leading to me developing my own form of problem-based learning using learning contracts (Knowles 1990) and learning activities involving business, engineering and three-dimensional graphic design students working on the same task from their own disciplinary and professional perspectives – great fun! And all designed to put the student as learner at the centre of the learning experience.

Thinking about my contribution to this chapter rekindled for me that feeling of transformation. I realised, too, that the adult learning literature, which so greatly influenced me, is sorely underutilised in making sense of learning and teaching in higher education. This also led to a re-reading of three books by one author, the highly influential Stephen Brookfield: *Becoming a Critically Reflective Teacher* (1995), *Discussion as a Way of Teaching* (Brookfield & Preskill 2005) and *The Skilful Teacher* (2006). The titles of the books say it all! They all recognise learners in university as adults, engaged in adult education.

Brookfield emphasises the chaotic unpredictability of teaching and how this is viscerally experienced, arguing that 'skilful teaching resembles a kind of contextually informed "muddling through" classroom experience that involves us negotiating moments of surprise as we grow into our own truth about the realities we face' (2006, p. xvii). He posits that:

> Teaching is in many ways the educational equivalent of white-water rafting. Periods of apparent calm are interspersed with sudden frenetic turbulence. Tranquillity co-exists with excitement, reflection with action. If we are fortunate enough to

negotiate rapids successfully, we feel a sense of self-confident exhilaration. If we capsize, we start downstream with our self-confidence shaken, awash in self-doubt.

(Brookfield 2006, p. 8)

Further, Brookfield makes three core assumptions about skilful teaching: first, 'Skilful teaching is whatever helps students learn.' Second, 'Skilful teachers adopt a critically reflective stance towards their practice.' And third, skilful teachers need 'a constant awareness of how students are experiencing their learning and perceiving teachers' actions' (2006, p. 17).

The challenge in most universities remains the tension between teaching that transforms students and their learning (Cranton 2006) and teaching which leads to easily measurable outcomes. Elton makes the distinction between 'doing things better (quality assurance) and doing better things (quality enhancement)' (Elton 2006). As a teacher, I sought to do better things and relished the challenges presented for me and the learners with whom I worked.

CHAPTER 3

DISCIPLINE-BASED TEACHING
Ray Land

Key words
discipline-based teaching, threshold concepts, signature pedagogies, pedagogies of uncertainty, interdisciplinarity

The nature of disciplines

The training and acculturation required to become a professional scholar, and gain entry to an academic tribe, is still concerned principally with acquiring deep knowledge in a specialised field. This disciplinary knowledge, as Kreber (2009) observes, is both the object of study which we look *at*, and also the lens which we look *through*. Moreover the disciplines within which the majority of these specialised fields are organised serve not just as sources of knowledge and expertise but as bases of personal identity (Henkel 2000). Indeed Henkel found that 'academics' own definitions of quality would seem to remain predominantly discipline-centred' (2000, p. 106).

Discipline-based teaching focuses on the strong primary influence of the disciplinary context, its signature ways of thinking and practising, its generally accepted conceptual structures and boundaries and the tribal norms and values of its community of practice.

Disciplines have developed their own conceptual worlds, with their own robust 'ways of thinking and practising' (McCune & Hounsell 2005, p. 255) and 'knowledge practices' (Strathern 2008, p. 11). Immersion within these worlds and practices constitutes the process of academic formation. We are what we know and do. Perkins has characterised these distinctive modes of reasoning and explanation as 'underlying games of enquiry' or 'epistemes', which are 'system[s] of ideas or way of understanding that allows us to establish knowledge ... manners of justifying, explaining, solving problems, conducting enquiries, and designing and validating various kinds of products or outcomes'. While epistemes may be left unspoken and tacit sometimes, Perkins emphasises 'the importance of students understanding the structure of the disciplines they are studying' (2006, p. 42).

Matthew and Pritchard suggest that it is virtually impossible for us nowadays to imagine a university which is not organised along disciplinary lines and some configuration of schools, faculties and departments: 'The division of knowledge and underlying epistemologies into defined disciplinary regimes is seemingly part and parcel of the post-industrial western university. We cannot think of it being any other way' (2009, p. 57). Certainly most academics seem to enter higher education because they are motivated by interest in their discipline. Wenger (1998) argues that the motivation for most learning is the desire to enter and be accepted by a specific 'community of practice' and to adopt and practise its ways, values and norms. In terms of forging academic and professional identities, Poole (2009) wonders whether disciplines, as powerful instances of communities of practice, represent a 'home' or a 'barricade'; that is, whether they are positive spaces that provide secure identities, generative sources of ideas and opportunities for mutual support and collaboration, or whether they serve as defended territories, places of resistance against corporate, managerial or even collegial 'others'.

YOUR THOUGHTS

- To what extent would you say your discipline has a distinctive way of thinking and practising?
- What might be its characteristic modes of reasoning and explanation?
- Is there a tacit or unspoken 'underlying game'?
- Do you consider your community of practice to be primarily your discipline or your university? How does one gain access to such a community?

Signature pedagogies

The former President of the Carnegie Foundation for the Advancement of Teaching, Professor Lee Shulman, once observed that 'if you wish to understand why professions develop as they do, study their nurseries, in this case, their forms of professional preparation' (Shulman 2005b, p. 52). He coined the term for such forms of teaching and learning 'signature pedagogies', namely the preferred fundamental ways in which future practitioners are educated for their new professions. Somewhat akin to 'ways of thinking and practising', signature pedagogies, according to Shulman, promote the three crucial aspects of professional work – thinking, performing and acting with integrity, though these dimensions do not receive equal treatment across the professions. According to Shulman, medicine, for example, is light on preparation for professional integrity and caring, and legal education fosters thinking like a lawyer but less so performing like one. The notion of signature pedagogies is an interesting one for analysing how this work is enacted.

In law, Shulman observes:

> Throughout the hour, the law professor faces the students, interacting with them individually through exchanges of questions and answers, and only occasionally writing anything on the board. The students can see each other as they participate, and can respond easily if the professor solicits additional responses. But it's relatively rare for students to address one another directly.
>
> (Shulman 2005b, p. 53)

Whereas in an engineering class on fluid dynamics:

> Although the teacher faces his class when he introduces the day's topic at the beginning of the session, soon he has turned to the blackboard, his back to the students. The focal point of the pedagogy is clearly mathematical representations of physical processes. He is furiously writing equations on the board, looking back over his shoulder in the direction of the students as he asks, of no one in particular, 'Are you with me?' A couple of affirmative grunts are sufficient to encourage him to continue.
>
> (Shulman 2005b, p. 53)

This, in turn, opens up what our pedagogies are intended to achieve. Donald (2009, p. 42) asks, 'Has law a signature pedagogy? Vested in cases, argument, statute and precedent, law is a pedagogy of uncertainty, of tension and negotiation, of multiple interpretations, and of risk.' Thinking like a lawyer requires a high degree of analytical ability, she suggests. In a study she undertook of teaching across a range of disciplines she found that law students need to acquire an abstract and nuanced technical vocabulary and to work within a framework of statutes and precedents which requires them to be 'both verbally proficient and aggressive'. One of her respondents commented that 'law schools are unruly places, where received wisdom and controversy vie for attention'. Legal concepts are highly abstract but tightly structured and logically related. Donald concludes that:

> The methodology of a legal expert consists of looking at the facts, looking at the issues, looking at the results and analysing the reasons, and critiquing these both distinctively and constructively. Lawyers must determine what was held and why to produce an argument.
>
> (Donald 2009, p. 42)

Pedagogically, this requires a pluralistic approach with discussion method integral to lectures, a combination of the case law method and Socratic method, seminars, moot courts (mock trials), workshops, field visits and simulated macro-analysis where students encounter problems similar to those they might face in a law firm's office.

Engineering on the other hand is concerned with applying structured knowledge to unstructured problems. The practice is beset with uncertainty. Donald observes that engineering students 'deal with unbounded problems, with too little or too much information, and must set the limits of their problem space'. The pedagogies are designed to help engineering novices estimate risk and take responsibility for their decisions. Becher (1989), observing them as an academic tribe, noted that they considered themselves hardworking, stable introverts, placing emphasis on creativity and inventiveness and valuing entrepreneurialism and a cosmopolitan outlook. Industry and the engineering professional bodies have considerable influence over content and the curriculum, with the danger that the latter becomes overstuffed with an expanding agenda of new issues. Teachers are concerned to develop their students' problem-solving skills, and their understanding of design and quality in real-life economic and industrial contexts. Teaching methods include lectures, class discussion, group design projects, cooperative inquiry-based learning, and active learning methods such as placements and internships.

In humanities subjects, such as literature, the signature pedagogy tends to be located within the debates, controversies, rifts and dialectic surrounding textual analysis, close reading and literary criticism. The emphasis is on interrogating practice, challenge of ideas and defending one's interpretation. As Martin argues, arts and humanities subjects generally 'do not understand themselves to be an education primarily structured around the imparting of skills and competences but one primarily structured around a series of engagements with a body of knowledge, or (in the case of the practical arts) a body of practice'. He maintains that these subjects are 'concerned with acts of continuous re-interpretation and revision' (Martin 2003, p. 302). Methods tend to be relatively conventional variants of the lecture seminar and tutorial, emphasising discussion and interchange.

Donald concludes that students in one program of study are experiencing a totally different education from students in another, with quite idiosyncratic organisation, practices, artefacts and even worldviews: 'All have a specific and abstract language to be learned. All have rules but the rules are different' (Donald 2009, p. 46). They also address quite different questions: engineering asks, 'Does it work?', law, 'Does it fit?', and literature, 'Do you agree?'

YOUR THOUGHTS

- To what extent would you say your discipline has a 'signature pedagogy'?
- How do the teaching approaches you adopt reflect the signature pedagogy of your discipline?

- How does assessment practice in your department reflect signature pedagogy?
- Might the prevailing disciplinary pedagogy benefit from being revised in any way?

Overcoming barriers to student understanding within disciplines

A threshold concept may be seen as a crossing of boundaries into new conceptual space where things formerly not within view are perceived, much like a portal opening up a new and previously inaccessible way of thinking about something. Successfully negotiating a threshold concept allows the learner to access a transformed way of thinking and practising, a fresh mode of reasoning and explanation and new understandings, perceptions, discourses and conceptual terrain, without which the learner would find it difficult to progress within a particular field of study. As a consequence of comprehending a threshold concept there may thus be a transformed internal view of subject matter, subject landscape or even world view.

The thresholds approach emphasises the importance of disciplinary contexts, as the conceptual boundaries that are crossed are part of disciplinary structures and formation. The learning of a threshold concept frequently entails an encounter with 'troublesome knowledge'. Depending on discipline and context, knowledge might be troublesome because it is ritualised, inert (unpractised), conceptually difficult and complex, counterintuitive, alien or tacit, because it requires adopting an unfamiliar discourse, or perhaps because the learner remains 'defended' and does not wish to change or let go of their customary way of seeing things (Perkins 2006). Encountering the troublesome knowledge of a threshold concept provokes a 'liminal' phase of transition (see below), in which new understandings need to be integrated and, importantly, prior conceptions relinquished. There is often double trouble, because both the acquiring of new knowledge and the relinquishing of old knowledge are difficult processes. The letting go of a prevailing or familiar view frequently involves an uncomfortable 'ontological shift' or a 'change in subjectivity', which, while advancing understanding, can paradoxically be experienced as a sense of loss (Meyer & Land 2003, 2005). Because we become, in many senses, what we know, letting go of something we know is like losing a part of ourselves.

Meyer and Land characterise such conceptual gateways as:
- *transformative* (occasioning a significant shift in the perception of a subject)
- *integrative* (exposing the previously hidden inter-relatedness of something)
- *irreversible* (unlikely to be forgotten, or unlearned only through considerable effort)
- *troublesome* (as discussed above)
- *reconstitutive* (they constitute a shift in the subjectivity of the learner).

These learning thresholds are often the points at which students experience difficulty. The transformation may be sudden or it may be protracted over a considerable period of time. Such transformations – which apply as much to habituated practices as to conceptual understandings – are often partial in their achievement, with learners 'getting' certain aspects of what is to be learned and not other aspects, leaving residual miscomprehension. They can incur resistance on the part of 'defended' learners or may lead to forms of mimicry in the application of new learning or adoption of new practices. In all disciplines such transformations seem to require and provide access to a changed use of discourse. Because of this combined reconfiguring of one's epistemological, ontological and discursive state, these transformations are usually irreversible.

Liminality

The notion of a threshold has always demarcated that which belongs within – the place of familiarity and relative security – from what lies beyond – the unfamiliar, the strange, the potentially threatening. It reminds us that all journeys begin with leaving that familiar space and crossing over into the riskier space beyond the threshold. This applies with any significant transformation in learning. All threshold concepts scholarship is concerned with stepping into the unknown and the discomfiting conceptual and ontological shifts which that entails. Difficulty in understanding threshold concepts may leave the learner in a state of 'liminality', a suspended transitional state or 'stuck place' in which understanding approximates to a kind of 'mimicry' or lack of authenticity. Illustrative examples of threshold concepts might be 'marginal cost', 'opportunity cost' or 'elasticity' in economics; 'evolution' in biology; 'gravity' in physics; 'reactive power' in electrical engineering; 'depreciation' in accounting; 'precedent' in law; 'geologic time' in geology; 'uncertainty' in environmental science; 'deconstruction' in literature; 'limit' in mathematics; and 'object-oriented programming' in computer science.

Transactional curriculum inquiry

Cousin (2008, pp. 269–270) maintains that the search for threshold concepts has the potential to open up discussions and co-inquiry among subject experts, students and educational researchers, creating what she terms 'forms of transactional curriculum inquiry' between these three parties. This holds out for these key actors a 'pursuit of shared understandings of difficulties and shared ways of mastering them'.

Cousin suggests that the thresholds framework, as one form of transactional inquiry, offers an approach 'which becomes neither student-centred nor teacher-centred but something more active, dynamic and in-between'. She has designed a practical process for the investigation of threshold concepts (Cousin 2009, pp. 201–212) within disciplines, which she terms transactional curriculum inquiry, given its emphasis on establishing dialogues between teachers, students and educationalists. This process explores the following questions:

- What do academics consider to be fundamental to a grasp of their subject?
- What do students find difficult to grasp?
- What curriculum design interventions can support mastery of these difficulties?

YOUR THOUGHTS

Drawing on a simplified version of Cousin's approach, establish a focus group of academics working within your disciplinary area and ask them to nominate threshold concepts which they consider essential to mastery of your subject and which are likely to cause conceptual or other difficulty for your students.

Investigate the threshold concept(s) in terms of the following questions:

- Why are they fundamental to a grasp of the subject?
- To what extent is mastery troublesome?
- What misunderstandings do students characteristically exhibit?
- Do students offer mimicked understandings rather than real mastery?
- What is the relationship between the various threshold concepts?
- How do they help to define disciplinary modes of reasoning and explanation?
- In what ways can mastery change the learner's relation to the subject?
- When does this mastery typically happen?

(Cousin 2009, p. 270)

Also consider:

- How do we typically teach these concepts?
- How do we typically assess these concepts? (see Chapter 5, Brown & Race 2012).

Issues for course design in the disciplines

The thresholds approach has significant implications for both course design and assessment (Land, Meyer & Smith 2008; Meyer & Land 2006a; Meyer, Land & Baillie 2010). The website maintained by Flanagan (2012) at University College London provides a frequently updated and comprehensive list of resources on this topic, with an alphabetical listing of resources by discipline. Key points that emerge are as follows:

- The thresholds approach draws attention to what most matters in a curriculum, and can serve to streamline curricula that have become 'overstuffed' (Chapter 2, Hunt et al. 2012). In this respect threshold concepts can be viewed as the 'jewels in the curriculum'.

- The approach indicates that learning requires a certain recursiveness (coming at the troublesome knowledge again through differing modes) which is not easily accommodated within 'short, fat' modules or semesters.
- There is a need for a more dynamic form of assessment capturing progression through the liminal phase at different points – a flickering movie perhaps, rather than a single snapshot.
- It also implies a listening for student understanding to which packed schedules and large class sizes are not entirely conducive.
- It seeks to identify the source of 'troublesomeness' and misunderstanding for students, which can point to the need for revisions in the course design.
- Learning incurs a reconstitution of self. Grasping a concept is never just a cognitive shift; it also involves a repositioning of self in relation to the subject. This means from the viewpoint of curriculum design that some attention has to be paid to the discomforts of troublesome knowledge.
- Learners tend to discover that what is not clear initially often becomes clear over time. So there is a metacognitive issue for students in terms of having to learn to tolerate uncertainty, complexity and ambiguity.

Encountering learning thresholds: student voices

Mathematician Sir Andrew Wiles gives an indication of what it feels like to have to develop a tolerance for uncertainty:

> Perhaps I can best describe my experience of doing mathematics in terms of a journey through a dark, unexplored mansion. You enter the first room of the mansion and it's completely dark. You stumble around bumping into furniture, but gradually you learn where each piece of the furniture is. Finally, after six months or so, you find the light switch, you turn it on, and suddenly it's all illuminated … Then you move into the next room and spend another six months in the dark.
>
> (Wiles, cited in Byers 2007, p. 1)

These students illustrate the unease of being in the liminal state:

> First student: I understood it in class, it was when we went away and I just seemed to have completely forgotten everything that we did on it, and I think that was when I struggled because when we were sat in here, we'd obviously got help if we had questions but … when it came to applying it … I understood the lectures and everything that we did on it but couldn't actually apply it, I think that was the difficulty.

> Teacher: Did you feel the same as Student 1?
> Second student: Yeah. I felt lost.
> Teacher: In lecture times as well?
> Second student: You know, I understood the concept for about let's say 10 seconds, yes, yes, I got that and then suddenly, no, no, I didn't get that, you know, suddenly, like this ...
>
> (Cousin 2010, p. 3)

Often students encounter new concepts but are not yet in, or through, the threshold, at a point where the new knowledge might make sense to them, as illustrated by a student of biology:

> Osmosis is counterintuitive, it goes the opposite way. When does it click? When you study marine fish in second or third year, you see what would happen; it's in a relevant situation. In first year you do mechanisms in blocks and there's no relevance.
>
> (Taylor 2008, p. 191)

But there is also the sense of gratification upon reaching the point of integration:

> Well, from not knowing what it is to knowing what it is, that is the big step one. So that can be knowing how to apply the concepts that we use. There are some things you learn, you suddenly think, wow, suddenly everything seems different ... you now see the world quite differently.
>
> (Cousin 2010, pp. 4–5)

Mapping understanding

One helpful approach to rendering more visible students' patterns of understanding in the liminal state is that developed by Kinchin and Hay (2000). They attempt to represent the gradual transformation of learners' understanding through simple concept-mapping techniques that make explicit current states of knowing and conceptual linkages (or misconceptions). Over a given period of time the structures of meaning-making are seen to change, with new elements being integrated, others being discarded, while further elements enter understanding but remain unintegrated. Fairly undeveloped understandings tend to take on a linear 'chain'-like pattern. Emerging or liminal understandings that are in transformation develop 'spoke'-like characteristics until a more expert 'net'-like structure is attained. This approach often surfaces understandings and misunderstandings which previously might have remained tacit. Kinchin et al. comment that 'the knowledge structures approach, facilitated by concept-mapping tools, provides a mechanism to go beyond making learning visible, towards making it tangible (i.e., not only can it be seen, but it can also be manipulated to support development)' (Kinchin et al. 2010, p. 83).

Tackling misunderstanding

In exploring the nature of student misconceptions in biology Ross et al. (2010) identified a range of potentially troublesome concepts within the discipline content knowledge, including 'cellular metabolic processes (e.g., photosynthesis and respiration), cellular size and dimensionality (surface area to volume ratio), water movement (diffusion and osmosis), genetics (protein synthesis, cell division, DNA), evolution, homeostasis and equilibrium' (p. 165). However, they also noted that difficulties in student understanding of these disciplinary concepts was compounded by a number of *procedural* threshold concepts such as 'energy, variation, randomness and probability, proportional reasoning, spatial and temporal scales, and thinking at a submicroscopic level' (p. 165). It was students' lack of such procedural abilities which further problematised the inherent difficulty in the subject content knowledge, causing misconceptions. Further to the assumption that threshold concepts reflect differences in ways of thinking and practising between acknowledged experts inside the subject and novices on the periphery (Wenger 1998), Ross et al. argue that students should be encouraged to become competent in procedural thresholds – in effect, the ways of thinking and practising – to facilitate their crossing of conceptual thresholds. This will enable us to understand 'whether students can subsequently transfer this thinking process to aid their understanding of other similarly difficult content (that is, to see if they have learnt how to cross unfamiliar thresholds)' (Ross et al. 2010, p. 174).

Decoding the disciplines: seven steps to overcome obstacles to learning

A similar, and helpfully pragmatic, approach is that offered by Middendorf and Pace (2004, pp. 4–10) in their work on 'decoding disciplines' in order to identify and help students tackle 'conceptual bottlenecks'. In their workshops for academic staff they employ a useful seven step approach which is repeated here in full as a strategy that you may wish to consider in the programs that you teach, to help you to open up what is often left implicit or unspoken within disciplines. Consider how you might answer the following questions:

- What is a bottleneck to learning in this class? Identify a place in the course where many students encounter obstacles (bottlenecks) to mastering the material.
- How does an expert do these things? Explore in depth the steps that an expert in the field would go through to accomplish the tasks identified as a bottleneck.

- How can these tasks be explicitly modelled? Show the students the steps that an expert would complete to accomplish these tasks.
- How will students practise these skills and get feedback? Construct assignments, team activities and other learning exercises that allow students to do each of the basic tasks defined above and get feedback on their mastery of that skill.
- What will motivate the students? Consider principles of student motivation that will enhance the learning environment.
- How well are students mastering these learning tasks? Create forms of assessment (Chapter 5, Brown & Race 2012) that provide specific information about the extent of student mastery of the particular learning tasks defined in Step 2. Are there other bottlenecks?
- How can the resulting knowledge about learning be shared? Faculty who have gone through the first six steps share what they have learned informally with colleagues or more formally in articles and presentations.

YOUR THOUGHTS

It has been observed that the notion of a threshold concept is, reflexively, something of a threshold concept in itself and may prove similarly troublesome (Meyer & Land 2005, p. 387).

- What is your own response to this approach? Is the idea of a threshold concept within your own discipline an idea that resonates with you or does it present problems for you?
- Have you ever personally experienced what is described here as a 'liminal' state in your own learning? If so what was the nature of that experience?
- Have you encountered instances of mimicry in your students' work? How do you recognise it?
- Do you consider that there might be threshold concepts in the process of becoming a university teacher? If so what form might they take?

Disciplines in the 21st century

Pedagogies of uncertainty

It is now becoming something of a cliché to discuss the 21st century as an age of uncertainty. Nonetheless, the world that students already face as they graduate is characterised by uncertainty in many spheres, as well as risk, unprecedented speed, and what Barnett (2000) has termed 'supercomplexity', a form of complexity which is ultimately irresolvable as it is predicated on fundamentally different value positions. To some extent disciplines have traditionally served to reduce the complexity and boundless nature of knowledge through establishing their own structures, internal logic and epistemes. How appropriate are they, then, as a vehicle through which to prepare students for such a challenging environment? Barnett has argued that:

> The student is perforce required to venture into new places, strange places, anxiety-provoking places. This is part of the point of higher education. If there was no anxiety, it is difficult to believe that we could be in the presence of a higher education.
>
> (Barnett 2007, p. 147)

Shulman similarly has coined the term 'pedagogies of uncertainty' as a positive description of robust classroom strategies to prepare students to cope with an unknown future:

> In these settings, the presence of emotion, even a modicum of passion, is quite striking – as is its absence in other settings. I would say that without a certain amount of anxiety and risk, there's a limit to how much learning occurs ... One must have something at stake. No emotional investment, no intellectual or formational yield.
>
> (Shulman 2005b, p. 22)

Atmospheres of 'risk taking and foreboding', he argues, produce excitement and anxiety, and foster both engagement and accountability.

The generic academic and employability skills, knowledge and attitudes that might be appropriate to help students cope with such challenging environments are often referred to as 'graduate attributes' (see Chapter 4, Chalmers & Partridge 2012). There is a link between pedagogies of uncertainty and such attributes in that the latter are in many respects the means by which students will learn to cope with an unpredictable world of risk and uncertainty. For example, a report by the Council for Industry and Higher Education (Fielden 2007, p. 19) drew attention to the need for students to develop the following capacities while at university:

- 'awareness of the complexity and interdependence of world events and issues'
- 'openness to learning and positive orientation to new opportunities, ideas and ways of thinking'
- 'tolerance for ambiguity and unfamiliarity'
- 'sensitivity and respect for cultural differences'
- 'empathy or the ability to take multiple perspectives'
- 'research skills to learn about the world'
- 'coping and resiliency skills in unfamiliar and challenging situations'.

Students, however, often can regard the teaching of such skills and capacities as somewhat irrelevant to their course of study ('I thought I came here to study engineering!'). This is particularly so if these skills are introduced as a 'bolt-on' study, such as an additional module on personal development planning, and not integrated into the disciplinary context of their program. These more generic attributes often make much more sense to students, and generate much less resistance, if they can be carefully woven into discipline-specific tasks that are clearly part and parcel of the learning of their subject.

Combining disciplinary and generic skills

You might like to reflect on how you could design discipline-based tasks in your own subject which will also serve to develop these broader skills and attitudes. Incorporating 'research-minded' activity (see Chapter 8, Jenkins & Healey 2012), such as inquiry-based learning or problem-based learning (see Chapter 9, Brodie 2012) can often be a good way to open up opportunities for the development of such skills. It has been recognised ever since von Humboldt's proposals for the establishment of the University of Berlin in 1810 (English translation, von Humboldt 1970) that research itself can provide a context and condition for the development of graduate attributes. Von Humboldt argued that what characterised learning in higher education was that it did not deal with settled bodies of knowledge (which would be more typical of secondary education perhaps) and therefore remained at all times in research mode, with teachers and students acting more like co-enquirers.

The following examples of discipline-based teaching give an indication of how generic skills might be interwoven with discipline-specific skills. They are instances in action, describing what this approach might look like at classroom level.

CASE 3.1: INTEGRATED TEACHING OF GENERIC AND DISCIPLINE-SPECIFIC SKILLS

The literature class

In this simulation exercise, derived from an approach originally created at Alverno College, Milwaukee, students, in groups of five, are asked to investigate a complaint from members of a local parent-teacher association that the novel *Jazz* by Toni Morrison be removed from the curriculum of the local girls' high school as being obscene and unfit for their 16-year-old sons and daughters to be reading. In the brief, the students are told that the school English staff defend their choice, arguing for the high literary merit and relevance of the text. The groups are asked to undertake an enquiry into this matter on behalf of the parent-teacher association of the fictitious school and report back in three weeks as to whether the novel should remain on the curriculum or not. The groups have to read the novel, form a working group, plan and chair meetings, determine what obscenity means in terms of literary publishing, how one assesses literary merit, and reach a decision on what is an open-ended situation with no prior assumption as to the desired course of action. They then have to prepare a written report and a presentation on the topic, not knowing which one of them will have to deliver it until shortly before (so they all have to be 'oven ready'). This approach offers a simple way of incorporating a variety of complex judgmental tasks and develops many useful attributes within one simple exercise which takes about 10 minutes to set up in class.

Forensic problem-solving

In a second-year pure and applied chemistry class, students are divided into small groups and given a case study of a (fictitious) student corpse found on campus. The students are given (partial) information in the form of lab reports from various official agencies. The students request analysis of the various types of evidence collected in order to determine the cause of death for which they will eventually have to deliver a simulated legal report 'in court'. A range of scientific reasoning and transferable skills are then exercised, with manipulation and evaluation of data to make realistic decisions on the evidence available. This occurs against a limited budget permitting a finite number of lab requests, and against a time deadline. They are obliged to tackle unfamiliar problems, apply forensic judgement, evaluate information, formulate and test hypotheses, and employ analytical and critical thinking. In all a broad set of graduate attributes come into play, and all have to be primed to give the final report.

Mechanical dissection

Drawing on an influential and successful model developed originally at Massachusetts Institute of Technology and known as CDIO (conceive, design, implement, operate) first-year engineering students are required, in groups of four, to undertake a mechanical dissection of a car. It is emphasised that the tasks they must undertake are related to the development of research skills for later in their course. Each student group spends a couple of hours selecting and removing a part of the car (for example, the front or rear suspension, or a part of the braking system). After doing this each group meets with two of the course lecturers to discuss the engineering theory that lies behind the particular component's function, and to identify particular parts of the component to be investigated and analysed in more detail regarding how they were made and of what materials. As the tutor of the course explains:

> These parts are examined under the microscope to ascertain the materials and processes involved in their manufacture. The students then have three weeks to research the functions, physics, manufacture and design of the components, and to produce a poster explaining these … They present their draft poster to two members of staff, who discuss the content with them and inform the students of any further work necessary to bring the poster to an acceptable standard. The students then have to produce a brief PowerPoint presentation covering the same material as the poster for a plenary session at which two students [from each group], chosen at random, describe their component to the rest of the cohort. After their presentation, each group has to field a couple of questions from students from the other groups. In preparing the poster and presentation students will need to explain topics not covered elsewhere in their first-year course.
>
> (Barker & McLaren 2005, p. 1)

For each of these three cases reflect briefly on the following issues:

- What is the disciplinary content being covered here?
- What disciplinary 'ways of thinking and practising' are possibly being developed here?
- What more general skills, knowledge, professional values or attitudes might the students be developing at the same time through engaging in these kinds of activities?
- How is evidence of the students' learning being gathered through these activities? (see Chapter 5, Brown & Race 2012).

You will notice in each of these cases that the students are required to be inquiring, to be actively engaged and somewhat enterprising, using their own initiative. Could you devise a similar teaching approach to a part of your own program?

Thinking beyond discipline: interdisciplinarity and collaborative pedagogies

The formative strength of disciplines, and the supportive social context they provide in which to practise, has traditionally served as the foundation of an academic career. The established scholarship on academic tribes and territories has amply demonstrated this (Becher 1989; Becher & Trowler 2001). However, as we increasingly find ourselves in an age of globalisation, uncertainty, risk and speed, the large pressing scientific, social and economic problems of our times – climate change, sustainability, terrorism, financial crisis, health, ageing populations – seem to demand more than one disciplinary lens to bring them more clearly into view. It is imperative that teaching crosses disciplines, to better allow students to master threshold concepts: interdisciplinary teaching and learning requires a sometimes troubling conceptual integration of different perspectives, a letting go of a previous stance, an ontological shift, and acquisition of a new shared discourse.

Interdisciplinarity and collaborative pedagogy at module and course level

A number of imaginative steps to promote cross-discipline teaching and learning are under way. Warwick University in the United Kingdom, for example, aims to explore different uses of learning spaces, alternative 'third spaces', which are seen as 'places where ambassadors of specialised knowledge recognise the explorative and pedagogical potential offered by other disciplines' (Blackmore 2010, p. 1). A new specialist centre has been set up to promote cross-departmental activity, at module level, that can combine disciplines in innovative ways, as the following cases illustrate.

CASE 3.2   SHAKESPEARE AND THE LAW
University of Warwick

This example of collaborative pedagogy combines law and English and 'focuses on trials in Shakespeare's plays and synthesising legal and textual history, and combining the forms of learning associated with the two departments (analysis of legal and textual evidence, mooting, performance)'. The module is assessed weekly by means of a 'weekly commonplace book' which acts as a learning journal and log (Blackmore 2010, p. 11).

CASE 3.3   POLITICS, LITERATURE AND IDEAS IN STUART ENGLAND
University of Warwick

This interdisciplinary module combines political science, literature and cultural studies by exploring key texts of major authors such as Bacon, Hobbes, Locke and Swift, drawing on biography, autobiography and diaries and addressing themes such as 'censorship of the press; the new, experimental science; news and its different forms; satire and polemic; radical consciences; women's writing; republicanism; and utopias' (Knights 2011).

Meanwhile, the Centre for Interdisciplinary Science at Leicester University provides full Bachelor of Science and Master of Science programs in Interdisciplinary Science.

CASE 3.4   INTERDISCIPLINARY SCIENCE
Leicester University

In the first year of a bachelor degree, for example, students complete eight core modules and one elective from a range including:
• Prophets and powers: Science from ancient to modern
• Science of the invisible: Molecules in chemistry, biology and physics
• Biosphere: An introduction to ecology
• Braining IT: Computer science and the human brain
• Near space: Earth, ocean and atmosphere.
    They also undertake four to eight hours of practical laboratory classes, two hours of mathematics classes, two hours of computing skills and fifteen to twenty hours of individual research. In the second year they cover:
• Time and energy: Dynamics and thermodynamics in physics and chemistry
• Habitable worlds: Cosmology from the big bang to the origin of life
• Forensic science: Detective science
• Molecules by design: Organic chemistry and pharmaceutical chemistry
• Man and machines: Physiology and biophysics.

Good practice in collaborative pedagogy

The Warwick University Centre that promotes collaborative pedagogy offers the following advice to academic staff for getting interdisciplinary initiatives under way (Blackmore 2010, p. 11):

- Make clear to students the purpose and rationale for interdisciplinary provision. Ensure provision is at the appropriate level for students.
- Consider provided interdisciplinary studies for the most able and interested students in 'high flier' courses.
- Establish a focal point to foster connections across schools.
- Ensure that interdisciplinary opportunities are (a) based on a nodal theme or problem approached from a variety of disciplinary perspectives, (b) linked to flexible and more collaborative teaching methodologies, (c) assessed appropriately, with assessment criteria made very explicit, (d) delivered through a variety of learning media and methods, and (e) highly reflective on the part of students and staff.
- Make clear to students in interdisciplinary programs where they should go for advice and support.
- Open discipline-centred modules to undergraduates from other departments to provide a rich and collaborative learning environment, where students feel valued for the perspectives which they bring from their own disciplines.

The centre recommends, moreover, that teachers should remind students of the 'five steps to great collaboration', which are:

1. Respect and appreciate your co-workers.
2. Practise your communication skills.
3. Make time and space for teamwork.
4. Be open to multiple perspectives and tolerant of discourses different from your own.
5. Make use of digital technology.

(McLeod & Dziegiel 2011)

YOUR THOUGHTS

Assess the extent to which your students gain experience of interdisciplinary work in your degree program.

- What form does this take?
- Identify aspects of interdisciplinary work that are done well and identify why these are aspects of good interdisciplinary practice.
- What might be barriers to interdisciplinary working for students in your field?
- How might these be overcome?
- What further possibilities might there be for collaborative pedagogy in your program?

Conclusion

It remains to be seen whether the changing modes of knowledge generation and exchange in a fast, globalised and digitised world will accelerate the rate of adoption of interdisciplinary practice and the design of new interdisciplinary programs amongst academics. As 18th-century author Dr Samuel Johnson once famously remarked: 'The chains of habit are generally too small to be felt until they are too strong to be broken' (cited in Bradley et al. 1969, p. 348). It may be that the current incentives, the patterns of reward and recognition which still predispose academics to keep within their disciplinary territories both conceptually and socially, may need to be rethought in order to engineer such a shift.

For the foreseeable future at least, however, disciplines will continue to serve as the main channel of engagement and remain the predominant conceptual terrain through which, and in which, students will encounter and attempt to integrate new knowledge and understanding in their university education. Consequently, the idea of discipline-based teaching – with its emphasis on disciplinary context, signature ways of thinking and practising, recognised conceptual structures and boundaries and strongly formative norms and values within its community of practice – offers an important lens through which you might analyse the concepts, topics and skills that, in the long term, will really matter to your students. It is a good lens also to bring into focus the difficulties and bottlenecks your students might be encountering and how your course design might be modified in order to help overcome these.

Your discipline – the area that both your students and you have actively chosen as your preferred avenue of study and inquiry – is also likely to be the most conducive space in which to help your students develop broader skills to equip them for their future careers and citizenship. It is the space where these more generic achievements tend to make more sense to them. Disciplines are always changing – some rapidly, others at a much slower pace – but all are always a provisional stability, and a continuingly interesting terrain in which to explore new directions in different ways. Ference Marton, a leading European theorist on learning in higher education, has argued that:

> The one single thing that would improve the quality of teaching and learning in higher education would be if academics in different disciplines took time to meet together and discuss what they should be teaching in their subject, and how they should be teaching it ... and I think the Threshold Concepts approach encourages people to do this.
>
> (Marton 2009, cited in Meyer, Land & Baillie 2010, p. xxiii)

This sounds like good advice and, if they are not doing so already, you might like to encourage your own disciplinary colleagues to join you in such a discussion.

CHAPTER 4

TEACHING GRADUATE ATTRIBUTES AND ACADEMIC SKILLS

Denise Chalmers and Lee Partridge

Keywords
graduate attributes, academic skills, employability, capability, integrating and
embedding

> There are obviously two educations. One should teach us how to make a living
> and the other how to live.
>
> (James Truslow Adams 1929)

Introduction

This chapter discusses how to integrate graduate attributes in discipline-based
teaching. It defines graduate attributes and shows that they must be included in
curriculum planning, teaching and assessment of student learning. It demonstrates that
developing students' graduate attributes will lead to better discipline-based learning
and enhancement of students' employability. The chapter discusses viewpoints about
embedding graduate attributes and presents strategies to teach them.

What are graduate attributes?

> Graduate attributes are the qualities, skills and understandings a university
> community agrees its students should develop during their time with the
> institution. These attributes include but go beyond the disciplinary expertise
> or technical knowledge that has traditionally formed the core of most university
> courses. They are qualities that also prepare graduates as agents of social good
> in an unknown future.
>
> (Bowden et al. 2000)

There has been a trend in universities to develop and declare a set of attributes that graduating students will have acquired. In part, the impetus for this trend arises from higher education accreditation and quality agencies asking universities to document the attributes and demonstrate how they develop and assess them. This reflects an international trend to require universities to demonstrate quality assurance processes and clear evidence of students' attainment of standards (see Chapter 14, Krause 2012). So, the graduate attributes that an institution aims to develop will include the external stakeholders' requirements, as well as sets of skills and attributes which universities agree are important for students to develop while studying for their degree. Therefore, an important first step for university teachers is to familiarise themselves with their institution's graduate attributes.

While the term 'graduate attributes' is used throughout this chapter, different universities may use other terms such as generic attributes, generic or graduate capabilities, core or key skills and employability capabilities. Regardless of terminology, they generally refer to the skills, knowledge, abilities and attitudes that students are expected to have developed as a result of their study for a university degree. They encompass discipline-specific knowledge and skills, broader professional and attitudinal dispositions related to the discipline, and the academic skills that underpin effective learning and inquiry. There is a remarkable consistency in the types of graduate attributes that each university wishes its students to develop, including effective written and oral communication and numeracy skills, critical analysis, independent learning skills and the ability to solve complex problems. There are also expectations that students will have developed behaviours and attitudes – specifically, these refer to ethical decision-making and citizenship skills – which they are able to apply in light of evidence and the global context in which they live. Barrie (2004) developed a framework that summarises diverse lists of graduate attributes.

FIGURE 4.1 Graduate Attribute Map (Barrie 2004)

This framework identifies two different levels of attributes: 'enabling' level attributes, which can be thought of as broader dispositions, and 'translation' level attributes which are more discrete, discipline specific attributes.

At the enabling level, there are three categories: scholarship; global citizenship; and lifelong learning. At the translation level there are five categories: research and inquiry; information literacy; personal and intellectual autonomy; ethical, social and professional understanding; and communication.

Each of these broader categories encompasses a number of subcategories. For example, research and inquiry encompasses the ability to undertake research and create new knowledge, critical analysis, discipline knowledge and problem-solving. The boundaries between categories are artificial constructs but the model is helpful because it encompasses all university graduate attribute statements identified in the Barrie (2004) study.

There are different national and sector approaches to the way in which graduate attributes are viewed and the means and mechanisms by which students acquire them. For example, in the United Kingdom, universities either attempt to embed skills within existing courses or offer stand-alone subjects. In the United States, academic skills tend to be taught in stand-alone subjects and are assessed in work-based or other co-curricular learning contexts. In Australia, graduates are expected to develop a generally accepted set of attributes as an outcome of engaging in their degree programs (Crammer 2006; Harvey & Bowers-Brown 2004). The attributes are, therefore, either explicitly or implicitly embedded as outcomes within individual subjects. There are also differences between the approaches taken by university and vocational education sectors, with vocational institutions focusing more on the acquisition and demonstration of competencies related to the workplace.

YOUR THOUGHTS

Find your university's statements and match them against Barrie's (2004) generic categories of graduate attributes, at the enabling level – scholarship; global citizenship; and lifelong learning – and the translation level – research and inquiry; information literacy, personal and intellectual autonomy; ethical, social and professional understanding; and communication.

Identifying graduate attributes to teach

The learning objectives (also called learning outcomes) of a subject are usually found in the subject outline or subject handbook and define what should be taught and assessed in a subject. They may be considered to be a learning contract between the student and the university. For example, the learning objectives shown below, taken from different subjects, relate to the category of graduate attributes shown in brackets.

Students will be able to:

- demonstrate proficiency within the laboratory by the correct use of the appropriate equipment' (research and inquiry)
- express their ideas coherently and logically when working both independently and cooperatively in both practical sessions and through assignments' (personal and intellectual autonomy and communication)
- demonstrate computer literacy by the use of internet resources and appropriate software in tutorial/laboratory sessions (information literacy)
- critically appraise the strengths and weaknesses of … , proposing solutions to problems affecting the implementation of … (research and inquiry, and ethical, social and professional understanding).

(University of Western Australia 2012)

YOUR THOUGHTS

Examine the learning objectives or outcomes for the subjects that you teach. Also read any available information about the program of study to which the subject(s) you teach contribute. Contextualise how your subject contributes to the students' overall development of graduate attributes.

List the objectives or outcomes that are discipline-focused graduate attributes in terms of content, knowledge and skills. List also the objectives focused on broader graduate attributes, such as students' communication skills, critical thinking and problem-solving capacity, ethical reasoning, or their understanding of socio-political and culture implications for their discipline.

If all of the objectives are focused on attributes of disciplinary knowledge and skills with no other graduate attributes listed, what broader graduate attributes are most closely linked to the learning required in the subject? For example, is there an opportunity to extend the students' ethical reasoning, cultural understanding or critical reasoning? Consider writing just one additional learning objective that describes the graduate attribute that you think students should develop while studying your unit.

Why is it important to teach graduate attributes?

Studies have shown that graduating students frequently fail to recognise and identify their development of graduate attributes during the course of their study (Scott 2005). This can influence their transition to employment and postgraduate research. It is, therefore, important for university teachers to assess the situation in their own institution and seek ways to explicitly signpost the teaching and learning of these skills and attributes.

Research by de la Harpe et al. (2009) found that while teachers generally accept the relevance of graduate attributes, many lack confidence in their ability to teach them. They were generally willing to teach graduate attributes that were strongly related to their discipline knowledge, such as critical thinking and problem-solving, but less willing, and less confident, in teaching attributes and academic skills such as teamwork, communication skills and ethical understanding. They felt these were outside their area of expertise. Accordingly, this chapter is designed to empower university teachers with some initial understanding and skills to teach a broader range of graduate attributes.

Stand-alone and embedded approaches to teaching graduate attributes

Barrie (2007) found that university teachers have different understandings of their role in developing their students' graduate attributes. Some viewed the development of such skills and attitudes as something that students should have acquired before coming to university. Others thought students should develop these outside of the subject and their own teaching, perhaps taught by student support or study advisors or in general introductory subjects. In contrast, some teachers consider it their responsibility to teach both disciplinary content and the underpinning graduate attributes that students require to learn the content effectively.

At the heart of these different points of view lies an implicit debate about the extent to which graduate attributes should be embedded in curriculum planning (the mainstream approach) and the extent to which they should be taught separately, as stand-alone, co-curricular topics (the separatist approach).

Research has shown that embedding graduate attributes in the curriculum leads to better quality student learning of disciplinary content, informed application of the knowledge and skills in the workplace, and greater student satisfaction with their study experience (Barrie 2007; Bath et al. 2004; Bowden et al. 2000; Chalmers & Fuller 1996; Crebert et al. 2004; Hager et al. 2002; Kelley & Bridges 2005; Treleaven & Voola 2008).

The following case has been adapted from Chalmers and Fuller (1996, pp. 127–131) and describes how one teacher's decision to trial embedding graduate attributes subsequently changed her practice and encouraged her to further incorporate the relevant skills within the subject content.

CASE 4.1   APPLIED SCIENCE
Monica Leggett, Edith Cowan University (adapted from Chalmers & Fuller 1996, pp. 127–131)

The course

Monica taught in the second-year Technology in Society course. Students attended classes (lectures, tutorials and site visits) for four hours each week. The course included three formal assessments: a group tutorial presentation, a written essay assignment and an end of semester examination. Important objectives of the course included challenging students' assumptions and beliefs about the connections between technology and society and developing their understanding of the complexity of interactions between science, technology and society.

The purpose of introducing the learning strategies program

Monica had identified two main problems that she wanted to address. Firstly, the low level of understanding and engagement with the subject that was evident in previous students' assignments, and secondly, the difficulty of getting students to integrate prior knowledge with new information. She decided to focus on how students acquired and worked with information and assessment. She aimed to integrate the teaching of knowledge-processing strategies into the teaching of the subject as students required these skills. For example, she presented note-making from text as a way of introducing students to a central reading required for tutorials and assessment activities. Then she taught students how to write a summary based on their notes. In this way, students learned about note-making and summary writing as they carried out the reading that was needed for their class work and their assignment. Students were also taught to generate questions to help them work with information. This strategy was first taught with lecture material that students had previously found challenging. It was later practised in the context of helping students revise for the examination by generating questions and writing summaries of important topics. Monica also involved the students in negotiating the criteria for assessing the tutorial presentation and essay assignment.

Successes

At the end of the course, the students demonstrated that they were better prepared to handle their third-year studies in science, both in terms of their understanding of the subject matter and their use of learning strategies. In tutorials students worked better in groups and presented work that addressed the relationships between technology and society more thoroughly than had occurred in previous years.

Students' initial complacency towards the introduction of learning strategies changed to a positive response to their introduction by the end of the course. Student feedback indicated that many believed the learning strategies were among the most important things learnt in the course. One student commented that 'the study skills were good and gave me a better idea of what I should be doing'.

As a result of introducing the teaching of learning strategies, Monica became more aware of the extent to which students do not know or use techniques expected of them in the course. She also felt that the program stimulated her to reconsider her own conception of teaching and her priorities as a teacher.

Difficulties

The main difficulty was identifying and allocating the appropriate amount of time needed to teach the various strategies. Initially Monica was hesitant and almost apologetic in teaching the strategies, for she expected that most students would have covered them at school. Later, as she became more aware of students' needs and saw that the integration of strategies and subject matter was working, she became more confident at teaching the strategies and less concerned that she was not devoting enough time to the subject matter of the course. Part way through she reviewed the program with the students and decided not to teach all the strategies that she had intended. Instead of teaching new strategies she began to focus on reviewing and practising those she had already taught.

Making notes from texts was particularly difficult for students. Monica had not realised how little some students gained from their reading, how long it took them to read, how many of them could not read flexibly, and how different it was for them to read and make notes in the recommended way. She became aware that she should facilitate reading by selecting different reading materials and by providing students with more guidance and practice on how to identify the main ideas and make notes from readings.

Students were reluctant to participate in negotiating the criteria for presenting and assessing assignments, and simply accepted her suggestions about the criteria that would be used and the marks that would be assigned. Despite this, Monica felt that the students obtained a better understanding of the criteria.

Future directions

Having tried the techniques, Monica now feels a greater sense of confidence and ownership of the program. She believes this confidence will allow her more freedom to adapt the techniques to fit the context and allow for better integration of the strategies and the content. She recognises that it is difficult for teachers to resist students' expectations that they should present factual content and information for students to learn and reproduce. However, she believes that if teachers integrate learning strategies with subject matter and help students work with information to develop understanding, it becomes easier to resist these expectations.

Embedding graduate attributes in your discipline

Biggs and Tang (2007) established a simple framework to assist university teachers to embed graduate attributes in the curriculum. It is a three-step process that involves customising graduate attributes, mapping them across the curriculum, and then aligning them with learning objectives and assessment. The first step is normally completed by the degree program team and/or program or subject coordinators. It involves customising generic graduate attributes so that they are relevant to specific disciplines. Table 4.1, developed by Dr Sara Hammer for the University of Southern Queensland, provides examples of what this might look like.

TABLE 4.1 Example of ways to describe graduate attributes in disciplinary terms

University-level descriptors	Discipline-based exemplars
Scholarship (discipline expertise) Evidence of analytical engagement with the theoretical knowledge of students' chosen disciplines	**Economics** A graduate in economics requires an awareness of the relationships between the main economic variables, an understanding of the nature and causal–chronological direction of those relationships and, finally, an ability to measure economic variables and utilise those measurements to assist decision-makers and policymakers.
Global citizenship Evidence of students' ability to connect discipline-based theory and practice to the sustainability of communities, economies and environments in a global context	**Mass communications** Upon completion of this program students will demonstrate the ability to understand the global implications of contemporary communication and media. Graduates will understand how the concept of sustainability impacts on their practice, value diversity, and possess a highly developed ability to communicate effectively with stakeholders, often with competing interests and from a wide range of cultural backgrounds.

TABLE 4.2 Example of graduate attributes of information literacy and interpersonal skills described at increasing levels of complexity (adapted from Chalmers et al. 2009)

Graduate attribute	Beginning	Developing	Advanced
Determine information requirements, identify credible and appropriate information sources, and interpret information accurately	Determine information requirements, identify a limited range of credible and appropriate information sources, and provide an accurate basic interpretation of information in area of study with extensive structured guidance	Determine information requirements, identify a moderate range of credible and appropriate information sources, and provide a competent interpretation of information within an area of study with limited structured guidance	Determine information requirements, identify an extensive range of credible and appropriate information sources, and provide an advanced interpretation of information within and beyond the area of study with little or no structured guidance
Demonstrate effective team and group skills: engage and participate effectively in team and group contexts; listen effectively and respond appropriately; self assess and provide and respond to constructive feedback	Demonstrate basic team and group skills in activities with structured guidance on effective team/group processes and skills which include listening, responding and providing constructive feedback	Demonstrate effective skills when participating in team and group activities with limited structured guidance. Assess contribution of self and others through providing and receiving constructive feedback	Consistently demonstrate: effective team and group skills in all contexts; effective listening and responses in all contexts; self-awareness of behaviour and engagement with others

After the graduate attributes have been customised to a specific discipline, they are mapped through all subjects that contribute to a degree program to ensure that students are provided systematically with opportunities to develop skills at increasingly complex levels. The levels may be described in broad terms as 'beginning', 'developing', and 'advanced'. Table 4.2, drawn from a communications skills framework, illustrates how two graduate attributes might be described at each of the three levels.

Biggs and Tang (2007) argue that effective teaching requires an alignment between the objectives or learning outcomes of the subject, the teaching and learning activities and assessment tasks (see Chapter 6, Angelo 2012). This same principle applies to the teaching of graduate attributes where the teacher plans to teach students the relevant graduate attributes, provide the students opportunities to practise and apply them in class and during independent study, and then assess the extent to which they can be demonstrated. An example of a plan of constructive alignment to teach graduate attributes within a subject is provided in Appendix 4.1.

YOUR THOUGHTS

Devise a table for your subject, similar to the table in Appendix 4.1, that identifies learning outcomes, student learning activities, assessment tasks and graduate attributes. This can also be provided to students so that the links between these components are transparent. This will help to identify repetition and gaps and can be used to refine and revise current and future teaching.

- Select a graduate attribute that is to be taught in one of your subjects.
- Write a learning objective or outcome that incorporates the graduate attribute.
- Define two teaching strategies that would address the graduate attribute and learning outcome.
- Design a piece of assessment that would measure your students' achievement of the learning outcome and provide your students with evidence of having addressed the graduate attribute.

Strategies to teach graduate attributes

It is necessary to develop a range of strategies specifically related to the teaching of graduate attributes. Table 4.3 provides examples of teaching and learning activities that enhance the development of graduate attributes and academic skills and can be used across a range of disciplines.

TABLE 4.3 Examples of teaching and learning activities to enhance the development of graduate attributes

Research and inquiry	Following teacher instruction and modelling, students: • compare and contrast different perspectives/theories/beliefs • undertake a literature review and conclude with questions that remain unanswered • generate questions designed to guide collection of relevant data • seek confirmatory and contradictory evidence to a posed question and conclude with an opinion based on the weight of evidence • take opposing positions and debate with others • examine an event drawing on evidence from several sources/perspectives.
Information literacy	Following teacher instruction and modelling, students: • undertake a search process using keywords and delineators • use an academic integrity tool (eg. Turnitin®) to review their referencing and citing skills and report on these • construct an annotated bibliography • identify a list of references on a topic or question and justify authenticity.
Personal and intellectual autonomy	Following teacher instruction and modelling, students: • assess their own work using reflective classroom activities • peer review other students' work • provide feedback to each other in collaborative projects • construct a personal viewpoint drawing on evidence.
Ethical, social and professional understanding	Following teacher instruction and modelling, students: • engage in work-integrated learning and service learning (see Chapter 10, Garnett 2012) • construct a small-scale research project involving collecting data from human subjects • practise completing the university's research ethics clearance process • role play or debate taking diverse ethical positions to encourage perspective-taking • participate respectfully in group activities with members from culturally and racially diverse backgrounds.
Communication	Following teacher instruction and modelling, students: • write for different audiences and in different professional roles • constructively critique other students' work • engage in group work and apply team processes • mentor other students • engage in a range of presentations for different purposes, e.g., persuasive, information, argument.

Modelling graduate attributes and academic skills

Teaching a graduate attribute or academic skill involves three types of knowledge: knowledge about the attribute or skill (declarative knowledge), knowledge of how to use it (procedural knowledge), and knowledge about when and why to use it (conditional knowledge). This implies that as well as telling students about the attribute or skill, you should show them how, when and why to use it. An effective way of doing this is to model the use of the attribute. Whereas a demonstration shows how an expert performs the process in a way that is free from hesitation and errors, modelling includes showing the decision-making components that help the expert (you) decide which process should be used and how to use it.

In teaching graduate attributes and academic skills, 'think aloud' modelling is often used. In this type of modelling, instead of just showing students how to use the strategy, the teacher verbalises and demonstrates what he or she thinks about when using the strategy. In addition to providing procedural knowledge about how to implement the attribute, this process provides conditional knowledge about how the decision to use the particular attribute is made, how progress is monitored, and how difficulties are handled. Think aloud modelling makes explicit the metacognitive aspects of the attribute use (Chalmers & Fuller 1996).

Assess and provide feedback on graduate attributes

The teaching and learning loop cannot be closed unless assessment, aligned with identified learning outcomes and teaching activities, demonstrates that learning has occurred. So, to ensure that students have developed their graduate attributes to the expected level, you must explicitly assess their acquisition of the attributes.

Thomas et al. (2009) provide specific examples of the progressive development of graduate attributes across a degree program through scaffolded activities and assessments. Beginning in first year, these broaden until in third year the assessments combine several graduate attributes. This process is designed to 'foster autonomous application of [graduate attributes] and reflection about them' (p. 325). Case 4.2 outlines the essential elements of this process which could feasibly be adapted to most disciplines.

CASE 4.2   TEACHING GENERIC SKILLS WITHIN THE BUSINESS DISCIPLINE
(adapted from Thomas et al. 2009, pp. 321–330)

The strategies listed in this case study were developed as part of an Australian Teaching and Learning Council project (Graduate Skills 2010) which focused on graduate attribute development in Business programs of study. The activities and assessments listed were trialled by 35 students from seven Australian universities during a three-day workshop. Further case studies and resources to support these activities are available on the project website (Graduate Skills 2010).

First-year activities and assessments

The graduate attributes of teamwork and critical thinking were addressed in two separate activities. The teamwork activity can be integrated into any group assessment. Teachers provided students with examples of team rules, then asked students to determine the rules by which their project team will operate. Students are subsequently asked to evaluate themselves and their fellow team members against the rules they developed. The critical thinking activities address the challenge that students face when asked to write their first university essay. Smaller activities such as those listed below are recommended to scaffold the required skills.

Activity 1: Evaluate sources. Teachers provide students with articles about a controversial topic or issue within the discipline from a range of sources (web, newspapers, Wikipedia, peer-reviewed journals) and a framework for evaluating the sources. The framework might include consideration of questions like: Who has written this source? Who has checked it to ensure it is correct? Why should I believe them? (Do they have any authority? Could they be biased in any way by belonging to a particular commercial enterprise or political party, for example?) Teachers should stress to students the importance of completing the reading individually prior to the tutorial session. In addition to learning to evaluate the quality of articles, students can use the references as a starting point for discussion.

Activity 2: Analyse articles. This is undertaken as a group activity, in groups of two to four students, in a tutorial. Outcomes of this activity include the abilities to analyse arguments, combine different ideas into one piece of work, and correctly reference a variety of sources. Students are asked to design a poster depicting the arguments for and against the issue discussed in Activity 1. They should include direct quotes and paraphrased statements from the articles, with the sources identified in the appropriate citation style. The most compelling arguments should be identified on the poster and the complete list of references used should be listed on the back using the correct format for the discipline.

Activity 3: Write a short argumentative essay. This activity is undertaken for individual assessment. Each student writes a 500-word essay which (a) presents points of view regarding the issue, (b) states and justifies the student's own position, and (c) uses correct referencing style. In addition students are asked to write a 200-word reflection on their learning in the three activities. Students can also be asked to peer and self-evaluate their writing.

Second-year activities and assessments

Teachers can continue to develop students' graduate attributes though the second year, but reduce the amount of scaffolding – that is, the teacher will not necessarily provide or signpost the requisite knowledge, skills and support the student needs to negotiate a new piece of learning; the student will have to discover some of this independently. This example involves a group assessment and employs the jigsaw method (see Chapter 2, Hunt et al. 2012 for a description of the jigsaw method). The teacher sets each student one reading from a selected list of readings that reflects a particular point of view on a topic. Students read, then discuss their understandings with others who have been assigned the same reading. These 'expert' groups discuss how they will negotiate their point of view with others. The groups are subsequently rearranged so that each group contains an expert on each of the topics or aspects. A series of questions are posed to each group which requires them to consider all viewpoints before negotiating a decision and making a short presentation to the class. For instance, on the question of sustainability in the context of a business, students can be asked to consider the viewpoint of various stakeholders including company worker, company management, government and community groups before answering a range of questions, which might include: What sustainability issues are relevant to the business? Did you reach a consensus? How did the group arrive at the consensus? What conclusion did you reach?

By asking students how they arrived at their conclusion, they are being required to reflect on the application of the negotiation and decision-making skills learnt in first year.

Third-year activities and assessments

This third-year assignment requires students to integrate various graduate attributes, and allows the teacher to reduce the amount of scaffolding provided for the students. The assignment is a team-based discussion on an ethical dilemma. The graduate attributes include critical thinking, teamwork, communication skills and discipline knowledge. Student groups are required to prepare a 15-minute presentation, discussion or debate that will engage the entire class. Topics might include: Should the government be bailing out the banks? Should organisations be able to monitor their employees' emails? Should organisations be able to drug test in the workplace? What is the role of public transport in the future? Teachers provide students with newspaper articles and reports on court cases to help them consider the issues.

Self and peer feedback

Self and peer assessment and feedback practices are critical processes to integrate graduate attributes into undergraduate teaching. Indeed, self and peer reflection and feedback are effective in supporting any form or content of learning. Nicol (2010) contends that the core requirement of acquiring graduate attributes is self-regulation. He reasons that 'the main characteristic of autonomy or self-regulation in learning is that students take some significant responsibility for setting their own learning goals and for evaluating progress in reaching these goals'(p. 4). He advocates a self and peer assessment approach to support intellectual autonomy, as 'it gives students skills needed to evidence their own attribute development' and 'it will help ensure the transfer of attributes and skills to other contexts and real-life situations beyond the university' (p. 6). Nicol (2009) describes four case studies of assessment and feedback practices in the first year of undergraduate study across a range of disciplines and where self and peer feedback is used to enhance the learning of graduate attribute skills. The examples include: online collaborative work in a large first-year psychology course; engagement and self-study in French language learning; encouraging time on task in first-year biology; and collaboration and reflection in software engineering (Nicol 2009, pp. 52–70).

Support for teachers and students to develop graduate attributes

Universities provide their staff and students with a range of services to support the development of graduate attributes. Teachers are often able to access personal, one-on-one support and advice from the staff in their university's teaching and learning centre. Support for teachers is also available from library staff, technical and administration staff. For instance, librarians are able to offer relevant information and are likely to provide resources and sessions to your students on aspects of information literacy and related research skills. Information technology and computer application assistance and training are also available for students.

University student services provide an invaluable resource for the development of graduate attributes and academic learning skills. These include focused workshops, study groups, peer mentoring and individual or group consultations. Some universities provide university bridging programs to assist students to develop learning skills before they embark on their degree programs, while others provide catch-up workshops for students at risk of academic failure. Proactive university teachers invite support service staff into their teaching programs to provide just-in-time assistance prior to assessments.

Many university student services organisations provide online information and advice for distance education students and for students to use on demand. Teachers interested in embedding graduate attributes in teaching and assessment practice should direct students to available services and refer to these in subject outlines and in feedback on students' assignments, to encourage students to work independently to address any emergent learning difficulties in regard to academic skills.

You may find it useful to attend some of the academic skills workshops offered for students that are particularly relevant to the learning skills required in your discipline. Subsequently, you can then adapt the examples to your subject. Alternatively, the academic advisor may be willing to run a tailored workshop in a tutorial session to provide just-in-time assistance for your students.

It is not always easy to work out what support is available to teachers. It may be useful to identify a more experienced colleague or mentor who is willing to assist and direct you. Case 4.3 provides an example of involving student support staff in the teaching of a first-year subject.

CASE 4.3   USING SUPPORT SERVICES IN YOUR TEACHING
Siri Barrett-Lennard, The University of Western Australia (Chalmers et al. 2009)

Introduction to Professional Engineering is a large first-year foundational subject for all engineering students at the University of Western Australia. The subject requires students to demonstrate and reflect on written, oral and presentation communication skills as well as critical information literacy skills and interpersonal skills. The focus on developing these skills is explicit, transparent and substantial.

Curriculum content

The subject introduces students to the social, cultural, environmental and economic contexts of professional engineering practice. Students learn to work in project-based teams to research, develop, write and present sustainable solutions to real-world design problems in developing countries. Lecture topics include project management, engineering design, international development, sustainability issues, risk management, cultural competency, report writing, oral presentations, teamwork, research skills and appropriate referencing and editing techniques.

Pedagogy

The subject typically caters for more than 650 students. Efficiencies are gained in lectures, which are run for the entire student cohort, and workshops, which cater for 100 to 150 students each. Extensive structured guidance is then able to be offered both in core tutorials, consisting of roughly 30 students, and in supplementary communication focus tutorials, which allow for roughly 15 students per group.

Lectures present information. Workshops complement lectures and assist students to construct designs they have developed. Tutorials are of two types: core tutorials that all students attend, which are conducted by disciplinary experts from the engineering faculty; and supplementary communication focus tutorials, conducted by staff with expertise in the theory and practice of communication skills from student services, that are recommended for students identified as at risk of failing the unit due to weak communication skills. Core tutorials allow students to investigate their design problems in teams and to communicate and receive peer and tutor feedback on their design solutions, reports and presentations. Supplementary communication focus tutorials provide additional embedded communication skills instruction and feedback linked to subject content and assessment tasks for those students who need it.

Assessment

Students complete an initial written task in the first week of classes, with at-risk students recommended to attend supplementary communication focus tutorials in addition to the core program. Throughout the semester, students demonstrate their learning through tutorial participation, problem-based assignments (investigative, progress and design reports) and oral presentations of their reports. Outstanding design reports are entered into the Engineers Without Borders design challenge, a competition open to first-year engineering students at all Australian and New Zealand universities. This competition provides external benchmarks for student learning performance.

Successes

This subject caters very well for at-risk students, while at the same time extends the communication skills of top-performing students. For example, UWA students out-performed more than 6000 students from 25 universities to win the Engineering Without

Borders design challenge in both years the university participated (2008 and 2009). This provides an external benchmark of the subject's success both in developing communication skills (students are judged partly on the basis of the quality of their written and oral reports) and in developing engineering design skills (students must demonstrate innovative, appropriate, sustainable solutions to design problems). At-risk students have also performed well. International students from non-English speaking backgrounds have also benefited from the additional supplementary communication focus tutorials. In 2005 the progression rate of international students was significantly lower than that of domestic students but, following the introduction of the communication tutorials, the progression rate of the international students rose to a level equivalent to domestic students. Students attending communication focus tutorials have also been among subject prize winners.

Faculty and student services staff members have collaborated on every aspect of curriculum development, tutor training, resource development, unit delivery, assessment and feedback over the years. This integrated approach between content and communication experts ensures that technical, professional and communication components of the unit are all addressed.

YOUR THOUGHTS

- Identify what support services and are available for your students.
- What will you do to integrate these services into your planning for teaching and assessment?

Conclusion

This chapter has stressed the importance of developing graduate attributes, skills and attitudes alongside discipline knowledge and expertise. It has demonstrated that the teaching of graduate attributes can be successfully integrated into disciplinary teaching. It has provided concrete examples of how to embed and assess graduate attributes and indicated the importance of aligning graduate attributes with the objectives of the subject, teaching and learning activities and assessment. Teaching graduate attributes can enhance student learning of disciplinary knowledge, and contribute to graduates' employability through developing qualities that employers value, such as the ability to communicate clearly in oral and written forms, work in teams, solve problems and demonstrate intercultural understanding (Hager & Holland 2006). Through integrating the teaching and assessment of graduate attributes within the teaching and learning activities of a subject, students will no longer report that they have graduated with little or no development of their graduate attributes during their study at university (Scott 2005) as they currently do. Instead, they will confidently be asserting not only their development but their demonstrable achievement, evident in their grades and illustrated in their job applications.

APPENDIX 4.1 Graduate attribute subject alignment matrix for a marketing strategy subject (Treleaven & Voola 2008, p. 163. © Lesley Treleaven & Ranjit Voola 2008. Reprinted by permission of SAGE Publications.)

Intended learning outcomes	Graduate attributes	Learning activities	Assessment tasks and assessment criteria				
			Seminar and online discussion board participation (10%)	Online reflective journal entries (10%)	Team-based written case study (20%)	Team-based computer simulation (20%)	Exam (40%)
Student is able to: • engage in lifelong learning, reflective thinking in marketing strategy • think critically about underlying marketing strategy theories, concepts and assumptions	• demonstrate personal and intellectual autonomy, including the ability to work independently and sustainably in a way that is informed by openness, curiosity and a desire to meet new challenges	• read texts and other materials and be prepared to critically analyse the topics • make notes and summaries before lectures • contribute constructively to discussion board topics • reflect and post online journal entries	• ask relevant and thought-provoking questions • be proactive in class participation	• question some of the traditional assumptions of marketing strategy • clearly articulate why he or she disagrees or agrees with a particular strategic topic or concept	• develop coherent and convincing arguments that require critical thinking	• work independently and in a group to solve any problems with the simulation or team process	• think critically and differently about key concepts and theories

			Assessment tasks and assessment criteria				
Intended learning outcomes	Graduate attributes	Learning activities	Seminar and online discussion board participation (10%)	Online reflective journal entries (10%)	Team-based written case study (20%)	Team-based computer simulation (20%)	Exam (40%)
• manage, analyse, evaluate and use marketing-related information efficiently and effectively • appreciate the changing nature of the frontiers of knowledge in marketing strategy through research and conduct research in archives, libraries and the web	• conduct research and inquiry to create new knowledge and understanding	• prepare for lectures by conducting research on the relevant topics beyond the textbook • gain access to library databases • apply the arguments in the articles to the classroom discussion	• transfer new knowledge into class discussion and online discussion by researching extant academic and/ or practitioner-related literature	• identify and discuss concepts that are strategic • develop coherent arguments when recommending solutions and critically evaluating theories in major fields of study	• summarise key articles and develop coherent arguments based on academic journals • identify, define and analyse strategic problems and recommend creative solutions	• manage, analyse and respond to vast amounts of information relating to the simulation	• conduct additional research to support arguments when answering the exam questions • apply business theories and concepts to problems and practice

Student is able to:

CHAPTER 5

USING EFFECTIVE ASSESSMENT TO PROMOTE LEARNING

Sally Brown and Phil Race

Keywords
assessment for learning, authentic assessment, formative assessment, summative
assessment

Assessment is integral to learning

In recent years, there has been a move away from the expectation that assessment
is (just) a measurement of the outcomes of learning, towards an acceptance that
assessment is an integral part of the process of learning. Even so, there remain
issues to address. University teachers still assess too much (Race 2010) and continue
to adopt ways of measuring students' achievement that were used when a smaller
proportion of the population participated in higher education. For students, there
can seem to be so much assessment that they become excessively strategic in their
learning – giving time only to those things that will 'count' towards their degrees.
So we know what's wrong with assessment and feedback, and what we need to
achieve by changing assessment to enhance student learning. The issue is: how
best to redesign assessment to make it fit-for-purpose?

Assessment is a complex, nuanced and intricate activity. To make it fit-for-purpose
it is necessary to take account of context, level, learning environment, students'
background, individual differences and learning content. As Sadler noted:

> The indispensable conditions for improvement are that the student comes to
> hold a concept of quality roughly similar to that held by the teacher, is able
> to monitor continuously the quality of what is being produced *during the act of
> production itself*, and has a repertoire of alternative moves or strategies from which
> to draw at any given point. In other words, students have to be able to judge the
> quality of what they are producing and be able to regulate what they are doing
> *during the doing of it*.
>
> (Sadler 1989, p. 121)

Sadler was a lead contributor to 'Assessment 2020' (Boud & Associates 2010), in which experienced practitioners agreed on seven recommendations at a national level in Australia for making assessment and feedback fit-for-purpose, noting that assessment has most effect when:

1. it is used to engage students in learning that is productive
2. feedback is used to actively improve student learning
3. students and teachers become responsible partners in learning and assessment
4. students are inducted into the assessment practices and cultures of higher education
5. assessment for learning is placed at the centre of subject and program design
6. assessment for learning is a focus for staff and institutional development
7. assessment provides inclusive and trustworthy representation of student achievement.

These chime clearly with Gibbs' (2010b) seven tactics for tuning assessment and feedback to learning, which propose that teachers should:

1. capture student time and effort, distributing that effort appropriately across topics and weeks
2. generate high-quality learning effort, oriented towards clear and high standards
3. provide sufficient feedback, often enough, and in enough detail
4. focus feedback on students performance, on actions under their control, rather than on students themselves or their characteristics
5. make feedback timely, while it still matters to students, in time for them to use it towards further learning, or to receive further assistance
6. link feedback to what students believe they are supposed to be doing
7. ensure that feedback is not only received, but is attended to, so that students act on it to change their future learning and performance.

Race (2010) argues that assessment can be improved dramatically by linking it to seven straightforward factors which underpin successful learning. He argues that we need to:

1. design assessment so that students *want* to learn, rather than assessing in ways that promote anxiety
2. help students to develop ownership of the *need* to learn by making clear to students the intended outcomes and associated evidence of achievement
3. use contact time with students to engage them in learning by doing (practice, trial-and-error, repetition) so that they become well-rehearsed in producing evidence of achievement
4. ensure students get quick and useful feedback – from university teachers and from each other
5. use assessment and feedback to help students to make sense of what they learn

6. get students to deepen their learning by coaching other students, and explaining things to each other, practising to communicate effectively what they have learned back to us in assessment contexts
7. allow students to deepen learning by assessing their own learning and that of others 'during the doing of it' (Sadler 1989). This can be achieved through self and peer assessment, helping students to see how assessment works in practice, so that they understand the rules of the game, and can give the game their best shot.

The qualities of assessment

Before delving further into a discussion of approaches to assessment, it is important to understand some of the key terms widely used in the literature on assessment:

- *Validity* is about how well we're measuring exactly what we're trying to measure, and boils down to how effectively we're measuring evidence of achievement of the published learning outcomes.
- *Reliability* is essentially about fairness, and getting away as far as possible from subjective judgements, especially in contexts where different assessors would be likely to award quite different marks or grades for a given candidate's essay, report or answer to an exam question.
- *Transparency* is about how well students themselves know how the assessment works, and how much they feel they can trust the processes used and judgements made on their work.
- *Inclusivity* is about the extent to which we can make assessment 'a level playing field' for all students, including those with particular needs, cultural backgrounds or learning problems.
- *Authenticity* is about two things – first, the extent to which it can be guaranteed that what is assessed is the work of the student concerned, and not plagiarised or copied; and second, how closely what is assessed links to the world outside universities and what students will need when employed.
- *Fairness* is critically important to students and assessors alike, and overlaps with several of the factors listed above (see overview by Flint & Johnson 2011).

YOUR THOUGHTS

Review an assessment activity that your students undertake and check the extent to which it aligns with each of the qualities.

To achieve all of these qualities in a single assessment element is almost impossible, but it may be possible to improve some aspects without radically altering design. The assessment profile of a subject – that is, the range of assessments conducted over the length of the course – can ensure that assessment design cumulatively satisfies each of the qualities. Assessment also needs to be manageable, for university teachers and students. It already takes considerable time, so efforts to diversify to match quality criteria should not add to the volume of assessment. Rather, we should replace long or repetitive assessment with shorter, sharper and more-focused learning opportunities.

A fit-for-purpose approach to assessment

Before designing an assessment strategy for a degree program, consider the following questions, which will help you to articulate how your assessment strategies are fit-for-purpose in terms of context, cohort of students, level of study and subject area:
- Why am I assessing?
- What am I assessing?
- How am I assessing?
- Who is undertaking the assessment?
- When should assessment take place?

The purposes of assessment

The purpose of assessment can vary from supportive, formative assignments in non-threatening contexts that we might use early to help students get the measure of how they are doing, through to final-stage summative assessments, designed to test whether the student is fit to practise in high-risk contexts like medicine or aviation. In-class group activities, including peer review, might be suitable for the former, while Objective Structured Clinical Examinations (OSCEs), where students demonstrate capability in a large range of short practical tasks, might better fit the latter (see Case 5.2 below).

Other purposes of assessment might include:
- enabling students to get the measure of their achievement (finding out what they know and what they don't yet know)
- providing feedback so that students can improve and remedy deficiencies, and become aware of strengths and weaknesses
- helping students to consolidate their learning (often students report not really 'getting it' until they construct an assignment on a particular topic)
- providing students with opportunities to demonstrate evidence of their competence and thereby employability
- motivating students to engage in deep learning (see Chapter 2, Hunt et al. 2012)
- helping students make choices to drop subjects where no consistent ability is demonstrated, or to continue with weaker subjects which are, nevertheless, essential to core study areas

- giving feedback to teachers on their own effectiveness (a few poor pieces of student work may reflect on your students; lots of weak assignments may reflect on the assessment design, task briefing, assessment arrangements or teaching)
- providing statistics for internal and external agencies (without which higher education systems will come to a grinding halt).

Choosing what to assess

When designing an assessment, we need to decide whether we are assessing product or process (or both), theory or practice (or both), subject knowledge as a discrete area or its application to professional or other contexts. Some areas lend themselves to computer-based multiple-choice tests, which can provide instant feedback to students on basic subject knowledge, while others require students to demonstrate critical thinking and reflection through, for example, critical incident accounts, where students identify two or three incidents from a reflective diary and report using a template proforma on the context in which they were working, what they did, what use they made of theory to choose particular lines of action, what happened as a result, what were the short- and long-term outcomes, what they learned from the experiences and what they would do differently next time.

We may also ask whether we are assessing what we've always assessed or what it's easy to assess. Authentic, relevant, assessment can be challenging to design and tricky to implement, but students tend to take it more seriously if they can see the sense of what they are doing and recognise how it fits into their overall programs of study, in what Biggs (2003) describes as a constructively aligned approach (Angelo 2012).

Choosing methods of assessment

Many universities rely on a small range of assessment methods: essays, unseen written exams, reports and multiple-choice tests (usually computer-based). Each has merit, but a wider range of assessment methods adds value in terms of student learning, as long as the range of methods is not so great that students never have the chance to get used to any single method (Gibbs & Dunbar-Goddet 2007). Using a range of diverse methods of assessment is valuable because each method disadvantages some students. Using a range of methods means that students are assessed across a range of abilities and skills, and that everyone has some opportunities to play to strengths.

Table 5.1 is intended to illustrate and explain ways of designing assessment. It is not exhaustive. Rather, the elements are a starting place from which to adapt and extend ideas, as appropriate, to different disciplines and contexts.

TABLE 5.1 Diverse assessment methods and approaches

Method	Advantages	Disadvantages	Notes
Exams Traditional unseen, time-constrained exams, which largely use essay style questions.	• regarded as fair, avoiding problems of plagiarism and cheating, and amenable to yielding data which can be handled quantitatively	• traditional exams only measure 'what comes out of students' pens' which is an inadequate proxy for 'what's in their heads' • a great deal of time is used in marking exams, often against the clock	• for a detailed discussion of the pros and cons of traditional exams and alternative exam approaches, see Chapter 2 in Race (2006)
Open-book or open-note exams Students can take into the time-constrained exam specified or unspecified texts and notes, so that the questions focus not on memory and recall, but on interpretation and analysis	• can take away the focus from memorising	• designing good questions for open-book or open-note exams is rather different from designing traditional exam questions, and is a skill which staff need to practise to develop fully	
Take-away papers Students are given, say, a week in which to prepare an answer to a given topic, effectively as a short-term course work assignment	• allows a more normal approach to researching and preparing answers than in traditional exams	• take-away papers can disadvantage students with hectic home lives	
Short-answer questions Students produce short responses to large numbers of questions, enabling high coverage of topics, with less reliance on elegance of sentence construction and argument	• moves away from 'speed of extended writing' as a necessary skill, and allows a wider range of subject material to be tested		

TABLE 5.1 (continued)

Method	Advantages	Disadvantages	Notes
Essays	• enables students to demonstrate the ability to construct an argument and to write fluently, coherently and at length	• essays are rarely used in mainstream occupations, so not an authentic means of assessment for most courses • readily plagiarisable • requires teachers to spend too much time marking • students may be graded on their essay technique, rather than their subject mastery	• one of the most heavily used methods of assessment on humanities courses, with least justification
Reports	• more authentic than essays, as students may enter careers where report-writing is a requirement	• reports are often based on practical and field work and done collaboratively by students, but are usually required as individual write-ups, so the report-writing itself may end up being assessed, when perhaps the collaboration was more important	• the fall-back means of assessment for many courses
Multiple choice questions with feedback responses	• excellent for quick testing of factual material • feedback on correct or incorrect choices can be given instantly, allowing rapid formative feedback on learning	• while suitable for formative purposes, it is much harder to design high-quality multiple-choice questions for summative assessment • questions must be piloted extensively to determine facility values and discrimination indices to select which questions are suitable to include in summative tests	• getting students to design multiple-choice questions and feedback responses is an excellent learning activity, and can lead to the development of substantial question banks for formative use
Sophisticated computer-based tests Using a wide range of question types including drop-down menu selection, drag and drop, clicking points on graphs, interpreting data from maps and diagrams etc.	• best suited to large cohorts and multiply presented courses, where it can be exceptionally efficient • helps new students build confidence as they self-test on new and familiar material	• tends to require considerable work to design good computer-aided assessment • when it is bad, it leads only to efficient guesswork	• needs expertise in question design, subject content and technology to support it

Method	Advantages	Disadvantages	Notes
Portfolios	• allows learners to present wide-ranging evidence of achievement, and to show originality and creativity alongside mastery of subject knowledge	• takes time to mark, and assessment reliability can be quite low as different assessors tend to look for different things when assessing wide-ranging evidence of achievement	• portfolios can be maintained and show development over a considerable time scale, and can be useful evidence of achievement to show to prospective employers
Viva voce individual oral tests or interviews	• allows probing questions to check for understanding • widely used for high-stakes assessment, such as at doctorate and masters levels • regarded as authentic, as many careers and professions may depend on face-to-face skills at answering questions and giving persuasive explanations	• some candidates can be let-down by nerves in face-to-face 'grillings' • evidence of achievement may be ephemeral, and it is hard to analyse retrospectively, unless recordings have been made • difficult to guarantee fairness between candidates, especially when variations in levels of probing occur • with large cohorts, it can be difficult to timetable oral assessment in ways which prevent 'leaking' of questions to forthcoming candidates	• Joughin (2010) proposes a strong case for increased use of oral assessment as part of a balanced range of assessment methods in present-day contexts
Presentations	• allows candidates to demonstrate oral communication skills alongside subject mastery • authentic, as oral presentation skills are often important in future employment • peer-assessment can make presentations a better learning experience for all • can include assessment of the ability to respond to questions from the audience	• time-consuming • may be hard to strike a balance between mastery of content and skills of presentation • 'raising the bar': expected standards can become higher over a series of presentations • unless recorded, presentations are 'ephemeral', making it hard to compare a series reliably	• 'impression' marks can be associated with the quality of presentation slides or handout materials

TABLE 5.1 (continued)

Method	Advantages	Disadvantages	Notes
Posters	• allow candidates to integrate a range of evidence of achievement in an agreed visual format • can be compared with each other in an amenable way • lend themselves to peer assessment, and assessment by third parties, for example professionals in the field or employers	• the visual appearance and design of the poster can rate too strongly in the overall assessment, as opposed to the thinking behind the poster • some candidates may have better availability of resources (colour, photos and so on), compromising fairness of assessment	• exhibitions of posters can be kept photographically or online, and used to train future candidates in the preparation of their own posters
Projects	• can be used for in-depth investigations that develop research skills (Jenkins & Healey 2012) • allow candidates to demonstrate originality and creativity	• reliability of assessment can be compromised when projects are quite different in scope and range • tendency for presentation to influence assessment unduly	
Case studies	• increased authenticity because they are 'real-world' scenarios	• written communication may dominate the assessment (unless an element of oral assessment is used as well) • it is impossible to have a range of case studies of exactly equal 'difficulty'	• a bank of case-studies can be built, to allow students the opportunity of rehearsal to develop the required skills and competences to do well
Simulations	• can measure a range of practical skills and competences beyond written and oral communication • highly authentic when relating to particular professions and contexts	• take time to design, which is offset by advantages when high numbers of candidates are involved	• heavily used in professional subjects like aviation and surgery to test competence in safe contexts
OSCEs (Objective Structured Clinical Exams)	• allow candidates to be tested on high-level skills, in authentic contexts (e.g., interpreting X-rays, interviewing patients (actors), interpreting case notes, making diagnoses, deciding on prescriptions etc.) • can be quite quick	• designing OSCE scenarios can be time-consuming, but the design can be done by groups of students in prize competitions – the real prize being that some of the scenarios they submit are actually used in their own OSCEs	• OSCEs are highly regarded as authentic, valid and reliable assessment processes in medical and clinical education, but the process can readily be extended to contexts such as business, policing, law etc.
Reflective journals	• deepens learning by reflection, and demonstrates analysis, creativity and originality	• risk being narrative rather than reflective	• when reflective journalling works well, students continually develop their learning on the basis of

Method	Advantages	Disadvantages	Notes
Critical incident accounts	• allows students the opportunity to choose particular incidents, analyse them in depth, and demonstrate creativity and problem-solving skills • can be word-constrained, thereby increasing 'cut-to-the-chase' writing or speaking • critical incidents are authentic, developing candidates' skills for real-world problem-solving	• incidents inevitably have differing levels of difficulty	• accumulate a bank of critical incidents providing students 'rehearsal' opportunities to develop skills at handling this assessment format • try presenting students with pre-determined incidents; their performance can then be compared
Assessed seminars	• ideally, seminars should be prepared and led by students (individually, or in pairs), and should involve peers and tutors as active audience participants • a series of seminars can give each student the chance to prepare in-depth an element of the curriculum, and present it to the group, and be questioned on it by the group • the assessment can be high in validity, relating to depth of knowledge, as well as communication skills and the ability to answer probing questions	• it is hard to allocate topics of equal difficulty to a large group of students • over a series of seminars, 'drift' occurs, as later presenters tend to bring in what they've learned from earlier seminars • difficult to assess audience participation at anything more than a basic level • students who have already presented may switch off and fail to contribute or attend later seminars	• students' continued participation in a seminar series can be increased if assessment is triangulated by the inclusion in a summative exam of one or more questions relating to things addressed only in the seminar series
Annotated bibliographies	• a useful way to engage students with the relevant literature, rather than just collecting information on it • candidates can demonstrate their depth of study of the sources and the breadth of the source material they have reviewed • plagiarism is limited; although students may choose the same sources, it would be easy to spot identical annotations	• the extent of the literature may mask the depth of thinking about the sources • avoid this by setting an exact number of sources to be included, and by asking students to include some elements of prioritisation of how well the respective sources measure up to two or three given criteria, alongside their own judgements about the sources	• annotated bibliographies can be turned into a resource-bank, and issued to future students as a starting place for them to develop their own bibliographies

TABLE 5.1 (continued)

Method	Advantages	Disadvantages	Notes
In-tray exercises For example, in an exam on ward management, students could find on their exam desks no questions, but a set of paperwork for them to study for a while, including logs of patients on the ward, doctors available, other facilities available on the ward etc. Then (say) 20 minutes into the exam, they each received a slip of paper, for example 'Incident at the airport. The following three patients will arrive in 15 minutes. What will you do?' The students write down their decisions, based on the information available to them. Other 'incidents' are given to them at different stages in the exam.	• this kind of assessment is strong on authenticity, as it measures the skills the candidates will need in their careers • reliability of assessment is high, as normally there will be 'best' choices in terms of the decisions and actions required • this kind of exam focuses on thinking, rather than merely writing • since all the students have the same in-tray exercises, the assessment is fair	• while exams based on in-tray exercises get away from measurement of 'speed of writing' towards 'quality of thinking', different students' 'speed of reading/ absorbing' the information provided can be a problem	• because of the relevance of 'in-tray' exercises and problems, a bank of such resource materials can be useful in the day-to-day teaching and learning of the subjects involved, and particular exercises can be used as examples to add variety to whole-class contexts such as lectures
Artefacts (e.g., sculptures, paintings, architectural designs, engineering models)	• assessment of artefacts such as these is high on validity and authenticity • artefacts are useful as evidence of achievement to show prospective employers	• assessment can be compromised in terms of reliability where different judges have their own idea of what constitutes excellence	• where the artefacts can be retained (or photographed) by the institution, they provide excellent indicators of the standards of evidence of achievement for new students to work towards

Choosing who is best placed to assess

The majority of assessment in higher education is based on university teachers undertaking the work, but other agents can make a valuable contribution. Students can assess one another's outputs as individuals or working in groups to assess the work of other groups (inter-peer assessment). An understanding of what the assessment criteria mean is essential (get the students engaging with brainstorming what the criteria should be as a preparation for the task). Students also need guidance on 'final language' (Boud 1995, p. 45) to avoid devastating their peers with thoughtless comments. Peer assessment also needs extensive briefing and rehearsal to avoid collusion and unfair practices. As students become sophisticated in its use, its value becomes more apparent.

To assess students' ability to collaborate, get them working together in groups and then ask students to rate one-another's input, based on evidence against clearly articulated criteria (intra-peer group assessment). This is a much better way to assess process than tutors trying to watch each group in action. Both forms of peer assessment provide a good grounding for students to learn to judge their own work and become competent at self assessment and reflection (Boud 1995). It is also an excellent means by which learners can get inside the assessment process, so that they take more seriously the feedback they receive from tutors.

Other agents for assessment can include clients in practical domains, for example, in legal practice surgeries where students provide walk-in clients with advice under the supervision of trained solicitors. Many disciplines already make use of employers, practice tutors and line managers, but there is significant scope for wider use of such colleagues in a broader range of subject areas.

When should assessment take place?

Significant amounts of assessment in higher education take place at the end of the learning process. Yet, it may be best to avoid excessive 'sudden death' assessment, where students remain un-assessed for long periods of time followed by only one high-risk opportunity to demonstrate their learning. Incremental assessment, where students provide elements of a large assignment over the period of its construction and receive feedback from tutors, peers or both is efficient in reducing student failure and underachievement, and is also a good strategy for reducing plagiarism. Continuous assessment, where students undertake a number of smaller, separately assessed, tasks also spreads the risk and enables students to learn from feedback to improve the next assignment.

When designing an assessment strategy, it is also important to avoid giving students no assessed work for some time and then giving multiple assignments with clashing submission dates (commonly known as 'Week 7 Blues'), which is stressful and risky for students.

Giving fast, effective feedback to students

Too often students seem interested only in their mark, avoiding interest in the detailed written comments that staff have provided. We therefore argue that staff should make time during orientation to help students to understand the importance of feedback and the value of spending time reflecting on it. Benefits can accrue from providing opportunities for students to respond to feedback, for example, by giving students follow-up tasks or giving them 'feed-forward' comments to improve their next assignment. Tactics that can help students to make use of feedback include the following (Race 2010):

- *Give students some immediate feedback when they submit work.* For example, get them to hand in their essays or reports at the start of a lecture, and immediately issue a short summary of likely 'frequently encountered problems' in the assignment concerned. Another useful tactic is to provide this even before they attempt the task.
- *Give students marks only when they've tried working them out themselves, making use of feedback given on their work.* Incentivise this by offering that if the mark suggested by the student is within (say) five per cent of the actual mark awarded by the assessor, the higher number goes forward. This also allows those students who really do need a chat with the assessor (e.g., those whose mark is more than five per cent away from the tutor's mark) to be identified, focusing time and energy of feedback discussions on those students who can benefit most from individual feedback.
- *Use much shorter assessments.* Rather than using one 3500-word essay, have two or three much shorter, sharper tasks, such as a 200-word (exactly) digest of what Smith and Jones say about Topic X, a 100-word summary of the main points in Chapter 2 of Bloggs, and a 300-word annotated bibliography of the five most important papers on Topic Y. Shorter pieces of work require higher-level thinking than a 'waffleable' essay. They are fast to mark, and have less likelihood of plagiarism.
- *Get students to make judgements on their work*, by filling in a short self-assessment proforma before they submit. This means they have the chance to reflect *before* it is assessed, and improve it before submitting. It also means that assessors know more about what the student thinks of the piece of work, and can fine-tune feedback accordingly.

Brown et al. (1994) indicated ways to give feedback promptly and efficiently. All the approaches can save staff time when assessing, but tend to involve additional time and skill in the design process. They include:

- Use *assignment return sheets*, showing how marks link to learning outcomes, and enabling students to indicate the extent to which criteria have been achieved by completing Likert scales, e.g., ranging from 'fully met' through 'partly met' to 'not yet met' and so on.

- Provide *model answers* which demonstrate good answers, and explain why they are good. Huxham (2007) demonstrated that model answers in formative feedback result in higher scores in summative assignments than personalised individual feedback.

- Give groups *oral feedback* on cohort performance, common errors and shared areas for improvement within classroom settings or as podcasts via the subject website. This makes feedback a shared learning experience.

- Provide a collective *written assignment report*, so that students see how to improve and how they compare to others.

- Build and use a *statement bank* of commonly used feedback comments which can be given to students electronically or in hard copy, enabling detailed formative feedback with minimum effort.

- Use well designed *computer-aided assessment* to maximise the speed with which students receive feedback. This is most applicable where there are large cohorts of students and frequently repeated curriculum materials.

- Incorporate elements of *self and peer review*, particularly formatively, so that students can measure the quality of work by applying criteria to each others' and their own work.

CASE 5.1   SUPER-FAST FEEDBACK ON INCREMENTAL ASSESSED TASKS
Sarah Nixon and Louise Williams, Liverpool John Moores University

---

The context is a third-year module on Business for Sport with around 40 students. Dissatisfied with their previous end-point assessment methods where students could not benefit from feedback, tutors decided to implement weekly tasks within the Friday whole-day sessions, which culminated in an assessment task which they marked over the weekend and returned on Mondays. Students were originally horrified at the idea, but nowadays appreciate the chance to achieve tasks and get regular really fast feedback.

Tutors were particularly keen that assignments be authentic and lead to learning. Some elements are individual, but most are group tasks including presentations and product development. Students take the work seriously and the teaching team is delighted by the high levels of commitment and creativity demonstrated by students, who are gaining employability skills. Attendance has improved to over 90 per cent, compared with parallel modules where attendance is as poor as 20 per cent on Fridays. Achievement is high, with one group convincing a supermarket chain of their marketing idea. Students find the workload heavy but enjoy the high levels of engagement. Some get annoyed if their grades are affected by low commitment and achievement of fellow group members, but each element of assessment carries relatively low weighting overall. It is indicated to them that in real life contexts overall performance will also be dependent on a team's weakest elements. Currently these assessed tasks are accompanied by short individual reflections and 1500-word essays, but the team is considering whether to reduce this to avoid over-assessing.

Using authentic assessment to promote learning

Students are more likely to take assessment seriously if they think staff are playing fair (Sambell et al. 1997) by assessing material from across the breadth of the curriculum rather than cherrypicking elements to assess, which carries high risk for students who try to guess which particular areas will come up in their assessment. Too often assignments test what is easy to test, rather than the heart of what has been learned. Effective assignments test students' capabilities in ways that are relevant to their own contexts, and which have a level of intrinsic value for learning.

Where students study professional or vocational programs, it is important to ensure that tasks use or simulate real-life practices, and that students are evaluated by demonstrating their competences rather than their ability to write about such competences. As Bloxham and Boyd (2007, p. 193) argue: 'Being able to reproduce knowledge in a decontextualised examination does not guarantee that knowledge can be used in a real-life setting'.

CASE 5.2   AUTHENTIC ASSESSMENT
Julia Tum, Leeds Metropolitan University

In the UK Centre for Events Management, teams of staff teach three second-year modules. One assessment uses Practically Assessed Structured Scenarios (PASS), adapted from Objective Structured Clinical Examinations (OSCE) which have been used effectively in medical and veterinary education for many years. An OSCE is a checklist marking approach to assessment that enhances consistency between multiple assessors. It also provides relevant and challenging short scenarios which can be used to assess students' understanding and the application of theories.

The reasons the assessment style changed were to:
* replace outdated formal examinations and a report writing assessment
* ensure validity and relevance for industry needs
* encourage a deeper understanding of the taught material and the relevance and usefulness of its application
* ensure that the assessment was realistic, challenging and reflected the everyday pressures of decision-making in the events industry
* minimise time for marking, moderation and recording of marks.

All three modules have their unique 20–30 minute assessment which is accessed by students successively entering different rooms pre-prepared with assessment scenarios, which they tackle individually. There is a tutor in each room, and 270 students pass through a suite of rooms and are assessed on the same day, with their marks standardised, moderated and recorded, within two days. Students can elect to have further feedback at a private meeting. Otherwise generic feedback is posted online.

Students report that the whole day is stressful, but authentic, and that each of the scenarios tests different elements of the modules in a practical way. The marks represent a good cross-section of grades, rewarding students for hard work and insightful comments, and not rewarding those who have failed to prepare for the assessment. Most of the scenarios are undertaken individually, but in one of the modules, students are assessed in small groups. Actors playing industry-relevant roles have been involved on some occasions to make the situations even more authentic.

Designing assessment to improve achievement and retention

Higher Education Statistics Agency data indicate that student drop-out is higher among students from low-participation neighbourhoods, students in receipt of Disabled Students' Allowance, mature-aged undergraduate students and students from lower socio-economic groups (Yorke & Longden 2004, cited by Brown 2011). In this context, it is important that your assessment strategy offers low-stakes, formative assessment in the first part of a degree program to enhance retention. Assessment should be formative, informative, developmental and remediable. Yorke argues that the links to assessment are crucial:

> Roughly two-thirds of premature departures take place in, or at the end of, the first year of full-time study in the UK. Anecdotal evidence from a number of institutions indicates that early poor performance can be a powerful disincentive to continuation, with students feeling that perhaps they were not cut out for higher education after all – although the main problems are acculturation and acclimatisation to studying.
>
> (Yorke 1999, p. 37)

Students, especially but not exclusively those from disadvantaged backgrounds, may need guidance at induction on understanding the various academic discourses that are employed within the subject and the institution if they are to be successful at learning through assessment (Northedge 2003, p. 173). It is also likely that we will need to help them to understand when writing needs to be personal and based on individual experience, such as in a reflective diary, and when it needs to be formal, using academic conventions like passive voice and third person, as in written reports and essays. Students who just don't 'get it' are more likely to fail early assignments.

Colleagues at Central Queensland University explored the impact that starting a course can have on student achievement and retention. They found only weak correlations between student performance and percentage attendance, but strong correlations between student performance and attendance in the first two weeks of class. In another study they found that students who missed the first two weeks received marks that were between seven and nine per cent lower than the average (Hamilton et al. 2007). Taken together, these findings reinforce the message that student orientation is critical. While it is important to have early assessment in a program, we need to ensure that late starters are not excessively disadvantaged.

Computer-aided assessment (CAA) can support retention effectively when it is used to let students know early on how they are doing; for example, through the use of weekly CAA tests incorporating feedback on right and wrong answers. Students like the chance to find out how they are doing, and attempt tests several times in an environment where no-one else is watching how they do. This approach allows first-year tutors to monitor what is going on across a cohort, enabling staff to concentrate their energies on students who are repeatedly doing badly or those who are not engaging at all in the activity. For example, Professor Bill Buchanan, School of Computing at Edinburgh Napier University, UK, designed 'So you want to be a millionaire?' – a computer-based, multiple-choice game, with hundreds of questions at various levels of difficulty. Easy questions are presented first with questions gradually getting more difficult. As soon as students get one wrong they are returned to lower-level questions for a while, until they work up to more difficult ones. Students work alone or in groups with the question bank, striving to get to the highest level questions, accumulating considerable practice and immediate formative feedback along the way.

Using assessment to improve student confidence

Dweck (2000) argues that students' self-theories about intelligence can affect learning and achievement (see Stewart 2012). Students who hold a fixed theory of intelligence – for example, 'I am no good at maths' – are more likely to interpret failure on an assessment as proof that they themselves are failures. Others have more malleable views of intelligence: when they get poor marks, they see it as a challenge to overcome rather than an insurmountable problem. Dweck suggests that students subscribing to a fixed theory of intelligence need 'a diet of easy successes' with incremental feedback to confirm their ability. Hence we advocate streamlining assessment to include early successes via regular, small assessed tasks with positive, constructive feedback.

Students may have difficulty in making the transition into higher education from school, college, work or other contexts and may find it problematic to decipher what is required of them. For non-traditional students to succeed in higher education, they have to become meta-learners, able to decode assessment requirements. Bowl's study of non-traditional entrants to higher education noted how difficult these students found it to penetrate the discourses of academic study. Issues included 'understanding what tutors wanted and what advice and support they were prepared to offer, and making sense of academic cultures and conventions' (2003, p. 88). As one student said:

> The hardship was not understanding. When they give you an assignment and say it was on this handout. But my difficulty is not understanding what to do at first … It's reading as well as putting what you read into your essay … I can read and understand it, but then you have to incorporate it into your own words. But in the words they want you to say it in, not just: She said this, and this is the way it should be. The words, the proper language.
>
> (Bowl 2003, p. 90)

Conclusion

Assessment is the engine that drives student learning, and it is your job to make this engine run smoothly and efficiently. As a university teacher, you have a responsibility to ensure that your assessment processes and instruments encourage students to take ownership of objectives and understand the standards of the required evidence of achievement. For, indeed, assessment is the basis of the qualifications students want to take away from higher education as their passport to the rest of their careers. Nothing you do for your students is more important than assessing their learning fairly, openly and in a well-planned way. Since assessment takes up a significant part of teaching time, it is important to spend this time wisely. We hope that the discussion in this chapter will help you to maximise the benefits of the time spent designing and implementing assessment, and hence help your students to demonstrate their optimum potential in the range of assessment opportunities they encounter.

PART 2
FOCUS ON
CURRICULUM

Good teaching is inextricably intertwined with good curriculum design, which is about planning and aligning what to teach, how to teach and how to assess so that students experience coherent learning.

For most university teachers, most of the time, curriculum design equals subject design. In Chapter 6, Tom Angelo offers practical, research-based principles and guidelines for effective, efficient subject design. The criteria and framework of key questions in this chapter provide step-by-step guidance for designing and redesigning subjects so that students learn more, without more work from teachers.

Thomas Reeves and Patricia Reeves in Chapter 7 focus on online and blended learning. They contend that the expansion of online learning means that all university teachers must now be prepared to design and teach online subjects and programs. Further, the advent of learning management systems means that on-campus, face-to-face teaching incorporates a sufficient degree of online opportunities to be called blended learning. Their strong message is that the fundamentals of effective curriculum development are paramount, regardless of how a subject is delivered.

Chapter 8 is the first of three chapters that focus on different types of curriculum. Alan Jenkins and Mick Healey distinguish between research-led, research-oriented, research-based and research-tutored curricula, as these reflect varying degrees of student engagement with research. The many cases of research-based teaching embedded in this chapter provide practical examples that can be adapted to different disciplines and university settings.

In Chapter 9, Lyn Brodie provides an overview, strategies and examples for implementing a problem-based learning (PBL) curriculum. Similarly, in Chapter 10, Jonathon Garnett outlines the principles of work-integrated learning (WIL) and describes the elements of WIL curricula, including recognition of prior learning, learning agreements and WIL research.

CHAPTER 6

DESIGNING SUBJECTS FOR LEARNING: PRACTICAL RESEARCH-BASED PRINCIPLES AND GUIDELINES

Tom Angelo

Keywords
subject, backward design, constructive alignment, course, curriculum design, intended learning outcomes, learning-centred, unit

Introduction

The purpose of this chapter is to help academics to promote deeper, more meaningful, longer lasting student learning – without increasing their workloads – through better subject design. Its underlying premise is that many subjects are less effective at promoting learning and less efficient to teach than they could and should be. This occurs because subjects are typically *constructed* based on unexamined, often implicit practices rather than *designed* according to explicit principles or criteria. To promote good subject design, this chapter outlines a process that is both principled and practical. This learning-centred design process combines 'backward design' (Wiggins & McTighe 1998) and 'constructive alignment' (Biggs & Tang 2007) and is supported by theory and research.

There are many excellent sources of 'how-to' advice – how to lecture, how to organise group work, how to assess, how to use technology – readily available online and in print (see Davis 2009 or Svinicki & McKeachie 2011, for example). Useful resources on the specifics of subject and course development also exist (Fink 2003; Grunert O'Brien et al. 2008). This chapter focuses, instead, on helping university teachers pose and answer the first-order or 'meta' design questions that should precede choices of specific subject content, techniques or technologies. It would, after all, make little sense for a builder to select construction materials and tools before knowing, in some detail, the design requirements of the structure planned. Similarly, it makes little sense for teachers to select specific content, teaching techniques or technologies without understanding, in some detail, the design requirements of the subject to be developed. This is, therefore, a chapter on how to make good subject design decisions.

This chapter will be useful to readers with a range of needs, priorities and interests. For example, if you are facing a looming deadline to design or redesign a subject, you may find it helpful to skip directly to the design questions and the text immediately following each. Similarly, if you find that some questions posed in this chapter have already been answered for you or are not relevant to your circumstances, you may choose to focus only on those to which your answers will matter most.

What are the core elements of a subject?

The terms 'subject', 'unit' and 'course' are used in different institutions – and sometimes even within the same institution – to denote a variety of curricular elements. In this chapter, a subject is defined as one element of many that constitute a larger degree program of study. Typically, students enrolled in degree programs must successfully complete a minimum number of discrete subjects in order to earn the desired qualification. Thus, full-time students in bachelor-level programs may be enrolled in four subjects each semester or term over three or four years. In this chapter when we discuss subjects, we are talking about, for example, Psychology 101 or Organic Chemistry 2A.

The great majority of subjects – whether taught face-to-face, fully online or in blended mode – have the following seven elements in common:

- *learning outcomes* (or goals or objectives) – the stated educational aims of the subject
- *teaching activities* – the specific types of work that teachers do to promote student learning; for example, lecturing, demonstrating, questioning and leading discussions (see Chapter 2, Hunt et al. 2012)
- *learning activities* – the specific types of work students are assigned by the teacher in order to learn, individually or in groups, in a classroom or outside it, in personal study or online; for example, reading, working problem sets, doing laboratory assignments and discussing assigned questions or problems
- *learning resources* – the time, staffing, workspaces, resources, tools and technologies made available to achieve the explicit aims of the subject; for example, timetabling, teachers, tutors, learning support staff, classrooms, laboratories, studios, libraries, learning management systems, websites, textbooks, readings and a host of more specialised resources depending on the discipline

- *feedback activities* – the types of work teachers do to provide learners with the information and guidance required to improve their current learning performance. Also known as formative assessment (Ambrose et al. 2010; Angelo & Cross 1993), feedback activities are typically employed before the summative assessment tasks and grading
- *assessment tasks* – the specific types of work teachers design and students carry out to demonstrate the quality and quantity of their learning in order to gain formative feedback or summative grades (see Chapter 5, Brown & Race 2012); for example, the learning activities listed above may be assessed for formative or summative purposes, and other common assessments include quizzes, tests, examinations, portfolios and performances
- *grading standards* (see Chapter 14, Krause 2012) – the explicit criteria and levels of performance used for evaluating and labelling the quality of student learning demonstrated through summative assessment tasks.

These seven core elements are minimum requirements in virtually every subject guide or syllabus. Therefore, it is not the elements, per se, but rather their organisation and sequencing, expression, relative emphasis and degree of alignment that differentiate effective from ineffective subject design. The design choices we make overall, and in relation to each of these seven elements, can raise or lower the odds that students will learn deeply and well. By analogy, we might note that while all houses are made up of the same basic structural elements – foundations, walls, roofs, windows, doors and so on – some houses, by design, are more elegant, practical and even sustainable than others.

It is of course possible for teachers to construct functional subjects without following explicit educational designs, just as it is for skilled builders to construct functional houses without architectural drawings. But, while it is increasingly uncommon, and often illegal, in modern urban societies for new houses to be built without plans, it is still very common for higher education curricula to be built on tacit assumptions.

In every state and locality, zoning ordinances and construction standards constrain housing design choices to a greater or lesser degree. Available materials, site characteristics and budgets impose further constraints. Skilled architects are well aware of those constraints and find ways to achieve their clients' and their own intended design outcomes with minimal compromise. Skilled teachers do much the same. In most universities, academic policies, procedures and guidelines – and the available resources – set the context and practical limits within which subject design choices can be made. For that reason, it is critical to become familiar with relevant policies, procedures, guidelines and teaching and learning resources before making specific decisions about your subject design.

Looking at your institution's curriculum and subject design policies, note the extent to which they include the seven core elements listed above.

• What other subject elements, if any, does your institution require?
• Do policies and guidelines make reference to any relevant educational research?

Why invest time and effort in subject design?

On one level, a subject is simply a sequence of activities organised to promote learning – an educational process. Like any other process, a subject may be well designed or poorly designed to achieve its aims. In poorly designed subjects, even highly skilled and experienced teachers and well-prepared, hard-working students struggle to succeed. Time, attention and effort that could have been spent on teaching and learning are wasted in clarifying unnecessary confusions, improvising solutions to inherent problems, recuperating from avoidable breakdowns and failures and, in the worst cases, dealing with students' complaints and grievances. For less-skilled and less-experienced teachers and less-prepared students, struggling to cope with poorly designed subjects can be demoralising and sometimes devastating.

Students' time is finite and valuable, so subjects should be designed to help them learn deeply, efficiently and effectively. In addition, a well-designed subject should be cost-effective and sustainable in terms of the amount and level of staff time it requires, since staffing typically accounts for 70 to 80 per cent of a subject's total educational costs. If a subject's costs exceed its revenues, then it will have to be subsidised by other more efficient subjects. While such cross-subsidisation is common and sometimes justifiable, particularly in the case of compulsory core subjects, it is difficult to sustain. Consequently, investing even a modest amount of time initially to design subjects well can advance effectiveness, efficiency, equity and sustainability in the long-term.

What is constructive alignment?

The 'constructive' in 'constructive alignment' refers to constructivist theory, which posits that students must actively construct rather than passively receive learning if it is to be meaningful and lasting. 'Alignment' refers to the explicit linkage of teaching and learning activities and assessment tasks to promote achievement of the intended learning outcomes. The premise is that a well-aligned curriculum can help students to construct their own learning more effectively and independently (see Biggs & Tang 2007, pp. 52–54).

While the focus of this chapter is mainly on within-subject alignment, most subjects are also elements of larger curricula. In a well-designed curriculum, individual subjects are well-aligned horizontally, complementing and reinforcing other subjects taught in the same year of a program with minimum unintended redundancy. They are also well-aligned vertically, with explicit and effective connections 'downward' to prior subjects or prior educational experiences and 'upward' to subsequent subjects. Horizontal and vertical alignment, however partial, can provide more educational coherence and efficiency for students and staff alike.

Why design backwards?

Notwithstanding the name, 'backward design' has a very straightforward logic. In essence, backward design requires that we begin by making clear what we hope to have achieved at the end. Virtually all contemporary buildings, products, campaigns and complex processes are designed backward from intended outcomes. For example, architects, often working with engineers and others, define exactly what a finished building should look like and how it should function before any dirt is dug or nails hammered.

As applied to the curriculum, 'backward design' is backward in two different senses. First, it starts with the end, not the beginning. The backward design process starts by defining what students must demonstrate they know and can do (intended learning outcomes) and how well they know and can do it (standards) by the end of the subject or degree program, and then works backward to determine how best to get there and where to start. In other words, only after the intended learning outcomes and standards are set does one decide what topics to teach and what teaching, assessment and feedback methods to use. Second, it is 'backward' in relation to common practice. Many, if not most, teachers still construct subjects by starting with the preferred topics, texts or teaching methods without explicit reference to intended outcomes or standards (see Wiggins & McTighe 1998, pp. 7–9).

Why take a learning-centred approach?

A dichotomy is often drawn between teacher-centred and student-centred approaches to education. There is, however, a third way: a *learning-centred* approach to curriculum and subject design. The learning-centred approach focuses on three key elements of the curriculum: what is to be learned (the intended learning outcomes); how well (the grading standards); and how to determine whether learning outcomes are achieved at the appropriate standard (the assessment tasks). In this approach, the quality of learning outcomes achieved is the desired end, and all other aspects of the curriculum design are means. Taking a learning-centred approach compels us to make design decisions, first and foremost, on the basis of what will most effectively and efficiently promote the intended learning outcomes, rather than on which teaching strategies and technologies staff and students might find most interesting and trendy or least demanding.

That said, staff and student perceptions and interests matter, as do those of other groups. In constructing subjects, it is common practice to attempt to balance the perceived or expressed interests and needs of the:

- teacher(s)
- discipline or field (see Chapter 3, Land 2012)
- stakeholders
- institution
- students.

Many subjects strongly reflect the particular research or scholarly interests, preferences and passions of those who teach them. Most subjects are also strongly influenced by the views of disciplinary leaders and associations about which topics and skills matter most. In professional fields, in particular, external stakeholders, such as accrediting bodies or employers, can significantly and directly influence the content of the curriculum. Each educational institution, and each faculty or college in turn, strives to put its own distinctive stamp on the curriculum. And the needs and interests of students can significantly influence enrolments and, thereby, the life or death of subjects and programs.

How to balance competing interests

These five different 'interest groups' exert competing and sometimes conflicting pressures on curriculum decisions. At any given moment, the pressures from stakeholders may outweigh those from the discipline, or the teacher's personal preferences may trump the students' interests. All of these interests are legitimate and worthy of consideration. Balancing these competing interests is a key curriculum design challenge, particularly in deciding what to include (and what to leave out) and how to teach. To make such decisions in a coherent, consistent manner, we need some overriding principles, or decision rules.

To help academics make those difficult curriculum design choices, the following three decision rules are proposed:

- put deep learning first
- take a scholarly approach
- design for your successors.

Put deep learning first

Deep learning is defined as learning that lasts and can be recalled and used effectively after the subject or course has been completed. To test if your subject requires students to demonstrate deep learning, you might apply the following 'parrot test'.

Suppose scientists had developed genetically modified African Gray Parrots which could not only learn, understand, remember and use the core vocabulary of your discipline, but could also type, using parrot voice-recognition software. Given their prodigious powers of rote memorisation and 'playback', could one of these parrots enrol in and somehow amass enough points to pass your subject? More realistically, is there any way that a student could pass your subject simply through rote memorisation – or by plagiarising or cheating – and without demonstrating deep learning? If the answer is yes, then the subject fails the parrot test and is probably not well designed to promote deep learning. If, on the other hand, there is no way students can pass your subject without demonstrating an appropriate depth of learning, then your subject passes the parrot test: bad news for parrots, but good news for you, your subject and your students.

Take a scholarly approach

The hallmark of higher education is its commitment to research and scholarship (see Chapter 8, Jenkins & Healey 2012; Chapter 15, Trigwell 2012). Turning that scholarly focus inward, on our educational programs, would require that we ask: What research-based, empirical evidence is there to support the way we design curriculum, teach, assess or give feedback? In some disciplines, a great deal of empirical research has been published on teaching and learning questions. (Disciplines such as economics, engineering, physics, nursing and psychology have been extensively studied.) To investigate research on teaching and learning in your discipline, apply the 'Google Scholar™ test'.

Set aside one hour to search the scholarly literature for research on effective teaching and learning in your discipline or field using an appropriate web search engine. If you have specific teaching and learning approaches in mind, such as group work or formative feedback, you can also search for research literature on those topics. Even better, convince a librarian, a postgraduate student or advanced undergraduate to collaborate on this web search with you. In most cases, after even one hour of focused searching, you are likely to know whether there is research to support your choices regarding content, approaches and techniques, research indicating better options, or no relevant research.

Design for your successors

In order to confirm that your subject is well designed, apply the 'bus test'. Suppose that the individual who developed a particular subject is hit by a bus – or a tram, or falls ill, goes on leave, takes another position or retires. If that individual's subject is well designed and clearly documented, other teaching staff with relevant disciplinary expertise can quickly and effectively prepare and carry on the teaching and assessing. By contrast, it is very difficult to take over teaching of someone else's poorly designed subject, or one in which the design is not explicit. Consider whether your colleagues would be able to take over teaching your subject with ease, if they had to do so. If not, why not? A well-designed subject is not person-dependent and, as a consequence, can pass the bus test.

Research-based guidelines for deep learning

There are authoritative summaries of research on teaching and learning on which to base good curriculum design and teaching practice. Three of the most often cited and used are *How College Affects Students* (Pascarella & Terenzini 2005), *How People Learn* (Bransford et al. 2000) and *Visible Learning* (Hattie 2009). Based on my own reading of these summaries, and many other sources, I have developed a set of seven research-based guidelines for designing and teaching, which are offered below.

Overall, research suggests that virtually all students can learn more – and more deeply – when our curriculum designs and teaching practices help them to:

- become explicitly aware of their own relevant prior knowledge, preconceptions, misconceptions, beliefs and values – and to *un*learn, as needed (see Chapter 3, Land 2012)
- set and maintain realistically high and personally meaningful learning goals and expectations for academic success
- learn how to study and learn effectively, so that they become increasingly self-directed, self-regulating independent learners
- understand the criteria, standards and methods used in assessing and evaluating their learning and how to make good use of feedback on their performance against those standards
- collaborate regularly and effectively with other learners and with teachers to achieve meaningful, shared learning goals
- invest adequate time and effort, effectively and efficiently, in their academic work
- seek and find connections to and applications of the concepts and skills they are learning to their lives and work (see Chapter 10, Garnett 2012).

YOUR THOUGHTS

- Which of the guidelines proposed above seem potentially most useful to your own teaching and subject design?
- What guidelines does your institution or your professional or disciplinary association provide for good practice in teaching and curriculum design?

Designing subjects for learning: 10 specific questions

The sequence of the questions below is absolutely intentional. In applying backward design to create or revise an academic subject, it is essential to begin with the overall purpose and context of the subject before setting the standards, related assessment tasks and specific content.

To assist in this process, consider the following 10 questions:

1. What is the overall purpose of this subject?
2. Where does this subject fit?
3. For whom is this subject designed?
4. What specifically should students learn and be able to do by this subject's end?
5. What standards will be used to assess their learning?
6. How will their learning be assessed?
7. What specific content will be taught and assessed?
8. What will motivate students to learn deeply and well?
9. What work will students do to learn?
10. What work will teachers and others do to help students learn?

What is the overall purpose of this subject?

If you had to sum it up in a few words, would the primary purpose of your subject be to promote:

- discipline-specific knowledge and skills?
- general graduate attributes or capabilities?
- work or career-related knowledge and skills?
- basic academic language or learning skills?
- personal awareness, development or growth?
- something else? (If so, what else?)

While most subjects are meant to serve multiple purposes, it is helpful to know which is foremost among them as you make the inevitably difficult decisions about what to emphasise, what to cut and what to keep. Understanding the purpose of your subject will influence the rest of the subject design process.

Where does this subject fit?

In most cases, a given subject has a place in the sequence, and a function in the larger context, of one or more degree programs. In a well-designed program, a given subject will function primarily as a *cornerstone, core, capstone, depth* or *breadth* learning experience.

Cornerstone subjects function as portals or bridges into the academic program. They are meant to ensure that students can demonstrate sufficient 'starting line' levels of competence in the key learning outcomes – the specific knowledge, skills and values required to succeed in the program.

Core subjects further develop and deepen students' competency in relation to those key program learning outcomes.

Capstone subjects are usually culminating experiences, designed to help students reflect on, integrate and apply what they have learned throughout the program. Capstones also often serve as portals or bridges out of the program into postgraduate studies or employment (Holdsworth et al. 2009).

While cornerstone, core and capstone subjects are all typically required or compulsory subjects, depth and breadth subjects are often electives. Depth subjects typically focus on one skill, as in writing- or research-intensive subjects, or one topic in the discipline. Breadth subjects, on the other hand, are meant to help students see the 'big picture' and are often, therefore, interdisciplinary in nature.

YOUR THOUGHTS

- Where does your subject fit in the sequence of the degree program – beginning, middle or end?
- What is its main function in the program: cornerstone, core, capstone, depth, breadth or other?

For whom is this subject designed?

When an academic is asked what he or she teaches, the response is typically the name of a discipline or field, such as physics, physiotherapy, philosophy, economics or early childhood education. Rarely do teachers reply that they teach students. Yet all experienced teachers know that the complex characteristics of each cohort of students have significant influences on how, how much and how well we teach and students learn. Among the most powerful factors in students' achievement is their prior learning, or lack of learning, in relation to the subjects they attempt.

If one is teaching introductory statistics, for example, it is useful to know in advance students' prior mathematics coursework and achievement test scores. If a large proportion of a cohort is relatively underprepared, then it would be wise to design-in more learning support. This additional support might be provided through tutorials, labs, workshops, the institution's learning support unit or through online resources. Conversely, if most of the incoming students are well prepared, designing-in a higher level of challenge would be reasonable. Quite often, introductory subjects have students whose preparation levels and language skills are diverse. Designing the subject to respond to diversity in students (see Chapter 11, Broughan & Hunt 2012) can lessen stress on teachers and improve outcomes for learners.

Institutions can normally provide teachers with useful information on the prior preparation and other relevant characteristics of the students in their subjects and courses. Department or school heads and administrators are good first contacts in seeking such background data. If data on incoming students is not available, then the overall profile of current students may prove the best predictor. And, if there is no data available in advance, one can always collect relevant information from the students via an informal survey at the start of semester.

YOUR THOUGHTS

- What kind(s) of students is your subject designed to serve?
- What kind(s) of students are actually enrolled in your subject?
- What useful data on your students' learning-related characteristics is provided to you by your institution or faculty?

What specifically should students learn and be able to do by this subject's end?

Backward design begins and ends with clearly written intended learning outcomes (ILOs), concise statements of what students are expected to demonstrate that they know and are able to do by the end of a subject or degree program. They are 'intended' in two senses. First, they represent an intentional approach to curriculum design by specifying the expected learning outcomes – what should be achieved – in advance. They are also 'intended' in contrast to what may or may not actually be the 'observed' student learning outcomes by the end of the subject or course. ILOs represent a commitment to be evaluated against a predetermined goal. There will be gaps between the intended (pre-subject) and observed (post-subject) outcomes. The smaller and less consequential those gaps, overall, the more effective the subject design.

The questions below provide a simple framework that may help in drafting and revising ILOs. To demonstrate the process, Case 6.1 takes the ILO 'Students will understand the causes of World War II' from a second-year history subject and revises it using the framework below.

CASE 6.1   REDRAFTING AN INTENDED LEARNING OUTCOME (ILO)

First-draft ILO
Students will understand the causes of World War II.

Who?	Each student
Will do what?	Identify what he or she believes to be the three most powerful factors leading to World War II in Europe or the Pacific, and explain and analyse the choice

103

For what audience?	Students in a first-year history class
When?	Between weeks six and eight
Where?	Online
How?	Through a five-minute maximum podcast recording
How well? (to what standard?)	At the 'meets expectations' level or above on the grading rubric as assessed by the tutor and by the majority of the first-year students who review the podcast
Why?	In order to demonstrate in-depth understanding of the readings, critical thinking and oral presentation skills

Revised ILO

Between weeks six and eight, each student will explain his/her identification and analysis of the three most powerful factors leading to World War II in Europe or the Pacific to students in a first-year history class through a five-minute (maximum) podcast, in order to demonstrate in-depth understanding of the readings, critical thinking and oral presentation skills.

Standard: The quality of the podcast must be assessed at the 'meets expectations' level or above, overall, by the tutor and the majority of the high school students who review it.

YOUR THOUGHTS

In relation to any subject you teach:
- To what degree are the ILOs in your subject vertically and constructively aligned with those of other subjects in the program?
- To what extent are the subject ILOs learning-centred?
- Could you improve an existing ILO or draft a new one using the question framework illustrated above?

What standards will be used

In addition to clarifying *what* students should know and be able to do, the subject design must specify *how well* students must know and do it. Standards indicate the quality of performance expected and help to set learner expectations. The power of high expectations to motivate better performance has long been documented in education research. The challenges arise both in setting appropriately high expectations and in communicating them in ways that lead to understanding, acceptance and, ideally, internalisation by the learners.

Standards that are developed and owned by professions, disciplines, faculties, programs or even small groups of teachers are likely to be more valid and persuasive than those developed by one individual. It is, therefore, useful to investigate whether there are existing achievement standards that are appropriate to your subject, or which could be easily adapted. Professional accrediting bodies, disciplinary societies and even government agencies can be sources. The Australian Learning and Teaching Council (ALTC), for example, sponsored projects that engaged academic staff in developing learning standards in a range of disciplines (ALTC 2011). Other potentially useful information and examples of standards can be found in relation to the Association of American Colleges and Universities Valid Assessment of Learning in Undergraduate Education (VALUE) Project (Association of American Colleges and Universities 2012); the European Union's project on Tuning Educational Structures (University of Deusto n.d.); and the UK's higher education Quality Assurance Agency (2011).

If you cannot find relevant or adaptable external standards that are appropriate for your subject, it may be worth contacting other academics, within or outside your institution, who teach the same or similar subjects and examining the standards they have set. Subject outlines or syllabi containing this information can often be found on the web. In the end, benchmarking your standards is likely to lead to clearer expression.

YOUR THOUGHTS

- How have the standards for student learning in your subject been developed? Against what other standards, if any, have they been benchmarked?
- Whom might you ask to review and critique your draft standards?

How will students' learning be assessed?

In a backward-designed, constructively aligned subject, all assessment tasks must be clearly connected to the intended learning outcomes, grading standards and learning activities. In practice, this means that assessment time and grading weight should be allocated to parallel the relative importance of subject ILOs. For example, if the development of critical thinking is more important than memorising facts and principles, then assessment tasks must clearly focus on and reward the former. All too often, subjects seem to assess not what is most important, but rather what is easiest to assess.

At the end of the last century, Gibbs (1999, p. 153) identified the following six functions of assessment in higher education:

1. capturing student attention and effort
2. generating appropriate learning activity
3. providing feedback to students
4. developing within students the ability to monitor their own learning and standards

5. allocating marks to distinguish between students or to distinguish degree classifications
6. ensuring accountability to demonstrate to outsiders that standards are satisfactory.

Gibbs noted that only the first four functions are relevant to promoting learning. He summed up his expert advice – based on a long career spent in academic development, research and policymaking in relation to teaching and learning improvement – in the following short paragraph:

> We need to use course requirements, portfolios, self and peer assessment and a range of other devices which are strong on functions (1)–(4) but which do not need to address functions (5) and (6) at all. If I was allowed a single message to improve student learning it would be to manipulate the assessment system so that functions (1)–(4) were performed as often as possible. Evidence from diary studies suggests that students are almost exclusively oriented to the assessment system, spending as little as 10 per cent of their time by year three on work which is not assessed (Innis 1996). If we want to change student learning that is where we have leverage. Being preoccupied by function (6) will not impact student learning in helpful ways.
>
> (Gibbs 1999, p. 154)

In essence, learning-centred assessment tasks are those which: motivate students to do the kinds of work required to learn deeply and well; provide useful and timely feedback required to further improve their learning; and help students to develop skill in monitoring and regulating their own learning. If assessment tasks are designed, first and foremost, to promote deep learning – for formative purposes – it is a fairly straightforward task to then apply subject standards to students' work for grading purposes – summative assessment.

In designing assessment for deep learning, a key question is: How can students effectively, authentically and efficiently demonstrate that they have achieved the intended learning outcomes at the appropriate standard? Once the ILOs and standard of performance have been set, there are many available resources that can help teachers choose assessment tasks that strike a good balance between authenticity and efficiency (see Chapter 5, Brown & Race 2012).

What specific content will be taught and learned?

Only now do we come to selecting the content. Backward design delays content selection until this point in the subject design process not because it is unimportant, but precisely because making the right decisions about content is critically important in promoting learning. While the ILOs and standards come first, and should generally focus on high-level concepts and skills, in order for students to learn and demonstrate that they can think critically and creatively, and can write and speak well, they must think critically and creatively, and write or speak *about* something. That something is the content.

A key premise of backward design is that the specific subject content is, nonetheless, a means to greater ends. In nearly every discipline and field, the amount of important information grows exponentially over time, whereas the key concepts and skills are much smaller, more slowly changing sets. Once one has considered the purpose, fit, audience, ILOs, standards and assessment for a subject, selecting the appropriate content to interest, motivate and assist specific types of students to achieve a given standard of performance is a much more focused, intentional task than simply deciding 'what to include'. In this task, once again, professional and disciplinary societies – as well as textbooks and web resources – can provide guidance and examples.

YOUR THOUGHTS

- If you were to revise one of your subjects through backward design, how would you begin?
- To what extent would backward design revision lead to the selection of different content and assessment?

What will motivate students to learn deeply and well?

Motivation is a much-theorised and researched topic in psychology and education (see Chapter 1, Stewart 2012; Svinicki 2004). Svinicki provides a succinct synthesis of the relevant literature that addresses practical issues of subject design and teaching in higher education. Her seven strategies for enhancing student motivation are as follows:

1. Be a good role model of appropriate motivation.
2. Choose learning tasks with utility, challenge and interest value.
3. Encourage accurate self-efficacy about the course.
4. Base evaluation on progress or absolute level achieved to produce mastery goal orientation.
5. Encourage attributing success to effort and interpreting mistakes as learning opportunities.
6. Provide choice and control over goals or strategies to the learner.
7. Communicate high expectations that are in line with student capabilities (Svinicki 2004, p. 167).

Designing even two or three of these strategies into a subject can increase students' motivation to take on and persevere in the challenging work of learning.

- How might you design some elements of choice into a new or existing subject?
- How might you design or redesign your assessment and feedback practices to encourage students to take risks, make mistakes and learn from those mistakes?

What work will students do to learn?

In order for students to learn deeply and well, in ways that lead to independence and further learning, they must engage in 'deliberative practice', that is, 'practice focused on improving particular aspects of the target performance, to better understand how to monitor, self-regulate and evaluate their performance, and reduce errors' (Hattie 2009, p. 30). Most of the deliberative practice students require to learn deeply must be done outside of class meeting time and without direct supervision from the teaching staff. Therefore, a key challenge in subject design is to create learning activities that will help students spend their study time productively. The most productive learning activities provide 'cognitive scaffolding', step-by-step guidance that promotes both the achievement of the ILOs and, at the same time, the development of transferable metacognitive skills, such as self-regulation.

CASE 6.2   SESSION PREPARATION ASSIGNMENTS

Session preparation assignments (SPAs) are specific and detailed written instructions provided to help students prepare for subsequent class meetings thoroughly, effectively and efficiently. Many teachers complain that the majority of their students do not prepare sufficiently – or at all – for their lectures, tutorials or laboratory sessions. To address this lack, session preparation assignments tell students not only *what* they are expected to prepare, but also *why, how, how much* and by *when*. Each session preparation assignment contains the following basic elements:

- a list of the intended learning outcomes (ILOs) to be addressed by the assigned work (the why)
- a list of ILO-related key questions, problems or prompts to be answered or addressed in writing (the what) before the next meeting (the when)
- a list of the assigned readings and problem sets to be used in responding to the questions (the how much)
- explicit tips on how to read and prepare for the next class meeting (the how)
- information on where and how to get help and support, if required.
- Session preparation assignments are used as the basis for in-class or online discussions and are marked very quickly and simply – often on a 0 to 3 scale (not submitted = 0, requirements not met = 1, requirements met = 2, requirements exceeded = 3) – contributing a very small number of points to a student's overall subject grade.

YOUR THOUGHTS

- Identify some examples of learning activities in subjects you teach that provide 'cognitive scaffolding' (structured guidance for student learning)
- How does your subject communicate expectations about the type and amount of learning work students are expected to do?
- How would you design a session preparation assignment for one of your classes?

What work will teachers and others do to help students learn?

According to Hattie, 'The aim is to get students to learn the skills of teaching themselves – to self-regulate their learning' (2009, p. 245).

At this point in the 21st century, we know quite a bit about how to promote deep, lasting learning. Summaries of the best empirical research indicate a number of teaching and learning strategies that work (Hattie 2009; Pascarella & Terenzini 2005). Among the most powerful teaching strategies are the following:

- providing timely, useful feedback – the primary educational justification for assessment tasks
- providing direct instruction on specific areas of confusion – typically to follow up feedback
- reciprocal teaching – that is, teaching students to teach each other
- teaching students metacognitive, self-regulatory strategies – strategies for managing and improving their own learning.

If there is time enough only to focus on one of these four powerful strategies, then feedback would be likely to provide the greatest learning returns on investment. Nicol and Macfarlane-Dick (2007, p. 205) offer useful research-based principles for facilitating self-regulation and effective learning through feedback. They suggest that good feedback practice:

- helps clarify what good performance is (specifying goals, criteria, expected standards)
- facilitates the development of self assessment (reflection) in learning
- delivers high-quality information to students about their learning
- encourages teacher and peer dialogue around learning
- encourages positive motivational beliefs and self-esteem
- provides opportunities to close the gap between current and desired performance
- provides information to teachers that can be used to help shape teaching.

109

The list above can serve as useful checklist for both feedback design and practice. Following such good practice guidelines is only possible if one focuses feedback on a very few critical assignments or assessment tasks; preferably tasks that students will be encouraged or required to resubmit, applying the feedback in order to learn and to improve their performance on summative assessment. Feedback is most effective when it is valued and consequential.

In conclusion: The seven Cs of successful curriculum design

Simply put, a well-designed learning-centred curriculum is one that helps all willing and able students achieve and demonstrate the expected standard of learning more effectively, efficiently and successfully than they could on their own. A short list of criteria for designing curriculum is proposed below, using alliteration to aid recall. Given that a single subject is usually one element in a larger curriculum – and typically makes up a rather small proportion of the whole program – it would be unrealistic to expect any single subject to meet all seven criteria fully. That said, in order for the parts (subjects) to align with and contribute to the whole (program of study), each element of the curriculum should be designed with the overall criteria in mind. To that end, subject-level design questions follow each criterion. Once you have drafted your subject design, you might give the draft a second look in light of the following criteria.

A well-designed curriculum is:

- compelling. To what extent does the subject focus on questions, issues or topics that interest and matter to students, staff and other stakeholders? In what ways will completing it successfully make any difference to students? A year after finishing the subject, how likely is it that students will look back on it as a meaningful and useful experience?
- conceptual. To what extent is the subject focused on 'learning that will last' rather than 'learning that will quickly pass'? To what extent do the subject's learning activities, assessment tasks and feedback activities focus on understanding and mastery of key concepts and skills – the conceptual level – and to what extent on the memorisation of facts and information?
- constructively aligned. How well aligned is the subject internally? How clearly are learning activities and assessments connected to the intended learning outcomes? And how well is it aligned externally with the rest of the curriculum, both horizontally – with other subjects at the same level or year – and vertically – with the subjects and experiences that come before and after?
- challenging. How well do the subject design, assessments and grading standards communicate high expectations to learners? Is the subject sufficiently

intellectually challenging to engage and benefit the best-prepared and most-able students? Is it sufficiently intellectually challenging to engage and benefit the teaching staff?

- consistent. To what extent is the design consistent with larger institutional values? For example, if the institution claims to value inclusiveness, equity and diversity, how well does the design provide all students with adequate scaffolding, support, feedback and access to learning support? Do all students who are allowed to enrol and who are willing to devote sufficient time and effort have a fair and reasonable opportunity to learn and succeed? Will all prospective students clearly see that this subject is offering them a 'fair go'?

- connected. To what extent does it help students make appropriate, useful connections to their course of study, to their current or future careers, to their roles as citizens? How well does the subject promote transfer and application of learning?

- cost effective. Is the subject financially sustainable in terms of its total cost per student enrolled? And is it sustainable in terms of the time and effort required of teaching staff and students? In terms of money, time and effort required, will the return on investment be sufficient for students and staff?

If your subject meets most of the criteria above then it is almost certainly well designed both for learning and for teaching.

CHAPTER 7

DESIGNING ONLINE AND BLENDED LEARNING

Thomas C Reeves and Patricia M Reeves

Keywords

online learning, blended learning, community of inquiry framework, learning management systems, instructional design

> The instructional approaches of choice in online environments are more collaborative, problem based, generative, exploratory, and interactive. There is more emphasis on mentoring, coaching, and guiding learning than in the past.
>
> (Bonk 2009, p. 33)

> The task of the online course designer and teacher now, therefore, is to choose, adapt, and perfect, through feedback, assessment, and reflection, educational activities that maximise the affordances of the Web. In doing so, they will create learning-, knowledge-, assessment-, and community-centered educational experiences that will result in high levels of learning by all participants.
>
> (Anderson 2008, p. 68)

The phenomenal expansion of online learning across all sectors of higher education means that virtually every new tertiary teacher must be prepared to design and teach subjects and programs that will be totally or partially online (Allen & Seaman 2010). Most tertiary institutions have invested enormous resources in providing teachers and students with access to one or more learning management systems (LMS). LMS such as Blackboard software (a commercial product sold by a for-profit company) or Moodle (an open-source program distributed freely and maintained by its worldwide user community) provide teachers and learners alike with easy-to-use online tools for presenting content, distributing assignments, enabling discussions and conducting assessments in ways that promote learning

(McGee et al. 2005). In fact, on many campuses, teachers are required to use the LMS provided by their institutions, if only to provide learners with access to a syllabus, academic calendar or their marks. As a result, most so-called traditional face-to-face subjects today are more accurately labelled as 'blended' in nature, depending upon the degree to which online resources are incorporated into a subject in ways that support student learning (Garrison & Vaughan 2008).

Numerous research-based principles and models for teaching online have emerged in recent years (Anderson 2008; Garrison 2011; Herrington et al. 2010; Means et al. 2009). The purpose of this chapter is to synthesise these guiding principles and instructional models into practical advice that teachers can use to plan, implement and evaluate effective online and blended learning opportunities for their students. The chapter is structured around five core strategies that teachers should follow when designing and teaching online or blended subjects. The five strategies are:

1. Attend first and foremost to the fundamentals of effective teaching and learning, keeping pedagogy ahead of technology (Hattie 2009).
2. Seek to maximise the alignment of the critical components of an effective online or blended learning environment (Biggs 1996; Reeves 2006).
3. Establish and maintain cognitive presence, social presence and teaching presence in the online or blended learning environment (Anderson et al. 2001).
4. Introduce new technologies selectively, seeking help from peers, learners and others (Bonk 2009; Marek 2009).
5. Conduct formative evaluations to refine the online or blended subject systematically each time it is taught (Reeves & Hedberg 2003).

Attend to the fundamentals of teaching and learning

The fundamentals of effective teaching and learning remain paramount, regardless of how a subject is delivered. For example, research indicates that teachers are more effective when they 'pay attention to the knowledge and beliefs that learners bring to a learning task [and] use this knowledge as a starting point for new instruction' (Bransford et al. 2000, p. 11). Much of the evidence about the fundamentals of effective teaching and learning is summarised in Hattie's important book, *Visible Learning* (2009), an evaluation of many meta-analyses about education. Meta-analysis is a statistical procedure that allows a researcher to integrate the results of multiple research studies that address similar research hypotheses. Hattie reviewed more than 800 published meta-analyses that examined the relationships between numerous instructional strategies and programs (which he labels as treatments). While most of the research studies that Hattie synthesised are related to achievement in school-level education, the findings have valid implications for higher education. Hattie concluded that the foundational building blocks of any robust learning environment, be it a face-to-face, a completely online or a blended model, should include:

- teacher clarity in explaining content
- high academic challenge
- time-on-task
- timely feedback to students
- positive teacher–student relationships.

By contrast, some of the least effective treatments according to Hattie's analysis are among the favourites of the proponents of educational technology, such as:

- computer-assisted instruction
- simulations and games
- audiovisual methods
- programmed instruction
- web-based learning.

At first glance, these findings might appear puzzling or even disturbing to teachers required to teach entirely or partially online. But it is important to distinguish between instructional methods that directly affect learning and instructional delivery systems that serve primarily as vehicles for the provision of instructional methods. 'Innovations' such as computer-based instruction or web-based learning can be highly effective if they are used to provide learners with pedagogical fundamentals, such as clear explanations, opportunities to practise new skills or apply new knowledge, and immediate feedback. It is helpful to think of instructional methods as analogous to the acid compound in aspirin that relieves pain. The acid compound can be introduced into the bloodstream through many different vehicles or media such as tablets, capsules, liquids or even chewing gum. Some delivery vehicles may be less expensive than others, some are easier to swallow and others are more appealing to children, but the important thing is to get the acid compound introduced into the bloodstream so that the pain is relieved. Drawing on this metaphor, an instructional delivery mode such as web-based learning may provide widely dispersed learners easier access to learning opportunities, but a subject offered via the web will not be effective unless the design of the subject exposes learners to clear explanations, allows practice and provides feedback (see Chapter 6, Angelo 2012).

Most teachers, even early-career teachers, are highly experienced and skilled in their respective disciplines, but not necessarily experts in the design and implementation of subjects that support effective learning. Accordingly, university teachers should be open to seeking the help of instructional designers or more experienced colleagues. Instructional designers are educational specialists with unique skills related to the analysis, design, development, implementation and evaluation of effective subjects and programs. Many universities provide teachers with access to instructional designers through a centre for teaching and learning or a similarly named unit. Whether teachers collaborate with instructional designers or more experienced colleagues to develop a new online or blended subject, they should not start with the assumption that it must include interactive games, 3-D videos or other high-tech components. Instead, they should begin by specifying the core components of the subject such as the learning objectives, content, learning activities and assessment strategies and how these are arranged to provide the fundamentals of effective teaching and learning (see Chapter 6, Angelo 2012).

YOUR THOUGHTS

- What learning technologies are available for you to use for your teaching? (For example, LMS, lecture capture and digital resources?)
- What support is available for you to learn how to integrate technology meaningfully into your teaching? (For example, professional development specialists, instructional designers, more experienced colleagues and library and information technology staff?)
- How can the technologies available to you enhance fundamental instructional strategies such as time-on-task and timely feedback that will allow your students to achieve the subject objectives?

Maximise alignment

Regardless of whether teaching is taking place in a face-to-face context, totally online or in a blended format, alignment is essential to effective teaching and learning (Biggs 1996; Reeves 2006). Alignment within the context of university teaching refers to the degree to which various components of a subject are synchronised with each other. For example, it should be obvious that the objectives of a subject are aligned with how the outcomes of the subject are assessed. However, alignment is a more complex problem than just matching subject objectives with learning assessment strategies. There are at least seven critical components of any learning environment that must be carefully aligned, including:
1. objectives
2. content
3. model of instruction
4. learner tasks
5. teacher roles
6. technology roles
7. assessment.

Misalignment of these components partially explains why students in higher education sometimes fail to learn (Arum & Roksa 2011).

Objectives

The objectives of a learning environment specify the knowledge, skills, attitudes and intentions that learners should develop as a result of participating in that environment. Ideally, objectives are stated as measurable outcomes. For example, in a subject on Climate Change and the Ocean, an objective might be: 'Students will be able to identify distinguishing properties of a climate system including the interactions among the atmosphere, the ocean and the biosphere.' Objectives associated with higher order thinking might indicate that: 'Students will exhibit a robust mental model of how climate change threatens the Great Barrier Reef in Australia.' The first objective relates to a lower order learning outcome involving recall of information whereas the second relates to the cognitive capacity to synthesise and evaluate scientific theories with evolving scientific data. The latter objective may require the use of technology as a cognitive tool (Jonassen & Reeves 1996). For example, students could demonstrate their mental model of climate change by building a concept map of the factors affecting coral growth on the Great Barrier Reef using a software program such as the open-source concept-mapping application Visual Understanding Environment developed at Tufts University.

Content

The content or subject matter included in a learning environment should be aligned with the nature of the objectives. In the past, content in higher education has usually been presented in highly structured formats such as textbooks and lectures. However, today, thanks to the internet, content can also be accessed in ill-structured, real-world formats such as scientific data from remote sensors, for example, earthquake sensing available from the United States Geological Survey, or political updates from newsfeeds such as the National Public Radio newsfeed in the USA. Indeed, the nearly ubiquitous nature of the world wide web means that the content encompassed within most disciplines is, for all practical purposes, limitless. Teachers can assemble their own content compilations from free resources, although it is good practice to seek the assistance of your institution's reference librarians and to ensure copyright and intellectual property rights are not breached. Students can also be enlisted in the process of defining and locating the content to be included in a subject. For example, for a decade, students at the University of Georgia enrolled in an online subject focused on learning theory have created their own electronic textbook, with students each year extending, enhancing and, where appropriate, deleting the contributions of earlier students (Orey 2002).

Model of instruction

The overall arrangement of activities, resources, structure and activities that an online or blended subject provides to promote learning should be organised in accordance with an effective model of instruction. Traditional didactic instructional models (direct instruction) found in universities are focused on teacher talk (lectures), static content (textbooks) and fixed assessment (tests that require one right answer), but evidence for the efficacy of these approaches is unacceptably weak (Arum & Roksa 2011; Fink 2003; Kuh 2003). Alternative instructional models include inquiry-based learning (see Chapter 8, Jenkins & Healey 2012; Lee 2004), problem-based learning (see Chapter 9, Brodie 2012; Hmelo & Evensen 2000), project-based learning (Markham et al. 2003), service learning (Butin 2005) and authentic tasks (see Chapter 10, Garnett 2012; Herrington et al. 2010). These alternative models often foster the innovative use of technologies in teaching. For example, Benz (2010) used the Google Docs^{TM} program to allow undergraduate students to contribute to the authentic task of writing a business information systems book.

Learner tasks

When designing an online or blended subject, teachers may be tempted simply to assign students to traditional academic tasks such as reading textbook chapters, discussing the readings, writing a short paper or two or taking quizzes. However, it is much more effective to engage students in tasks that reflect the ways their knowledge, skills, attitudes and intentions will be applied in the real world (Herrington & Herrington 2005). For example, students enrolled in a blended Master of Instructional Design and Development program (mostly online but incorporating optional face-to-face workshops on weekends) at the University of Georgia primarily learn by working as apprentice designers and producers for real-world clients (Clinton & Rieber 2010). In short, they learn instructional design by doing instructional design, using the technology relevant to their discipline under the guidance and supervision of their teachers and more advanced students enrolled in the same program.

Teacher roles

Bain (2004) described how the very best academic teachers often surrender some of their power as subject matter experts and become co-learners with their students. Teachers can foster better collaboration among learners by nurturing a sense of community among them, intervening if conflicts about workload expectations among students are not realised, and incorporating authentic tasks that are inherently motivating. For example, a graduate-level online subject at the University of Georgia allowed learners from countries as widely dispersed as Australia, South Africa, Sweden and the USA to collaboratively plan, conduct and

117

report evaluations of e-learning products for real clients. The role of the teacher in this subject has shifted from the delivery of information to the nurturing of group collaboration and supporting of self-regulated learning among diverse learners separated by time zones and cultures (Oh 2011).

Technology roles

Web 2.0 technologies such as cognitive tools, visualisation software, simulations, serious games and other interactive resources have enormous potential in higher education (Lee & McLoughlin 2010; Thomas 2011) as long as they are aligned with an appropriate instructional model. Teachers should consider the 'affordance' of resources. The affordance of an object (whether it be a door or a computer program) is the type of interactive possibility provided by the object in the real or cyber world. Some doors have the affordance of being pushed or pulled whereas others only have the affordance of being pushed open because they lack a handle or doorknob. Similarly, some computer programs have an affordance of automating some process, such as writing with a word processor, whereas others have an affordance that allows people to see previously unimagined relationships, such as allowing people to calculate alternative budgets with a spreadsheet or detect the effects of industrial pollution on climate change using web-based databases.

Cognitive tools, programs that help humans think and learn in more powerful ways, can be especially useful in higher education when employed within the context of alternative models of instruction such as inquiry-based learning (Jonassen & Reeves 1996; Kim & Reeves 2007). Multimedia resources are also valuable in providing the cognitive scaffolding many learners need in challenging subjects. Amaral and Shank (2010) described how they make 'extensive use of multimedia resources such as instructor podcasts, animations, short videos, modules (tutorials with practice exercises), and simulations' in a blended chemistry subject at Pennsylvania State University. Students in this undergraduate chemistry subject were failing to come to class prepared to engage in meaningful inquiry until these online resources were provided along with detailed guides about how to use them. Examples include podcasts that allow the learners to listen to more detailed explanations of core chemistry content on their own time and animations that allow learners to perceive the complex interactions involved in chemical bonds.

Assessment

Online and blended subjects can incorporate several unique approaches to assessment including electronic portfolios, authentic tasks and simulations (Oosterhof et al. 2008). In the blended Master of Instructional Design and Development program at the University of Georgia (Clinton & Rieber 2010), students compile an online portfolio of all the digital products they create throughout the three-semester program of study. All products ranging from design documents to fully-realised interactive learning materials are accompanied by critical reflections written by the learners themselves, their peers and their teachers.

Woo et al. (2007) described several online subjects offered by the University of Wollongong that incorporate authentic tasks for learning and assessment purposes. In one master's-level subject, learners work in small teams to create a design document (blueprint) for an online learning environment and then individually produce prototype interactive components of the environment. Both the design documents and prototype components are assessed using rubrics, or scoring guides that allow teachers to assess aspects of student work using clearly stated criteria and standards.

Simulations are regularly used as high-stakes assessments in areas such as pilot and surgical training. Although not widely used yet by university teachers, simulations and 'serious games' that assess skills as diverse as classroom management for teacher education students and international diplomacy for political science students are beginning to be more widely adopted in university online and blended subjects (Shute et al. 2009).

YOUR THOUGHTS

Thinking of a subject you will be teaching, how can you use technology in each of these components?

- Objectives – Can your objectives encompass relevant technology skills along with subject related content outcomes?
- Content – How can students gain access to the most accurate and timely content using digital libraries and the web?
- Model of instruction – How can technology foster the effective integration of an innovative model of instruction?
- Learner tasks – What roles will communications technologies play in enabling students to engage in collaborative group work to complete complex tasks?
- Teacher roles – How will your communications with students be enabled by the features of the LMS at your university?
- Technology roles – What can you do to make sure that any technology incorporated into your subject is aligned appropriately with the other essential components?
- Assessment – How can online portfolios, automated test scoring systems and other technologies enhance the learning value of assessment activities in your subject?

Maintain cognitive, social and teaching presence

Anderson et al. (2001) developed the community of inquiry (COI) framework to guide the research and development of online learning environments. The COI framework is grounded in two primary theories: constructivist learning theory (Jonassen 1999) and collaborative learning theory (Roberts 2004). According to constructivist learning theory, learners construct different cognitive structures (for example, a mental model of climate change) depending upon their previous personal experiences and the learning activities in which they are engaged. According to collaborative learning theory, people can engage in especially productive learning when they are involved in solving ill-structured problems or tackling complex tasks (for example, preparing public service television segments concerning the impact of climate change on the local economy) with others who are also interested in learning. Teachers can use the COI framework to help them to think about and design their online and blended subjects as a learning community, which is a group of individuals who collaboratively engage in purposeful critical discourse and reflection to construct learning that is personally meaningful.

The COI framework includes three forms of 'presence' that must be attended to within the context of teaching and learning online: cognitive, social and teaching presence. The framework's developers define cognitive presence as 'the exploration, construction, resolution and confirmation of understanding through collaboration and reflection in a community of inquiry' (Garrison 2007, p. 65). Social presence is defined as 'the ability to project one's self and establish personal and purposeful relationships' through 'effective communication, open communication and group cohesion' (Garrison 2007, p. 63). Teaching presence is defined as 'the design, facilitation, and direction of cognitive and social processes for the purpose of realising personally meaningful and educationally worthwhile learning outcomes' (Anderson et al. 2001, p. 5). Teaching presence has three components: (1) instructional design; (2) discourse facilitation; and (3) direct instruction.

Establishing and maintaining cognitive presence

From the cognitive presence perspective, the teacher must seek to ensure that all learners (including the teacher as co-learner) share equitably in collaborative discourse and reflection. Below are several strategies for establishing and maintaining cognitive presence within an online or blended subject.

Clarify the structure of the learning environment for the learners

This can be done in several ways, but the aim is always to help the learners comprehend their roles and responsibilities within the overall learning environment. For example, the seven components of the subject that must be aligned (objectives, content, model of instruction, learner tasks, teacher roles, technology roles and assessment) can be explained to the students through provision of a clear syllabus. Of course, it is not sufficient to simply load the syllabus onto the LMS with the expectation that students will read and understand it. Instead, the teacher must seek to engage the learners in consideration of and reflection upon the syllabus. For example, students can be assigned to small groups with each group having the responsibility to share its understanding of one component of the syllabus with the rest of the participants via a tool for online communications, such as the discussion forum provided as part of the LMS.

Incorporate a mix of individual and small group assignments

The capacity to collaborate is an important outcome for all learners. Small group collaboration to accomplish meaningful learning tasks heightens cognitive presence within a subject, but teachers will find that most learners need support to collaborate effectively. Oh (2011) revealed several design strategies to support collaborative learning in online and blended subjects, including:

- Facilitate the group work process by carefully selecting a leader and participating in initial group meetings to model good teamwork and clear communications.
- Provide opportunities for establishing positive interdependence by making sure that each team member does an equitable share of the group work. Detecting individual contributions to group work is not easy and often requires periodic peer and self assessments. For example, a weekly email can be sent to learners asking questions such as – How satisfied are you with the progress of your team project? What have you done in the last week to contribute to the team project? What do you plan to do next week to contribute to the team project?
- Enhance individual accountability, motivation and engagement by acknowledging the positive collaboration of individual participants when it is evident. Sending a 'you are doing great work' email to a learner who is contributing to teamwork above the normal expectation enhances the learner's motivation and satisfaction.

Bring the content of the subject to the fore

This should take place within the discourse that occurs via email, discussion, chat and other spaces used for communication within an online or blended subject. For example, seek teachable moments when questions are asked about subject objectives, assignments or assessment procedures. Suppose a student posts a question about whether some specific content or material will be 'on the test'. Instead of simply responding 'yes' or 'no', use this as an opportunity to clarify the relevance of the material to the overall objectives of the subject.

Establishing and maintaining social presence

From the social presence perspective, the teacher must strive to establish rapport with and within the community of learners engaged in a subject by maintaining open and clear communications and nurturing a sense of cohesion among the learners. Here are several tips for establishing and maintaining social presence within an online or blended subject.

Begin a subject with an opportunity for a self-disclosure activity

For example, learners can be asked to post something personal about themselves to the subject online discussion forum along with a picture. A popular ice-breaking activity is called 'three truths and a lie'. In this activity, each participant (including the teacher) posts four 'facts' about themselves with one of the facts being untrue. Participants post their guesses about which of the facts is untrue, and after everyone has posted, the person reveals the 'lie'. Ice-breaking activities like this enable students to become comfortable with the mechanics of the online discussion forum within the LMS while at the same time beginning to form a community of learners (Palloff & Pratt 2005).

Acknowledge the online contributions of each learner by name

It is especially important to compliment participants on the questions they ask even when some of the early questions in an online discussion forum might reflect a failure to read the subject syllabus or other online materials. Adopt an attitude that 'there are no stupid questions'.

Refer to other messages or postings and quote from them when appropriate

Whereas in a face-to-face classroom discussion misunderstandings may be detected by observing facial expressions or body language, online perceptions are more subtle. It is generally better to be much more detailed in online discussions than in normal communications.

Establishing and maintaining teacher presence

From the teaching presence perspective, the teacher must work to design, facilitate and guide the cognitive and social processes that more directly influence learning. Strategies for establishing and maintaining teaching presence in an online or blended subject include the following.

Identify areas of agreement and disagreement

Provide students with opportunities to explore areas of agreement and disagreement about subject topics and seek to build consensus when appropriate. Most students arrive in a subject with misconceptions or incomplete knowledge that must be reduced or amplified as indicated by the nature of the content and the skills to be learned. Whereas in a face-to-face subject it is sometimes difficult to track the learning exhibited by individual students within the context of classroom discussions, discussion tools in blended and online subjects allow teachers to examine the contributions of students for evidence of cognitive growth and higher levels of discourse as a subject proceeds. For example, Moodle, a popular open-source LMS, allows teachers to see an individual student's contributions over time. In large classes, examining a sample of student responses will be sufficient for the teacher to gain a sense of the level of understanding.

Provide direct instruction when needed

Shea et al. (2006) described direct instruction as 'presenting content and questions, focusing the discussion on specific issues, summarising discussion, confirming understanding, disposing misperceptions, injecting knowledge from diverse sources and responding to technical concerns' (p. 181). Learners engaged in authentic tasks and collaborative group work online should be allowed adequate time to learn by doing, but, if they flounder, it is important for the teacher to provide direct instruction to allow them to progress.

Maintain teaching visibility by providing encouragement and feedback

It is important to do this to the greatest extent possible. Most learners crave feedback about the quantity and quality of their assignments, contributions to discussions and overall participation within a subject. In classrooms, teachers provide subtle feedback in many ways such as a smile, a nod or an utterance. In online contexts, feedback is necessarily more overt. Emoticons (typed symbols for smiles or other expressions) can accompany communications in discussion forums and other tools to provide unobtrusive feedback.

Ideally, feedback should be timely and formative (Espasa & Meneses 2010). Timely feedback is given as soon as possible after a question is asked or an assignment is completed. Formative feedback provides learners with the opportunity and basis for refinement of their questions, work or other contributions.

Writing individualised feedback for each student in an online subject can be tedious and time-consuming, especially in subjects with large enrolments. Therefore it is useful to maintain a database or spreadsheet with feedback options that can be cut and pasted and perhaps tailored (e.g., adding a student's name) so that the teacher's workload is decreased, but the feedback is still timely.

A principle of effective teaching is that people learn more by discussing questions and issues than by simply being told (Carroll 1968). According to the proponents of the COI framework, discussions must be carefully planned and supported to promote learning within online and blended subjects.

Anderson et al. (2001) argue that there are unique strengths of online discussions that enable richer and more reflective learning from discussion than is

possible in face-to-face settings. Garrison and Vaughan (2008) encourage teachers to:
- provide both public and private discussion opportunities
- expect different levels of participation, but seek to engage all learners to a sufficient degree
- focus on acknowledging and nurturing the value of the learning community.

Discussions are important in most models of instruction, but they are especially important when online subjects are built around 'authentic tasks' that allow people to learn by completing real work or simulated tasks in collaboration with others. Research summarised by Herrington et al. (2010) demonstrated that online discussions within the context of completing authentic tasks are both natural and productive because learners must engage in rich, meaningful discussions to accomplish their collaborative work. In her multi-year investigation of an online subject that utilised authentic tasks as its primary instructional model, Oh (2011) found that the most successful teams engaged in authentic tasks for real-world clients were able to communicate clearly and respectfully using the affordances of whatever tools they felt most comfortable with (for example, online discussion forums, the Google Docs™ program, chat rooms or wikis). In the effort to establish and maintain cognitive, social and teaching presence, teachers are advised to allow some flexibility among learners with respect to the communication tools they use, as long as the teachers themselves also have access to the tools.

YOUR THOUGHTS

- What learning technologies can you use to establish and maintain cognitive presence within an online or blended subject? (For example, how can the LMS scheduling functions be used to maintain student focus on the primary learning tasks to be accomplished in a subject?)
- What learning technologies can you use to establish and maintain social presence within an online or blended subject? (For example, how can social media tools such as Twitter be used to keep students aware that you are engaged as both the teacher and a co-learner in an online or blended subject?)
- What learning technologies can you use to establish and maintain teaching presence within an online or blended subject? (For example, what online tutorials are available to help students lagging behind or enrich the learning of students pushing ahead in an online or blended subject?)

Introduce new technology selectively

There is a lot of buzz in the online learning research and development community today about the potential of web 2.0 social media tools to support learning in online and blended subjects. Facebook, Twitter, the Blogger™ web publishing service and other social media tools are being endorsed by a variety of proponents as tools that can help teachers reach the so-called Net Generation – those born after 1985 (see Dunlap & Lowenthal 2009). However, there is a lack of consensus on the characteristics of this (or any other) generation sufficient to be used as a solid foundation for designing adaptive learning environments (Oblinger & Oblinger 2005; Reeves & Oh 2007). Instead of using speculative assumptions to justify the adoption of popular web 2.0 tools, serious games and the latest high-tech gear to teach the young learners described as 'digital natives' (Prensky 2010), approaches to integrating technology in higher education should be determined by considering the potential pedagogical effectiveness of a technology in relation to specific teaching and learning contexts. Clearly, today's higher education institutions have highly diverse student bodies and faculties, and it is as important to consider the needs of older participants in learning with technology as it is to consider those of the younger participants. In addition, it may well be that students accustomed to using Facebook, Twitter and other social media in their personal lives may actually resist incorporation of these tools into educational pursuits (Minocha 2009).

Unless they are highly skilled 'digital natives' themselves, teachers are advised to master the affordances of the LMS their institutions provide before rushing to bring the latest social media tools into their online or blended subjects. Social media tools have a relatively short shelf life and what is today's rage may be gone tomorrow. If, however, teachers perceive that one or more online tools have unique capabilities for supporting engagement and learning, they should seek as much assistance as possible from technology experts, peers and the students themselves. As one example, Oh (2011) found that having more technologically advanced students within a graduate program enabled the teacher of an international online subject, involving authentic tasks and extensive group work, to use an open-source LMS, Moodle, that was not supported by the normal information technology systems in the institution. Without the additional technical support provided by the advanced students, the teacher would have been so burdened by the demands of mastering ever-changing technologies that he would not have been able to focus adequately on maintaining cognitive, social and teaching presence in the online subject. Although many teachers will not have access to students with advanced technical skills enrolled in their own subjects, students in technically oriented programs may be recruited to provide help as part of a service learning activity (Butin 2005).

Evaluate for enhancement

Even the best-designed learning environment can and should be improved through rigorous formative evaluation (see Chapter 14, Krause 2012; Reeves &

Hedberg 2003). Hattie (2009) reported that providing formative evaluation to teachers is one of the most powerful treatments of the 138 variables examined in his meta-evaluation of meta-analysis studies. It is common practice to divide evaluation into two types: formative (conducted to 'improve' a subject) and summative (conducted to 'prove' the effectiveness of a subject). Reeves and Hedberg (2003) recommended that academic teachers should invest much more heavily in formative evaluation than summative because the former has a much greater and more direct impact on the quality and effectiveness of teaching and learning. The overall purpose of formative evaluation is to provide information to guide decisions about 'debugging' or enhancing an online or blended subject during various stages of its development and implementation.

Although it is common for online or blended subject students to be asked to complete an online 'subject evaluation' questionnaire at the end of the subject, this information provides teachers with inadequate information for making timely formative decisions about how to improve a subject (Frick et al. 2010). Brief surveys can be directed to students at strategic intervals (for example, at the midpoint of a subject or after each significant assignment has been completed) to garner information for enhancing their experience, engagement and learning. Some LMS enable one or a few questions to pop up at random or at pre-planned intervals. Imagine this scenario: a student has just posted a query to the discussion forum. A pop-up questionnaire could ask the student about the purpose of the posting, the student's confidence that the posting will receive a useful response, and whether they have any specific questions that the teacher can answer outside the context of the discussion forum.

Numerous studies have indicated that online subjects are just as effective as traditional face-to-face subjects (Bernard et al. 2004; Hattie 2009; Means et al. 2009; Tallent-Runnels et al. 2006). But the question university teachers, experienced and inexperienced, should ask is: 'Is "just as good" good enough?' The potential of online and blended subjects is not just to extend access to higher education, but to increase the effectiveness of the subjects. The impact of online and blended subjects will not be realised without careful and ongoing formative evaluation. Teachers are encouraged to ask their peers or advanced students to contribute to the evaluation of their online and blended subject. For example, advanced students can be invited to serve as mentors within the context of a subject while at the same time they provide insight into the relative effectiveness of various teaching and learning activities (Reeves & Hedberg 2003). Whatever data collection strategies are used, teachers who seek specific formative feedback regarding the efficacy of their teaching will become more effective (Hattie 2009).

- How can you systematically evaluate various instructional design and technological components of your online or blended subject so that its effectiveness is optimised?
- How can you recruit colleagues or more advanced students to collaborate in conducting rigorous studies of the integration of technology into your online or blended subjects through engagement in the scholarship of teaching and learning (see Chapter 15, Trigwell 2012)?

Conclusion

The bottom line is that effective teaching and learning in online or blended environments requires a multifaceted approach. First and foremost, teachers must pay attention to the fundamentals of any effective learning environment such as clear objectives and valid assessment.

Second, teachers must carefully examine the alignment of seven critical components of the online or blended learning environment: objectives, content, instructional design, learner tasks, teacher roles, technology roles and assessment.

Third, when designing online or blended subjects, teachers should take into consideration the community of inquiry framework and attend to maintaining effective levels of cognitive, social and teaching presence within a subject.

Fourth, teachers should be very selective about adopting new social media tools into their online and blended subjects and should seek the help of information technology experts, more experienced peers and even students.

And fifth, teachers should engage in systematic formative evaluation to enhance the quality and effectiveness of their online and blended learning subjects.

Following these five principles will not guarantee a perfect subject, but will assist a teacher to begin to harness the enormous potential of online and blended subjects to enhance the outcomes of higher education.

CHAPTER 8

RESEARCH-LED OR RESEARCH-BASED UNDERGRADUATE CURRICULA

Alan Jenkins and Mick Healey

Keywords
undergraduate research, teaching–research nexus, research-led, research-based, curriculum

> The research universities have often failed, and continue to fail, their undergraduate populations, thousands of students graduate without seeing the world-famous professors or tasting genuine research.
>
> (Boyer Commission 1998, p.3)

> Universities need to set as a mission goal the improvement of the nexus between research and teaching ... The aim is to increase the circumstances in which teaching and research have occasion to meet ... Examples of strategies to increase the relationship between teaching and research include the following: increase the skills of staff to teach emphasising the construction of knowledge by students rather than the imparting of knowledge by instructors ... develop strategies across all disciplines that emphasise the uncertainty of the task and strategies within the disciplines ... ensure that students experience the process of artistic and scientific productivity.
>
> (Hattie & Marsh 1996, pp. 533–534)

> All providers of higher education that gain registration [must demonstrate] the commitment of teachers, researchers, course designers and assessors to the systematic advancement of knowledge.
>
> (Commonwealth of Australia, p. 11)

Introduction

What does the phrase 'a research-led curriculum' mean to you? Does it attract, repel, intrigue or confuse? What might it mean for your students? Would it attract them? Do you think they would gain from a research-led subject? Is it a perspective on curriculum design that is relevant to university teachers at the beginning of their careers? Or would terms like 'research-based', 'research-active', 'problem-' or 'inquiry-based' better describe what you think is desirable or possible in the contexts in which you teach?

This chapter recognises and values the range of such approaches and explores associated issues by establishing a tension between curricula focused on students learning about current research in their discipline, including the research done by those teaching them, an approach we call 'research-led', and curricula focused on students learning through doing some form of research or inquiry, which we call 'research-based'. Consider the questions above before and after reading this chapter.

The central focus in this chapter is on undergraduate curricula, though the discussion is equally applicable to postgraduate subjects and doctoral programs. The chapter is interspersed with practical examples of subject designs that will inform your practice. Its focus is on the relationship between teaching and research in universities; evidence associated with the teaching–research nexus; frameworks for research-led and research-based curricula design; and strategies for getting started with research-led and research-based curricula including working with first-year students, extending the research skills and orientations of upper-level students and embedding research-led and research-based teaching and learning throughout degree programs.

What are the roles of research and teaching in universities?

The relationships between teaching and research have long been debated in universities. Some see the central role of the university to be teaching, and consider a focus on research as obscuring the primacy of that teaching role. Others argue that a university is an institution in which teaching and research are interconnected through the 'teaching–research nexus'. These issues are becoming more important to analyse and manage in a mass higher education system in which governments, and some university leaders, want to concentrate high-level research in selected research elite universities. Correspondingly, other institutions are encouraged to focus curricula on professional and employment outcomes for students and to appoint teaching-only staff with no allocated time to conduct research. These issues are particularly important for staff at the beginning of their careers as they seek to define their academic roles as teachers and researchers, managing two different roles with conflicting pressures on their time (Colbeck 1998). This chapter aims to help university staff to integrate their teaching and research functions by engaging in the development of research-based curricula.

The evidence on teaching–research relations

Much early research on the teaching–research nexus focused on the attributes of individual teachers and the extent to which being an effective university teacher also means being an effective researcher. Such studies normally used student opinion data as a measure of teaching effectiveness and measures of research productivity as indicators of research effectiveness. In an influential study, Hattie and Marsh (1996) undertook a meta-analysis of 58 such studies, and concluded that 'the common belief that teaching and research were inextricably intertwined is an enduring myth. *At best teaching and research are very loosely coupled*' (Hattie & Marsh 1996, p. 529, emphasis added).

The research by Hattie and Marsh has been used to cast doubt on the benefit of disciplinary research to teaching. Thus a report by the UK Department for Education and Skills (2003), *The Future of Higher Education*, used the research by Hattie and Marsh to justify the development of what came to be called teaching-only or teaching-intensive universities. However, Hattie and Marsh (2004) argued that this was a misreading of their evidence. Rather, they suggested their research indicated that more needed to be done to strengthen the links between good teaching and high research productivity. 'The fundamental issue is what we wish the relationship to be, and we need to devise policies to enhance this wish,' they wrote, adding that 'to better ensure effective teaching research links we need to increase the skills of staff to teach emphasising the construction of knowledge by students' (Hattie & Marsh 1996, pp. 533–534).

More recently, a study of 37 Australian and UK research-active teachers analysed the relationships between individual conceptions of teaching and research, the extent to which teaching and research were seen as relatively separate activities, and the influence of disciplines on such perceptions. The conclusion was that:

> it is the focus on wholes – the overall conceptualisation of subject matter – that is associated with quality of teaching. *It is not how active one is as a researcher, but what form of activity the research focus is on.* On the other hand, it may be that the non-research-active academics who, through scholarship within their discipline, are able to keep a focus on the developing overall conceptualisation of their subject matter, may also experience their teaching from a more student-focused

conceptual change perspective. This suggests that it is not the quantity of research that is associated with quality of teaching, but how scholarship in the discipline or profession is maintained and developed that is important. *This may apply equally to non-research-active as well as to research-active academic staff.*

(Prosser et al. 2008, pp. 12–13, emphasis added to final sentence)

Much of the recent research on teaching–research relations has centred on understanding the student and staff experience of the teaching–research relationship and how institutional and departmental cultures shape that experience (Healey 2011b; Jenkins 2004). A study at the University of East Anglia, UK, concluded that: 'While students value being close to research, and to the idea of a university as a research community in which they are included, there are many ways in which they feel excluded' (Zamorski 2000, p. 1). Pulling together this research, and drawing on her own research conducted at the University of Sydney, Brew (2006, p. 52) concludes that current practice continues to keep students 'at arm's length' from the world of university research. Even so, teachers can do much through the way they design their subjects to bring students into research but they do need an understanding of how institutional and national policies shape the extent to which this can be achieved.

Research on university academics' experiences generally reveal that national systems and institutional policies conceptualise teaching and research as separate activities. While national, institutional and departmental mission statements often proclaim the value of students' learning in a research environment, the potential interconnections between policies for research and teaching are often not sought or realised. A study of departmental organisation in the UK found that

> heads of departments and other managers of staff time indicated that, on a managerial level, it is more convenient for teaching and research activities to be treated as separate activities. On an intellectual level, however, academic managers would rather perceive the two to be synergistic.
>
> (Coate et al. 2001, p. 162)

Mayson and Schapper (2010) analysed interviews with senior staff members at Monash University to gauge the staff's understandings of, and commitment to, the institutional strategic directions in regard to research-led teaching (RLT). They concluded that:

> The discourse of RLT privileges research and assumes a desired link with teaching to raise the quality and value (to the university) of teaching. However the assumed link is one which is expressed through the discourse as a vastly

> simplified and one-sided relationship – that research and researchers will improve and benefit teaching and teachers. The discourse constructs teaching as a lesser valued activity.
>
> (Mayson & Schapper 2010, p. 478)

This research offers a bleak picture to academics hoping to bring a research orientation to their teaching because it suggests that the institutional context may obstruct that aim. Even so, undergraduate research programs and curricula are now a significant feature of many US and Australian universities (Brew 2010), and they have been shown to be effective in promoting students' learning. For example, US studies researching the impact of summer intensive programs demonstrate 'a broad set of benefits ... arising from engagement in authentic research'. In general, undergraduate research experience offers 'a constellation of gains that collectively reflect students' personal, intellectual and professional growth' (Laursen et al. 2010, pp. 33–34).

A framework for curriculum design and teaching and research links

Investigations indicate that research-based teaching and learning curricula can be used for varied purposes (Levy 2011; Levy & Petrulis 2012; Spronken-Smith & Walker 2010):

* *research-led*, involving learning about current research in the discipline. Here the curriculum focus is to ensure that what students learn clearly reflects current and ongoing research in their discipline. This may include research done by staff teaching them.
* *research-oriented*, developing students' research skills and techniques. Here the focus is on developing students' knowledge of and ability to carry out the research methodologies and methods appropriate to their discipline.
* *research-based*, requiring students to undertake research and inquiry. Here the curriculum focus is on ensuring that, as much as possible, students learn in research or inquiry mode. This means that students become producers of knowledge, not just consumers. The strongest curricula form of this is seen in special undergraduate programs for selected students, but such research and inquiry may also be mainstreamed for all or many students (Healey & Jenkins 2009).
* *research-tutored*, engaging students in research discussions. Here the focus is on students and staff critically discussing research in the discipline as, for example, in many seminar-based subjects.

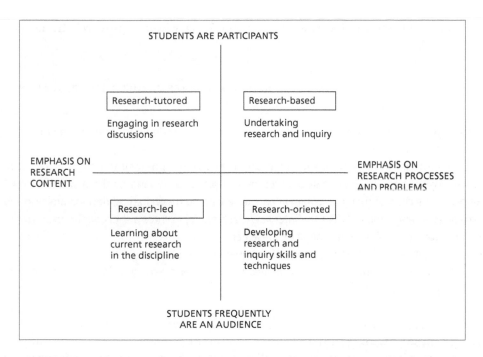

FIGURE 8.1 The nature of undergraduate research and inquiry (Healey & Jenkins 2009, p.7)

The model shown in Figure 8.1 has two axes: the first classifies the ways students may be engaged in research and inquiry according to the extent to which students are treated primarily as the audience or as participants, while the second classifies the approach as emphasising research content or research processes and problems. All four ways of engaging students with research and inquiry are valid and valuable, and curricula can and should contain elements of them all. So the question becomes not so much 'Do you engage your students in each of these ways?' as 'What proportion of their time do they spend in each category and is this an appropriate balance given the students you teach, the type of subject and discipline, and the departmental and institutional culture?' We argue that in much of higher education too much teaching and learning is in the bottom half of the model, and students would benefit from spending more time in the top half. This framework provides a language to analyse and discuss such issues.

The four ways of engaging students with research and inquiry are not independent. So if you use this framework to analyse the case studies included in this chapter you will see that many subjects contain elements of more than one approach. For example, Case 8.1 is clearly *research-led*, in that it is based on current research by the staff who are teaching the students. Yet, from another perspective, it is *research-based*, in that students are inquiring within a research framework designed by staff.

CASE 8.1   GEOGRAPHY STUDENTS INTERVIEW STAFF ABOUT THEIR RESEARCH
University College London, UK (Dwyer 2001)

An assignment in a first-year, term one subject requires students to interview members of staff about their research.

Each tutorial group is allocated a member of staff who is not their tutor.

Tutorial groups are given three representative pieces of writing by the member of staff along with a copy of their curriculum vitae. Students read the materials, develop an interview schedule, arrange and conduct the interview. Each student writes a short paper on:

- the objectives of the staff member's research
- how that research relates to the staff member's earlier studies
- how the staff member's research relates to his or her teaching, other interests and the discipline as a whole.

In a similar example, students in a community health program at Rutgers University, US, were sent out in small groups to interview professionals working with AIDS patients and asked to inquire the extent to which and how their work was shaped by current research.

YOUR THOUGHTS

- To what extent are subjects that you teach:
  - ◊ research-led? In which ways can you introduce your students to current research in your discipline?
  - ◊ research-based? How can you engage your students in research and enquiry?
  - ◊ research-oriented? How can you assist your students to develop research and inquiry skills and techniques through the learning and assessment activities in your subject?
  - ◊ research-tutored? How might you engage students in research discussions?
- Looking across the whole departmental program, which teaching strategies are already in use and which need strengthening?

A further useful distinction may be made between *information-oriented* and *discovery-oriented* inquiry (Levy 2011). In the former, students investigate mainly existing knowledge, which is new to them, while in the latter they are engaged in discovering knowledge which is largely new to society. If you restrict your conception of research to discovery-oriented activities then you are likely to advocate an elite model of engaging selected students in research. If you also accept information-oriented inquiry as a form of research, then you will create opportunities to mainstream research-based learning into the curriculum for all or many students. The following suggestions should help you start on this journey:

- Make student understanding of how research is continually reshaping our understanding of complexity central to the curriculum and the wider student experience of higher education.
- Develop practical approaches to *what* and *how* you teach and how you assess your students based on the research evidence about the relationship between teaching and research.
- Consider the potential to support student learning through your own research.
- Integrate research projects into the curriculum.
- Explore with your colleagues how a research-based curriculum might be embedded on a whole-of-program basis.

Getting started with research-led and research-based curricula

There are a number of strategies to introduce research-led and research-based curricula. The following list provides some initial pointers:

- Decide on which ways of engaging students with research and inquiry are particularly relevant to the needs of students in your subjects, considering their year level and the discipline. Map where each might be included in your current teaching and assessment practices.
- Identify what changes would be needed in the degree programs in which you teach to implement new approaches to linking research with teaching.
- Identify what *you* bring to this agenda, for example, knowledge of how research is used in professional practice. Identify how you might help your students develop such knowledge, skills and understandings of knowledge complexity.
- Consider how the case studies presented in this chapter might be adapted for your subjects. Evaluate their specific features, but also consider how they might be changed to meet the particular needs of your students and discipline. For example, return to Case 8.1, about geography students interviewing staff. Note that this assignment is for first-year students. So, if you teach a first-year subject, use that case study to interrogate practice in your subject group teaching. If you teach in health care and professional disciplines, consider the relevance of the example of the health care students at Rutgers University, for here the focus is not on the research done by staff but on how research shapes professional practice.

- Recognise that students in some disciplines, particularly those with a strong professional or employment focus, may not immediately see the relevance of a research perspective to their learning (Booth & Harrington 2003). For such students ensure that the importance of a research perspective is made transparent to them with respect to their university studies, future employability and their involvement in civic society.
- Make assessment fit how research is conducted and communicated in your discipline. For example, research posters would be particularly appropriate in science subjects as many science research conferences feature poster sessions.
- Seek the support, where appropriate, of subject librarians and learning technologists in the design and delivery of 'research as learning' in your subjects.

Start at the beginning: Introduce first-year students to research

Traditionally, undergraduates are most frequently engaged in research in their final year where many undertake a dissertation or research-based capstone subject (Healey 2011a; University of Gloucestershire 2012). However, it is important to give students research experiences from the day they enter higher education so that they begin to think like historians, chemists, lawyers and so on. Three examples of research being embedded in first-year subjects follow.

YOUR THOUGHTS

Take a look at the following cases and:
- identify which research skills and understandings of knowledge complexity the first-year students might develop as they engage with the learning activities
- assess the relevance of these skills for students studying your subjects
- consider ways in which such skills might be introduced into first-year subjects in your department.

CASE 8.2   PSYCHOLOGY STUDENTS RESEARCH STUDENTS' QUALITY OF LIFE
York St John University, UK (Akhurst 2006)

First-year, non-specialist, psychology students undertook an eight-week project in which each student collected data from him- or herself and three other students using four short inventories and a biographical questionnaire. Research topics related to students' quality of life. This project provided students with the opportunity to collect live data, contribute to a developing database, select data for analysis and write up findings. The topics available for selection by students were linked to the research interests of the lecturer, making the project mutually beneficial. A departmental technician provided assistance with questionnaire design, the development and maintenance of a database, data entry and tutoring on some portions of the project.

CASE 8.3   REINVENTED ENQUIRY LABS IN FIRST-YEAR CHEMISTRY
Warwick University, UK (Taylor & Geden 2008)

Student experience surveys found that fourth-year chemistry students did not feel prepared for their final-year projects. The students felt that the style of the experiments taught in earlier years was formulaic, and did not encourage original thought. Students also reported that classes gave the impression that most chemistry works; after a research project, they appreciated that the reality was somewhat different.

Based on this feedback, the university chose to reinvent a first-year, second-term laboratory subject explicitly to support inquiry-based learning. This involved major changes to the laboratory manual and the pre-lab activities. The new manual posed each experiment 'as a problem to be solved, with all references to the expected outcome removed', and presented experimental procedures 'in the style of methods published in research journals, insofar as was sensible with safety considerations in mind'. Marking schemes were completely revised to support the revised subject goals. In addition, the previous whole-class, didactic pre-lab sessions were revised to a more open discussion and inquiry approach.

CASE 8.4   WRITING RESEARCH AND CONTEMPORARY CULTURES
Miami University, Ohio, USA (McKee 2009)

Students in a first-year writing and cultures subject investigate how the forms of writing, and the methodologies for researching writing and culture, are being transformed through web-based communication. Through this reading and writing intensive seminar, students investigate how digitised technologies are transforming the forms of writing and communication. The subject culminates in a group assignment in which students, using secondary and primary sources, investigate an aspect of contemporary culture (e.g., dating, shopping) to ascertain how the forms of communication are being reshaped by the internet. They produce a multimodal website that presents their findings through text, digital images, audio and video.

The value of cases such as these is that they provide specific strategies that you might adapt to your context, but they also illustrate general issues. The strategies employed in these examples help students gain an initial understanding of general research skills and dispositions, such as asking questions, collecting and analysing data and drawing out preliminary interpretations. The strategies also require students to be active learners in contexts where there is strong staff support. We could then expect that later courses will require students to take greater control of research. For example, they could define the questions and select and refine research methodologies. Further, these strategies help students to understand and participate in research as 'a community of practice' (Smith & Rust 2011). Clearly these students are not involved in high-level research, but they are being guided into research. Implicitly the students are also experiencing something of the particular styles and approaches to research of particular disciplinary communities. Thus, in the psychology case, students might confront issues of confidentiality, an issue that is unlikely to be central to the chemistry case study. And, while dissemination of research is important to all disciplines, the form of that dissemination may well vary by discipline – an issue implicitly introduced in the writing and cultures case study.

Extend research skills in upper-level studies

The following cases from a range of disciplines and upper-level subjects incorporate a stronger focus on students developing their own questions and hypotheses and choosing research methodologies. They are being supported to enter further into the research of their disciplinary communities.

CASE 8.5   ASKING QUESTIONS IN PLANT BIOLOGY

Australian National University (Centre for Higher Education, Learning & Teaching 2012)

A practical exercise designed for a second-year subject involves students:

- making observations in a botanical garden
- coming up with 10 questions each (for example, why do eucalypt leaves dangle?)
- sharing one of these questions with a group of other students
- as a group, coming up with hypotheses based on the question (for example, eucalypt trees in arid environments have leaves that dangle at steeper angles than those in wet environments)
- thinking of ways of testing the hypotheses
- writing-up, individually, their 10 questions and one hypothesis as a 750-word mini-proposal for a research project.

CASE 8.6   HISTORY STUDENTS CONTRIBUTE RESEARCH FINDINGS TO A WEBSITE
University of Victoria, Canada (Lutz 2009; University of Victoria 2010)

History 481: Microhistory and the Internet is a learner-centred and research-oriented subject in which the main activity is primary archival research on various aspects of life in Victoria, British Columbia from 1843 to 1900. Initial subject activities include orientation to the historical archives in Victoria and basic website creation skills. Students work in small groups on a research project and the final research 'product' of the subject is a website, not a standard research paper. The subject has been developed with the support of local community groups and another university. It is one of the international innovative examples of digital history where the web is used as a research tool, a means of disseminating research and developing student web skills.

CASE 8.7   COMMUNITY OUTREACH RESEARCH PROJECT TO PRODUCE A MEDIA DVD
Southern Cross University, Australia (Coyle 2008)

Students in their second or third year of a media studies degree research a topic and record interviews with relevant members of the community to produce a DVD. Students are assessed on their project plan, progress and DVD.

There is a strong focus on research dissemination which, for many, is central to the research process. This focus will help students gain ownership of the research and feel its importance to them and the wider community.

CASE 8.8   TOURISM STUDENTS' VIRTUAL CONFERENCE
University of Lincoln, UK (Hughes 2009; Hughes & Heitmann 2011)

Every year, final-year tourism students at the University of Lincoln participate in a live virtual conference. This is part of their assessment for the final semester-long unit. A conference is a useful vehicle for extending insight into the process and practice of research creation and dissemination and for students to participate as research disseminators. A virtual learning environment has made it possible: during the specified timeframe of one week, students do not have to be assembled in one place and can participate at any time. Two qualified web designers built the site and have been on hand to deal with technical issues. Teaching staff have provided support for the conference throughout the unit. Students submit a full conference paper, with a summary that appears on the conference website. Each student is also required to post a comment on another conference paper. Recently the conference has been extended to students at another university.

What can you do to engage your second- and third-year students in:
- the development of hypotheses and research questions
- the formulation of research proposals with particular reference to ethical issues and dissemination of research outcomes
- presentation of results
- dissemination through conferences and publications?

Departmental approaches to research-led and research-based curricula

Specific strategies to promote research skills and orientations with students in your subjects are but a first step in the development of research-led and research-based curricula because outcomes may be limited and ephemeral without a whole-of-program approach (Jenkins et al. 2007). Ultimately individuals, subject teams and institutions must decide what makes university teaching different from high school or vocational education. In brief, what makes higher education higher? Barnett (2000a) concludes that university education should focus on supporting students' understanding of, and ability to investigate, the 'supercomplex world' in which we live and work.

> A *complex* world is one in which we are assailed by more facts, data, evidence, tasks and arguments than we can easily handle *within* the frameworks in which we have our being. By contrast, a *supercomplex* world is one in which the very frameworks by which we orient ourselves to the world are themselves contested.
>
> (Barnett 2000a, p. 257)

From this, Barnett developed a perspective on program design. He sees teaching and research as separate and distinct activities, but argues that:

> research is a strong condition for teaching: being engaged in research of a frame-developing kind and projecting those frames to wide publics is a strong – although not exactly necessary and certainly not sufficient – condition of teaching that is aimed at bringing about supercomplexity in the minds of students. … *The issue, then, is whether … the lecturers … adopt teaching approaches that are likely to foster student experiences that mirror the lecturers' experiences as researchers.*
>
> (Barnett 2000b, p. 163, emphasis added)

Case 8.9 illustrates one approach to research-led curricula that does mirror university teachers' experiences as researchers, namely, involving students in departmental research.

CASE 8.9   RESEARCH PROJECT LINKED TO STAFF INTERESTS
Australian National University (University of Sydney 2008, p. G5)

Students at ANU have the opportunity to participate in a research project based on current research being conducted by members of the Faculty of Law, the Australian Institute of Criminology and the Research School of Social Science. Criminal Justice is an advanced law elective which critically examines the principal institutions, processes and legal rules relating to the administration of criminal justice. The iLearning project is an assessable option that allows students to devise research projects which have both academic value and practical outcomes.

....

Ideally research-led and research-based curricula are embedded in degree programs and particular research skills and orientations are mapped at increasingly complex levels through all subjects in much the same way that graduate attributes are included in curricula (see Chapter 4, Chalmers & Partridge 2012). For example, Case 8.10 shows a set of linked interventions to bring students into the worlds of research in their discipline.

CASE 8.10   COORDINATED INTERVENTIONS IN ZOOLOGY
University of Tasmania, Australia (Edwards et al. 2007a)

The department has developed a set of linked strategies. In a first-year workshop on the use of animals in research, students are put in the position of researchers, exploring experimental design and animal ethics. Students have access to a website linking to zoology lecture material and other resources.

In second-year, the curriculum and assessment centres on an exercise in which students are given real unpublished data for analysis, supported by workshop practice sessions and one-to-one tutorials. Students are required to write-up their findings in the form of a manuscript for publication.

Third-year subjects include group research projects, critical reviews of current literature, writing research grant applications, lectures from scientists outside the school and training in scientific communication. Students taking the zoology research unit are matched with academic supervisors to complete a semester-long research project. Selected students work with staff to prepare a research paper for publication in the university's *Nexus: Journal of Undergraduate Science, Engineering and Technology.*

All students in second and third year zoology subjects are invited to participate in the student research volunteers program. Volunteers are matched with mentors, usually postgraduate or honours students in the school, for short-term, in-house research placements that may offer either laboratory or field experiences.

Reach into Research seminars are held several times each semester, open to all students. Speakers from industry and collaborating institutions' postgraduate students present their research, and then the speaker or a facilitator leads an extended discussion, open only to undergraduate students.

Willinson and O'Reegan (2007) have proposed a research skill development framework as a way to conceptualise research skills across a student's educational lifetime. It can be used to monitor students' research skill development and autonomy, from level one, where students research at the level of a closed inquiry and require a high degree of structure and guidance, to level five, where students research at the level of an open inquiry within self-determined guidelines in accordance with the discipline. It has subsequently been applied to a large number of disciplines and institutions in Australia (Willinson 2011).

Another way to think about mapping research across degree programs is to consider the work of Baxter Magolda (2009). Drawing on a longitudinal study started over 20 years ago, she has developed a framework for analysing the intellectual growth of students through the lens of self-authorship. She suggests that students' construction of meaning, or ways of knowing, progress from absolute knowing, through transitional and independent knowing, to contextual knowing or self-authorship:

> Moving away from uncritical acceptance of knowledge to critically constructing one's own perspective, however, is more complex than learning a skill set. It is a transformation of how we think – a change in our assumptions about the certainty, source and limits of knowledge.
>
> (Baxter Magolda 2006, p. 50)

This influential framework is complementary to Barnett's call for students to understand complex ways of knowing. An interesting application of Baxter Magolda's concept of self-authorship to one discipline, geography, has recently been published, though much of the analysis is transferable to other subjects (Moore et al. 2011). It shows that the concept of 'self-authorship' is a useful guiding principle in supporting curriculum revision and reform. A series of international case studies illustrate how self-authorship can be enacted in different ways within curricula in a range of contexts.

Early career university teachers may feel daunted by the prospect of leading program-level or departmental change to promote research-led and research-based teaching, but Blackmore (Chapter 16, 2012) considers leadership to be a significant building block in the development of teaching careers:

> A starting point for developing one's capacities as a leader is to recognise the central importance of leadership in academic work and the opportunities we have to lead, at whatever level in the university we find ourselves ... Indeed, academic work is inherently an act of leadership because academics should always be at the forefront of what is being thought and done in their domains of knowledge and practice. This is intellectual leadership ... of which teaching forms a part.
>
> (Chapter 16, Blackmore 2012, pp. 268)

This being so, the following questions, adapted from Jenkins et al. (2007, p. 59), might help when working to promote research-led and research-based teaching across departments and degree programs:

- What is your departmental and disciplinary understanding or conception of 'research-led', '-based' or '-informed' learning?
- What forms of pedagogy and assessment do you consider appropriate to support these conceptions?
- Can you clearly identify where research-based learning is integrated in the program?
- Where is current research in your field presented in the program? How does research relate to program design and program outcomes; curriculum content and delivery in the modules; and assessment methods?
- Where are research methods, skills and ethics taught and practised? Is this progressive? Is a variety of appropriate skills and methods taught?
- Are the research knowledge and skills the student should acquire made clear in the module learning outcomes?
- Can and do students participate in departmental research projects, for example, as research assistants?
- Where is the scope for students to conduct independent research in their programs and in what ways do the programs allow progression?
- How are research skills and the links between teaching and research embedded in monitoring and review of subjects and programs?
- How are students supported in making explicit how this research training and knowledge increases their employability?
- How are undergraduate students made aware of postgraduate research opportunities?
- How does the department's research strategy explicitly support undergraduate students' learning through and about research?

YOUR THOUGHTS

- Identify the research skills and orientations that are appropriate to teach at different levels of one degree program in which you teach.
- Identify the appropriate assessments at these different levels that would facilitate student learning of such skills.
- How might you arrange for students of each year to work together to collaborate in the development of the identified research skills?
- What might be done to engage your students actively in inquiry and investigation associated with current departmental research?
- What are the current strengths, weaknesses, opportunities and threats to embedding research-led and research-based curricula in your department?
- Which aspects would you want to strengthen immediately?
- Which aspects would you want to strengthen over the next two to three years?

Conclusion

We started this chapter by asking you: What does the phrase 'a research-led curriculum' mean to you? Or would terms like 'research-based', 'research-active', 'problem-' or 'inquiry-based' better describe what you think is desirable or possible in the contexts in which you teach?

As this chapter has focused on providing you with an evidence base, frameworks and cases about research-led and research-based curricula, it should now be possible for you to formulate your own responses to these questions. The chapter has also provided subject- and program-level strategies to develop undergraduate student learning through and about research, but the principles also apply to postgraduate subjects, including doctoral programs. Whatever the level at which a research-led or research-based curriculum is taught, the aim is to contextualise learning and make it relevant in ways that foster students' growth and development so that your students can say:

> 'Choose a topic of interest and it is so much easier to apply and remember when the context in which it is done is interesting to you.'

> 'Research can be interesting! Before this class I thought research to be boring.'

> 'The term "research methodology" isn't a bad one, but rather very interesting and exciting. Even I can do it!'

> (students, cited in Hunt 2002)

CHAPTER 9

PROBLEM-BASED LEARNING

Lyn Brodie

Keywords
problem-based learning, problem design, facilitation, reflection, teamwork

Dear colleague,

Professor Crammer is taking sabbatical next semester and you will be required to teach her first-year subject. Semester starts in four weeks, so please have your subject outline ready for approval at the next faculty academic committee meeting.
In line with new faculty guidelines we are focusing on retention and progression of first-year students. The student evaluation results have been disappointing for this subject so this is a good opportunity to increase student engagement and motivation.

Regards
Head of Department

Welcome to problem-based learning, commonly referred to as PBL. You have just been given an 'ill-structured' problem; you must deconstruct the problem, find your own resources, develop a solution to the problem using discussion with your colleagues, test your solution, see how it compares to other situations and, at the end, think about what you did, what you learned and how the subject might be improved. In short, you have worked through the stages of PBL.

PBL is based on the principles of adult education and cognitive psychology (Knowles 1990; Norman & Schmidt 1992) which include acknowledging the prior knowledge and experience adults bring to the learning environment; providing real-life problems rather than theoretical situations; and developing active and self-directed learners. Barrows (1984) describes a cycle of three phases of PBL. First, students encounter a problem, as opposed to a fact or theory; they discuss and deconstruct the problem, usually in a small group setting. Second, the problem and discussion motivates students to undertake self-directed study and research framed by prior knowledge, understanding and identified gaps in their knowledge. Third, students apply their new knowledge and summarise their learning by reflection, either formally in a portfolio or informally in team discussion.

These steps may be repeated with a new problem, or an iterative approach to the initial problem may be used. Koschmann et al. (1994) extended the process, identifying five fundamental steps for students in problem-based learning:

1. project or problem formulation
2. development of a solution through a self-directed learning approach
3. alignment of examination of the problems to test the proposed solutions
4. abstraction, where the solutions are contextualised with other known cases
5. reflection, where the students reflect and critique their learning process seeking to identify areas for future improvement.

Introduction to PBL

The first PBL program was developed in the medical school of McMaster University, Canada, in the 1960s. The program's developers had no background in either education or psychology; they simply thought that learning in small teams, using authentic cases and problems, would make medical education more interesting and relevant for their students (Barrows 2000; Newman et al. 2001). This PBL methodology is now currently used in more than 80 per cent of medical schools in the USA (Ribeiro & Mizukami 2005; Vernon & Blake 1993) and is an entrenched component of medical school programs in Canada, the United Kingdom, the Middle East and Asia (Blight 1995; Finucane et al. 1998). In Australia, more than 50 per cent of Australia's doctors graduate from schools with PBL-based curricula. PBL has now been incorporated into a wide range of professional studies including nursing, dentistry, social work, management, engineering and architecture (Boud & Feletti 1997).

YOUR THOUGHTS

Do a quick scan of the internet. You may find it helpful to use the Google Scholar™ program. Search PBL and your discipline area.

- What seem to be the key issues associated with the use of PBL in your discipline?
- Identify three strategies to help you to develop PBL curricula in your discipline.

In the internet search you may have discovered that the literature presently discusses problem-based learning, project-based learning, inquiry-based learning and project-orientated problem-based learning, among others, as quasi separate themes. These are all used to describe a range of instructional strategies with conceptual similarities. The common core is that all rely on open-ended scenarios, which have more than one approach or answer, and they stimulate student interest. Learning is defined as being *student centred*, while the teacher or instructor takes on the role of *facilitator*. Students work in cooperative groups and individually and collectively seek and use multiple sources of information. Learning is active and self-directed, and it fosters key skills of problem-solving, communicating, researching, acquiring knowledge and transferring knowledge to new situations. Group work develops students' skills in peer collaboration, mentoring and peer assessment. Formal teaching, as such, does not occur, but facilitators pay close attention to the *process* of enabling students' autonomy and self-direction in undertaking the problem or project.

There are two main distinctions that can be made between problem-based and project-based learning. In problem-based learning, teachers set the overall goals and problems (although not the solution pathways). In project-based learning, students set their own learning objectives and learning strategies. In addition, project-based learning typically supports the goal of producing a product or artefact. Problems will be encountered, which add to the learning experience, but these problems may or may not be solved. Projects reflect real-world practices and the *process* of producing the product is as valuable as the end result itself (Brodie 2008).

The instructional strategies of problem- and project-based learning are widely considered to provide students with opportunities to develop skills in communication, collaboration, self-direction and informed decision-making. A number of contemporary studies and meta-analyses show that while learning remains consistent between traditional and problem- or project-based delivery, students report greater motivation and experience in PBL scenarios than in other learning environments (Greening 1998; Newman 2003; Newman et al. 2001; Thomas 2000).

Traditionally in universities, teachers tend to approach learning by presenting concepts in identifiable blocks, in a linear, or at least logical, sequence. Implicit in this approach is the belief that learning amounts to acquiring a set of 'rules' which must be practised separately to be learned and only then applied. The 'practice' relies on applying the rules to similar situations. With enough practice comes understanding, and then the knowledge and rules can be applied to new situations (Norman & Schmidt 2000).

Presenting students with the knowledge they need in a lecture format is efficient and relatively easy for both student and university teacher. It is a transmission model which presents the content to potentially large numbers of students at one time. However, lecturing does not take into account the ability of the student to remember, reason and apply the knowledge even in a similar situation; in short, to *learn* the content. When information is presented out of context, or for some unspecified possible future use, students may not appreciate the importance of the information, which may affect their motivation to learn. The lecture format also does little to help students develop skills required for self-directed learning (Barrows 1984; Perrenet et al. 2000).

Educational psychology research of the last decade has shown that a 'student is not an empty vessel waiting to be filled with new knowledge' and many traditional teaching practices result in surface learning (Sawyer 2006, p. 2). In a traditional lecture situation, it is the lecturer who is active in preparing and delivering material and the student who passively receives the content (Brodie & Borch 2004). However, productive and 'deep' learning is an active process. Students must engage with the material, deconstructing, constructing and reconstructing ideas and knowledge. PBL is an approach consistent with these needs.

Planning for PBL

Developing a plan to implement PBL in the subject you teach may be an opportunity for you to practise PBL yourself. How might you go about this?

Figure 9.1 shows a flowchart of actions and decisions which may help. The first step is to identify the goals and key learning objectives of the subject. Having well-defined goals and learning objectives is critical to the development of content and assessment. These need to be clearly understood by teachers and students for effective learning to take place. A subject goal is a broad statement about the outcomes of the subject. The goal normally incorporates skills and knowledge. Learning objectives answer the question 'What do you want your students to know and do at the end of studying this subject?' They focus on student outcomes and use action verbs such as describe, list, compare, demonstrate and analyse. They describe what students will be expected to achieve. Specific content and topics arise from the objectives. An example is shown in Case 9.1.

CASE 9.1   A CORE FIRST-YEAR ENGINEERING SUBJECT

Lyn Brodie, University of Southern Queensland (University of Southern Queensland 2012)

This subject introduces the student to some important measurement and analytical tools that will provide the basis for future work. Students will be introduced to the concept of a system and to the need for teamwork in most engineering activities. Aspects of physical properties are explained together with statistical concepts and both of these are applied to the analysis of complex systems. The use and understanding of teamwork is emphasised throughout. All students are expected to contribute to and interact in a positive manner with other team members.

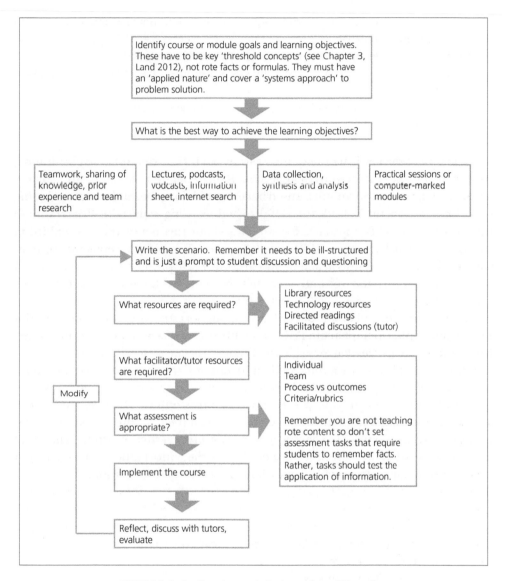

FIGURE 9.1   Flowchart to help determine a PBL outline

On successful completion of this subject students will be able to:
- cooperate and participate in a team working on technical problems
- seek and evaluate the input of other team members
- apply prior knowledge and experience to assist in solving a problem as part of a team, recognising the value of such prior knowledge from team members with diverse backgrounds

- identify and use appropriate scientific and mathematical techniques and procedures to explain physical phenomena
- outline the requirements for measuring physical properties
- apply basic statistics to analyse measurements and examine the variation that occurs in properties
- apply systems analysis to well-defined simple systems and problems.

Once you have the key learning objectives you can refine topics and begin weaving the problem and the resources together. Remember that lectures and formal learning opportunities can still be used but the problem and stimulus material come first. Often, academics think the self-directed learning aspects of PBL translate into a 'do-it-yourself' approach for students – but this is not the case. Shifting from traditional learning to PBL involves more than simply replacing content with problems; it requires teachers to carefully craft problems and scenarios in which students will uncover and construct the required knowledge and skills for themselves. The learning is self-directed but appropriately supported.

In PBL, lectures and other formal learning support structures are opportunities to provide 'just-in-time learning'. This means that relevant material is presented when the students need it or at least discover the need for it. This is a tricky dimension of PBL as different student teams will realise the need for more information and even different information at varying times. An ideal way to circumvent this problem is to present the resources online, allowing students to access the information when they need it. This can include information that you have prepared, directions to specific material or internet sites or stimulus material to encourage students to source unspecified further information. Consideration should also be given to providing a variety of formats of information.

YOUR THOUGHTS

Below are some ideas for providing information or stimulus materials:
- digital recording of a lecture
- selected readings from textbooks
- newspaper reports
- plans, maps, videos (including through the YouTube® video community) and photographs
- survey results and statistics
- reports (e.g., government papers)
- selected internet sites
- workbooks
- dialogue or conversations.
  What other formats might suit your subject?

Problem design

Having defined learning objectives you can now begin formulating a scenario which integrates these into a problem with appropriate triggers to stimulate discussion and move students into a particular direction as illustrated in Table 9.1.

TABLE 9.1   An example of turning topics into problems

Main learning topics	The problem will advance students' understanding of heat, temperature, experimental methodology, statistics, errors and uncertainties, ethics and the role of engineers in society. It will also develop students' skills in teamwork and communication.
Problem scenario (in brief, originally presented in the form of a memo emailed to student teams)	We now have another job on the books. The client is Legal Eagles and Co and the contact person is Ms Jane Solicitor. The client needs technical advice to help with a case and wants to have an understanding of the basic physics involved. The case has to do with the death of a baby in a car; you may have read about it in the paper. The team of legal staff assigned to the case would like a presentation from us. I know you will be away on holidays but if you could prepare a PowerPoint presentation with complete notes I can get one of the staff members to deliver it ...
Stimulus material	(Newspaper clipping) **Baby dies in stolen car** By Jon A List A two-month-old baby was found dead in an abandoned stolen car on Friday afternoon after an intensive search by police and emergency services. Local police received a call at 11.51 am from the hysterical mother, saying that her locked car had been stolen from Major-urban Shopping Centre and her child was still in the car. She told police that she was gone from the car for only about 15 minutes and had left the sleeping child in the baby capsule. Police immediately launched a massive search operation, aided by emergency services. The car was found locked and parked in a nearby suburb about two hours later. A person has been arrested over the theft of the car and is still being questioned by police over the death of the infant. Police have issued a statement in which the suspect has admitted to the theft but claimed that they did not know that the child was in the car. 'I drove that car for about five minutes before I noticed the baby capsule. When I checked inside the baby was dead, then I panicked and dumped the car,' the suspect has claimed.
Resources	Data set of measured temperature in a variety of cars, different days and under different circumstances.

Gijselaers and Schmidt (1990) have shown that the problem design itself has the greatest overall effect on student learning outcomes. A good problem or project is engaging and orientated to the real world, is ill structured and has multiple outcomes or hypotheses, requires team effort, builds upon previous knowledge and experiences, is consistent with desired learning outcomes and curriculum objectives and promotes the development of higher-order cognitive skills (Kolmos 2002).

While you can carefully define the problems and resources required, the social dimension of PBL cannot be underestimated. In PBL, the problem is discussed and deconstructed, usually in a small group setting, which assists students to develop teamwork and communication skills. It is effective, especially as an introductory activity, for the student group to set the rules of engagement. Depending on the learning objectives, you may decide to make the teamwork aspects part of the assessment.

Case 9.2 emphasises to students that teamwork is a key learning objective. The team code of conduct is assessed and throughout the semester subject teams and individuals are asked to reflect on how well the code of conduct is working. It is made clear to students that the code of conduct is the foundation on which the team sits and as the team matures and changes, so too should the code of conduct. It is regularly applied, refined, reviewed and updated, which requires the group to regularly reflect on actions and outcomes and seek avenues to improve both individual and group outcomes. This can be honed by the assessment strategy which emphasises *processes* and *improvement* as well as outcomes.

CASE 9.2   STUDENT ACTIVITY AND ASSESSMENT TASK

Everyone has been a part of a team at some point in their lives. Ask the students to discuss the types of teams in which they have participated. Standard answers are sporting teams, work teams and family. From this discussion ask students to:

- list the advantages of teamwork and the disadvantages of teamwork
- define strategies to minimise disadvantages and maximise the advantages
- summarise these in a team code of conduct.

This can be a facilitated large group exercise, a small team ice-breaking exercise or formal part of the assessment strategy, depending on your identified learning objectives.

An extension activity involves researching team roles and discussing how team roles apply to your team. A good starting point when looking at team roles, but by no means the only theory, is Belbin's definition of team roles (Belbin Associates 2007). Belbin's team roles identify 'clusters of behaviour' and discuss how people interact in a team. The Belbin theory predicts that success of a team is dependent on these behaviours and that by understanding behaviours and roles, many problematic team dynamics can be avoided.

The activity can follow the principles of PBL: begin with research and identify team roles from the literature. A team discussion activity follows, focusing on what types of team roles have been found and how this will affect the team. After the team has worked together for a while, ask its members to reflect on how accurate they now think the initial team role characteristics were.

PBL, technology and online learning

Implementation of PBL can be standard face-to-face, technology supported, or entirely online. Elements of online and distance education can easily be expanded or slightly modified and applied to PBL. For example, a modified version of Anderson's (2008) model for online learning, Figure 9.2, can serve as a foundation for online problem-based learning and team-based PBL becomes not only possible but a way of overcoming the isolation sometimes felt by distance education students and even those studying on-campus. The model provides a framework for the interactions between multiple students and the academic facilitator via synchronous and asynchronous communication. Technologies can deliver resources and content required to support individual student learning in a small group setting and teamwork in a virtual or online environment. However, online implementation of PBL requires early 'scaffolding' of individual students and student teams – that is, teachers ensure that students have the requisite knowledge, skills and support to negotiate each new piece of learning.

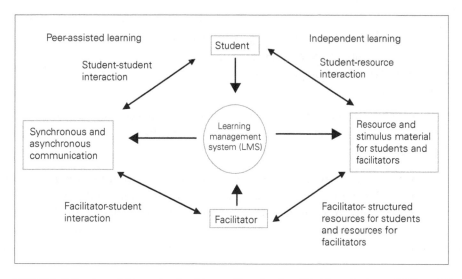

FIGURE 9.2 A model for online teaching and learning (modified from Anderson 2008, p. 61)

Using Anderson's modified model as a basis for an online PBL subject, the teacher becomes a *facilitator* and guides students and teams. Stimulus and content material can be provided for easy, just-in-time access and students can communicate via a team discussion forum (asynchronous) or team chat forum (synchronous). In the early stages of the subject, scaffolding students' understanding of the subject and how it will operate is very important, otherwise it becomes overwhelming. This may include, in the beginning, some specific lists and 'how-to' information. Resources and communication for online PBL can be integrated into learning management systems (LMS). Wikis, LMS group discussion boards and chat rooms, Skype and instant messaging all offer varied opportunities for interactions: student-to-student and student-to-academic facilitators.

One of the strengths of PBL is that prior learning, skills and experience can be easily integrated (see Chapter 10, Garnett 2012). However, these aspects are often overlooked in traditional subjects and hence remain unrecognised by the students themselves. Ask students to identify their strengths and weaknesses and then determine some individual learning goals with respect to the subject objectives and topics. This information can then be used to group students into teams where skills and knowledge can be complemented within the team. As a team activity, students can then negotiate a mentoring plan based on learning goals and their strengths. In an online environment, this is a great introductory activity helping students develop trust and setting a framework for further collaboration.

YOUR THOUGHTS

Your students have identified the following weaknesses in their prior learning:
- reading and analysing tables of statistical data
- summarising key points from discussions
- listening skills.

Write individual learning goals for each weakness and identify some learning activities that could be used by a group of 30 students in a PBL setting to enhance students' confidence and abilities in these areas.

The next step is to encourage teams to develop online meeting strategies. Setting meeting strategies requires more than just agreeing on times and places to meet. The strategies must state how the meetings will improve students' learning, efficiency and effectiveness and contribute to the learning community. Teams should also take into consideration the technology available to each team member and the technological literacy of each member. Team members have to identify these possible barriers and work with them.

TABLE 9.2 A sample assessment scheme to include adequate reflection

	Task	Components	Points available
Teamwork	Team report 1	Team code of conduct	5
		Team meeting strategy	5
		Peer assessment strategy	5
		Project choice and mentoring plan	5
	Team report 2	Team reflection and evaluation, assessed on problem-solving strategy, management plan, evidence of mentoring and skill sharing, team dynamics and analysis and critique with view for improvement	10
		Technical report, including introduction (problem definition and context), objectives, alternative solutions and evaluation strategy	10
	Team report 3	Completed report, assessed on accuracy, clarity, depth, scope, structure and presentation	12
		PowerPoint presentation	2
		Team reflection and evaluation	6
Individual work	Portfolio 1	Personal learning goals	6
		Contribution and reflection on discussion topic	2
		Set task – Harvard referencing	2
		Reflection on teamwork	2
	Portfolio 2	Contribution and reflection on discussion topic	2
		Demonstration of progress towards individual learning goals	2
		Design task description, self and team review	10
	Portfolio 3	Set task – professional goals and attributes	2
		Reflection on lifelong learning	2
		Review and evaluation of progress to personal learning goals	5
		Final reflection	5

The role of reflection and assessment in PBL

Reflection by both staff and students is an important part of the PBL learning process. Theory on learning and reflection arises from a number of different sources. It is founded on Kolb's work on learning cycles (1984) and Schön's theory about reflection (1987). Students must be given time to synthesise their new knowledge and reflect upon what they have discovered. This is particularly important in PBL where learning is sometimes covert – problems and projects are solved without the student being aware that skills and knowledge have been acquired and enhanced (Brodie 2007).

Reflection is a key part of any PBL implementation and assessment plan. The literature on the topic of reflection in PBL tends to focus on individual reflection. What did I learn? How did I learn? What could I do better? However, students also need opportunities to reflect as a group, as well as individually, in order to develop sufficient grounding in team and group *processes*. This can be achieved through a structured PBL approach that builds students' reflective skills over the course of the subject and by including reflection in marking criteria. Table 9.2 illustrates how the weighting attached to reflection might encourage students to address the reflective tasks and take them seriously.

In PBL students take control of their own learning, deciding what they know and need to discover to solve the problem. Assessment can take this control away from students, forcing them to concentrate on what the instructor wants them to learn, or at least what they *think* the instructor wants them to learn. Therefore assessment in PBL should establish the individual's knowledge, skill and competence rather than testing for factual knowledge (de Graaff & Kolmos 2002).

There is great variety in the assessment literature on methodologies (see Chapter 5, Brown & Race 2012) congruent with the aims of PBL. It is best if assessment is authentic (real world) and embodies a range of non–traditional assessment techniques. These include a mixture of written reports, oral presentations, written examinations, peer and facilitator assessment (of contributions and behaviour) and portfolios (of both reflections and individual work) (Acar 2004; Brodeur et al. 2002; Brodie 2007) and can focus on process, outcomes or a mixture of both.

In summary, authentic PBL requires assessments of *process*, which, if structured correctly, have a beneficial effect on student learning (Swanson et al. 1997). However, assessments of process alone are not sufficient for a valid measure of student learning. Assessments of *outcomes* are also required, but the assessment items must focus on the *application* of knowledge in a *problem-solving situation*. These assessment items, while mainly used for traditional grading purposes, can also provide an effective and efficient way for students to self-assess their strengths and weaknesses which, in turn, should assist their self-directed learning. This ultimately is the goal of PBL.

Case 9.3 demonstrates how setting-up team strategies can be linked with assessment. This reinforces with students the need for planning and commitment to the PBL tasks in any mode of operation.

CASE 9.3 ASSESSMENT TASK: TEAM MEETING STRATEGY
Lyn Brodie, University of Southern Queensland

The team is to discuss and finalise a team meeting strategy.

Decide on a method of regular weekly communication, either face-to-face meetings (considering the time and place) or through a common virtual team-meeting technology (a particular instant messaging service or discussion forum, for example).

This section is more than 'we will meet at 7pm on the MSN® *internet service*' or 'at 2pm in the library'. On-campus and distance (virtual) teams will need different strategies to make the meeting efficient, effective and inclusive.

Discuss options for running and conducting your team meetings so that they are effective and efficient. These may have implications for your code of conduct (e.g., come prepared for meetings, read agendas and so on). Try looking for resources in a library or on the internet on how to organise meetings (resource videos on the LMS may be useful). As always, if you use a resource such as this, ensure it is correctly referenced in your report.

One key part of your strategy is to aim for more effective meetings, but fewer of them.
On-campus teams should consider:
- Will you set agendas and take minutes? Who will be responsible for these?
- Do you want a very formal meeting with a chairperson?
- How will you let your facilitator know things like participation, outcomes, problems and progress?
- How will your facilitator monitor participation efficiently?
Distance teams should consider:
- How does a virtual meeting differ from a face-to-face meeting?
- Is it effective to hold a meeting on the discussion forum over a weekend (asynchronous) rather than a virtual meeting (synchronous)?
- Remember, not everyone has the same level of keyboard skills or knowledge about chat technology.
- Past virtual teams have reported difficulties with staying on task and students being logged on, but not in the meeting. How can you fix this?
- How will you let your facilitator know about things like participation, outcomes, problems and progress?
- How will your facilitator monitor participation efficiently? (Is what you are doing visible?)

TABLE 9.3   Sample assessment rubric of team meeting strategy for Case 9.3

0–10 marks	11–20 marks	21–30 marks	31–40 marks
The team has: • not clearly demonstrated or discussed a team meeting strategy in sufficient depth • discussed team roles in a generalised manner, but has not specifically defined and designated any roles • made insufficient references to the literature in their team meeting strategy to demonstrate an awareness of team needs	The team has: • discussed a simple team meeting strategy but has only considered times and media (e.g., chat or discussion board) • discussed team roles and specifically defined and designated some roles • made some references to the literature in the team meeting strategy	The team has: • discussed an appropriate team meeting strategy • discussed how research can be applied to the team's particular circumstances • discussed team roles and specifically defined and designated most roles • made sufficient references to the literature in the team meeting strategy to demonstrate knowledge and understanding of team needs	The team has: • researched and documented an appropriate team meeting strategy • considered how the strategy will be applied, evaluated and improved • discussed team roles and specifically defined and designated all roles • made excellent reference to the literature in the team meeting strategy, demonstrating awareness of specific team needs

YOUR THOUGHTS

Many of the activities you expect of students can also be mirrored by the staff team.

- Invite your academic facilitators to write their own code of conduct and meeting strategies.
- At the end of semester reflect, as a team, on all aspects of the subject including design, implementation and assessment. This provides valuable information to either support staff in their new role or make improvements in the subject.
- Over the course of the semester, keep a reflective journal of your learning. After all, you are a student of PBL as well.

What skills do you need to develop for PBL?

Facilitation skills

Facilitation skills are crucial to the successful implementation of PBL. Facilitators help learners to manage the learning process: the facilitator does not lead, but guides the team by helping members to clarify communication and establish directions for themselves while still ensuring that the team will meet all required objectives. Facilitators scaffold student learning. Where traditional educational paradigms have focused on lecturing and tutoring, PBL places a greater emphasis on problem design and class preparation, student guidance and support, and managing and delegating learning to students.

Facilitators need to know how to ask open-ended questions to challenge thinking and raise issues that might need to be considered. They also need to know how to help students and teams to reflect (Woods 1997). They must focus teams on monitoring progress against agreed plans, and provide a safe, encouraging and stimulating environment in which students are willing and able to share ideas and experiences. However, facilitators do bring their own attributes and beliefs to their work and this can influence the role they play. Not surprisingly, perhaps, the 'content expert' facilitator takes a more directive approach, using content knowledge to direct group discussions, whereas non-content experts take a supportive role and use their process-facilitation skills.

Hmelo-Silver and Barrows (2006) provide excellent guidance on goals and strategies for problem-based learning and suggest that facilitators set educational and performance goals. These include the educational goals associated with students' ability to:

- develop factual, procedural and conceptual knowledge and awareness of the links among them
- employ an effective reasoning process
- show awareness of knowledge limitations
- meet knowledge needs through self-directed learning and social knowledge construction
- evaluate their learning and performance.
- The performance goals for facilitators include:
- keeping all students active in the learning process
- keeping the learning process on track
- making apparent to students the depth of their understanding
- encouraging students to become self-reliant.

The overarching aim of these goals is to scaffold the PBL process. Scaffolding makes the learning easier for each student 'by changing complex and difficult tasks in ways that make these tasks accessible, manageable, and within student's zone of proximal development' (Hmelo-Silver et al. 2007, p. 100). There are some commonly used and pedagogically sound scaffolds that will assist facilitators, such as the tripartite problem-solving exercise (TRIPSE) (Rangachari 2002), the Secondary Teacher Education Project (STEP) (Steinkuehler et al. 2002), the architectural structures of the tutorial process (Barrows 1988), the triple jump and the problem-solving process (Toohey 1996). These provide a more detailed breakdown of the processes with further support in the intervening steps. Scaffolding is particularly useful in the early stages of group work, when students are less familiar with the PBL process and with working with others in the group.

Facilitators need to be aware of the problem-solving process inherent in PBL. This has been discussed widely in the literature and a simple outline of the process is given in Figure 9.3. While the process is stated in a step-by-step fashion it is important to note that it may not be followed in such a rigid manner. For example, reflection may be used after any stage to encourage deeper thought and critical analysis of either self or team, and regular return to 'What *is* the problem?' may also help keep students on task and focused.

Good preparation for implementing such a scaffold includes thinking through problems that might be encountered at each stage. Table 9.4 shows a partial list of potential problems that students and facilitators could encounter. It offers a starting point and a 'watch list 'for those beginning PBL.

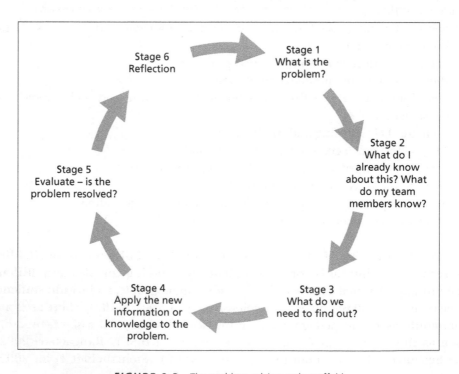

FIGURE 9.3   The problem-solving cycle scaffold

TABLE 9.4   Framework for supporting the problem-solving cycle scaffold

Stage	Potential problems
1	Students struggle to unpack the problem due to its ill-structured nature, leading to: • poorly defined specifications (for a design problem) • no thought to an evaluation strategy • not enough thought to the context of the problem, for example, social, economic, environmental aspects • poor time management • focusing on a 'solution' too early, thinking 'I know the answer to this' • lack of team and individual aims and goals • lack of time and effort in forming the team.
2	Students do not feel safe in sharing their knowledge. Students think they know more than they do and are not willing to investigate.
3	Students exhibit: • lack of information literacy skills • lack of team 'brainstorming' • too much or too little information • lack of critical evaluation of information • losing focus.
4	Students try to make *their* solution fit the problem – 'What was the problem again?' Students don't understand how to apply their ideas or solutions to the problem.
5	Stduents do not consistently apply evaluation criteria to all solutions. Students neglect their time-management plan. Students do not sufficiently critique their process and outputs.
6	Students do not incorporate reflection as part of the process, or 'gloss over' reflection.

YOUR THOUGHTS

Use Table 9.4 to guide your preparation and jot down your thoughts on where you think facilitators and students may encounter obstacles and identify what strategies or resources might be necessary to keep going in the right direction.

Reflective practice

Reflective practice develops and hones facilitation and teaching skills and leads to cohesive and dynamic PBL teaching teams. Frameworks for developing facilitator reflection abound in the literature but the 5Rs reflective scale (Bain et al. 2002) is simple and easy to use:

1. reporting – give a brief account of a situation
2. responding – assess your personal response to the situation (feelings and questions)

3. relating – make connections between the situation and your skills and knowledge
4. reasoning – explain the situation in terms of relevant theory or experience
5. reconstructing – draw conclusions and make future action plans.

Reflection, supported by keeping a diary, will help facilitators to build experience and strategies to cope with students' problems and the reflective diaries from all facilitators will, over time, build capacity in the teaching team. Engaging facilitators in reflection can be supported by providing a framework, something as simple as the following questions:

1. What were the strengths that I brought to the teaching team?
2. What was my role in teaching this subject?
3. In my facilitation role, what did I work on and how did I work with students?
4. What are my impressions of the way in which this subject was taught with reference to course design and content?
5. What does the evidence of students' achievements and feedback indicate about how this subject was taught?
6. Based on the answers to questions 1 to 5, what points for improvement can I identify in regard to:
   ◊ problems (academic or administrative)
   ◊ positives (what things went well, and what should we definitely keep?)
   ◊ priorities (what should we be focusing on, for example, problem-solving, technical aspects or teamwork?)
   ◊ processes (how can we structure the course to minimise the problems, keep the positives and hit the priorities?).

Conclusion

In PBL the effort is not in the delivery but in the formation of the problem or project, the provision of resources necessary to scaffold student learning, the alignment of assessment with process and the progress of students, and the integration of technology sufficient for student interaction and learning. For distance learning students, the transformation from well-known classroom teaching to a virtual classroom learning environment is not difficult but the developer must turn the class teaching into self-learning processes. This can be done by guiding and motivating students along with self-tests, team reflections and peer problem-solving.

PBL requires students to participate actively and to interact with other students and the facilitator and to take charge of their own learning. The facilitator should carefully explain PBL to students, and should ensure students feel they have a voice throughout their learning. In a team situation, developing a team code of conduct, meeting strategies, individual and team learning goals give the students this voice. However, the facilitator must lend his or her wisdom to the process. Successful facilitation requires the teacher to strike a delicate balance of guiding, mentoring, assisting and supervising all students.

To summarise, the key components for successful PBL include:

- a high level of research and development on the scenarios and resources given to students
- a focus on creating problems and projects that are real-world, ill-structured, applicable to the profession and include a wide range of disciplines
- recognition of the difference between PBL and problem-solving
- commitment from staff
- appropriate assessment
- time and recognition of the need for reflection by both staff and students.

With careful planning, PBL offers many advantages best summarised by the following student comment:

> This subject has challenged my ideas of learning, and through the application of problem-based learning [the subject] has taught me what no other subject has before ... As such, I feel confident in my basic knowledge of all the areas covered in this subject, and I am confident in my ability to learn what I don't already understand.

CHAPTER 10

AUTHENTIC WORK-INTEGRATED LEARNING

Jonathan Garnett

Keywords
work-integrated learning, negotiated program, learning agreement, recognition of prior learning

Introduction

This chapter describes the elements of work-integrated curricula. It draws on 19 years of operational experience of work-integrated learning (WIL) at Middlesex University in the United Kingdom (Garnett et al. 2009), which has demonstrated that WIL is not just about vocationally orientated subjects. Rather, it concerns a broad interpretation of professional development and learning through work itself. This chapter defines WIL and considers the elements of constructing a negotiated WIL curriculum including learning agreements, reviews, projects and reflective practice.

What is authentic work-integrated learning?

The integration of learning and work is not a new concept. From the middle ages, professions such as medicine and law developed their skills in practice and then took their learning into the academy to codify and transmit a body of professional knowledge. Since then, WIL has been adopted by other professions such as engineering, nursing and teaching, often starting as an apprenticeship model, but increasingly moving into delivery by higher education with universities defining the curriculum. Today, WIL at higher education level acknowledges not only that work has learning needs (i.e., workers require specific knowledge and skills) but also that high-level learning can take place at work, through undertaking work and for the specific purposes of work.

WIL has a focus on higher education level knowledge, skill acquisition and application. This distinguishes it from simple work experience, which is not necessarily integrated into a theoretical and research-based university program. Universities have sought to integrate higher level learning with work in a variety of ways, notably by the:

- incorporation of work-based assessment and projects in university subjects
- development of 'sandwich' degree programs incorporating six months or one year of supervised and assessed work placement, normally after the second year of study
- provision of opportunities for students to work in industry, without supervision or assessment, for a year after their second year of study
- voluntary or compulsory inclusion in degree programs of work experience subjects assessed by workplace mentors or university staff
- development of complete degree programs at undergraduate and postgraduate level which are aimed at full-time workers and stem from the learning needs of work.

This variety of forms of engagement with work can be seen as a continuum of practice. At one end of the continuum WIL is dominated by disciplinary knowledge created in universities and applied in the workplace by full-time students studying individual modules sometimes during an extended period of work placement. For an overview of a range of ways to integrate practice-based experiences into the curriculum, see Billett (2011).

At the other end of the continuum, WIL is primarily concerned with knowledge created by full-time workers engaging with the university in programs specifically designed with employers to meet the knowledge and skill requirements of work. This form of WIL is often referred to as work-based learning. The current definition of work-based learning as understood and used by Middlesex University is:

> A learning process which focuses university-level critical thinking upon work (paid or unpaid), in order to facilitate the recognition, acquisition and application of individual and collective knowledge, skills and abilities, to achieve specific outcomes of significance to the learner, their work and the university.
>
> (Gibbs & Garnett 2007, p. 411)

The key feature of authentic work-integrated learning is that it focuses on work itself as a learning activity rather than work as just a placement activity for the knowledge of the academy to be put into practice. This could be at the level of part of a subject or the whole degree program. The distinctive feature is the recognition of the potential of the activity, context and purposes of work to develop high-level knowledge and skills. The knowledge and skills derived from work will often be informed by and interact with disciplinary knowledge but such work-based learning may not always fit neatly into subject boundaries. Portwood (2000) argued that work-based learning should be regarded as a 'field of study' in its own right, rather than just a 'mode' of study. This allows students to create their own individually negotiated program, starting with accreditation of their learning from work, where work itself becomes the subject, rather than traditional subject disciplines.

Boud et al. (2001, p. 3) drew on evidence from Australia and the UK to argue that the work-based learning approach to integrating university-level learning with work could be seen as 'one of the very few innovations related to the teaching and learning aspects of post-secondary education that is attempting to engage seriously with the economic, social and educational demands of our era'. They identified the following distinctive features:

- First, a partnership between an external organization and an educational institution is specifically established to foster learning.
- Second, learners involved are employees of, or are in some contractual relationship with, the external organization [and] negotiate learning plans approved by representatives of both the educational institution and the organization.
- Third, the programme followed derives from the needs of the workplace and of the learner rather than being controlled or framed by the disciplinary or professional curriculum.
- Fourth, the starting point and level of the program is established after learners have engaged in a process of recognition of current competencies and identification of the learning they wish to engage in rather than on the basis of their existing educational qualifications.
- Fifth, [work-based learning projects] are oriented to the challenges of work and the future needs of the learner and the organization.
- Sixth, the educational institution assesses the learning outcomes of the negotiated programmes with respect to a [transdisciplinary] framework of standards and levels.

(Boud et al. 2001, pp. 4–6)

The work-based learning described by Boud et al. and practised at a range of UK universities (e.g., Chester, Derby, Glasgow, Leeds, Middlesex, Northumbria) is at one end of the WIL continuum. As the form of WIL which is most removed from the traditional discipline-based curriculum, it is particularly helpful in highlighting features which all forms of WIL need to consider. At the heart of the distinctive 'work-based' form of WIL is the role of the external organisation as a partner with the university and the individual learner in the planning of learning activities which are responsive to the needs of a specific workplace. This contests the supremacy of the role of the university in curriculum design, delivery and validation of knowledge and suggests that authentic work-integrated learning should seek alignment with thinking and practice relating to knowledge creation and use in the workplace.

Work-integrated learning at higher education level draws on adult learning theories (Knowles et al. 2005) and humanistic theory (Rogers 1983; see also Chapter 1, Stewart 2012), and includes aspects such as communities of practice and multifaceted contexts of learning such as social, economic and psychological factors. The practice of WIL has been significantly informed by the experience of higher education institutions in offering 'independent study' routes to university qualifications (see Osborne et al. 1998). Such programs would often stem from the specific interest of the learner who would be allowed to negotiate, within rules specified by the university, for program construction and assessment, a route to a specific target qualification. Where the learner already had significant knowledge in the area, for example, of local history, that might be formally recognised via a process often referred to as recognition of prior learning (RPL) or accreditation of prior experiential learning, negotiation of subject content or possibly an entire program would often take the form of a 'learning agreement' or 'learning contract'. The negotiation of module content and assessment would normally be facilitated by the use of project 'empty shell' subjects or modules. These provide a generic shell specifying size, level of complexity, generic learning outcomes and indicative forms and weight of assessment to be fleshed out by the student as part of the process of negotiation. WIL provides the added complexity of the needs of specific work contexts.

Elements of a negotiated WIL curriculum

Review and recognition of prior learning

The starting point for WIL programs is often a forward-focused review to establish what relevant knowledge and skills the individual brings to the program, which can lead to formal accreditation via recognition of prior learning (RPL). The student undertakes a review of their experience to date in order to identify demonstrable learning achievement. Many universities regard the process of reflection upon experience to identify and evidence high-level learning as a significant intellectual activity in its own right and have developed university subject outlines to structure and support the process. Typically the learner will put together a portfolio consisting of:

- a current résumé or curriculum vitae, highlighting specific activities that were of particular significance in the acquisition and development of their personal learning
- a current job description, highlighting the knowledge and skills required to undertake the job
- areas of learning achievement; if accreditation is being sought these will often be focused to demonstrate how the learning outcomes of specified subjects have been met
- a range of evidence in support of the learning achievement claimed.

The role of the university teacher is to help students reflect on their experience in order to identify the learning involved. Individuals often take for granted their learning from experience and may not think that it might be of interest or at higher education level. Using the résumé and job descriptions as the initial basis for an online or group discussion can elicit details about the learning underpinning effective work performance. Given the personal nature of this process, there may be reservations about group work and it is worth considering using anonymised or fabricated examples of CVs and job descriptions as prompts for discussion. Some key prompts to facilitate identification of learning from experience are as follows:

- Identify something that went particularly well at work and consider why it was successful – what did you learn from this?
- Think of the first time you were in a new role – what did you need to find out in order to be effective in the role?
- Think of a situation at work which did not go well – what would you do in future to try and avoid the situation arising again?
- What types of work issues do colleagues seek advice from you about?

CASE 10.1   RECOGNITION OF PRIOR LEARNING
Middlesex University (Garnett 2009b)

The case of 'Bob' from the Animal Reception Centre at one of the UK's busiest airports illustrates the use of RPL to recognise learning achievement from work and to provide the basis for the development of a negotiated, work-integrated program. Bob was referred to the university by his employer following an appraisal where it was agreed that it would be beneficial for him to engage in higher education. Bob had a broad range of knowledge and skills in the area of animal husbandry which would not normally be associated with higher education. The challenge for the RPL process was to identify and assess a diverse range of achievement extending from snake and crocodile handling to complex knowledge of animal welfare and legislation.

Bob worked with an academic facilitator to put together an RPL portfolio following a standard Middlesex University format. The portfolio included a curriculum vitae extended to focus upon key learning episodes, for example, establishing a wildlife park in Africa, and a current job description expanded to focus upon the knowledge and skill requirements to perform the job. These documents served as the background for the university adviser supporting the development of the claim and helped Bob to differentiate between recounting the experience and identifying the learning from experience. The documents put the accreditation claim in context for the assessor. The heart of the portfolio is a number of claimant-defined 'areas of learning'. For each area the claimant will identify a title (e.g., animal health and welfare) and explain how they acquired knowledge and skills in the area. Often this will be a combination of short training courses and learning through carrying out a work role. The claimant is required to identify clearly what it is that they know and are able to do.

Bob claimed achievements in areas of learning related to knowledge of animal classification and characteristics, knowledge of legal procedure, management of resources and management of people. He was able to draw on a range of evidence including major reports for national bodies, photographic evidence supported by explanatory text and line manager statements. It is noteworthy that the only formal certificated learning Bob held was a Diploma in Zookeeping gained more than 25 years before engaging with the university. While this certificated learning had contributed to the claimant's professional development, it clearly no longer represented the level or range of his learning achievement. As a result of the RPL process Bob was awarded academic credit at both final honours-degree level and at postgraduate level. Upon this basis the university gave Bob the opportunity to negotiate a work-based program of study at master's level.

Critical reflection

Developing the reflective capacity of the student is a key concern of the WIL academic facilitator. Schön (1987) highlighted the value of reflective practice in the early 1980s and this has been reasserted by an international team of writers (Boud et al. 2006). Reflection is held to be a key human mechanism in understanding our experience and deriving lessons from it. Key to reflection is the notion of standing back from experience to derive meaning with a view to informing future action. Two vital parts of self-reflection for students are the ability to critique their own thought processes and to take into account their feelings, for example, the role of inference and distortions of reality. Coghlan and Brannick describe reflection as:

> the process of stepping back from experience to process what experience means, with a view to planning further action ... it is the key to learning as it enables you to develop an ability to uncover and make explicit to yourself what you have planned, discovered and achieved in practice.
>
> (Coghlan & Brannick 2001, p. 31)

Reflection on practice is a key theme of work-based learning. Reflection develops self-knowledge – that is, informal theorising about personal learning patterns and styles that a student can take into future life experiences. WIL has at its core *reflection* on experience in order to make sense of that experience by relating it to *abstract concepts* or theories. WIL also provides the opportunity to *test out theories* through active experimentation and engagement with real world problems.

Some key prompts to facilitate student reflection upon the process of review and recognition of prior learning include the following:

- What were your initial expectations of the learning review process? Did these change during the course of carrying out the review?
- What did the process of assembling the claim for recognition of prior learning involve? The emphasis should focus on any problems encountered and how you coped with them, how did the process develop?
- Have you discovered anything about yourself or your work role from undertaking the review?
- Has undertaking the review changed the way you approach or think about your work?
- Have you discovered new areas of learning that neither you nor your employer had previously recognised or fully used, or has the process confirmed what you already knew?
- How easy or difficult was it to identify learning and provide evidence of it?
- Has the identification of areas of learning made you think about areas you wish to focus on in future?
- Has the learning review influenced or altered how you view yourself, your work roles or your career aspirations?

Learning agreement

Once the individual starting point has been established by RPL, the next stage in a negotiated WIL program is program planning. A student's experience of WIL is based on the construction of a higher education program which is a personal learning journey addressing real-life work issues. The WIL program is typically the product of a three-way negotiated learning agreement between the student, their employer or sponsor and the university.

Typically a program-level learning agreement might include negotiation of the:

- level and title of the award
- timing and duration of the program
- program composition, including the rationale for the inclusion of any accredited learning
- content and output of negotiated project modules
- program outcomes.

The university needs to have a process for the formal consideration and approval of such negotiated learning. Program approval would typically include consideration of:

- content, coherence and level of the program
- appropriateness of the title
- feasibility of the program
- conformity to university and program regulations
- appropriateness of the program in terms of personal, career and professional development
- relevance and potential significance of the program to the interested third party (often the employer, but it might be a professional body, union or client)
- ethical considerations raised by the proposed work-based project activity.

Facilitation of the construction of a learning agreement focuses on supporting the identification and consideration of stakeholder interests and requirements as well as the use of the key resources of time, information and materials. Often, particularly at postgraduate and doctoral levels, the learner is more informed about their area of practice than the academic facilitator, but the facilitator is in a position to translate academic demands to fit the needs of the workplace and intervene in response to work or academic constraints (Boud & Costley 2007). The challenge is to produce a customised program demonstrating coherence and progression from learning identified and certified via RPL to a work-integrated program designed not only to meet the academic requirements of the university but also to be of value to the employer or stakeholders. The learning agreement identifies the learning that will be undertaken in the form of work-based projects and taught subjects where applicable. Therefore appropriate methods of learning and assessment for each student's program will depend on negotiations with the academic facilitator to align the proposed learning and assessment strategies.

CASE 10.2 LEARNING AGREEMENT

Tom is a database manager and stock controller of a branch of a major retailer and wishes to develop a work-based honours-degree program. In the first instance, he registers for the module Recognition and Accreditation of Learning. This takes one semester, and the results of the module are encouraging. Tom has identified, described and provided evidence for a number of areas of work-based learning, which are assessed as carrying higher-education-level academic credits. Tom has now seen that his work-based learning to date is credit worthy. The next step is to design a program of study leading to an honours degree. In order to design this program, he takes a Program Planning module. He takes as his starting point the areas of learning which have been accredited by the university and argues the case within his learning agreement that these areas underpin and therefore form a coherent part of an honours-degree program which incorporates conventional subject-based modules in resource management and database design and two linked work-based projects. Tom has discussed the timing and content of his program with his line manager and they have agreed on project areas that would not only enhance Tom's expertise but be of direct relevance to the current business objectives of the company.

Work-integrated learning and academic research

WIL is concerned with development and change at the level of the individual and the work context. At honours-degree and postgraduate levels WIL often involves the generation of new knowledge for practice and possibly the development of new practices. These activities require methodological approaches to development and systematic change. This implies that WIL involves practitioner-led research undertaken by students. However, in WIL the context and purposes of work have consequences for the value and use of knowledge as the nature of knowledge claims that have value will to a large part be determined by the norms of the work or organisational context. This has important implications for designing professional inquiry as part of WIL (see Costley et al. 2010).

University-constructed paradigms of knowledge and the systematic process by which new knowledge is created and judged are increasingly contested and work-integrated learning is one dimension of that debate. The empirical, positivist paradigm associated with scientific enquiry is deeply rooted in our understanding of academic research; consider our emphasis on research as a systemic process subject to tests of validity and reliability. The researcher is a detached and objective observer of the object of study. This is to be expected given that this is the traditional paradigm for knowledge production in universities and holds sway over much of the general research literature, as well as the assumptions and expectations of university research.

Academic research concentrates upon description and explanation, is conducted systematically and logically, occurs within defined structres and parameters, and is governed by explicitly stated theories and hypotheses. Work-integrated learning is often by design and necessity concerned with knowledge which is unsystematic, socially constructed and focused on actions carried out by the worker–researcher in order to achieve specific outcomes of significance to others.

Work-based knowledge and definitions of knowledge reflect different interest groups. In the context of work, the value of knowledge is performative; it thus follows that sufficiency and timeliness of information to inform or bring about action are key considerations for WIL research projects.

Proposal for a work-based project

The key role of the academic facilitator in WIL is to stimulate project ideas and consideration of the work-based context, the work-based inquiry and its intended use. The following series of questions provides a good start to promote individual or group consideration of work-based projects:

- What do you want your project to achieve?
- What is the potential for impact on the organisation of the project activity as well as the project outcome?
- What difference does it make that it is *you* undertaking the project? Ideally you want to focus on something which you know already is a major issue for you. How might you personally benefit from the project? Is there a downside?
- What sort of knowledge are you drawing upon – including your own pre-understanding? What sort of knowledge are you trying to create? For example, is it a question of knowing what to do and how to do it? The work context will often mean that knowledge of 'who' and 'when' will be far more important aspects of knowledge than in traditional subject-based research.
- In what ways might your project need to draw upon the learning resources of the workplace? This might include knowledge of key individuals, professional knowledge or procedural knowledge held by an employer or professional body. In what ways might your project enhance the knowledge of others in the work context? How can you take this into account in your project design and activity as well as outcome?
- Who else is involved? What is in it for them? Are they fully informed? Are they active participants?
- Are there individuals or groups which may see your project as threatening? If so, how are you going to deal with this? How can you construct your enquiry in a way which will be ethical and provide an appropriate duty of care to individuals acting as 'informants' to your inquiry?
- If your project is to have significance for your organisation do you have to convince key decision-makers? If so, what sort of case do you need to put forward? What is the decision-making process? Be aware that the espoused process for decision making may not be what actually happens!
- How might the knowledge you have created be used, disseminated and updated when your project is finished? How might this have implications for the type of data you collect and how you analyse and present it?

CASE 10.3   DEVELOPING A PROPOSAL FOR A WORK-BASED RESEARCH PROJECT

Sue is studying an undergraduate teacher training course. She has been asked to work with a senior teacher at the school where she is on teaching practice to undertake a small-scale research project. Aims of the project are to determine how issues of transfer from primary to secondary education influence the school's teaching of information and communication technologies (ICT). The findings will inform decision-making about future ICT curricula in the first year of education at the secondary school. Sue uses the checklist given above to heighten her awareness of the work context for the research project. This highlights issues of her credibility and professional authority to undertake the project and the need to determine the type and format of information that would be of value to the school. This, in turn, leads her to have detailed discussions with the senior teacher as a major stakeholder in order to determine the key research questions which she, as the enquirer, needs to address in order to deliver on the project aims.

Work-based project

The concept of the real-life, work-based project is a central feature of work-integrated learning. The need for the project must be grounded in the knowledge needs of work. Thus the project is not an artificial device solely to demonstrate the learning achievement of the student; rather, it explicitly addresses the needs of work and demonstrates learning achievement of the students in the process. The work-based project is the vehicle to focus university support and higher-education-level critical thinking to achieve learning outcomes not just of significance to the learner and the university but also to the employer and other stakeholders.

WIL projects involve focused activities in the work situation which are based on methodological competence and demonstrate a range of practical and intellectual capabilities. A WIL project may concern, for example, practical ways to improve organisational systems, procedures, processes or practices that draw upon and demonstrate the student's abilities as a work-based learner. Some common features of a WIL project are as follows:

- The project may have been aided or unaided in its conception and realisation, giving scope for the student to undertake broad consultation and work in teams.
- The project focus is of at least potential interest to one or more work-based stakeholders.
- The starting point for planning the theme of a project is often a sense that there is room for improvement in the work environment within a specified area of the student's own authority and autonomy.
- The project incorporates a pragmatic justification of its intended outcomes – why a particular approach has been used and not another; methodological understanding; and a coherent train of thought.
- The project entails analysis and synthesis, which explores what is being generated in a work-based situation, often using empirical knowledge as its source.

- The project demonstrates a range of practical and intellectual abilities as specific features, usually some creative, unusual or particular points relevant to the work-based context of the project.
- The knowledge produced by the project is relevant to a work-based as well as academic audience.

Work-based projects will often include a product of direct use to the workplace, for example a manual for project managers, technical instructions for firefighters, business plans for bank managers. They will also give rise to a written document in the form of a critical commentary on the product addressed directly to the academic audience. The structure for the critical commentary should include:

1. *an introduction.* Give the work context and your position. What was the background to the creation of the product? To what need or opportunity was the product a response?
2. *terms of reference.* What was the specific aim of the product? What objectives did you have to address in order to produce the product?
3. *details of product development.* How was the product developed? What research and development activity underpinned the creation of the product? What was your role? How did the product development draw upon and extend your knowledge and skills? What resources were involved?
4. *details about the use of the product.* If the project includes a pilot or actual use of the product, how has the use been planned? How has feedback been received and how has it been evaluated? If changes have been made, what are they and why are they required?
5. *conclusions and recommendations.* What is the outcome of your evaluation of the product and how will it inform future use or revision of the product? Reflect upon your personal and professional learning from the development and use of the product you have created.

The new knowledge or product engendered from the project contributes to the work organisation, and the learning from the process has the potential to provide insights into organisational behaviour and equips the worker–student with new understanding of the work organisation and professional area. The knowledge that is required in such a project may contain only a limited amount of disciplinary knowledge, perhaps newly applied to changing and enhancing practice (Costley et al. 2010).

CASE 10.4   A WORK-BASED PROJECT

Valerio is the captain of a drilling ship working in 10 000 feet of water off the coast of Brazil. This is a world record for this type of drilling. The company has a vision of 'Operations conducted in an incident-free workplace – all the time, everywhere' and has procedures to consider the implications of all decisions affecting the ship, but was still having accidents in manual handling. Valerio took a WIL master's degree over two years. He was able to gain substantial accreditation for his learning from experience, gaining 80 of the 180 credits required for his award. Valerio's project was to research the type of accidents that occurred and the reasons they occurred. It appeared that risk analysis was conducted at a senior level but those involved in manual handling had not enough training or experience in anticipating what could go wrong in manual handling of heavy weights on a moving ship. Having identified the type of accidents that occurred and the reasons, he devised training so that manual workers were required and able to do their own risk assessment.

Working with employer organisations

Middlesex University's work with major corporate clients has highlighted the potential of work-integrated learning to combine individual learning with organisational development (Garnett 2009a). This puts the employer at the centre of the work-integrated curriculum. The following case study shows how the elements of an individual WIL program have been adapted to meet the needs of a major employer partner.

CASE 10.5 CUSTOMISING WORK-INTEGRATED LEARNING FOR A MAJOR EMPLOYER

Middlesex University (Garnett 2009b)

The Middlesex University Work Based Learning Studies subject area provided an existing validated framework for the development of a postgraduate scheme for transnational construction management company Bovis (Garnett 2007). The joint development of the work-based learning partnership program ensured that the Bovis management development program and the Bovis core competencies were central components of the scheme. These two components and the program planning module were important in the provision of a high degree of customisation at the level of the employer organisation. The jointly designed scheme had four main components which combined learning already produced and valued in the workplace in the form of training programs and organisational competencies with the university work-integrated learning modules.

The first compenent was program planning. A Middlesex University module enabled participants to negotiate a work-based learning program with the university and their employer. The participants produced a learning agreement detailing the proposed composition of the program, duration and sequencing and a customisation of the title of the target qualification. This began as the standard Middlesex University learning agreement between the individuals, their employers and the university. It soon became apparent that in order to ensure employer commitment to the program the signature obtained from the central Bovis training department had to be supplemented by the signature of the Bovis head of the local business centre. Employer commitment emerged as a significant strength as it reinforced employer involvement and helped ensure the relevance of the program at the operational level of the business.

The second component was a management development program. The program, focusing on general management principles and human behaviour, was designed and delivered by a private training provider in a residential training centre. Each participant built up a file of course notes and submitted two reports on the application of learning gained from the course to their own work situation.

The third component was core competency development. Participants selected a number of Bovis core competencies that were relevant to their personal expertise and project work. They took a recognised prior learning module, which had been customised by the university to suit the Bovis scheme. The module provided a structure and materials to support participants to build portfolios. Using the skills and processes learnt in the module, participants gathered evidence into portfolios which demonstrated that they had the knowledge and skills required to underpin competent performance. The process of portfolio building was used to develop reflective practice, with participants encouraged to reflect upon the full range of their experiences (i.e., not just paid work). A key concern of the academic facilitator during this process was to emphasise the holistic nature of the core competencies: that real-life tasks would require participants to use combinations of competencies, not individual competencies in isolation. The facilitator encouraged participants to use short case studies of real-life issues to demonstrate how each participant had applied learning from across several competency areas in order to achieve competent performance. Participants were encouraged to reflect on the learning process of making a claim for university accreditation based on the Bovis core competencies.

The fourth component was work-based research and development. A Middlesex University professional inquiry module was adapted to the Bovis context. The aim of the module was to introduce a range of research approaches and data collection techniques appropriate for projects of a research and development nature carried out by workers as part of their work. Middlesex University had to devise strategies to present this module in a relevant and accessible form. One successful strategy was to ask a group of Bovis managers to identify the attitudes, skills and knowledge required of a manager and of a researcher and then to compare the two. This highlighted the range of generic skills which researchers and managers had in common.

Learning from work-integrated learning to enhance student employability

During the development and operation of work-integrated learning at Middlesex University, graduate employability has emerged as a dominant concept for measuring the success of higher education in general and specific universities and programs. Employability skills are not just the skills required to gain employment but also to enable individuals to achieve their potential at work and to contribute to the enterprise in which they are engaged. In the context of higher education, such skills include high-level cognitive skills and critical thinking. Employability skills are typically detailed (e.g., Department of Education, Science & Training 2002; Oliver 2011) to include:

- communication
- teamwork
- problem-solving
- self-management
- planning and organisation
- use of technology
- lifelong learning
- initiative and enterprise skills.

WIL provides the opportunity for students to develop and apply these skills in a real-life context and thus to have genuine workplace experience as a part of their academic program.

Indeed, the increased importance of employability as an attribute of higher education has encouraged a broadening of student market for work-integrated learning from mature, well-established learners to graduates entering the labour market, often for the first time. While such undergraduates are generally less likely to be able to make a claim for recognition of prior learning, the need to develop an understanding of work as a site for learning and for knowledge creation, dissemination and use is no less relevant. Students will have learning experiences to draw upon: part-time work, voluntary activity, social and sporting activity, and the experience of being in higher education. All these can be harnessed as the basis for developing reflective practice.

WIL can play a major role in developing graduate skills and demonstrating that they can be applied in the context of work. For example, a Professional Practice in the Arts honours-degree program at Middlesex University uses reflection on real-life experience to develop the understanding of the professional context, what it means to be a professional and how to develop and utilise professional networks using social media.

Queensland University of Technology, Australia, has used WIL across all disciplines in the Creative Industries Faculty at undergraduate and postgraduate level. Students undertake WIL on placement with a focus on real-life professional projects. The work-based project can be the means for the student to draw on a facilitating support structure provided by the university to develop their own career aspirations and first steps into professional practice. For example, a student taking the Professional Practice in the Arts program at Middlesex University used the final project as the vehicle to develop and launch her own dance company.

Conclusion

Although work-integrated learning has a considerable track record in Australia, the UK and the USA, its full potential is still to be realised. This chapter suggests work-integrated learning requires the lecturer to be a facilitator of adult and organisational learning as well as a subject expert. Once this challenge is recognised and engaged with, then work-integrated learning has much to offer; it combines a learner-centred approach with an understanding that learning is a socially constructed activity, and this has potential benefits not just for the individual learner but also for those affected by the learner's work.

PART 3

FOCUS ON
STUDENTS

Many governments around the world have policies that seek to widen participation in university study. In part, this is for social justice reasons, but it also reflects the need for highly educated populations to compete in global knowledge economies. This means that university teachers now work with increasingly diverse cohorts of students. The chapters in Part 3 show how this might be done. In so doing, they characterise diversity among both staff and students as a rich resource on which to draw in the preparation, design and delivery of inclusive curricula. The chapters on inclusive teaching and international and Indigenous students all focus on how diversity can extend and enrich the learning experience of all students. They avoid a one-size-fits-all approach. Rather, the chapters chart the terrain and help university teachers to plan inclusive teaching approaches in local contexts.

Charting the terrain challenges conventional academic perceptions of knowledge and research and gives rise to opportunities for reflection about creative curriculum and teaching initiatives. The question to address as you read the chapters in Part 3 are: Who are my students and how can we work together to maximise student learning outcomes?

In Chapter 11, Christine Broughan and Lynne Hunt provide an overview of inclusive teaching practices with reference to the practical teaching and learning implications of the widening participation agendas in higher education. It notes the importance of teacher self-awareness and students' transition to university, including social engagement and inclusive and flexible curriculum design.

Whether they travel abroad or enrol in a university through distance education, international students have particular needs arising from lack of familiarity with the expectations of different sociocultural and academic contexts. In Chapter 12, Michelle Barker examines issues associated with teaching international students. She notes that international students create a cultural diversity that enriches the experience of sojourners as well as domestic students, especially at a time when internationalisation of the curriculum and global citizenship are imperatives in higher education. The chapter discusses good-practice approaches to address international students' needs with particular reference to participation in group work, written and verbal communication, academic integrity and managing intergroup relations in the classroom.

In Chapter 13, Michael Christie and Christine Asmar discuss how teaching western academic knowledge can be enriched and extended by bringing Indigenous knowers and knowledges into postcolonial classrooms. Defining Australian Indigenous knowledge as performative, contextual, owned, collective and renewable, they foreground the voices of Aboriginal and Torres Strait Islander practitioners in suggesting new approaches to teaching and learning. Engaging with similar issues and strategies in readers' own local settings, they suggest, will bring exciting learning opportunities for students – and their teachers – everywhere.

CHAPTER 11

INCLUSIVE TEACHING

Christine Broughan and
Lynne Hunt

Keywords
inclusive curriculum, widening participation, transition to university, flexible learning, social engagement

> Inclusive learning and teaching in higher education refers to the ways in which pedagogy, curricula and assessment are designed and delivered to engage students in learning that is meaningful, relevant and accessible to all. It embraces a view of the individual and individual difference as the source of diversity that can enrich the lives and learning of others.
>
> (Hockings 2010, p. 1)

Introduction

The worldwide trend in government policies to promote wider participation in university study has increased the diversity of student populations and given rise to renewed considerations of inclusive university teaching, which has both moral and legal dimensions for universities, as noted by Gravestock:

> When considering diversity and inclusion in higher education it is often tempting to consider the areas that are covered by legislation, such as: 'race'; disability; sexual orientation; religion or belief; age and gender identity. However, students have multiple identities and all students have aspects of their personal lives that will impact upon the classroom context (such as having to act as a carer for a relative or partner, or having to work extra hours to earn additional money). An inclusive curriculum not only addresses groups of students who are covered by

legislation, but also allows flexibility to accommodate issues that can potentially be faced by a much larger group of students … 'good practice for disabled students is good practice for all'.

(Gravestock, cited in Craig & Zinkiewicz 2010)

Widening participation in university study is not just about recruiting more students; it is also about keeping them engaged in their degree programs, and about successful completion. In short it is about retention and progression. This means that all university teachers, regardless of discipline, need to address students' varied learning needs through inclusive teaching practices. It also requires some understanding of university life as a culture in itself, to which *all* students must have some introduction to support their transition to university study. This chapter explores how to do this, focusing on three elements:
1. teacher self-awareness, competence and confidence about inclusive teaching
2. inclusive curriculum and teaching approaches
3. university-wide organisational initiatives.

Widening participation

A number of recent reviews into higher education attest to the importance that governments attach to university education (e.g., Bradley 2008; OECD 2010a; Spellings 2006). Such interest in higher education is due, in part, to the global transition to knowledge economies. This requires nations to have highly educated populations if they are to participate, compete and prosper in the international market. As a consequence, governments have sought to widen participation in higher education and to make university study accessible to a wide cross-section of the population. Beyond economic considerations, universities are expected to contribute to the development of a just society. In the UK, for example, a government report noted that: 'universities are integral to our national culture and a cohesive society. They create a broad community of learners willing to question conventional wisdom and foster progress, while also nurturing the shared values that bind us together' (Denham 2008).

So, for economic and social reasons, government policies have widened participation in university study, which has resulted in the so-called 'massification' of higher education. As a consequence, enrolment rates in degree programs have increased and student cohorts have become more diverse. Despite these initiatives, some social and cultural groups remain under-represented. The Spellings Report in the USA, for example, noted persistent inequitable access to post-secondary education, finding 'troubling' gaps in university participation and graduation rates between students from low-socioeconomic backgrounds and more affluent students, and between students of different racial or ethnic backgrounds (2006, p. 1). Gender is also a factor. The gender parity index, which measures the ratio of male to female participation across nations, reveals a picture of female participation in higher education that is made complex by the relationship between gender, poverty, class, caste, race and occupation. In some countries, the number of women enrolled in universities exceeds the number of men, but clear gender patterns persist between disciplines (Ramachandran 2010, p. 12). Research also shows that the simple provision of access to university education does not necessarily lead to the widening of *successful* participation in higher education (Higher Education Funding Council for England 2010). University enrolment rates have not been matched by retention rates and successful completion of degree programs for some groups of students. This suggests that there is something that universities and university teachers can do to enhance *successful* participation in university studies – starting with personal reflection.

Teacher self-awareness

Growing numbers of university teachers are from diverse backgrounds; indeed, some universities have employment strategies to increase that diversity to better to reflect their student populations. However, Gillborn (2010) cautioned that, while teachers from traditionally under-represented groups can be inspirational role models for students, they need to be wary of becoming pigeonholed as the 'token' minority put forward to deal with issues of equality and diversity. The important issue is for *all* university teachers to be aware of the values and attitudes, hopes, expectations and even stereotypes that they bring to the teaching and learning context. This includes an awareness of the cultural basis of pedagogy, because students may not always understand your teaching processes in the way you intend – as this third-year botany student from Thailand observed, 'If the lecturer does not answer a student's questions in class but asks the other students what they think, in my country we would think that teacher is poorly qualified or lazy. But in Australia this way of not giving the answer … is common in our class, even when the Professor is our teacher' (cited in Ballard & Clanchy 1991, p. 1). This signals a strong message about the need for transparency in teaching and learning processes, both face-to-face and online, to avoid misunderstandings.

The need for teacher self-awareness is not necessarily widely understood as an important first step in inclusive teaching. Yet, as McCutcheon observed, 'As teachers we do not shrug off these aspects of ourselves as we remove our coats and hang them on pegs outside our classrooms' (1988, p. 198). Accordingly, there is a need for university teachers to reflect on their own values, and how these apply to university teaching. Fenton's (1967) values schema still offers a useful framework for reflection about the distinction between personal and professional values. He distinguished between behavioural, procedural and substantive values:

- *Behavioural values* refer to university cultures and agreed ways of behaving in university learning environments. Students are or are not required to attend, assignments and marking criteria will or will not be negotiated and dialogue will be conducted in an evidence-based manner and with intellectual respect for everyone's contribution.
- *Procedural values* refer to ways of thinking that are central to disciplines. Scientific method and rigour might be central to many disciplines, while critique or creativity feature in others.
- *Substantive values* are those to which individual teachers and students adhere as a consequence of being raised in particular regions or cultural, religious or political value systems. It is these values that are often addressed in sensitivity training sessions to alert staff to their own implicit world views, as Case 11.1 illustrates.

CASE 11.1 COURAGEOUS CONVERSATIONS ABOUT RACE

Malcolm Fialho, University of Western Australia (Fialho 2012)

The University [of Western Australia] has identified cultural competence as a critical attribute for both staff and graduates, and absolutely vital for a globalised university striving for international excellence. Working with staff and students from different cultures is both rewarding and challenging. This [Courageous Conversations about Race] workshop deepens the dialogue by challenging members of the University community to think through the various ways race and culture affects their life and professional practice. It will provide an opportunity to increase your comfort, confidence and capacity to work effectively with people from culturally diverse backgrounds …

The workshop will offer participants an opportunity to:

- unpack their own unique racial story, linking it to the local, national and global context
- understand the concept of race privilege, and how to examine its influence
- utilise the insights gained to develop a more meaningful and targeted response around race and culture in a University context.

Key activities:

- presentation of information
- group discussion and opportunities to raise questions
- interactive activities
- case studies.

Inclusive curriculum and teaching approaches

This section of the chapter explores how to plan, design and deliver learning experiences that embrace diversity and engage *all* students in successful learning. The discussion seeks to avoid a deficit model in which diversity is constructed as a problem to be fixed. Rather, it assumes that diversity is a resource that can enrich learning because:

> From both the students' and staff perspectives, interaction among students from diverse backgrounds potentially leads to: increased awareness and understanding of different perspectives; better preparation for the workplace; improved English language skills of international students; and a greater feeling of belonging.
> (Arkoudis et al. 2010, p. 6)

The effects of interactions between diverse peers, however, depend on the nature and quality of the interactions. To ensure that they teach inclusively and support successful learning for a diverse group of students, university teachers can focus on:

- improving students' transition to academic skills and discourse
- designing a flexible curriculum
- enhancing students' social engagement
- inclusive planning
- viewing diversity as a resource
- inclusive language
- inclusive assessment.

Transition to academic skills and discourse

Students enter university from diverse backgrounds and find themselves in an academic culture that has been characterised as monolithic and even described as 'educational imperialism' (Shaw 2005, p. 7). This academic culture exists because, traditionally, university students have been drawn from privileged backgrounds that prepare them to meet exacting standards for evidence-based academic discourse, oral and written communication and academic honesty, with little need for additional explanation. Manifestly, this is not the case for everyone. One student surveyed by Wilson and Lizzio, for example, described the despair of an early university experience: 'I had no idea what a laboratory report was or how to write one! I believed that everyone else in the class understood the task but me. I felt lost and cried. Yet I forced myself to ask my peers how they were going and to my amazement they too were feeling uncertain' (psychology student, cited in Wilson & Lizzio 2011, p. 13). To prevent such situations, many universities now induct students to university life and study through bridging programs (see Case 11.2), university orientation programs and academic skills support for students including workshops and individual and peer support – both face-to-face and online. University teachers can address their students' learning difficulties in collaboration with such support services.

CASE 11.2 TRANSITION PROGRAM

The University of Central Lancashire (Cook 2009)

The University of Central Lancashire (UCLan) initiated a Flying Start program in 1999 in response to the low retention rates of students entering UCLan from vocational courses. The program was designed to address discontinuities in teaching and learning styles between the independent autonomous learning style of higher education and the highly prescriptive, bite-size, competency-based, vocational curriculum with high class contact time. The Flying Start program is delivered in a lecture/seminar style by academics and a team of trained peer-assisted learning mentors, who are second- and third-year students at UCLan.

Flying Start offers prospective students a three-day residential or non-residential event to prepare them before they enrol in their degree program. These events offer sessions in academic and social activities, networking and explanations of university procedures and academic discourse and the expectations associated with university study. The free residential summer school introduces students to the realities of independent learning; including an introduction to the library and electronic resources, orientation to the campus, life-skills such as time and budget management and experience of the range of support on offer at UCLan.

UCLan has tracked the students who attended the program to see how they subsequently performed at university and compared them with vocational students who did not attend. The dropout rate for the students who took the Flying Start program is now lower than for almost any other category of student including regular-entry students. Accordingly, UCLan opened the program to all students – the events remain free and places are offered on a first-come first-served basis. The program continues to have a substantial positive effect on the retention of students.

Useful though university academic support services are, it has been shown that embedding university academic skills in the curriculum gives rise to more effective student learning (Chalmers & Fuller 1996; see also Chapter 4, Chalmers & Partridge 2012). This can be done by working with the university's academic skills advisors, who can assist with point-of-need learning for student groups embarking on assignments. Alternatively, such skills can be embedded in learning design and associated teaching, assessment and feedback processes as illustrated in Case 11.3.

CASE 11.3   LOW-RISK WRITING

Lynne Hunt, Edith Cowan University (Hunt 2002)

I create frequent opportunities for students to complete low-risk writing in class. This is not for assessment but to help them to develop a personal style, formulate their ideas, and compare their work to that of other students. For example, when teaching 'Abstract' writing in my Health Research unit, I ask students to draft anonymously an Abstract and to pin their draft on the notice boards (discussion board for online students). Students are invited to walk around and read the abstracts and to identify the best three, saying why they are the best. This process encourages students to interact and to be reflective about the writing process and also shows them, in concrete terms, what 'good' means.

The need for induction extends beyond academic skills into acculturation into disciplines, as noted by Land, who acknowledges 'the strong primary influence of the disciplinary context, its signature ways of thinking and practising, its generally accepted conceptual structures and boundaries and the tribal norms and values of its community of practice' (Chapter 3, Land 2012, p. 38). Yet, encountering new ways of thinking can be challenging, as Northedge observes: 'Many come to academic discourse expecting it to complement the knowledge produced in their other life-worlds, but instead find it discordant and unsettling' (Northedge 2005, p. 20). To address this, Northedge makes academic discourse transparent. In his Understanding Health and Social Care subjects at the Open University, he teaches students to distinguish between everyday, professional and academic discourses, as shown in Table 11.1.

TABLE 11.1   An Open University example to explain academic discourse (Northedge 2005, p. 20).

	Everyday discourses	Discourses of care practice	Academic discourses on care
Source	Tabloid headline	Hospital spokesperson	Journal article
Issue: Scarcity of resources for care	'Is baby Julie's life worth $50,000?'	Achieving maximum good with limited resources Priorities, difficult decisions	Debate on alternative models of care financing Debate on shifting of resources from cure to prevention

Studies by Yorke et al. (1997) and Wilson and Lizzio (2011) have shown that integration has positive outcomes for students. Yet, processes that induct students to university study have been criticised because they:

translate all too easily into little more than 'remedial' support for the 'weak' students, so that non-traditional students are effectively treated as 'charity' cases, rescued from ignorance. The existing edifice of elite education is simply extended by adding a large paupers' wing. 'Proper' students continue to define the norms, while the rest tag along behind. Yet such a response fails to meet the underlying aims of broadening education. Instead, it creates an underclass of students, who become alienated from the knowledge dangled beyond their reach and eventually emerge from their encounter with education with a sense of personal inadequacy rather than empowerment.

(Northedge 2005, p. 13)

Yorke et al. (1997) found that universities that integrated students into university culture early in their studies significantly reduced students' risk of failure and non-completion of degree programs; and Wilson and Lizzio (2011) have shown that with appropriate support and teaching, early disadvantage and insufficient preparation for university study dissipates by the end of the first year. They note growing evidence that these students perform better than their peers as they progress through their degree. This indicates that student success is due in large part to their preparation for and engagement in university, not to any innate ability to learn. It might be concluded, therefore, that the remedial approach to student support is necessary but not sufficient. The best approach is to embrace the opportunities created by diversity, and respond with innovative curriculum design and teaching, to minimise barriers that all students may face.

Inclusive curriculum design

First-year experience programs demonstrate inclusive curriculum responses to the needs of diverse student cohorts because they facilitate the transition to university and enhance student retention. An Australian first-year initiative focused specifically on curriculum issues and the articulation of a transition pedagogy comprising the following six principles, summarised from Kift (2009):

- *transition* – 'the first-year curriculum should be designed to mediate and support transition'
- *diversity* – 'the first-year curriculum design should recognise that students have special learning needs by reason of their social, cultural and academic transition'
- *design* – first-year curriculum design should 'support students' engagement through the intentional integration and sequencing of knowledge, skills and attitudes'
- *engagement* – 'learning, teaching, and assessment approaches in the first-year curriculum should ... enable active and collaborative learning ... peer-to-peer collaboration and teacher-student interaction'

- *assessment* – first-year students should 'receive regular, formative evaluations of their work early in their program of study to aid their learning and to provide feedback … on progress and achievement'
- *evaluation and monitoring* – 'the first-year curriculum should also have strategies embedded to monitor all students' engagement in their learning and to identify and intervene with students at risk of not succeeding'.

YOUR THOUGHTS

Consider the first-year subjects taught in your department:
- What activities are planned to facilitate students' transition to university in each of the subjects?
- How are teaching and learning activities varied to accommodate students' diverse learning needs?
- How are academic learning skills integrated into teaching and assessment processes?
- What peer-to-peer collaborations and teacher-student interactions are planned?
- When in the semester are students assessed? Is this early enough to give students diagnostic feedback?
- What opportunities for formative evaluation are provided to students? (see Chapter 5, Brown & Race 2012)
- What do the subject teachers and your department do to monitor students at-risk of non-completion?

Flexibility is a key to inclusive curriculum design, particularly where the design offers opportunities for students to study at their own pace. For example, providing learning materials online, and in advance, through your university's learning management system (also known as virtual learning environment) assists all students, particularly those with dyslexia and visual or hearing impairment, who can access such resources in ways suited to their needs. Further, synchronous and asynchronous blended learning opportunities (see Chapter 7, Reeves & Reeves 2012) allow rural and remote students, studying by distance education, to engage meaningfully in online discussion groups and group work with on-campus students at times of their own choosing. In short, the provision of resources online allows students to revisit learning materials in their own time and at their own pace.

Inclusive curriculum design offers choices not just in when learning takes place, but also in how to learn. Figure 11.1 shows a variety of teaching and learning strategies that you might include in your teaching plans to afford choice for students in when, where and how to learn.

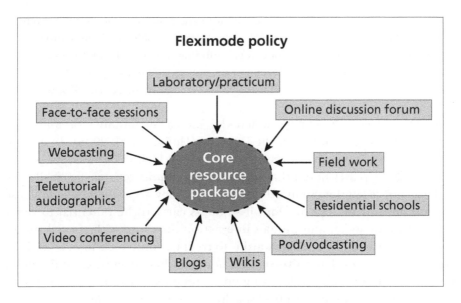

FIGURE 11.1   Flexible learning options of core resource packages (University of Southern Queensland)

YOUR THOUGHTS

Compare the range of learning activities in the subjects that you teach:
- To what extent does the range of learning activities respond to the diverse learning needs of your students, be they mature-aged, rural and remote, international, or students living with disability?
- Are there opportunities for you to increase the range of learning activities? If so, how?

While the use of a variety of learning opportunities can accommodate students' diverse learning needs, an Australian study sounded a note of caution about the use of learning technologies and web-based learning materials:

> The study found that there are [sic] a range of factors – physical, experiential, economic and institutional – that inhibit computer access for students from equity groups. These include: lack of reliable on-campus access for students who have no other access options; lack of modified equipment and enabling software in mainstream labs for students with particular disabilities; the cost of purchasing and upgrading home computer equipment for students of low socioeconomic

status; the cost of remote connection for rural and isolated students; poor levels of information literacy leading to lack of confidence in older students; culturally inappropriate computing environments inhibiting Aboriginal and Torres Strait Islander students and students from non-English speaking backgrounds.

(Barraket et al. 2000, p. xiv)

To this list of factors might be added the increasing number of students in prison who are denied access to the internet (Huijser et al. 2008). In addition to problems associated with access to learning technologies, Veenker and Cummins (2005, p. 81) noted that learners from equity groups 'generally need more face-to-face support than other students'. They argued that the increased use of online learning options for all students carried the potential to reduce opportunities for social and human interaction for those with special support needs. They suggest that a way forward is to treat learning technologies only as a means to an end, and that university teachers should concentrate on the design and development of inclusive learning environments. This includes flexibilities in time and place of study, variety of teaching and learning strategies and social engagement.

Social engagement

After analysing more than 150 000 feedback comments about university study by Australian graduates, Scott (2005) concluded that 'learning remains a profoundly social experience'. This means that establishing social connectedness and a positive learning environment forms a part of inclusive teaching practice. Wilson (2009) advocates strategic initial orientation and early student engagement strategies to increase attendance and participation in online study. In brief, students need to be engaged in their studies, in university culture and with each other from the beginning of their university studies. Wilson argues that for universities to achieve this, they might:

> think beyond traditional and passive notions of front-end orientation to more comprehensive and active processes of 'facilitating transition'. The key idea is that building student engagement requires 'an ongoing process' not just an 'orientation event'. The key aspects of this strategy involve a substantive school-based Orientation Day program in the week prior to semester, followed by an ongoing within-semester transition process ...

(Wilson 2009, p. 14)

Connectedness can be fostered through teaching strategies that are interactive and that introduce students to each other (Hogan 2007). It can be facilitated by specific cultural transition strategies (Hogan 2012) or through something as simple as getting to know students' names. This might be achieved by icebreaker exercises or by use of name tags. Some university teachers develop 'cheat sheets' of students' names and photographs. However, this may risk privacy issues and would need to be locally negotiated. Further, whole subjects can be introduced to foster students' social engagement. The Engelhard Project at Georgetown University, USA, for example, sponsors social wellbeing, including students' awareness of their personal growth, as a foundation for effective learning. The project embeds wellbeing topics into course curriculum through reading and writing tasks, discussions led by university health professionals, and social justice and local community projects. The project 'strives to create meaningful connections between faculty, students and campus health professionals' and encourages the university's principle of *cura personalis*, or care for the person (Engelhard Project 2011).

Inclusive planning

There is no one teaching approach that will meet the needs of all students all of the time. However, there are some general considerations associated with an understanding of students' religious calendars, disability issues and family commitments, as well as the learning needs of part-time, rural and remote students. For example, there are approximately 160 major religious festivals and days each year and, while it is impossible to take account of them all, it is worthwhile checking that assignment deadlines and examination dates avoid clashes with significant religious events – depending on the major religious affiliations of your university's student population and the community in which it is situated. Similarly, it is important to be aware of school holidays, as students who are parents may have difficulties in studying and meeting deadlines at these times. If there are alternative timeslots for repeat on-campus lectures, tutorials and workshops, then ensure that they are dispersed through morning, afternoon and evening timetable slots to facilitate attendance by part-time students working in paid employment. Alternatively, record lectures, make them available online and incorporate follow-up discussions via your university's learning management system. This will allow students to learn at times convenient to them and reduce the need for multiple repeat sessions on campus.

When planning field trips or work-integrated learning, university teachers may need to organise alternative learning activities for students who have mobility or access difficulties. Computer simulations provide a way to allow all students to participate in field work. For example, the biosciences team at the University of Gloucestershire developed an ecology computer program based on real data collected from previously published field research. The interactive program, Virtual Rocky Shore, allows students to manipulate variables to simulate realistic experiments. University staff also developed a website that explains how to design and conduct an experiment, how to get the most out of the computer simulation, how to carry out statistical analysis, and how to write up the experiment's result in the style of a scientific paper (Stafford 2010).

Diversity as a resource

There is a significant body of research on the impact of diversity on student learning. It shows that the value a university places on diversity has a positive effect on the quality of learning, as does interacting with students from different backgrounds (Antonio 2001; Gurin 1999; Gurin & Nagda 2006; Hurtado et al. 1998, 1999; Inoue 2005; Pascarella et al. 2001; Terenzini et al. 2001; Umbach & Kuh 2006). Hu and Kuh (2003) found that students who collaborate with peers from different cultures and backgrounds self-report positive gains in learning. Other research showed that facilitated discussion about commonalities and differences among students from diverse backgrounds improved students' sense of shared identity and citizenship (Gurin & Nagda 2006). Further, Inoue (2005) found that diversity experiences are likely to enhance critical thinking and cultural sensitivity.

University teachers can demonstrate how they value diversity by including content that reflects a diverse range of interests and perspectives. It is important to consider not only what content is included, and whose perspectives are heard, but also what content is excluded and whose voices silenced, and what messages this might send to students. If curriculum content does not reflect diversity, this signals to students that diversity is unimportant, and that the people who are not being represented are not important. For example, research shows that working class women can find university curricula alienating and disempowering simply because women are either invisible or presented in terms of deficit (Quinn 2006).

Inclusive language

Language is a powerful tool that can marginalise students or engage them in learning. Labelling or stereotyping ascribes characteristics to groups that cement expectations, despite intra-group differences. This can interfere with individual learning and runs the risk of alienating students. Indeed, one of the difficulties of discussing inclusive teaching is that it implies that 'we' (university teachers) need to include 'them' (students from diverse backgrounds). The binary concepts of 'traditional' and 'non-traditional' students risk being unhelpful: they imply that it is these students who have problems in regard to university study; that 'they' should conform to 'us'! This suggests a compliance model that is antithetical to the nature of universities defined by open enquiry and intellectual engagement. Such thinking by a strongly established group can serve as a set of blinkers and stifle creativity and change in university teaching. Rather than understanding diversity as a deficit, diversity may be seen as a resource that enriches university education. If students are not constrained by rules and stereotypes they may be in a much stronger position to challenge taken-for-granted notions or 'the way things are done round here' (Deal & Kennedy 1982).

Inclusive assessment

As Gravestock (2009) noted, 'good practice for disabled students is good practice for all', so the principles of good assessment practice espoused by Brown and Race (2012) apply to inclusive assessment. These have been summarised as (Chapter 5, Brown & Race 2012, p. 76):

- *Validity* is about how well we're measuring exactly what we're trying to measure.
- *Reliability* is essentially about fairness, and getting away from subjective judgements.
- *Transparency* is about how well students themselves know how the assessment works.
- *Inclusivity* is about the extent to which we can make assessment 'a level playing field' for all students, including those with particular needs, cultural backgrounds or learning problems.
- *Authenticity* is about ensuring that what is assessed is the work of the student concerned and, secondly, how closely what is assessed links to the world outside universities and what students will need when employed.
- *Fairness* overlaps with several of the factors listed above (see overview by Flint & Johnson 2011).

Given that inclusivity features as a key principle, the task for university teachers is to explore how to establish a 'level playing field'. Validity, reliability, transparency and fairness are part of this process. Authenticity has particular relevance to inclusivity because it directs attention to the importance of designing assignments that draw on the varied life experience of all students. This values and honours everyone's experience and accords with Knowles' principles of adult learning (Knowles et al. 2005). These incorporate the life experiences and knowledge that adults bring to learning environments and direct attention to the need for relevant and practical approaches to learning and assessment.

Inclusive university teaching practice prepares students for assessment. For example, Kift's transition pedagogy (2009) advocates early low-stakes assessment so that students can identify points for improvement. Clear guidelines and marking criteria, developed with students, make transparent the requirements of academic work. Facilitating connectedness through peer interaction is important, yet group assignments can be risky, especially if the assignments carry high marks and if they assume that students have opportunities to meet as a group. Students in paid employment and parents of small children can find it difficult to meet outside of timetabled learning activities. Even so, teamwork is normally listed in university statements about graduate attributes or generic skills, so it remains important to create the conditions of success for students to show that they can work effectively in groups (see Chapter 2, Hunt et al. 2012). This can be done by providing a range of opportunities for interaction, including online, by engaging students in the process of establishing clear group processes, and by making contribution to group work part of the marking criteria (see Chapter 9, Brodie 2012).

Organisational approaches to inclusivity

In many countries around the world, government legislation requires that universities treat students equally and diversify student populations through equal access and positive discrimination strategies. A Universities Scotland web-based resource characterises typical organisational responses to such legislation. It 'encourages the institutions to develop the corporate strategies necessary to support individual lecturers and departments in mainstreaming race equality issues' (Universities Scotland 2010). The website addresses many of the matters discussed in this chapter such as inclusive curriculum, learning and teaching and assessment. It also addresses the need for institutional action, because, as Budge has argued, 'the changes needed to sustain the expanded and diversified student cohort require a sophisticated whole-of-organisation approach and response, and not just change at the individual academic level' (2010, pp. 5–7).

Hunt and Peach argue that universities should view each individual student 'as a whole person, as opposed to the student as the subject and object of a series of unrelated interactions with an organisational bureaucracy'; should encourage connections between students' lives and their studies; and should allow students flexibility rather than imposing a 'one size fits all corporate strategy' (2009, p. 20). Essentially it is about getting the context right to support students' learning, however that manifests itself in local settings. To this end, and with particular reference to students living with disabilities, Gravestock (2009) collated resources you may find useful. These suggest ways in which universities might ensure all students have equal and easy access to a range of resources and activities, including: information and e-learning resources; enrolment processes; subject and curriculum design; lectures, seminars, tutorials and practical classes; placements, study abroad programs and field trips; and assessment. Many universities, for example, provide hearing loops in lecture theatres to assist those with hearing difficulties. In regard to hard copy and e-learning resources, special facilities enable visually impaired students to read and write with large print or Braille. University assessment and examination offices can make special provision for students living with disabilities, such as viva (oral) examinations or extra time to complete exams.

Inclusive, whole-of-university approaches facilitate the development of seamless processes to support students. To be effective, these approaches must be embraced by all staff, including admissions and graduation staff, library and technical support staff, learning skills advisors and university teachers. A holistic approach might involve the provision of crèche services, to facilitate study for parents of young children; prayer rooms for students of different religious backgrounds; and coordinated communications strategies that avoid overly solicitous situations in which students are bombarded with communications from their university. The development of appropriate, user-friendly learning spaces is also an organisational responsibility, but university teachers can plan for inclusiveness by booking appropriate rooms and reorganising seating arrangements to maximise interaction.

Inclusive organisational approaches can also include positive discrimination projects with which individual university teachers can align their curriculum and assessment practices. The award-winning Go Women in Engineering, Science and Technology (Go WEST) project at the University of Southern Queensland, for example, provides support for female students and professionals in discipline areas in which females are traditionally under-represented. The project 'aims to:

- establish a university wide network to build cross-discipline links to foster the success of academics and students in SET [science, engineering, technology]
- provide a virtual support structure of professionals and academics
- identify female SET student concerns and priorities
- implement strategies to address student issues
- link network members to Queensland Government Office of Women and industry initiatives
- establish mentoring relationships with SET students
- establish an annual Go WEST awards scheme
- maintain a community collaborative site for students, professional women and academics in SET disciplines
- administer Go WEST Equity and Social Justice and Go WEST Women in Engineering or Surveying scholarships.' (University of Southern Queensland 2011a)

YOUR THOUGHTS

- What special services are provided by your university to support students' diverse needs?
- What positive discrimination projects currently exist at your university?
- What special projects might be needed at your university?
- Does your university provide equity funding to develop equal opportunity initiatives and inclusive teaching?

- Work backwards to an understanding of inclusive contexts:
  - ◊ Imagine a non-inclusive university. What would the entry criteria be? What support services might it offer? What would the curriculum and assessment be like?
  - ◊ Compare your non-inclusive university with the one in which you work. What additional resources and processes are required in your university to fully support staff and students in an inclusive teaching environment?

Conclusion

Universities have increasingly diverse student populations, reflecting government initiatives to widen participation. As a consequence, universities have a responsibility to ensure they are inclusive of all students. Strategies to improve inclusivity can focus on developing teacher self-awareness, inclusive curricula, flexible teaching and learning strategies and organisational change. While some warn against heroic individualism that can result in burn-out for committed university teachers, this chapter recognises the power of one – you – to make a difference to individual students.

CHAPTER 12

TEACHING INTERNATIONAL STUDENTS

Michelle Barker

Keywords
international students, internationalisation, international education

The changing face of university teaching

University teaching has changed as the enrolment of international students number has increased from 1.1 million in 1980 to 3.7 million in 2009 (OECD 2011a). This increase has occurred as economic growth in countries such as India and China has put international education within financial reach of more students. At the same time, countries such as the United States, the United Kingdom and Australia have dramatically expanded their enrolment of international students which has resulted in increased cultural diversity of campuses, while simultaneously enhancing the revenues of their institutions. Terms such as offshore campuses, transnational education and student mobility were relatively unknown in the early 1990s. Now they are commonplace, and universities around the globe vie to recruit the best and brightest students. So teaching international students has become an important consideration for university staff whether they teach on-campus or online.

This chapter examines the nature and extent of international student cohorts and the internationalisation of the curriculum. In so doing, it explores issues associated with cultural adjustment, social integration, language proficiency, academic integrity and managing intercultural conflict. The chapter aims to help teachers to respond to the needs of international students from culturally and linguistically diverse (CALD) backgrounds, and to feel confident that their teaching approaches are grounded in accepted principles of effective and inclusive teaching (see Chapter 11, Broughan & Hunt 2012; Chapter 2, Hunt et al. 2012). The focus is sharply on curriculum and teaching approaches that promote the learning of international students and on international students as a resource that can enrich learning. It carries the strong message that good teaching for all students, especially international students, makes the implicit explicit.

What do we know about international students?

Madge, Raghuram and Noxolo (2009) note that the concept of an 'international student', which uses a student's cultural background or home country to explain that student's behaviour, is questionable in an age of globalisation. Even so, most countries use the Organization of Economic Cooperation and Development (OECD) standard which defines international or foreign students as 'those who travel to a country different from their own for the purpose of tertiary study' (OECD 2001). Possession of a visa to study in another country is a useful, if crude, way to categorise that which sets international students apart, because it directs attention to the fact that higher education provision for international students is regulated by legislation such as the Australian Education Services for Overseas Students Act. Regulations relate to students' enrolment hours, the amount of paid work permitted in addition to academic studies and whether the visa holder may remain in the country to work after graduation (see also UKCISA 2011), all of which have implications for how these students engage with their learning. It is important, therefore, for university teachers to have some familiarity with the legislative framework within which they work.

While there are peaks and troughs in overall numbers of international students, millions of students worldwide seek an international higher education. The main destination countries are the United States, the United Kingdom, Germany, France and Australia. Between 2000 and 2009, Australia doubled its enrolments of international students at tertiary level (OECD 2011a). Numbers of international students are also growing rapidly in destination countries within Latin America and Asia (OECD 2011a). Malaysia aims to become a regional hub for higher education, and sees international students as 'a potential new source of growth and export revenue' (Tham 2010, p. 99). Middle Eastern countries have also attracted increased numbers of international students in recent years (Institute of International Education 2011).

The main source countries for international students are China, India and Korea, with more than 50 per cent of international students coming from Asian countries (OECD 2011a). In 2009–2010, there were more than 200 000 new international student enrolments at US institutions. The largest source countries for these students were China (the source of 18 per cent of international students) and India (the source of 15 per cent) (OECD 2011a). In Australia there were more than 200 000 international student enrolments in the higher education sector in 2010 (Studies in Australia 2010). In Europe, the student mobility scheme Erasmus – the European Commission's flagship education and training program – enables 200 000 students to study and work abroad each year (European Commission 2010).

International education agencies and universities are continuously analysing students' motivations to study abroad and their satisfaction levels with their university experience. In 2007, the British Council launched the online global Student Decision Making Survey (British Council 2010), which captures why students are interested in studying abroad or pursuing a foreign qualification in their home country, what they look for in an institution, location and course, and where they look for information about study destinations. The results showed that:

- 59 per cent of students heading for the UK nominated the quality of education as a priority
- 38 per cent of students heading for the US nominated their career prospects as a priority
- 25 per cent of students heading for Germany nominated low tuition fees as a priority
- 24 per cent of students heading for Australia and Canada nominated the opportunity to work while studying as a priority.

Regardless of the country or the university they select, international students will normally share one characteristic: They have taken the step to leave primary support networks to undertake an academic program, often in a new linguistic and cultural context. Yet, international students, like domestic students, are not a homogenous group and differ markedly in terms of gender, ethnicity, class, age, ability, previous education, social status and work experience. So, like any generic label, the category risks grouping disparate individuals.

Diverse teaching contexts

Diverse international educational options are now available so university teachers may find themselves teaching students studying though distance education (with or without local support), twinning programs, articulation programs or branch campuses (McBurnie & Pollock 1998). Distance education allows students to remain in their home country and either enrol in universities abroad or study at offshore campuses of international universities. These students continue to have the benefits of home country support networks but they share with those studying abroad the need to adjust to the requirements of their international university.

The implications of diverse, transnational educational options are that university teachers may have to teach in a 'branch campus' overseas as well as at their home university, because many universities have franchised operations in partnerships with foreign governments (Dunn & Wallace 2008). They may find themselves interacting by email or teleconference with locally employed university teachers to ensure cross-campus consistency of subjects. They may also be involved in twinning programs, whereby students study the first two years of their undergraduate degree in their home university, completing the later years of their program at an overseas university. It is clear that teaching internationally diverse student cohorts in a variety of learning environments is a significant issue for contemporary university teachers.

What are the needs of international students?

A fundamental issue for university teachers concerns the extent to which teaching international students is seen as a challenge or as a rich learning resource. If international students are seen as bringing problems that need to be 'fixed', then teaching practices are centred in a deficit model. Promisingly, a recent survey of academic staff at a London university found a shift towards positive views about international students because they were seen as adding a fresh perspective to learning environments (Kingston & Forland 2008). However, Arkoudis notes that 'much discussion of international students has focused on stereotypes: a presumed reluctance to talk in class, a preference for rote learning and an apparent lack of critical thinking skills' (2006, p. 5). Such stereotypes establish 'us' and 'them' dichotomies that classify international students as those with educational and social deficits. This positions domestic students as more capable learners than their international peers, yet Arkoudis reports that 'international students are some of the highest achieving students at the university' (2006, p. 5). Clearly, international students have particular needs arising from their status as sojourners unfamiliar with the expectations of different socio-cultural and academic contexts – but these are needs, not deficits.

Ryan (2005) notes that teachers do not have to change their teaching style when teaching international students. Rather, it is about being culturally sensitive when making curriculum choices and seeing students' cultures as a resource for creating rich learning environments. It is a question of balance – neither overemphasising cultural differences, nor ignoring the needs of international students (Louie 2005). The needs of international students may include support to develop language proficiency, to learn about living in a new culture and to understand the academic discourse of their discipline (Arkoudis 2006).

YOUR THOUGHTS

- What differences (if any) have you noticed between international students who study abroad and those who study by distance education in their home country?
- What differences (if any) have you noticed in the learning needs of international and domestic students?

Internationalisation of higher education and the curriculum

The OECD (1999) defines the internationalisation of higher education as the inclusion of an international dimension in all university activities. This concept is echoed in other definitions; for example, Bremer and van der Wende indicate that internationalised curricula have 'an international orientation in content, aimed at preparing students for performing (professionally/socially) in an international and multicultural context, and designed for domestic students and/or foreign students' (1995, p. 10). Internationalised curricula result in graduates with the awareness, knowledge and skills to interact in culturally diverse and international working environments (Bourn 2011; Clifford 2011).

It is helpful to distinguish between 'internationalising content' and 'internationalising teaching and learning' (Arkoudis 2006). Internationalised content refers to the selection of global and intercultural subject matter and assignments that focus on variations in professional practices across cultures. For example, engineering and information technology students may research global usability of (and access to) modern technology, cross-cultural software and engineering designs, intercultural human-machine systems, multilingual websites and internet options. In science disciplines, students might examine emerging global issues such as climate change, international patents and transnational research and development.

Internationalising teaching and learning provides opportunities for university teachers to model respectful behaviours and show how understanding different cultural perspectives can be beneficial (Caruana & Ploner 2010). For example, teachers might show respect for the significance of sacred days or religious holidays, especially those which may have implications for classroom practices, such as Ramadan, when Muslim students fast from dawn until sunset, and need to eat and drink before they can concentrate during evening classes. Some teachers negotiate alternatives with the whole class, such as starting class a little later or taking a longer break. What the teacher models, in terms of respect for all, provides a rich learning experience.

Learning and teaching in a new academic culture: make the implicit explicit

International students must adjust to local language and culture and to the academic context of their new university. They may find the pedagogy and curriculum at odds with prior learning experiences and educational traditions of their own culture (Dunn & Wallace 2008). As a consequence, they may not display behaviours expected by teachers in their host university. For example, being self-effacing may be appropriate in a student's home country, but ineffective in a seminar or student practicum in the host country. Similarly, descriptive essays may have been rewarded in a student's previous academic institution, but the lack of critical analysis can result in low grades in their host country university. In other words, when international students and university teachers interact, both are influenced by 'systems of belief, expectations and practices about how to perform academically' (Cortazzi & Jin 1997, p. 7). Both parties need to be aware of their assumptions – what is considered 'normal', what is valued, and what is seen as 'rule-breaking' behaviour. Differences in assumptions commonly relate to teaching methods, academic writing, assessment processes, teacher-student relationships (Carroll 2005) and expectations of appropriate behaviour in tutorials, lectures and staff consultations. Even so, researchers caution against rigid views about the effect of culture on students' approaches to learning because 'cultural knowledge is so fluid and constantly changing that it is impossible to "gather" it as if it were a pure and static thing' and 'many students come from rapidly changing cultures and those who succeed in life learn to manage the cultural changes within their own cultures skilfully' (Louie 2005, p. 23). Not only is culture a dynamic phenomenon, but individual differences between students from the same culture make generalisations unhelpful (Chalmers & Volet 1999).

A particular area of misunderstanding arises from the belief that students from cultures with Confucian philosophies rely on rote-learning methods. However, Kingston and Forland (2008, p. 206) note that 'numerous researchers have argued that what Western researchers mistake for rote learning is, in fact, learning through memorisation, which often involves deep learning strategies' (Biggs 2003; Shi 2004). Over-attributing cultural explanations to behaviour has meant that 'researchers ... have allowed their sweeping assumptions of an entire culture to ... overshadow their conclusions' (Kingston & Forland 2008, p. 207). Borland and Pearce agree that 'teaching approaches that focus primarily on cultural difference do not seem particularly useful in assisting lecturing staff to address issues of student performance' (1999, p. 59). Indeed, all students need to adjust to the disciplinary and academic cultures of their universities, so it is important to make the expectations for tertiary study transparent to all, regardless of background. Ways for university teachers to make academic expectations explicit include:

- stating specific standards and expectations in learning outcomes in subject outlines, group contracts and assignment instructions (see Chapter 5, Brown & Race 2012)
- elaborating in subject notes and websites what students can expect of you and what you expect of them – this may include what you prefer to be called, average response time to email queries, and your role in facilitating learning rather than providing answers

- peer mentoring schemes pairing domestic students with international students or later-year international students – for example, students enrolled in a third-year leadership or group facilitation course could be given an assessment item that required them to undertake a mentoring or coaching role and to write a reflective journal about tiered learning experiences (Hills et al. 2010).

YOUR THOUGHTS

- What are some of the academic 'rules of the game' that you expect students to know?
- How did you learn these 'rules' when you were a student?
- What are the consequences for your students when these 'rules' are broken?
- How do you make the 'rules' and the consequences of breaking them known to your students?
- What improvements (if any) can you make to ensure that students, especially international students, understand the 'rules' of academic culture at your university?

Ensuring academic literacy and integrity

Academic literacy is clearly one of the most important 'rules of the game' for students to learn. It may be defined as:

> the ability to read, write, understand, analyse, interpret, create and communicate in a formal scholarly context. It involves being capable of critical/independent thought, being able to work alone and knowing how to acknowledge the work of others.
>
> (Whitelaw et al. 2010, p. 6)

Academic dishonesty and plagiarism, which includes failure to acknowledge sources correctly, are ongoing challenges for university teachers to address with students (Montgomery & McDowell 2009). According to Chanock (2004), international students may have greater difficulties because they are 'writing in a second language and also, often, from a cultural background of different assumptions about the correct use of sources'. A survey of university websites about academic dishonesty and plagiarism (Whitelaw et al. 2010) found four common characteristics: a statement of the university policy on plagiarism; a strong focus on penalties for committing plagiarism; a highly academic style of describing plagiarism 'clearly written by academics for academics' (p. 7); and some helpful hints (technical instruction) on how to paraphrase and cite correctly. The survey noted the lack of discussion of the principles underpinning academic honesty, especially plagiarism. In response, Whitelaw and colleagues (2010) developed a public website that includes five video clips with interactive questions that address aspects of academic literacy, while taking into account the particular needs of international and, especially, Chinese students. In one video, 'The road to academic literacy', two students step into the world of academia and learn that 'success at university involves using advanced principles such as critical thinking, creativity and academic honesty that they must master'. The tone of the resources is educative rather than punitive, and they are designed to be incorporated into the curriculum and assessment tasks.

The 'Teaching International Students' website (Higher Education Academy 2011) provides institutional, program and subject level strategies to address plagiarism including the need for university teachers to:

- provide information on the difference between paraphrasing and plagiarism, and the exact rules for acknowledgement of authorship
- promote academic learning services workshops to students at the start of each semester
- scaffold what is required in assessment tasks by providing exemplars, model answers and frameworks (see Chapter 5, Brown & Race 2012)
- model good practice by referencing and acknowledging other authors' work in lecture material and handouts
- offer clear feedback about referencing, including suggestions for improvement
- develop practical assessment tasks that draw on students' experiences and creativity, rather than focus on 'finding an answer'
- use internet-based plagiarism-detection programs such as Safe Assign or Turnitin to teach students about plagiarism. These can be incorporated in a developmental way that allows students to self-assess written drafts for unintended plagiarism prior to assignment submission.

Case 12.1 illustrates one way to help students understand the rationale for academic integrity.

CASE 12.1   PLAGIARISM IN LITERATURE

Dr Maria E Jackson, University of Glasgow (Jackson 2010)

I have been teaching students 'good scientific writing' for years as part of [a Master of Science] in Medical Genetics. The students, most from overseas, sometimes seemed convinced that regulations associated with plagiarism were designed to make life more difficult. They resented learning the necessary skills for what some saw as local rules.

Then I introduced an editorial by David Barlow (editor-in-chief of the scientific journal, *Human Reproduction*, 2000–6) which explained why articles were retracted and manuscripts rejected from the journal … We also look at 'Instructions for Authors' from prominent journals and at the criteria for publication. I wanted students to see that getting to grips with the issue of plagiarism and good scientific writing was part of making the transition to becoming scientists.

Once I have their attention, I give them a published article to review, which is almost wholly plagiarised. Discussion is prompted by asking whether the authors have shown understanding? Originality? Scholarship? I ask them if the article conforms to the criteria for publication. Finally, we explore the tricky question of whether or not the article is ethically acceptable.

Since I started using this activity, antagonism from students has disappeared. Some still find it hard to avoid plagiarism, but they can, I think, now see it is a professional skill that they need to acquire.

YOUR THOUGHTS

- What strategies do you use to help students understand acceptable academic literacy skills?
- What resources exist in your university to assist your students to avoid unintentional plagiarism?
- How can you include university academic skills resources in your teaching and learning plans?

Responding to language proficiency needs

International students will normally study through the medium of a foreign language, as will migrant domestic students who do not speak the local lingua franca as a first language at home. This section addresses some of the challenges of studying in a foreign language, particularly English language proficiency, revealing specific strategies that university teachers use to facilitate international students' written and oral language skills.

International students are expected to meet specified standards in the language of instruction before enrolment at a foreign university. In Germany, sufficient knowledge of the language has to be proven, unless applicants have passed their high-school diploma at a German school abroad (German Academic Exchange Service 2007). According to China's University and College Admissions System (2011), degree courses taught in Mandarin Chinese require applicants to provide Chinese Proficiency Test (HSK) results to prove the applicants' Chinese-language proficiency.

Enrolment in anglophone universities requires specified levels in one of two standardised assessments: the Test of English as a Foreign Language (TOEFL) or the International English Language Testing System (IELTS). TOEFL is designed to test whether prospective students can use standard American English at tertiary education level, while IELTS is the preferred test in the UK and Australia. Most universities have as their minimum requirement an average IELTS score of between 6.0 and 7.0 on the four areas of reading, writing, speaking and listening for social sciences and arts courses, and 6.0 and 6.5 for other courses. There is much debate about the extent to which these minimum scores equip students to manage the demands of their academic subjects. For example, the research of Edwards et al. (2007b) on Chinese students' English competence found that 'university teachers expressed uncertainty about whether the acceptance of levels of written English, which fall far short of native-speaker competences, is an ill-advised lowering of standards or a necessary and pragmatic response' (p. 387).

Most students from non-English speaking backgrounds need English language skills assistance despite achieving required entry test scores (Arkoudis & Tran 2010; Harryba et al. 2011; Johnson 2010). Universities do provide this, but students report that using such services is not their highest priority because they are feeling too time-pressured. The solution lies in integrating language and academic skills development within disciplinary learning and teaching. This can be achieved by mapping such skills through the curriculum (see Chapter 6, Angelo 2012; Chapter 4, Chalmers & Partridge 2012), by working with learning support staff in your university to incorporate skill development in your subjects, and by drawing on the following suggestions in ways suited to your students' learning environments (Arkoudis 2006; HEA 2011; Rochecouste et al. 2010).

To communicate clearly in university learning environments:

- speak slowly and clearly because students may struggle to understand your accent and word usage
- break information into manageable but meaningful chunks to assist students' comprehension
- present information verbally and visually
- use concept-checking devices, such as verbal or written questions and self-assessment worksheets – for example, ask students to summarise in two or three sentences what you have just explained
- develop a glossary of terms for your subject and encourage students to add to their personal copy of the glossary
- modify use of humour because it is a difficult for second language learners to comprehend.

To help students to improve their communication:

- encourage them to express themselves fully, even if they feel like giving up – for example, if a student says, 'It doesn't matter' after being misinterpreted, ask him or her to write the problem

- use paraphrasing and perception checking to ensure that you understand students' needs accurately – for example, use phrases such as 'What I understand you mean is ...'
- offer praise when students participate actively in class discussions
- use one-minute written papers to give shy students an opportunity to communicate anonymously and to check their understanding of concepts
- refer students to English academic assistance workshops, or invite academic skills staff into lectures early in the semester or when assessment is outlined
- encourage students to read English material, listen to the radio and watch television, participate in peer mentoring programs or become a volunteer in a community group to increase their confidence.

It may also help to refer students to the English Language Growth (ELG) resource (Rochecouste et al. 2010). The ELG contains five modules that students can address at their own pace. The first shows students that motivations and beliefs can affect language learning. The second focuses on confidence in speaking English. The third provides strategies that students can employ to facilitate language development. Later modules outline the expectations of university teachers:

> At Australian universities many lecturers see themselves as facilitating your learning. When someone facilitates, they make it possible – they don't do it for you and they do not tell you what to do. If you are not applying yourself to your learning, you need to take responsibility for the consequences. ... One of the biggest problems among students is not asking for help. All academic staff expect students to communicate their difficulties in understanding course material.
>
> (Rochecouste et al. 2010)

Social integration

Newcomers to a culture need specific guidelines about navigating verbal and non-verbal communication in the host society (Westwood et al. 2000). One approach is to use intercultural skills resources such as 'cultural maps' (Mak et al. 1998), which are succinct descriptions of appropriate behaviour (both non-verbal and verbal) in specific social contexts. Cultural maps can include social values and historical reasons underlying why some behaviours are preferred in local cultures. ExcelL (Excellence in Cultural Experiential Learning and Leadership) is an intercultural teaching resource built around six social competencies: seeking help, making social contact, participation in a group, refusing a request, expressing disagreement and giving feedback (Ho et al. 2004; Mak et al. 1998; Ward 2006). The following case illustrates how such resources can be used to promote competence in social and academic situations.

CASE 12.2   USING SOCIAL INTERACTION CULTURAL MAPS

Karen Commons and Xiaodan Gao, Victoria University of Wellington, New Zealand

---

Learning advisers use ExcelL cultural maps to help incoming international students successfully adapt to their new learning communities. International students, helped by local students, construct cultural maps that explain in detail how to communicate successfully in the host country. These cultural maps relate to specific scenarios such as participating in a group meeting to discuss a group assignment, or initiating conversation with another student outside a lecture hall. The maps include appropriate words and body language, as well as the values underlying these behaviours. For example, a cultural map for a group meeting would explain how to enter a fast-flowing conversation, how to acknowledge the previous speaker before moving on to make a contradicting point, how much eye contact is appropriate and so on. It would also list the values underpinning this interaction: for example, the importance of showing initiative in a relatively individualistic culture. After such a cultural map is constructed, students practise the interaction using the suggestions in the map. They are given feedback by their local student peers on anything they can do 'more of' or 'less of' in order to improve their chances of successful communication in their host culture.

To facilitate students' social integration, start by correctly pronouncing the names of international students. Name tags may be helpful. Avoid stereotypes and over-generalised descriptions of other cultures and, as Case 12.3 illustrates, use every opportunity, including assessment, to introduce students and their cultural backgrounds (Ruth & Houghton 2009).

CASE 12.3   USING PERSONAL WEB PAGES AS ASSESSMENT

Dr Alison Ruth, La Trobe University and Dr Luke Houghton, Griffith University

---

As part of the development of online editing skills in a first year Management Information Systems course, students are asked to develop a personal page in a shared wiki space. This page has requirements that demonstrate the skills needed to present collaborative work in later assessment items. The minimum requirements included using headings, bold and centred text, inserting an image and inserting a table (often their study timetable). The text is self-constructed and biographical in nature. The assignment is completed early, by Week 4 of a 12-week semester, and is worth five per cent of the total mark. The marking criterion is for execution only (that is, fulfilling the minimum layout requirements). This provides low-risk opportunities to build confidence and to get to know other students.

The benefits of intercultural engagement for international and domestic students include social cohesion within the university (Smart et al. 2000), improvement in socio-cultural adjustment for international students (Ward & Kennedy 1999), less stress and depression, plus higher levels of life satisfaction, happiness and self-esteem (Ward 2001). For all students, intercultural engagement has been associated with improved intercultural knowledge, attitudes and skills; a decrease in the propensity for stereotyping; an increase in world-mindedness and intercultural problem-solving skills; and higher assignment marks (Doyle et al. 2009; Summers & Volet 2008; Ward et al. 2005). Zepke and Leach's (2005) review of 17 studies reported benefits for students who engaged in social activities outside of the classroom in university sporting clubs or networking groups. Similarly, Colvin and Jaffar (2007), Leask and Carroll (2011) and Dunne (2009) argue that formal and informal curricula should be utilised to enhance intercultural interactions between students.

Despite the benefits, student surveys report that meaningful interactions between domestic and international students are generally low. An Australian study showed that 81 per cent of the 3500 international students surveyed would like to be friends with more Australian students, and 46 per cent of the 7000 Australian students surveyed also expressed a desire to be friends with international students (Australian Education International 2007). The United Kingdom Council for Overseas Students Affairs (UKCOSA 2004) reported that the majority of international students in the UK form friendships with people from similar cultural heritage. For example, only 15 per cent of Chinese students reported friendships with local people. However, Mak et al. (1994) indicated that if international students feel pressured to assimilate to their host culture, it may be counterproductive for cultural engagement because they can feel that their cultural identity is threatened. Overall, it seems that the mere presence of international and domestic students in the classroom is not enough to facilitate effective intercultural contact (Brown & Daly 2005; Hibbins & Barker 2011; Nesdale & Todd 1998; Volet & Ang 1998).

A useful way for university teachers to promote meaningful interaction between international and domestic students is to teach students how to manage multicultural groups. For example, the Finding Common Ground project (Arkoudis et al. 2010) outlines why working in such groups is beneficial and suggests strategies to promote interaction. The Higher Education Academy (2011) site also offers helpful approaches to managing assessed group work including: explaining to students the purpose of using group work and interactive learning; knowing when to let students choose their group members and when to assign group membership; and choosing the types of assessment tasks most suited to groups. Case 12.4 illustrates assessed group work in which cultural diversity forms part of the assessment (Woods et al. 2011).

CASE 12.4   DRAWING ON STUDENTS' CULTURAL BACKGROUNDS
Dr Peter Woods, Griffith University

The subject was designed to facilitate effective multicultural teamwork … the learning objective [was] that students would 'be able to apply international Human Resource Management values and techniques to real-world situations … [and] apply these values to the practice of multicultural teamwork'. The module comprised:

- a one-hour presentation on the theory and practice of effective multicultural group work
- a group selection exercise in which students selected team members, based on set roles, by sharing their résumés with each other
- a series of group facilitation activities including guided discussion on factors that make multicultural teams effective
- the development of a process framework for multicultural team functioning, and guided group development exercises centred on the completion of a group presentation project.

Group facilitation exercises included groups evaluating their processes using worksheets on: factors enhancing effective global teams; achieving task and relationship balance on a global team; and frameworks for developing high-performance teams. Students earned a group mark for their group presentation which comprised 30 per cent of the total subject assessment plus structured, non-assessable feedback from all student peers at the completion of each presentation.

The presentation task required students to form groups of five and to compare and contrast the practice of a human resource management function between two countries considering the practical, cultural, historical, religious (where relevant) and legislative contexts. As the majority of students were international they usually presented on their country of origin, thereby sharing their countries' historical, religious and legislative contexts as applied to a human resource management function.

Managing intercultural conflict

University teachers must be alert to tensions between students of different religious or ethnic groups and to sensitivities that surround nationality, for example, in relation to the People's Republic of China and Taiwan (the Republic of China). If conflict is not addressed and is allowed to escalate it may lead to hostile learning environments in which students do not feel safe to participate. Dealing with conflict effectively requires communication and listening skills, assertiveness, mutual respect and sensitivity towards others. Strategies that teachers can employ to minimise the possibility of conflict include:

- anticipate topics that may cause controversy and actively plan how to manage it
- plan learning activities that encourage students to understand issues from alternative perspectives

- teach students to address the evidence
- establish ground rules about how to treat each other
- include ice-breaker activities that focus on students' common interests to minimise perceived differences between students
- use controversial statements made by students as a resource for intellectual development (ask the class, for example, 'Does anyone have another perspective on this?').

YOUR THOUGHTS

- What are the causes of intercultural conflicts in your classes (if any)?
- What approaches do you find helpful in managing intercultural conflicts?

Conclusion

International students comprise a significant cohort within universities across the globe. Teaching them is rewarding, especially when diversity is seen as a resource. This chapter has presented curricula and teaching approaches that respond to international students' needs in areas such as language development, academic literacy and integrity, and enhancing interaction between domestic and international students. So now, what will you do next week to enhance the learning experience for each of your international students?

CHAPTER 13

INDIGENOUS KNOWERS AND KNOWLEDGE IN UNIVERSITY TEACHING

Michael Christie and Christine Asmar

Keywords
Aboriginal, Indigenous, Indigenous pedagogy, Indigenous epistemology, 'both-ways' education, cultural safety, postcolonial

Introduction

An exciting thing about being a teacher in a university in Australia (as in other former colonial countries) is the ongoing and stimulating presence of Indigenous[i] students, academics and their communities who interact with non-Indigenous people and their knowledge practices. Around the world, particularly in North America, southern Africa, Australia and New Zealand, universities are working to integrate traditional knowers, their knowledge practices and perspectives into the academy. Several Australian universities now specify that *all* their graduates should, for example, 'respect Indigenous knowledge, cultures and values' (University of Melbourne 2010); while in New Zealand, universities are formally committed to the contribution of Māori knowledge to scholarship across disciplines (see, for example, Victoria University of Wellington 2009). This work has resulted in significant changes to university teaching and learning – strikingly illustrated by the fact that the medical deans of Australia and New Zealand have now established a national joint framework for the inclusion of Indigenous health into core medical curricula (Phillips 2004).

For those 99 per cent of Australian academics who are not of Aboriginal or Torres Strait Islander background, working with Indigenous knowledge and practitioners is a privilege and a responsibility. Australian Indigenous people have their own ways of making and understanding knowledge, of validating knowledge claims and of understanding intellectual property and ethics, which require quite different practices of knowledge production and accountability. These characteristically

Australian practices come with unique social and political ways of being and doing, implicating all people who come into contact with them: Indigenous and non-Indigenous staff and students at personal and institutional levels. Yet it is not always easy to appreciate the differences between a western academic knowledge system and the systems shared and celebrated by Indigenous people around the world (see Denzin et al. 2008; Smith 1999). Even when there is recognition of knowledge differences, practitioners do not always know what to do about them. New teachers may be inhibited by fear of getting things wrong or of offending someone. Fortunately, the rewards of engaging with Indigenous knowledges and ways of seeing the world are as great for teachers as they are for students.

In this chapter some of the teaching and learning implications of this 'Indigenising' work are addressed, with a particular focus on the Australian experience. Our task is to help readers understand the undeniable complexity of the issues; and at the same time to provide guidelines and resources for successful and enriching professional practice (Asmar 2011a). The chapter is structured around four key areas: understanding Australian Indigenous knowledge; Indigenous pedagogy; approaches to teaching and learning in the postcolonial classroom, including cultural safety, 'both-ways' education and bringing Indigenous knowers and knowledge into the curriculum; and engaging with Indigenous centres.

Understanding Australian Indigenous knowledge

The first thing to understand is that Indigenous knowledge, like all other knowledge, is found in the routine practices of everyday life and makes those practices possible (see Christie 2008). In some contexts, *representations* of knowledge become codified in particular ways, as in art and painting, and in databases, university textbooks, websites and research papers, but normally knowledge is embedded in the ways people live out their daily lives. It is *performative*. It is something that you *do* rather than something you *have*. Embedding Aboriginal knowledge in the curriculum is not so much about embedding *what* Aboriginal people know about the environment, for example, but rather *how* they know – their *practices*, knowledge in action. Learning to be an Aboriginal knower involves learning how to construct, rehearse, implement, perform and celebrate knowledge collectively and in place, more than it has to do with specific content, such as the names of places and species or with facts about their usefulness.

The fact that Indigenous ecological knowledge is performative and located means that incorporating it into university teaching requires a new approach to curriculum. Resource management students in northern Australian universities, for example, learn about Aboriginal 'firestick farming'. This is the way in which careful early dry season burning has over millennia (until colonisation) maintained the biodiversity of the area, which is currently threatened by poor burning practices. This sort of environmental management requires an intimate practical knowledge of the land, the winds and moisture in the air at different times of day in different places, the grasses currently dominant, the topography and the previous history of burning in that area.

Second, because of this grounded performativity, Aboriginal knowledge practices differ from place to place. They derive from and enable *culturally-specific, context-specific* practices. Specific Australian languages (and their people) belong to and derive from specific estates across the country. All through Australia the creating ancestors changed their language as they moved from place to place. Australian Aboriginal knowledge is possibly different from many other Indigenous knowledge systems around the world, because language, land and identity are interdependent in a unique way in the Australian Aboriginal world and in a unique way in each context. Aboriginal knowledge is not universal, so it is unreasonable, for example, to ask a student for '*the* Aboriginal perspective' as if there *were* a unified position in such a diverse population. (In any case, it is good teaching practice to avoid 'spotlighting' individual students.) Aboriginal knowledge is fundamentally local. It comes from place and relates people to place in their everyday lives. When it is abstracted and generalised, it loses some of its richness, quality, holism and usefulness. It is at work in urban as well as remote settings, embedded in place and practice.

Third, Australian Indigenous knowledge is *owned*. Laws concerning who can say what, who has a right to access information and who can profit from particular performances existed throughout Australia for millennia before colonisation. Western laws cannot define Aboriginal intellectual property adequately nor accommodate its requirements. They may go some way towards linking traditional knowledge systems with Australian law, but will never replace or take precedence over the need for local respectful agreements over what knowledge is, who it belongs to and how it can be put to use. In university teaching, for example, the fact that Aboriginal and Australian intellectual property laws are incommensurable needs to be considered carefully, as there are two regimes to be accounted for. See, for example, Gurruwiwi and Guyula (2010), who discuss the problems of protecting their *performances* of Yolngu Aboriginal knowledge in a university teaching context, through an Australian legal system which protects only *content*.

Fourth, as Gurruwiwi and Guyula (2010) point out, Australian Indigenous knowledge is in many respects *collective*. It is owned and performed by groups of people and its continuance depends upon the collective memory at work in their languages, social practices and structures and performance traditions, as well as in the physical features of their land, its species and other natural phenomena. The natural environment is an embodiment of both ancestral and recent histories. The species it holds participate in making the world both intelligible and meaningful. People are only part of the knowledge system at work in the world. In many places

Aboriginal knowledge is also protected by a system of 'managers' or 'caretakers' who have rights through kinship to supervise and control the production of knowledge. People who share it must account for their right to represent it. People who receive it must account for the use to which it is put. Laws and acceptable practices that govern knowledge use are local and need to be understood and negotiated at the local level. Social groupings are constituted through shared knowledge, and Aboriginal identity depends as much upon practices of exclusion – making only some knowledge available freely and controlling the availability of other knowledge – as it does upon sharing and inclusion. None of this changes when Indigenous knowledge and its holders find a place in the university, but it can be severely compromised unless its unique epistemology is understood. The collaborative teaching model used in the Faculty of Education at Monash University is an excellent example of a shared understanding provided by Indigenous and non-Indigenous lecturers working together in the classroom, as academics Zane Ma Rhea, Henry Atkinson and Peter Anderson explain:

> There is an important issue in the nature of the distinction between Indigenous Knowledge and Indigenous people – they are not separate. The three of us have permission to speak of different things – quite a lot of things, between us – but we cannot all speak of the same things, and in fact we sometimes disagree with each other, in front of the students. We deliberately model this, so students can learn from it … We have an interrogative approach to teaching; the questioning by one of us goes on while the other one is talking about the content, in a kind of meta-cognitive way, for example Henry will intervene to say: 'The reason Zane is saying that, is …' In the end, the use of this 'critical meta-narrative' means that students develop the ability to reflect on their own practice. And we model the possibility that you can have normal relations [between Indigenous and non-Indigenous people]. [ii]

Co-teaching is recommended as a pathway towards such shared understandings on the part of teachers. Students' cognitive abilities will also be extended as they learn to view the world – and disciplinary knowledge – from multiple frames of reference (see Kincheloe & Steinberg's 2008 concept of 'critical multi-logicality').

Finally, Aboriginal knowledge is *responsive*, active and constantly renewed and reconfigured. It continues to embrace and make use of new technology and find new sites of activity. It does not solidify as facts which can be stored. It is eco-logical. What becomes sequestered on a database or a DVD or a curriculum document is only ever a trace of some previous knowledge production episode and some of these traces have a significant role to play in Australian tertiary education even while they are still 'owned' by their authors. There is understandable resistance (for ethical, political and epistemological reasons) to the 'harvesting' of Indigenous knowledge – particularly knowledge about the environment and its resources –

or even the 'documentation' of Indigenous knowledge – as if knowledge can be made into *documents* without compromise. Understanding documents as *traces* of knowledge work is one way of maintaining the connection between the artefact and the people, place and moment of its production.

To summarise: Indigenous Australian knowledge is performative, contextual, owned, collective and renewable. The next question to consider is: what happens when Indigenous knowledge practices interact with academic knowledge? As the Torres Strait Islander scholar Martin Nakata (2007, p. 8) sees it: 'In the academy it is not possible to bring in Indigenous knowledge and plonk it in the curriculum unproblematically as if it is another data set for western knowledge to discipline and test.'

Indigenous pedagogy

Indigenous epistemology, that is Indigenous understandings of the 'nature, source(s), and limits of knowledge' (Maffie 2005), implies particular understandings of learning and teaching (see Maffie for a useful discussion on ethnoepistemology). Often based on a conceptualisation of knowledge production as collaborative and performative work, Indigenous pedagogies and epistemologies are relevant for understanding research, teaching and learning. As a young Indigenous academic from Macquarie University explains:

> It's tough ... Elders in the classroom. You've got the concurrent knowledge systems running. You've got the high-level educators in the classroom – in their communities they have the knowledge – and then there's me, the lecturer, who's twenty years younger. It takes a lot of skill to manage that, so I try to incorporate their knowledge in the teaching.

There are few 'magic bullets' for the incorporation of such knowledges. A flexible approach to what has to be 'covered' in class is necessary, with time allowed for student voices. The essential precondition is an awareness of, and respect for, the non-western knowledges some students bring.

Some universities are fortunate to have, from time to time, Indigenous teachers teaching Indigenous students through Indigenous knowledge practices. Such examples are instructive for non-Indigenous academics and managers as they help us to see and reflect upon the complexities and differences in an alternative pedagogy. See, for example, the work of Payi-Linda Ford (2010), whose quest was to find a way to institutionalise her traditional Indigenous (Tyikim) knowledge practices in a university teacher education course. The authority of her Elders, the agency of the metaphors for agreement-making (and knowledge-making) which emerge from her own ancestral land, the Tyikim epistemology, metaphysics and ontology, the histories, the local systems of authority and accountability, the evidential practices, intellectual property and ethics all find their way into the classroom of Indigenous students.

Many Indigenous theorists and philosophers have used traditional metaphors to elucidate understandings of how knowledge traditions come together and work respectfully and productively, for example, the inmixing of fresh and salt water in Worby et al. (2006) and Marika et al. (1990). Some of these Indigenous theories have much in common with socio-constructivist theories in western learning theory. The Yolngu metaphor of the *garma* – 'when people with different ideas and values come together and negotiate knowledge in a respectful learning environment'(Yothu Yindi Foundation 2006) – emphasises the importance of context, good faith and collaboration in producing new, workable, useful and right knowledge (Ngurruwutthun 1991).

How might a garma pedagogy be introduced into, say, the teaching of medical students studying the epidemic of renal disease in Aboriginal communities? We suggest establishing a forum to explore Indigenous perspectives on the body, health, life, death and disease to balance the biomedical model of the body and its treatment. This could be done by inviting a renal nurse and maybe a nephrologist for discussion with a renal patient, family member or social worker. Good treatment takes seriously the fact that the patient knows her body intimately, and integrates the medical with the social, the nutritional, the spiritual and much else. Indigenous pedagogy takes seriously the parallel collaborative agreement-making taking place and being modelled in a tertiary classroom, while still in the context of rigorous evidence-based biomedical research (see Cass et al. 2002).

Such an approach to teaching represents a stark contrast to the 'conduit metaphor' (Reddy 1979) in which messages are somehow transferred from one mind to another as if by magic along a conduit. Kincheloe and Steinberg, in their stimulating discussion of Indigenous knowledges in education, address this issue directly: they suggest that, in positivist Eurocentric education, teachers might say: 'Give me the truth and I will pass it along to students in the most efficient manner possible.' By comparison they propose an 'Indigenously informed' approach which would have teachers (and students) saying: 'Please support me as I explore multiple ways of seeing and making sense of the world' (2008, p. 149). We come now to consider how those explorations may occur in the classroom.

Approaches to teaching and learning in the postcolonial classroom

Nakata (2007) has argued that 'Indigenous people are entangled in a much contested knowledge space at the cultural interface', and this is particularly

219

apparent when considering approaches to teaching and learning in the postcolonial classroom. In talking about teaching in the postcolonial university classroom, the term 'postcolonial' is used to describe contexts and practices where Indigenous and non-Indigenous knowledges are each taken seriously, respectfully and in good faith. The emergence of such postcolonial learning spaces requires careful insight and dedication by non-Indigenous tertiary educators. This work is not so much learning to include and engage Indigenous people and their knowledge as it is learning to appreciate the culturally and historically contingent nature of one's own academic knowledge and its practices. When an Indigenous lecturer, student or guest speaker enters a mainstream university classroom, there are (at least) two knowledge practices seeking visibility and acceptance. Even Indigenous students of hard sciences, like mathematics or physics, who have fully mastered the western scientific approach, may still struggle with the directions in which their Indigenous knowledge practices lead them.

Two key principles – cultural safety and both-ways education – are proposed and illustrated below, followed by practice-based discussion of how to bring Indigenous knowledge into the curriculum. (For more approaches and exemplars, see Asmar 2011b.) Note that 'Indigenous teaching' involves not only Indigenous students but also teaching Indigenous topics to any group of students.

Cultural safety

The concept of cultural safety was first developed by Irihapeti Ramsden, a Māori scholar in nursing who set out an educational framework analysing power relationships between health professionals and those they serve (Ellison-Loschmann 2003). The concept requires teachers to reflect on – and respect – the fact that cultural values and norms of the students are different from their own (Polaschek 1998).

Consider, to begin with, that the group labelled 'Indigenous students' encompasses students with a range of experiences: from school-leavers going straight into mainstream courses to mature-age students already employed in their (often remote) communities who come onto campus for short, intensive, 'block-mode' courses to further develop their professional skills (Asmar, Page & Radloff 2011; DiGregorio et al. 2000). Some of these learners may have been brought into university study without much preparation in academic skills, through 'alternative entry schemes' (see for example, Nakata et al. 2008; Douglas 2005). Some may bring a strong and proud tradition of Indigenous culture and governance. Some may be part of or descended from the Stolen Generations[iii] and be struggling to pull together a sense of personal identity. Many will have had experiences of marginalisation (and even racism) at school (Craven et al. 2005). Many will speak 'Aboriginal English'. On the other hand, those who speak English as their first and only language, or come from an urban middle-class background, or have a fair complexion, may find that others judge them as inauthentic – not like the *real* Aborigines in very remote Australia.

Indigenous students, therefore, may well be nervous on entering the classroom. The need for building trust is, of course, relevant to all students (non-Indigenous students are often anxious too), but it's highlighted for Indigenous students by the often tragic experiences of Indigenous communities during Australia's colonial past, and by the fact that Indigenous communities – and students – remain affected by those legacies today. A teacher from Macquarie University describes one example:

> Sometimes you've got people walking into the classroom who are wounded from things that have happened to them and to their families – it's like an iceberg, you can't see it. You have to bide your time, you have to be kind ... So it's trying to juggle all of that. And I believe a lot of heart has to come into your teaching ... When I first met one of the older students, she asked if we could change the seating so the chairs weren't in rows. It reminded her of her bad experiences at school. So I moved them into a circle and afterwards I asked her if it was OK for her. She said yes – she had tears in her eyes. She had to feel trust in me in order to be able to say what she said.

Indigenous students are sometimes affected by things going on in their communities today. Reading about the legacies of colonisation can help inform teachers' responses to such student behaviours, as a teacher from the Academy of Sport, Health and Education in Victoria explains:

> Students sometimes come in seeming very low, flat, apathetic, depressed ... The very first thing is to work out their mood. I use the warm-up activities to get them into the mood, sometimes, but I don't waste their time if they don't need it, if they are ready to go.

Some (though not all) Indigenous students have had few opportunities to develop formal academic skills, and for such students, 'scaffolding' – providing a framework for their learning - is vital. Case 13.1 shows how one lecturer used teaching skills to create a safe learning space for her students: Sally Farrington, with 15 years' experience of teaching Indigenous students, describes her approach to teaching and assessment in preparatory courses in anatomy.

CASE 13.1   TEACHING INDIGENOUS STUDENTS FROM NON-TRADITIONAL ACADEMIC BACKGROUNDS

Sally Farrington, The University of Sydney

The students were always very clear about my expectations of them. I have structured the learning and assessments in a workbook – it's all in there. I observed that students can't do what we take for granted, for example, managing pieces of paper – so I put it all in there for them.

I try to link new material back to previous material we have done. I try to use learners' own experiences. I use advance organisers with them. I demonstrate ways in which they are already masterful, and I use their own experiences. I try to be encouraging, I listen respectfully to students' questions – which can be a challenge when they feel confident enough to ask all kinds of questions about the body!

Sometimes you can't cover all the content – the class dynamics can be slow. With a subject like anatomy, I'm careful to decode the language – to teach them about the terminology. I make sure I orientate the diagrams – 'This is a diagram of … It's from this angle … ' What seems easy to me is not, for new students. I've developed some plain English notes – it's scaffolding. Note-taking is a challenge for people new to learning, especially in my area where there's a lot of terminology. Their level – say, in the preparation programs – is often below the level of the textbook. I spend time on process skills, for example on looking up glossaries, and I give formal feedback on those things, so some of the teaching is on formal academic skills.

For school leavers who are in support programs, I don't use a lot of assessment, and the assessments are formative. So I'm preparing them for formal assessment – it's scaffolding again. In courses where I had to grade students, I ensured the subject outline had the assessments front-ended. There are templates. I spend a lot of time talking about the assessments. Part of the assessment was a draft, and then a redraft after feedback. I try to encourage students to use something from their workplace, something relevant to them. About the submission of assignments – that hoary old subject of deadlines – I always accepted that students might find it hard to meet them. Students did not always meet deadlines, so I gave them the time they needed to get the work done – without penalty. On feedback: students need detailed feedback – then if they haven't met the criteria they can resubmit.

In particular subject areas, students may be upset by the subject matter itself – for example in the study of the history of Australian colonisation. There are ways of preparing students for this confronting work. At Charles Darwin University, a five-week pre-law program for Indigenous students gives them an opportunity to meet other Indigenous students and think through together the injustices of 'the lie of the law' (*terra nullius* [iv] for example) before entering the undergraduate law program (Hussin 2002). Individual teachers, aware of student vulnerability, also devise their own in-class pedagogies, as described by an experienced teacher at the University of Newcastle:

> I've taught in contexts of the Stolen Generations and so on. At one level [with non-Indigenous students] it's important to set out the consequences of those policies and so on. But at the same time, if you're teaching Indigenous students, you have to acknowledge their responses will be different. And so I say to my

Indigenous students: 'You may find this material disturbing' and 'You don't have to attend this lecture.' It's good pedagogy to recognise these things – that knowledge is not all going to be consumed in the same way.

Cultural safety can also be informed by Indigenous and postcolonial theory (see for example Anderson et al. 2003). Good respectful relationships at the interpersonal level can reverberate out to produce effective, generative organisational culture, as a teacher from Monash University explains:

> Working together, we have created an environment of safety for young Aboriginal students. We have changed the way Monash [University] thinks about 'Indigenous'. Flying the [Aboriginal and Torres Strait Islands] flags is now done here – it's important.

There are cultural safety issues around non-Indigenous students as well. There is no denying that teaching Indigenous studies and history – especially to students who would not voluntarily have enrolled in any such class, but are (increasingly) obliged to do so – can meet with resistance. Experienced teachers know that some of that hostility can spring from feelings of 'political correctness' or anxiety, and carefully plan accordingly, as these three real-world examples show:

> We tell the students 'There are no stupid questions' and encourage openness. Some students will say what they think the tutor wants to hear, but mostly they are ready to ask any question they need to know. I always say that the tutorial situation is a perfect opportunity to ask a question, and if I can't answer I will do my best to find the answer. I freely admit that I don't know everything.
>
> (teacher from the University of Sydney)

> The premise, which I've developed over years, is that I make a safe and respectful environment for them, where they feel safe, and where they don't get jumped on for not knowing things. It's the not knowing that creates friction – the fear of not knowing – so I say: 'You can ask anything.'
>
> (teacher from the University of New South Wales)

> If someone says something stereotypical, I put it out to the other students to think about, rather than taking it on myself. Other students will respond to it, but they need a comfortable space to feel free to do so. I always try to respond with empathy, that: 'I can see where you are coming from, I can see why you might think that.' I try to acknowledge that there is some legitimacy to their

views from a certain perspective, but then I emphasise there are also other ways of viewing the situation and will proceed to explore these with the students.

(teacher from the University of Sydney)

All students bring to university study particular ways of knowing learnt in the home and community. Aboriginal students have a strong sense of how they do their knowledge work differently (how they ask questions, and of whom, who has the authority to speak, when and why to speak up, when and why to remain silent) (Harrison 2011). At the same time they may feel that their knowledge might be undervalued, marginalised or misappropriated. They may be keen to have their Indigenous knowledge make contributions to class discussions, or they may wish to keep it to themselves. Uninformed opinions voiced by 'mainstream' students may make it even less likely that Indigenous students will participate. This can be at odds with university norms for group participation. The lecturer may need to accept Indigenous students' right to remain silent, and find alternative ways to engage them; for example, via online or written contributions. Once trust is established, a teacher might be able to ask students *before* the class if they would be willing to contribute their view. One teacher's dilemma – and response – is well captured by Sam Cook, of the Victorian College of the Arts and Music:

> We have students from the Daly River and the Northern Territory – they're not exactly loud in projecting their voice. But at the same time, the things they know are integral to the learning of the whole group, so we have to weigh that up. We have one student who, when he does talk, it's absolutely central and important. We have to be mindful that we don't lose voices. With our Indigenous students, if you put them on the spot, that can result in a very short response, like – 'It's OK', or 'Yeah, good'. Some students have a stronger inner dialogue than an outer one. There is quite a lot of one-to-one teaching and mentoring of such students.

Finally, non-Indigenous teachers should not feel daunted by any of this discussion, but are encouraged to tackle nearly all Indigenous topics (such as history, land rights, conservation, technology), providing there is, wherever possible, consultation with and participation by Indigenous experts. Topics best left to Indigenous people would include ceremony, spirituality and men's and women's business (for further discussion, see Craven et al. 2011, p. 296).

Both-ways education

Many Indigenous scholars – such as Canadian First Nations scholar Marie Battiste (2000) – argue eloquently against the under-valuing of Indigenous knowledges in the disciplines. Both-ways education attempts to right this imbalance (see Case 13.2). Australia's Batchelor Institute of Indigenous Tertiary Education, for example, has formally adopted a both-ways educational philosophy 'which enables exploration of Indigenous Australian traditions of knowledge and Western academic disciplinary positions'. In every discipline, Batchelor graduates are expected to 'value learning, critical analysis, creativity and Indigenous scholarship' (Batchelor Institute of Indigenous Tertiary Education c. 2010).

If our education practice is to be genuinely both-ways, there are two pitfalls to avoid: first, teaching as if academic knowledge is objectively true, and Indigenous knowledge is mere 'folk knowledge'; and second, adopting the relativist position that each system is as good as the other. They are distinctive knowledge practices which can still be brought to work productively together (Christie 2006), as the following two examples show.

In New Zealand, the work of Ocean Ripeka Mercier (2011) (the first female Māori PhD in Physics) embodies both-ways principles. Mercier's course at Victoria University of Wellington, 'Science and Indigenous Knowledge', explores initiatives to bridge the philosophical gap between western science and Indigenous Knowledge. For their assessment, students research and document 'local knowledge' in a way that explores the tensions inherent in 'capturing' local, Indigenous and/or oral knowledge with electronic media, as these examples show:

> One student geo-referenced Google Earth to a 1917 map of Te Whanganui a Tara (Wellington Harbour), then used Elsdon Best's *The Land of Tara* to map old Māori placenames, sites of pā (fortified villages), and resources.

> Another student mapped the Native Schools and the Kura Kaupapa (Māori-language immersion schools) of earlier centuries. She incorporated narratives from each school, illustrating the massive shift in the education of Māori children since the introduction of immersion schools.
>
> (Victoria University of Wellington 2011)

In another science example, medical students in Victoria were 'immersed' in a rural Aboriginal community, supported by Aboriginal facilitators who travelled with students to cultural sites, as well as to community agencies where they learnt first-hand about Indigenous health and social issues. As one student wrote later: 'I've been getting cynical about the medical course, but over the weekend I couldn't help but think: "Hey, this is what medicine should be about!"' (Rasmussen 2001, p. 131). In Case 13.2, Michael Christie describes a unique both-ways course in languages and culture.

CASE 13.2   THE YOLNGU STUDIES PROGRAM
Michael Christie, Charles Darwin University

When the program for teaching Yolngu (north-east Arnhem Land Aboriginal) languages and culture was set up at the Charles Darwin University, it took around a year to negotiate permission, agree upon governance and curriculum, and develop appropriate resources. A team of senior Yolngu Elders from six different communities and six different clan groups was appointed to act as advisers to the program, and the team developed some principles for teaching: the languages cannot be taught without the culture (and vice versa); students should be exposed to all the different Yolngu languages, not just one; they should learn about the stories of creation and the environment in the languages to which those stories belong, told by people to whom those stories belong; nothing of a secret or sacred nature should be taught; and the university should maintain its obligation to 'mutual benefit' by ensuring that Yolngu students receive good quality education, especially in English.

We built up a digital collection of texts, videos and audio files in various Yolngu languages, and appointed a Yolngu lecturer to take the 90 minutes of every lecture. The Yolngu lecturer talks around a theme, mostly in English, but with the aid of videos, bark paintings, old documents and photos – or a walk in the bush tucker garden, or even a hunting expedition on the weekend. The talk might be about a place or a piece of history, always carefully told within the laws of what can be said and what can't. The tutorial immediately after is led by non-Yolngu with background linguistic and cultural knowledge to help explain the complexities of morphology and grammar, or the fundamental mechanisms of the kinship system. The Yolngu aim for non-Yolngu students is very much to 'teach students to really know about themselves, who they are' (Gurruwiwi 2010), so the assessment largely involves students learning to write (and talk) about their own experience and life history using Yolngu languages and kinship terms, or (for more advanced students) collaborative research with a Yolngu knowledge authority on a topic of mutual interest (for example, dogs in Yolngu history). The Yolngu studies pedagogy is perfectly acceptable by Yolngu as a garma pedagogy, and by the university as a rigorous academic practice – provided, of course, the mutual benefit and the agreed governance arrangements continue in place. It has been going strong since 1995.

Bringing Indigenous knowers and knowledge into curriculum

Perhaps the most common configuration of Indigenous knowledge and knowers in a university is when non-Indigenous lecturers teach topics to do with Indigenous knowledge – history, art, education, health, languages, environment. In the past, much of this work *about* Indigenous people was found in departments such as anthropology, history, linguistics. Much of that teaching is now being reclaimed by Indigenous schools and centres, but many non-Indigenous academics will still need to work out how to bring Indigenous knowledge and its practices into their curriculum respectfully and rigorously. One of the very best ways to do this is by inviting Indigenous people directly into the classroom. Other ways include arranging for students to spend time in community contexts, as well as accessing the wide range of electronic, visual and other resources now available to us. Whatever the approach, engagement with Indigenous knowledge practices entails making a commitment to Indigenous community practices and aspirations to the mutual benefit of the university and the community (Campbell & Christie 2008, 2009).

Guest speakers

A key feature of (Australian) Indigenous knowledge is that it is owned. So how might the custodians of Indigenous knowledge be brought to share their knowledge with students? Lecturers with good connections to local communities (and funding) often ask guest lecturers to come and tell their stories. While developing such connections and trust can take time and effort, and organising payment through the university system is onerous (Christie 2010), the outcomes are often transformative, especially for students who have rarely met Indigenous people. Student evaluations regularly show that hearing the complex stories of people's experiences, especially if combined with personal interactions, can lead to profound attitude shifts. In the words of a medical student: 'Meeting and talking with Koori people, discovering the positive things happening in the Aboriginal community ... reaffirmed my desires to get involved in Aboriginal health' (Rasmussen 2001, p. 131).

Excursions, field trips and placements

Engaging local community Elders as guides on excursions in the local area allows students not only to understand Indigenous perspectives, but also to reflect upon their own assumptions and preconceptions. Who gets to tell which story? How does memory work? What are the formative influences on how we think about particular groups? History professor Richard Broome, of La Trobe University in Victoria, explains how his students' learning is enriched by opportunities which his own long-standing community relationships can facilitate for them:

> The community took [the international students] to rock art sites, they gave them a bush tucker lunch, and then the Community Manager spoke to us about contemporary Aboriginal issues and problems ... The liaison with the Budja Budja came out of my research – so it all bent back on that relationship – it was wonderful.

> (see also Broome 2009)

227

In another example from environmental health, Clark (2002) developed an on-the-job pedagogy for Aboriginal environmental health workers whose training involved the disciplines of 'law, microbiology, public health engineering, health promotion and food handling to name but a few'. Clark was interested in the connections between the disciplinary understanding of environmental health and the context in which is taught, and how those connections affected the way it was taught by lecturers, perceived by students and ultimately received by the community. On-the-ground problem-based training engaged community leaders in identifying appropriate students, supervising the training and working with the health inspector. The ownership which emerged from this pedagogy allowed for long-term structural and behavioural change in everyday community life.

Film, web, media and other resources

When it is not possible to bring students into direct contact with Indigenous knowers and communities, what other resources are available? Exploring libraries and curriculum resources (including online) will yield authentic representations of Aboriginal knowledge and history, made by people who own those languages and histories on their own terms. Using film and video will privilege the voices of Indigenous people as they talk about their own histories and cultures, as one teacher from Wollongong University explains:

> In Aboriginal Studies, film is a really important driver to represent the diversity of Aboriginal voices, their geographical locations, their language groups … Film is a powerful pedagogical tool – but you need to cue it right, so it doesn't go on and they get bored.

When Indigenous knowledge authorities come as guest lecturers, short video recordings can be made of what they say, for teaching purposes in other contexts. Naturally this needs to be done carefully, and the Indigenous person must be aware of the different uses to which the resource will be put. Encourage them to talk about who they are and where they come from before they tell their story, and remember to remunerate them. Building up your own collection of such authoritative digital resources is well worth the investment, especially if the resources are available to the community as well as the students, and can be used to maintain and consolidate the engagement between the university and its community (see for example Christie 2011).

Other great resources for university teachers include: Indigenous media and literature; internet resources such as the Australian Broadcasting Commission's website; statistics from the Australian Bureau of Statistics; teaching kits from Reconciliation Australia; songs, films, music and art. A teacher from the University of Newcastle explains how such resources can be used:

I bring in multimedia to class so that the students get a snippet of Aboriginal people talking, singing, doing artwork. A lot of the best political comment is not in *text* – so if all you were doing was text [you'd miss things] … It's much more visual, engaging, emotive [this way].

Finally, the importance of consultation is reiterated. Commonwealth-funded Aboriginal Education Consultative Groups exist in every Australian state. Smith's (2011, p. 201) 'considerations for effective consultation' are a useful reminder that educators need to be clear about what they need; and also be ready to make changes as a result of consultation. Indigenous colleagues and centres in one's own institution are yet another resource, as will be seen below.

Graduate attributes

Teaching associated with Indigenous perspectives may be included in all disciplines as part of the teaching required for the development of graduate attributes (see Chapter 4, Chalmers & Partridge 2012) associated with ethics, cultural sensitivity and critical thinking. For Indigenous and non-Indigenous students alike, learning to 'walk in the shoes of others' is a powerful learning experience, as shown in Case 13.3 by Bill Genat's multi-layered approach to teaching and online learning about issues in Indigenous health. Community involvement is an important dimension.

CASE 13.3   ONLINE ROLE PLAY AND COMMUNITY FORUM

Bill Genat, The University of Melbourne

I think that teaching Aboriginal Health – what's really interesting is that it constantly raises questions about things like ethics … and it pushes our consciousness to places it probably didn't want to go. It pushes us into new frontiers of thought. I run an online role-play, where students walk in the shoes of the colonisers, and of the colonised. Most of it is online [but] in the last class they do it in class, they enact a range of roles. That's different, I guess. That's powerful. Students respond very positively, they acknowledge they have learnt something.

It's all online stuff. Students correspond with one another, they go to public meetings, they get different information depending on their role, they get involved in issues which are still with us today. It's a bit of an 'immersion' project. It's based on diaries, Royal Commission transcripts, letters to the newspapers. They get a personal engagement with the material – it's not just history as a set of secondary documents. It's good. And it goes beyond the History Wars[v] – they have to understand the disparity of views that exist. The role-play is only part of the subject. The assessment for that is a reflective journal – their key insights, the things that challenged them, their understanding of what they glean from the popular media.

And I organise a public forum – there might be a researcher, a service provider, policymakers and a community member. They all come and speak to a particular issue; it might be the justice system, the Intervention[vi], family violence. Two or three of the speakers are Aboriginal. The audience can ask questions. The students are in the audience too, and they come back later, after tea, and deconstruct everything they've heard. The students get a lot out of it. It's a way of bringing public servants, people in the field, into contact with people in the community. It also brings Aboriginal people into the University, it encourages access. It's comfortable for them because there's a bunch of other Aboriginal people there.

Engaging with Indigenous centres

Most of Australia's 40 universities have dedicated centres for Indigenous students (for a list and contact details, see Asmar 2011c). The various centres have different philosophies and roles, but are known to provide many Indigenous students with support crucial to completing their degrees (Asmar, Page & Radloff 2011; Farrington et al. 1999; Page & Asmar 2008). Support includes pastoral care, academic tutorials, and the provision of resources such as computer labs, as well as safe spaces where Indigenous students can study and relax together. Some centres are able to provide research support as well (Trudgett 2009). University teachers who want to understand and engage respectfully with their Indigenous students would do well to find out the institutional support for students at their university, such as the special tutorial arrangements available for Indigenous students.

There is also an increasing trend for such centres to evolve into schools or departments, in which the (mainly) Indigenous academics have teaching and research roles like all other academics. The expertise of Indigenous academics is a wonderful resource for universities as well as for non-Indigenous staff who regularly ask Indigenous academics to teach into their courses, or ask for their help in making contact with local communities (Asmar & Page 2009). Yet sending an email out of the blue may not elicit much of a response. Relationships are the key. New academics might, for example, show support for the work of Indigenous centres by attending events such as seminars, orations and ceremonies, and getting to know their colleagues that way.

Conclusion

Effective Indigenous teaching, like all good teaching, involves careful planning, a variety of teaching techniques and sensitivity in managing classroom interactions.

In this chapter, however, we have tried to show that it is more than that. Going beyond the mere inclusion of Indigenous content or material, it requires an ongoing willingness to *learn* – including refining an awareness of how one's own epistemology, values and culture might affect how one goes about teaching. As one experienced teacher put it: 'You can't teach Indigenous students without recognising your own values.' This may mean setting aside one's academic assumptions in order to be open to new learning. A central part of that learning will be about relationships, inside and outside the classroom.

Dealing respectfully and productively with Indigenous knowledge and Indigenous knowers constitutes a postcolonial Australian academic knowledge practice (McConaghy 2000) as does ensuring the 'cultural safety' and welfare of Indigenous students. This work ideally involves Indigenous lecturers and their communities (as for example in the Yolngu languages and culture program at Charles Darwin University – see Christie 2011; Yolngu Advisors to ACIKE 2005), but more often it is done by working with representations of Indigenous knowledge, such as film, images and texts, used with proper acknowledgement and permission. The research-based exemplars provided here, while relevant to all our tertiary students, are particularly significant for work with Australian Indigenous students. Ultimately, however, each new teacher will do their own work of learning from and with Indigenous knowers and knowledges in their own local context, over years of sometimes challenging but always exciting and ultimately rewarding relationships. We hope that all our teaching colleagues will experience the excitement expressed by one Indigenous lecturer: 'I get satisfaction out of my students. They teach me heaps. I love them.'

Notes

[i] The term 'Indigenous' in this chapter refers to Australians of Aboriginal or Torres Strait Islander descent. 'Non-Indigenous' refers to all other Australians. Indigenous Australians constitute less than three per cent of the Australian population; about one per cent of Australian university students; and about one per cent of Australian university teachers.

[ii] All the comments from teachers in this chapter are drawn from interviews with teachers in Australian universities (see Asmar 2011b) and are reproduced with their permission.

[iii] The forcible removal of Aboriginal and Torres Strait Islander Australians, as children, from their families and communities by government, welfare or church authorities and their placing into institutional or foster care (see Reconciliation Australia 2012).

[iv] The Council for Aboriginal Reconciliation (2000) explains *terra nullius* thus:

> British colonisation policies and subsequent land laws were framed in the belief that the colony was being acquired by occupation (or settlement) of a terra nullius (land without owners). The colonisers acknowledged the presence of Indigenous people but justified their land acquisition policies by saying the Aborigines were too primitive to be actual owners and sovereigns.

[v] The term 'history wars' refers to 'an ongoing public debate over the interpretation of the history of the British colonisation of Australia and development of contemporary Australian society (particularly with regard to the impact on Aboriginal Australians and Torres Strait Islanders)' (History wars 2012).

[vi] The Australian Government's controversial Northern Territory National Emergency Response Act 2007, a reaction to alleged child abuse in the Northern Territory (see ABC 2012).

PART 4
FOCUS ON QUALITY AND LEADERSHIP

Government initiatives to educate more university students are commonly referred to as the 'massification' of higher education. This has coincided with reduced funding to universities, typically resulting in students being required to contribute more through tuition fees. With more students in higher education and with governments contributing a significant proportion of their national budget towards higher education, governments, university administrations and students expect there to be transparency, accountability and quality in university teaching. Further, the competition for international students has resulted in governments scrutinising university teaching standards because they seek a positive national reputation to continue to attract international students.

More than 70 countries have established quality assurance agencies to monitor the quality of tertiary education institutions and courses. As Kerri-Lee Krause observes in Chapter 14, these developments matter to university teachers because they have influenced university level processes related to quality assurance and standards. In distinguishing between quality assurance and standards, she focuses on: why the quality of teaching matters in universities; quality management frameworks; the connection between quality and standards in university teaching; and multidimensional notions of standards, including curriculum design and delivery standards, student learning outcomes and student support standards. She also explores strategies that university teachers can use to monitor quality and assure standards in the subjects and degree programs for which they are responsible, explaining how to build a portfolio of teaching achievements that will facilitate consistent quality improvement of curriculum design and delivery, and how to present evidence of good teaching practice in performance reviews and applications for promotions and teaching awards.

Universities have their own culture and expectations, including a strong research emphasis. Indeed, academic career processes such as appointment, performance appraisal and promotion may be weighted to reward research achievements to

233

the detriment of comparable achievements in teaching. Even so, the majority of western-styled universities seek evidence of teaching achievements when appraising academic careers. Accordingly, Part 4 aims to support university teachers to build their careers through an integrated approach to teaching and research. In Chapter 15, Keith Trigwell argues that the scholarship of teaching is 'about making transparent, for public scrutiny, how learning has been made possible'. He focuses on the needs of university students, arguing that the scholarship of teaching and learning 'is first about improving student learning … and second about scholarship (a systematic, peer-supported, research-like scholarly process). Together they lead to higher quality teaching.'

Paul Blackmore's discussion of leadership in Chapter 16 is an important signal for all university teachers, and particularly early career teachers, that they have a leadership role not least because they are tomorrow's leaders. In particular, he demonstrates that even small changes to promote university teaching involve some kind of leadership, observing that 'academic work is inherently an act of leadership because academics should always be at the forefront of what is being thought and done in their domains of knowledge and practice'. His research has revealed that many academics equate teaching leadership with the administration of getting teaching done rather than with change to transform students' learning. He seeks to shift this commonly held perception by focusing on leadership in teaching at university from the outset. He does this by exploring the dimensions of leadership, by demonstrating what leaders do to enable students' learning, and by showing how university teachers can learn to lead.

CHAPTER 14

A QUALITY APPROACH
TO UNIVERSITY TEACHING

Kerri-Lee Krause

Keywords
quality, quality assurance, quality enhancement, teaching standards, teaching portfolios

Introduction

The quality of teaching in universities has received increased attention over the last two decades as government-mandated accountability mechanisms, such as quality audits, have grown in importance. Governments, students, industry and the broader community now expect universities to provide evidence of the quality of their activities, including teaching and its contribution to successful student outcomes. This chapter explores some of the ways in which these developments influence your work as a teaching academic. The first section focuses on why the quality of teaching matters in higher education. It provides a brief overview of developments in the areas of quality assurance and enhancement, followed by consideration of implications for institutions and their quality management frameworks. The next section explores the connection between quality and standards in university teaching. A key part of your commitment to high-quality teaching involves monitoring and assuring standards. It is important to be aware of the multidimensional notion of standards. These dimensions include inputs, such as curriculum design standards and support standards to enhance the quality of student learning; processes, such as curriculum delivery standards; and outcomes, in the form of academic achievement. Strategies for monitoring quality and assuring standards in the units and degree programs for which you are responsible are outlined in this section.

The chapter then turns to practical ways in which you might engage with a quality approach to teaching in your day-to-day work. This section outlines strategies for gathering and documenting evidence of the quality of your teaching, including the use of different forms of evaluation and feedback from students and peers. It also addresses practical ideas for documenting evidence of good teaching as well as a case study on peer review of teaching. The final part of the chapter includes a checklist for assuring and enhancing the quality of your teaching.

Why quality matters in university teaching

Quality developments in higher education

The early 1990s marked a turning point in the intensity with which governments in the developed world focused on evidence of quality in higher education (Newton 2010). In 1990, the United States Department of Education added the requirement that higher education institutions must provide evidence of the assessment of student learning outcomes in order to meet the standards for institutional accreditation (Ewell 2010). In the United Kingdom, the Higher Education Quality Council was introduced in 1992 and became the Quality Assurance Agency for Higher Education in 1997. Similarly the Australian Government established the Committee for Quality Assurance in Higher Education in November 1992 to 'provide advice on quality assurance issues, to conduct independent audits and to make recommendations to the government on the allocation of annual quality-related funds'. The committee conducted three rounds of quality assurance reviews between 1993 and 1995 (DETYA 2000, p. 2). These developments coincided with the massification of higher education on a global scale.

There is no doubt that market forces and global financial pressures have contributed significantly to increased government scrutiny of quality processes and outcomes in higher education (Krause 2009). This includes a focus on all core business, including research, teaching and community engagement. However, as many higher education commentators note, the notion of quality in higher education is multifaceted and contested (Gibbs 2010a; Harvey & Williams 2010). Quality may be perceived differently depending on whether you are a front-line academic, a student, a government policymaker or an employer. One of the most contested quality assurance domains is that relating to measurement of the quality of teaching, accompanied by the growing imperative to provide concrete evidence of student learning outcomes (Ewell 2010) and the value that institutions add to student learning.

The common understanding of 'quality' might include concepts of excellence, consistency, value for money or fitness for purpose. On the other hand, interviews with academic staff in the disciplines suggest that many attach situated meanings to the term. These include quality as 'ritualism', 'tokenism', 'impression management' and 'lack of mutual trust' (Newton 2002, p. 46). Anderson's (2006) interviews with academic staff across 10 Australian universities revealed a similar scepticism about the notion of quality, with many interviewees observing that their institutions seemed to spend more time focusing on the quality assurance system than on the actual goal of assuring quality (p. 168). Academic staff reported resistance to quality assurance mechanisms, which they perceived to be undermining the idea of quality as excellence, replacing it with 'instrumental, minimalist' (p. 171) notions of quality. Anderson concludes that there appears to be considerable misalignment between university managers' views of quality assurance systems and those of academic staff in her study, who typically perceived these systems as being ineffective in assuring quality in practical ways.

Blackmore (2009) supports Anderson's conclusions, highlighting that generic student evaluations of teaching, in particular, are typically consumerist in their approach, concerned more with accountability and marketing than with enhancing teaching and learning. Blackmore notes the limited nature of teaching quality indicators which rely primarily on student satisfaction. Instead, she calls for alternative approaches to student evaluation of teaching that are situated in the intellectual traditions of the disciplines and that are aligned with the graduate capabilities we value so highly, such as compassion, care and a sense of social justice. To achieve these goals requires a suite of meaningful and timely measures of teaching and learning performance that Blackmore argues are not captured by simplistic student feedback tools.

Given these contested notions of quality and the tendency in some quarters to equate quality with bureaucracy, managerialism and an erosion of trust (Knight & Trowler 2000), how might academic staff engage positively and proactively with the quality agenda in the interests of their students and their own academic career paths?

Productive ways forward in a contested landscape: quality as transformation

While quality remains a contested construct with the potential to alienate and disaffect academic staff (Blackmore & Sachs 2007), there are many merits to engaging productively with the quality agenda in your institution. One positive way forward is to consider quality as a transformative process that places students at the centre of the learning process (Harvey & Green 1993). It focuses on students and academic staff working together to enhance the quality of the educational experience through strategic use of student and peer feedback to improve the curriculum and assessment.

Houston (2007) cites a study of academic staff and students' perceptions of quality processes in one New Zealand university, highlighting the mismatch between their respective views of the meaning of teaching quality. Academic staff interviewees equated quality with 'teaching well' (p. 71), though none identified measures or data to support their views. Student interviewees equated quality with staff commitment to student learning. For students, quality teaching included making expectations clear and carrying out stated learning goals. Given the potential discrepancy between staff and students' views of the quality of teaching, a further productive way forward is to discuss with your students their notions of

237

quality, what they understand quality teaching and learning to be, and how these might differ from your own views. Such conversations provide an opportunity to explore possible differences in expectations and understandings of what it means to learn and teach in university settings. These interactions may also help to clarify mutual expectations, establish respect and consolidate learning partnerships. These activities exemplify a commitment to improving the quality of your teaching and of student learning, and they should be integral to your practice.

While accountability and quality assurance mechanisms have a role to play in higher education, there is value in extending the notion of quality to include quality enhancement and the improvement of learning and teaching. Quality assurance tends to concentrate on accountability and evidence of the effectiveness of the educational process (Brink 2010), while quality enhancement is concerned with making improvements. For some academics, quality assurance and quality enhancement are seen almost as antithetical rather than complementary concepts. According to Middlehurst (1997), however, quality enhancement is part of a wider framework in which quality control, quality assurance, quality enhancement and transformation are stages in the management of quality.

Engaging with quality as transformation requires a partnership among all parts of the institution (Krause 2011b). This is a systems approach to the use of data – such as student evaluations of teaching – to enhance quality. In your academic work, you will need to engage with your university's quality assurance reporting requirements and to comply with student feedback processes.

At the same time, the institution has a part to play in supporting you with timely access to data – both quantitative and qualitative – and with professional development resources to assist you to analyse and interpret these data for the purposes of quality improvement. With the support of your institution, you can go beyond a focus on compliance by taking purposeful steps to improve the quality of your students' learning. This commitment to enhancing the quality of students' experiences and outcomes is central to providing an empowering and transformative approach to quality for you, your colleagues and your students. The key is to integrate these two perspectives into your personal plan for quality assurance and enhancement of your teaching and curriculum practice.

Connecting quality and standards in learning and teaching

The connection between quality and standards in tertiary learning and teaching is an important one. The name of Australia's new tertiary regulator – the Tertiary Education Quality and Standards Agency (TEQSA) – represents a timely reminder of the inter-relatedness of the two constructs. The Universities UK guide to quality and standards distinguishes between the two concepts as follows:

> Academic 'quality' describes the effectiveness of the learning experience provided by universities to their students, i.e., the appropriateness and effectiveness of learning, teaching, assessment and support opportunities provided to assist students achieve their learning objectives ... Academic 'standards' describe the level of achievement (i.e., threshold) that a student has to reach to gain a particular degree or other academic award.
>
> (Universities UK 2008, p. 23)

Standards, then, are the 'benchmark by which quality can be judged' (Brink 2010, p. 142). Just as quality is a contested area, so too is the issue of standards in higher education. Brink (2010, pp. 143–144) raises several 'difficult issues' relating to standards. These include the issue of who makes judgements about standards and how one compares quality and standards between different universities and over time. The issue of academic standards in higher education is a highly politicised matter. In 2009, the UK House of Commons Select Committee produced a report that was critical of existing approaches for protecting quality and standards in UK higher education. Issues such as grade inflation and the comparability of standards between institutions were among the concerns expressed. As a result, quality assurance arrangements across the UK were reviewed, though the jury is out with respect to the impact of these new arrangements (Brown 2010). This example provides a salutary reminder of the high stakes around the monitoring and assuring of standards in higher education and, indeed, in your own teaching and subject or program delivery.

Accreditation and standards

A number of mechanisms currently exist for assuring standards in university learning and teaching. Many of these will affect you directly. For instance, on a national and international level, discipline-based accreditations in such areas as business, nursing, teaching and engineering represent objective, expert endorsement that:

> a professional preparation course meets the needs of a particular profession; that the course is able to produce graduates who reach standards for entry to the profession, and are therefore competent to begin practice. Accreditation is a key mechanism for assuring the quality of preparation courses in the professions.
>
> (Ingvarson et al., 2006, p. 1)

In the disciplines of business and accounting, for example, the Association to Advance Collegiate Schools of Business (AACSB) is an international accrediting body with standards that were first adopted in 1919 and have progressively been revised to 'ensure quality and continuous improvement in collegiate business education'. In order to secure AACSB accreditation, business schools are required to demonstrate that they meet accreditation standards in three domains: strategic management standards, participant standards and assurance of learning standards (AACSB 2011).

Similarly in the discipline of engineering, Engineers Australia (2011) accredits all undergraduate engineering programs, ensuring that 'academic institutions consistently meet national and international benchmarks':

> The primary objectives of the accreditation process are the maintenance of internationally benchmarked standards, the promotion and dissemination of best practice and the stimulation of innovation and diversity in engineering education. Assessment of any particular academic program for accreditation is based on the following criteria:
> * the teaching and learning environment
> * the structure and content of the program
> * the quality assurance framework.

Likewise, in the field of nursing, a suite of registration standards defines the requirements to be met in order for students to be registered with the Nursing and Midwifery Board of Australia (2011). In the area of teacher education, the Australian Institute for Teaching and School Leadership (2011a) has published national professional standards for teachers, comprising seven standards outlining what teachers should know and be able to do (p. 3). In addition to these individual level standards, a suite of national program standards outlines a framework for standards in teacher education programs across Australia (2011b).

Alternative approaches for monitoring and assuring standards

While external accreditation bodies represent one external reference point for making judgements about academic achievement standards, there are several other points of reference that should be considered as you seek to monitor and assure standards within the subjects and degree programs for which you are responsible. External reference points that you might consider as you design and deliver your curriculum and assessment tasks might include:
* the Australian Qualifications Framework (Australian Qualifications Framework Council 2011)
* the Australian Learning and Teaching Council discipline-specific academic standards (2010)
* feedback from employers
* input from external degree program advisory committees and reference groups
* your university's graduate attributes
* the results of school or department reviews

- benchmarking of subject and program content with comparable universities nationally and internationally
- student feedback and survey data, both quantitative and qualitative.

In addition to these reference points, you may monitor your students' academic achievement outcomes through the use of internal moderation of assessment items with colleagues who teach in the same subject, or through external inter-university moderation. Krause, Scott and colleagues (2011) are trialling a sector-wide model for assuring final year subject and program achievement standards through inter-university moderation across nine disciplines. There are several other Australian examples of discipline experts – for instance in law (Kift & Israel 2011) and accounting (Freeman 2011) – pilot-testing approaches to providing evidence that standards are being monitored and assured within and across universities. International strategies include the Tuning USA project (American Council on Education 2010), which seeks to 'define what students must know, understand, and be able to demonstrate after completing a degree in a specific field', and the Assessment of Higher Education Learning Outcomes project (OECD 2011b), which involves a feasibility study test of what students in higher education know and can do upon graduation. It involves assessing student performance in a range of areas including generic skills and discipline-specific skills in economics and engineering, in the first instance. In the UK, the external examiner system represents another model for monitoring and assuring standards across the sector (Universities UK 2011).

Within your institution, you will be involved in annual monitoring of the quality and standards of subjects for which you are responsible. Many universities also include three- to five-yearly reviews of degree programs. These usually include external discipline experts who review the quality and standards of your program against a range of indicators, including comparative analyses of retention, progression, overall student satisfaction, graduation and employability rates. As part of your teaching quality assurance and enhancement plan, it is a good idea to become familiar with these data early on. Be sure to keep records of relevant data and to track them over time in order to assist with reporting when required.

A framework for assuring standards in learning, teaching and curriculum design

Just as quality comprises several dimensions, so the construct of standards in higher education is multidimensional. The University of Western Sydney in Australia has mapped these dimensions as part of its quality management framework (see Figure 14.1).

241

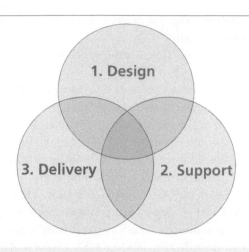

Curriculum design standards: includes evidence of alignment between learning objectives, graduate attributes and assessment; relevant and up-to-date content; clear assessment criteria and feedback mechanisms; active learning activities; online resources available and use of blended learning to enhance learning and flexible access; evidence of alignment with external reference points and disciplinary standards.

Support standards: refers to a range of support mechanisms that are objectively evaluated and expected to meet threshold standards. This may include student orientation programs, library support, unit outlines and learning guides, learning management system support, peer support programs for students, learning support. Support standards also include evidence of rigorous staff recruitment, training programs and support roles in the form of First Year Advisor and Program Leader.

Delivery standards: includes evidence of staff accessibility, responsiveness and skills; consistency and quality of curriculum delivery of provision of support for students (as outlined in support standards above). Evidence of consistency and quality may be shown through benchmarking, peer review and moderation within the university and between institutions.

Impact and outcome indicators: includes evidence of achievement of academic achievement standards through benchmarking and moderation, validation of assessment outcomes, retention, student progression, employability, industry feedback and further study.

Institutional quality management system

FIGURE 14.1. University of Western Sydney Learning and Teaching Standards Framework (adapted from University of Western Sydney 2011, p. 23)

This framework is particularly instructive for highlighting how partnerships across the institution and among academic and professional staff throughout the learning enterprise ultimately contribute to positive student outcomes (Krause 2011a).

Figure 14.1 highlights that standards are inherent in each stage of the learning process, from curriculum design through to curriculum delivery and support for learning. Each phase is interconnected and contributes in some way to the impact of the learning experience, as evidenced by students' achievement outcomes.

The framework is not designed to be prescriptive; rather, it provides an indicative outline of the value of monitoring and maintaining standards at each stage of the learning process through a combination of inputs, processes, outputs and outcomes in relation to student learning. The framework complements the work of Chalmers (2007), who highlights the value of identifying indicators of quality teaching and learning in such areas as assessment, engagement, learning community, diversity and inclusivity. These quality areas align with the University of Western Sydney's emphasis on the design, support and delivery of learning and teaching. Together, these quality dimensions have an impact on student learning outcomes, as evidenced through such indicators as overall student satisfaction, moderated and benchmarked academic achievement standards, progression to further study and positive employability rates.

Documenting teaching quality and monitoring standards: some practical strategies

Gathering and documenting evidence of teaching quality and ways in which you assure standards is central to academic work. It is important for university teachers at all stages of their career to document their teaching development and achievements for such purposes as performance review meetings and promotion. Evidence of success in the research domain is determined through well-defined criteria including the number of refereed journal articles published and the amount of external competitive funding received. However, evidence of excellence and success in teaching is often more complex to define and document. As a starting point, your evidence base may include the following (adapted from McAlpine & Harris 2002):

- subject matter expertise
- skills in curriculum and assessment design
- skills in classroom teaching, lecturing and student advising
- management and organisational skills
- mentoring and supervision of colleagues, graduate students and students in practical or professional workplace settings
- personal and professional development intended to enhance your teaching practice
- departmental development that enhances teaching policies and practices at department level
- contribution to the wider community through teaching and sharing of expertise beyond the university.

Planning your approach to teaching quality assurance

As you develop your plan for quality assurance and enhancement in teaching, consult with your supervisor, mentors and experienced teachers in your department. Look for resources to guide you and talk with colleagues in your university's teaching and learning unit (or equivalent). Adopt a purposeful approach to documenting teaching quality. An electronic or paper-based portfolio is a useful mechanism for gathering and documenting your evidence (Seldin 2006). Organise your portfolio of materials in a manner that makes it as easy as possible to trace your development and to track your progress.

You might find the widely used plan, implement, review and improve (PIRI) cycle a useful model to guide your practice as part of a continuous improvement strategy. It comprises the following steps:

- plan your curriculum or a particular initiative or innovation you wish to trial
- implement the plan and gather data in a range of ways, including from students and peers
- review the success of your initiative and consider areas for further enhancement, as you repeat the process
- improve your practice.

Evaluating your teaching

There are several methods available for evaluating the quality of teaching. It is worth taking time to find out more about these and how they might suit your purposes and disciplinary context. This section explores two of the most commonly used approaches: student feedback in the form of surveys, and peer feedback in the form of peer review and observation of teaching. Those who wish to read further in this area may refer to Knapper and Cranton (2001) and Seldin (2006). Both of these resources provide practical strategies associated with teaching portfolios, conducting self-review and evaluations of your teaching, and the value of formative evaluation in your practice.

Gathering student feedback

Blackmore cautions that 'standardised teaching evaluations encourage lecturers to focus on the narrow range of outcomes that are measurable, on style rather than substance, to minimise the discomfort by reducing contentious readings and watering down substance to produce "thin" pedagogies' (Blackmore 2009, p. 868). For this reason it is important to consider the use of student feedback as but one source of data. Nevertheless, it is a valuable source of information and one on which governments and institutions rely heavily. Despite the recognised limitations of student surveys (Halonen & Ellenberg 2006), these forms of feedback can be instructive, particularly when the feedback is provided in a mutually respectful culture in which students receive 'feedback on their feedback'. In other words, student feedback on teaching – whether quantitative or qualitative – is more likely to be taken seriously if students know that their feedback is analysed and acted upon. This does not mean that all their requests – or even demands – are necessarily met. However, it does mean that a feedback loop is evident in subject outlines, in-class feedback or teachers responding to student comments as part of an ongoing dialogue of quality improvement. This may be achieved through relatively informal mechanisms at the beginning or end of lectures, or formally as part of each semester's subject outline or website. Closing the loop with students helps to develop a culture of quality that encourages meaningful student feedback and engagement.

In addition to the mandated university surveys on student evaluation of teaching and units, there are many other forms of student feedback that may assist you in evaluating your teaching. Table 14.1 summarises some of the main instruments designed to gather data on students' learning experiences in different contexts and for a range of purposes.

TABLE 14.1 Student survey types, purposes and typical levels of application (Krause 2011b, p. 62)

Survey type	Purpose	Typical levels of application
Student evaluation of teaching/subject	Summative student evaluation of a subject/ unit, focusing on day-to-day experiences of a particular teacher or teaching team, typically conducted at the end of a teaching session. Locally developed formative instruments are also used to supplement summative data.	Individual and/ or teaching team, subject/unit
Student evaluation of degree program (e.g., Course Experience Questionnaire (CEQ))	Students' retrospective evaluation of whole-of-program experiences (e.g., CEQ: conducted post graduation)	Degree program within or across departments or faculties
Student satisfaction surveys (e.g., National Student Survey, UK (NSS))	Students' evaluation of the overall experience of higher education, including extra-curricular dimensions (e.g., NSS: distributed to final year students). Institutionally developed satisfaction surveys are also used to target specific issues (e.g., satisfaction with information technology provision or student services)	Institution-level, national
Targeted student experience and engagement surveys (e.g., Australian Survey of Student Engagement (AUSSE), First Year Experience Questionnaire (FYEQ))	Students document behaviours, experiences within and beyond the formal curriculum and amount of time spent on study-related and other (e.g., paid work) activities (e.g., AUSSE: distributed to first and third year students; FYEQ: distributed to first year students)	Institution-level, national, international

For a more detailed discussion of types and purposes of student surveys and how they might be used to enhance the quality of learning and teaching, see Krause (2011b) and Barrie, Ginns and Symons (2008). In addition to student feedback surveys, you may also consider the use of student focus groups to gather qualitative feedback. In some cases, it may be desirable to invite a colleague or a research assistant to conduct these interviews in order to provide some distance between yourself and the interviewees. It is important to look for complementary sources of data and feedback on your teaching. These range from informal methods, such as talking with students after class or via email, to formal mechanisms, such as surveying. As you demonstrate to your students that you are committed to creating the best possible learning experience and outcomes for them, this will contribute to a culture of quality and respect in your teaching practice. It may take time to foster this culture and not all students will contribute positively, but your commitment to quality improvement will be evident and valued.

Peer review of teaching

Complementary to student feedback mechanisms is a growing emphasis on the use of peer feedback on teaching and curriculum design and delivery. Many universities now recognise the value of peer review as a valid component of teaching evaluation strategies and several projects in the Australian higher education sector have yielded valuable practical resources on the subject (see for example Harris et al. 2008; Crisp et al. 2009).

CASE 14.1   PEER REVIEW AND OBSERVATION OF TEACHING PROJECT
Dr Steve Drew, Griffith University

Dr Steve Drew leads the Peer Review and Observation of Teaching Project as a developmental resource for academic colleagues, dubbed 'PRO-Teaching' (literally: 'for' teaching). He recognised the dangers of associating peer review with judgemental behaviours that might deter academics from participating. Yet he also understood that observation notes from 'buddies' are often not acceptable to promotions committees as evidence of quality and achievement.

To address these challenges, he developed a pilot project in the education faculty, then in science, environment, engineering and technology discipline areas at Griffith University, comprising collaborative, developmental peer review of teaching, using protocols that engage academics in two action-learning cycles at least two weeks apart. Academics undertake training prior to their engagement in order to become familiar with the process and the instruments used.

The PRO-Teaching process begins with an academic staff member volunteering to participate. An observation team is assembled comprising a discipline expert from the same school as the teacher under observation and a teaching and learning expert from a different area of the university. The mix of relevant discipline knowledge and recognised teaching and learning expertise provides a balanced range of views and ideas.

The observation team attend one of the teacher's classes. At the end of the session student volunteers are invited to submit anonymous written feedback in the form of a teaching and learning 'minute paper' (as part of the process, volunteers also complete an informed consent form). Observers complete the peer feedback form and the teacher records his or her reflections.

The team meets soon after the session to consider key questions such as:

- What do you think went well?
- What do you think you would do differently?
- How do you think you might improve ... ?
- Were there any aspects that you did not feel confident about?

The observers then share their observations in a factual yet sensitive manner. A commonly used approach is to first summarise the strengths of the observed session, then discuss any perceived points for improvement.

The focus is on peer-to-peer interaction and on sharing knowledge. Enthusiasm and the interplay with discipline-based and learning and teaching colleagues can be central to reducing perceived threat or criticism and to increasing the likelihood of quality improvement in teaching practices.

A friendly, personal approach to engaging academics' involvement and to deal immediately with their questions and remove perceived roadblocks to their participation is of paramount importance. Evaluation to improve the peer review process is undertaken each semester using a plan, implement, review and improve (PIRI) cycle to collect data from participant experiences, student perceptions and project reference group input. The evidence of quality teaching generated by peer review can be used to support teaching award, promotion and job applications.

CASE 14.2   PEER REVIEW IN ONLINE ENVIRONMENTS
(Swinglehurst et al. 2008)

Swinglehurst et al. (2008) have investigated the challenges of peer observations of teaching in online environments using online focus groups as part of an action research framework. While participants agreed that many of the principles of effective teaching were common in both face-to-face and online contexts, they acknowledged that one of the unique characteristics of effective online teaching was the ability to engender trust in an otherwise potentially remote and impersonal learning environment. The sense of teacher 'presence' emerged as a distinctive quality of engaging online teaching. The researchers in this study highlight the importance of clarifying the purpose of peer review and observation of teaching: is it for monitoring and evaluation (i.e., quality assurance) or for reflection on practice and staff development (i.e., quality enhancement)? (p. 390) These are valuable issues to clarify, along with the importance of adapting evaluation strategies to learning modes and teaching contexts.

Documenting your teaching achievements

While it is important to gather a range of data on the quality of your teaching and on the outcomes of student learning, it is equally important to document these data methodically. This process represents an important part of your teaching quality enhancement strategy as you trace developments and improvements over time. The documented evidence also forms a valuable record of your achievements for such purposes as performance review and promotion. Six strategies are suggested. You may wish to adapt these according to your career stage, your discipline and your individual teaching and learning goals.

1. Articulate your teaching philosophy:
- Develop a brief introductory statement of your intentions as a teacher in higher education. This statement may evolve over time as you teach in different contexts and develop more expertise.

2. Keep systematic records of your teaching, course reviews, leadership and service:
- Keep a record of subjects taught and of learning and teaching materials developed.
- Include student numbers, teaching mode and resources you design such as subject notes, student workbooks or problem sheets.
- Systematically collect and respond to student evaluations of subjects and teaching.
- Keep copies of evaluations for future purposes. For each set of evaluations, document what you have done and any improvements made in response to feedback.
- Comment on the currency of your curriculum content and learning objectives. How and when do you review content and learning objectives? What are your sources for benchmarking?

3. Describe how you implement a student-centred approach to teaching:
- Reflect on your availability to students and strategies for connecting with students.
- Document the strategies you employed to facilitate student contact and advising.

- Keep a record of your students' accomplishments beyond the classroom.
- Make a note of students' professional or research achievements, awards and publications.
- Document your strategies for working with individual students or special student groups. How do you cater for international students, students with disabilities or students from diverse cultural backgrounds?
- Document approaches to providing student feedback. When and how do you provide feedback to students and what is the impact of this approach?

4. List examples of scholarship in your discipline and in learning and teaching:
- Provide evidence of your scholarly approach to teaching. This may include your research into learning and teaching or evidence-based approaches that inform curriculum design or implementation of priority areas.
- Document professional development you have undertaken, including courses completed, conferences attended or online professional development.
- Articulate how and why you use technology in your teaching. What impact has the use of information and communication technology had on student learning, attitudes and outcomes? Have colleagues reviewed your use of technology? What are their views?
- List your conference papers and research publications related to learning and teaching. Include reference to formal feedback and recognition from peers.
- Keep track of all awards, citations and invitations to speak on teaching – for example, 'My national reputation as a teacher is evident in the regular invitations I receive to ... '
- Include findings from evaluations and comment on actions taken in response to these. This could include student surveys, peer review, observations and self-review.

5. Outline innovations you have developed in your teaching:
- Document innovations in teaching or grants received for innovation.
- Outline successful applications for funds to address issues in relation to student learning in your discipline.
- Comment on how you achieve teaching–research links in your practice.
- Outline your strategies for ensuring that students benefit from your disciplinary research program.
- Describe how you have adapted curriculum to address the learning and teaching priorities of the university, as appropriate.
- Explain how you have adapted curriculum to include international perspectives or blended learning approaches.

6. Describe examples of your leadership in learning and teaching:
- Identify your leadership in teaching in the discipline. Provide details of any textbooks you have written or to which you have contributed. Who uses them? How many universities? What is their international distribution?
- Document your influence on the departmental context (and beyond). Outline any changes you have influenced in programming and operations in your department.
- Document subjects and programs designed, reviewed and revised.
- Look for opportunities to demonstrate leadership. Document your role in developing new subjects or programs in your discipline. Outline your strategies and achievements in initiating change in teaching, curriculum design and academic culture in your department.
- Document your postgraduate supervision responsibilities. List the number of students you have supervised and the outcomes of their research in terms of completions and publications.

To summarise this section on documenting your teaching achievements (adapted from Krause et al. 2008):
- View your documentary evidence as an argument and a narrative – tell the story of your teaching and its development. Provide compelling evidence.
- With regard to your contribution to teaching, focus not only on the scope, quality and effectiveness of your work but also the increasing sophistication of your contribution. Trace the increasing complexity of the tasks, document the leadership demonstrated, and identify the growing knowledge base required.
- Keep returning to your main theme or organising principle – aim to bring coherence to your argument.
- Strategically select supporting evidence and examples and be sure to keep documenting your evidence in a methodical, easy-to-access way each semester.

Conclusion

This chapter has explored issues and strategies designed to assist you in enhancing the quality of your university teaching. The following checklist (Table 14.2) draws together many of the key messages of the chapter. It may be a useful reference point as you develop your strategies for quality assurance and enhancement in your teaching practice.

TABLE 14.2 Checklist to develop strategies for quality assurance and enhancement of teaching practice

Strategies		Check box
Make connections with the people, policies and processes of your institution	• Attend induction sessions to find out more about the institution, its mission, its values and its approach to quality assurance and improvement.	☐
	• Find out about teaching communities of practice and opportunities for improving the quality of your practice through professional development.	☐
Familiarise yourself with your institution's quality framework and its implications for you	• Locate your institution's policies relating to the quality of teaching, including the promotion policy, policies on subject and program review and institutional expectations regarding student evaluations of teaching. How often do you need to evaluate? What are the institutional expectations of your teaching performance?	☐
Develop your personal teaching quality assurance and improvement plan	• Before the academic year begins, develop a big-picture plan for assuring and improving the quality of your teaching. This will include: ◊ addressing the minimum institutional expectations on teaching quality assurance, including regular use of student feedback surveys ◊ supplementing these with other forms of feedback such as peer review of your teaching and formative student feedback strategies to improve your practice ◊ gathering peer feedback on your teaching 'inputs' including curriculum and assessment design at subject and/or program level ◊ engaging in assessment moderation as part of your commitment to assuring academic achievement standards in your subject or program.	☐
	• Consider working with a mentor as part of your strategy. Some institutions allocate mentors to early career academic staff but if this is not the case for you, speak with your supervisor to find out more about mentoring opportunities.	☐

→

TABLE 14.2 (continued)

Document the outcomes of your teaching quality assurance and enhancement plan	• Develop a simple, methodical system for keeping records of your teaching evaluation and improvement activities, including student and peer feedback on your teaching, along with your teaching achievements. This may take the form of a paper-based or electronic portfolio or similar.	☐
	• Keep a record of your teaching evaluation and feedback data each year. This may include: 　◊　an analysis of quantitative and qualitative student feedback – both formative and summative 　◊　feedback from peers – including the outcomes of peer observations of your teaching, feedback from your supervisor and from your mentor.	☐
	• Document the strategies you have used to gather evidence each year.	☐
	• Track developments and improvements in your teaching, including improvements in students' overall satisfaction in your teaching, as well as enhancements and achievements noted by peers, your supervisor or senior managers.	☐
	• Consider taking your teaching evaluation activities one step further by writing them up for a conference paper or journal article as part of your engagement in the scholarship of learning and teaching.	☐
Close the loop on teaching evaluations with your students	• Let your students know the outcomes of their feedback – for instance, if you make changes to your practices or to the subject content or assessment based on their feedback, tell your students about it. They will appreciate knowing that their feedback has made a difference.	☐
Benchmark and network with professional associations and colleagues	• Look for opportunities to work with disciplinary colleagues in other universities as a way to peer review your subject or program curriculum design, assessment and teaching practice.	☐
	• You may extend inter-university collaboration to more formal benchmarking of your subject content and assessment items through inter-university peer review and moderation. These are invaluable opportunities to monitor the quality of your teaching and curriculum design and to assure standards.	☐
	• Where relevant, document your contribution to benchmarking and moderation to demonstrate a growing body of evidence of your leadership in teaching.	☐
Engage with quality and standards issues beyond your institution	• Keep up-to-date on national developments and debates on enhancing quality and assuring standards in tertiary education and their implications for your teaching.	☐

CHAPTER 15

SCHOLARSHIP OF TEACHING AND LEARNING

Keith Trigwell

Keywords
improving student learning, SoTL, scholarship of teaching and learning, standards of scholarship, scholarly investigation

---

CASE 15.1   TRIALLING A NEW APPROACH TO ENGAGING STUDENTS

When grappling with the dilemma of how to encourage her students to be more engaged with her subject matter, Miranda picked up an idea from the start of a TV program. It began with three people talking about their experience of the topic of the program. She wondered if she could ask a student, mid-way through each teaching session, to present a scenario that showed how they thought her topic was of relevance to them (and other students). She drafted an outline of how it might work – how the students would be selected, what notice they would be given, how long they would be asked to talk in each class, what she expected to happen and why? Before trying it she sent a copy by email to an experienced colleague. She explained that she thought the student experience would be enhanced because they may be able to connect more with the topic if they experienced it as being more relevant. Her colleague agreed to observe her using the idea and on judging it to have been successful, suggested she write up a two-page outline of the process as a teaching tip.

This is the first of five cases in this chapter that are illustrative examples of forms of the scholarship of teaching and learning (SoTL). In this case, Miranda is engaging at a basic level, but one that includes the key elements of SoTL. She has an idea of how to improve learning using the concepts of relevance and links to prior experience; she describes to a colleague how she hopes to help make learning happen in the subject; and the colleague peer reviews (observes) the idea in practice. Adopting the process improves her teaching and her students' learning and leads to an artefact (a teaching tips sheet) which creates the possibility of the idea being adopted by other teachers in their own context.

While being simplistic, the form of scholarship described here may lead to a greater enhancement in student learning than the effects of most research papers in the leading education research journals. The scholarship of teaching and learning is first about improving student learning (mostly enacted through teaching) and second about scholarship (a systematic, peer-supported, research-like scholarly processes). Together they lead to higher quality teaching.

The scholarship described in most research journals is about making transparent the scholarly processes used to reach the reported research conclusions through a publicly available artefact that can be scrutinised by the peers of the researchers. This perspective is similar to the ways Shulman (1987) describes scholarship and it applies both to research and to the scholarship of teaching and learning. Andresen (2000) sees a scholarly process as involving personal, but rigorous, intellectual development, inquiry and action built on values such as honesty, integrity, open-mindedness, scepticism and intellectual humility. This also applies to scholarly work in teaching. So if teaching involves a scholarly process aimed at making learning possible, it follows that the scholarship of teaching is about making transparent, for public scrutiny, how learning has been made possible (Trigwell et al. 2000; Trigwell & Shale 2004). It is this process that is described and illustrated in this chapter.

Making transparent how learning is being made possible means describing how it is intended that learning will happen, and gathering evidence to show that learning is happening, or that an intervention is working. Alternatively, the evidence may be gathered to make transparent why intended learning may not be happening, as shown in Case 15.2.

CASE 15.2   RESEARCHING EXPLANATIONS FOR POOR STUDENT PERFORMANCE

After observing an unusually poor performance by students in the mid-semester test in their second-year law subject, Suzanne and James decided to search for reasons why. They noted that the students' answers were listings of facts, lacking internal logic and the required argument, and generally illustrative of a poor understanding. In a teaching program James had completed nearly 20 years earlier, he was introduced to the work of Perry (1970) who showed how students develop intellectually through a degree program, and how in the early years many were more likely to see knowledge as being about facts and factual accuracy rather than a consideration of a range of positions and making a case for the 'best one'. Thinking that slow development might be an explanation for the students' results, Suzanne and James consulted with the Centre for Academic Development in their university to ask how they might check this hypothesis. The advice they received was that this was unlikely to be the reason, but that Suzanne and James could look for this or other explanations by interviewing a group of current students. They decided to use a nominal group technique (a group discussion method) with nine students who volunteered to participate, and they asked 'What are the issues that are related to your learning progress this semester?' It quickly became clear that almost all the students identified a curriculum clash as the reason for their poor test performance, as a subject they were taking in parallel had newly introduced a group project and presentation task with a high assessment weighting, timetabled over the month leading up to the time of the mid-semester test. Suzanne and James drafted a note to the Teaching and Learning Committee containing three years of test results, a summary of students' comments and a conclusion requesting that the department establish a coordinator to oversee assessment of the program as a whole. The committee were convinced by the argument and established the position. The changes resulted in improved student learning.

The process of SoTL

The first two cases, though basic in the nature of their inquiry, focus squarely on improving learning in a local (their own) context. Both cases also illustrate the key components that constitute the SoTL procedure.

The scholarship of teaching and learning, as a process, usually starts with an idea of *how* student learning might be enhanced (or made possible), and often develops through a six-step process:

- using a theory, model, framework or possibly even a substantial teaching tip to ground the initiative and provide the justification for action
- identifying an intervention designed to enhance learning, or a current practice thought to be affecting learning, or a collection of information that might lead to enhanced learning (the approaches identified are usually derived from the model or theory)
- formulating an investigative question related to teaching and/or student learning in the chosen context
- conducting an investigation (empirical, theoretical or literature-based) designed to address the question
- producing a result and some form of public artefact
- inviting peer review on the clarity of each of the theory, practice, question, method and result steps of the procedure.

There are clear parallels between this process and those that many of you will be familiar with from your own research programs. In this sense there is integration between research and teaching with the skills and ways of thinking used in high-quality research providing a substantial platform from which to build an evidence base for effective student learning.

Like good research, SoTL relies on the use of a framework, model or theory to drive the directions of change, observation and interpretation. Several examples of suitable models are used in the five cases in this chapter. In Case 15.1, Miranda's relevance intervention could be seen as the application of cognition research, which emphasises the importance of linking new knowledge with prior understanding and of exploring relationships between the two. In Case 15.2, Suzanne and James see the work of Perry as a possible explanation for their observations, and while the explanation turned out to be more about relations between workloads and learning, it served as a way of framing their investigation. The ideas of constructive alignment and student learning models are used in the more substantial examples of SoTL in Cases 15.3 and 15.5. Getting started with SoTL means finding one or more models of teaching/learning that suit your own ways of thinking about university teaching in your context. The 'Understanding learning: theories and critique' chapter in this book contains many ideas (see Chapter 1, Stewart 2012).

A more complete case of SoTL, illustrating the full procedure and the ways of thinking described above, is presented in Case 15.3.

The scholarship of teaching and learning is as much about a way of thinking about teaching and learning as a practice. Table 15.1 contains 10 items from a scholarship of teaching and learning questionnaire. If you would like to check your progress in SoTL thinking and practice, note whether you agree or disagree with these statements, or whether (in some cases) you don't know.

TABLE 15.1   Items from a Scholarship of Teaching and Learning questionnaire

Scholarship of Teaching and Learning item	Disagree	Agree	Don't know
I often ask other teachers to comment on my teaching ideas.			
I find the literature about teaching and learning useful in teaching my subjects.			
I often investigate questions related to how students learn in my discipline.			
I usually try to make public my innovative teaching ideas.			
My main aim in investigating teaching is to improve my students' learning.			
I usually try to share my scholarly teaching and learning ideas with my students.			
I usually try to find a theory or framework on teaching to work with when thinking about teaching in my subjects.			
In developing my teaching, an improvement in student learning is at least as important an outcome, as a journal article.			
I usually participate in conferences, meetings or courses about teaching and learning.			
I can explain what concepts, models or theories underpin my thoughts about teaching.			

Most university teachers who are active in SoTL respond by agreeing with all 10 statements.

A more complete case of SoTL, illustrating the full procedure and the ways of thinking described above, is presented in Case 15.3.

CASE 15.3 CONSTRUCTIVE ALIGNMENT

Li, a lecturer in engineering, has been introduced to the idea of constructive alignment (Biggs 1996; Biggs & Tang 2007). Constructive alignment is achieved when students perceive that what is being assessed is in alignment with the intended learning outcomes and the teaching/learning activities designed to achieve those outcomes. Li notices that the learning activities she provides are mostly passive, and not aligned with the actual engineering problems students address in the assessments. She decides to introduce inquiry-based learning and adopts an approach in which students work through five inquiry stages (asking, investigating, creating, discussing, reflecting) on a range of engineering issues (Sincero 2006). Her own scholarly inquiry question is holistic: What is the experience (locally) of my students, myself and my peers, and more broadly as described by other engineering teachers using inquiry-based learning? This approach is informed by Brookfield's four lenses (1995) in which the outcomes of reflections from four perspectives (students, peers, self and literature) are integrated to give a more holistic analysis. Li invites her colleagues to participate in the change process and seeks their feedback. She surveys the students for their response and does a critical self-review that includes thinking about her own satisfaction with the process. On consulting the literature, she notes that Friedman et al. (2010) report a trial of inquiry-based learning in engineering in which student learning was shown to be enhanced. Together with three of her peers, she drafts a teaching grant application to extend the inquiry-based learning idea to the teaching contexts of her three peers. The grant application is supported.

As in Cases 15.1 and 15.2, the focus of Li's work in Case 15.3 is on the learning of her students, though in this case she also has in mind her own satisfaction in teaching as an outcome. The other five SoTL procedures are all present. She uses constructive alignment as the concept behind the learning improvement plan, and changing the teaching/learning activity as the means of achievement. She addresses her investigation question using a process of multi-source reflection based on Brookfield's four lenses, and shows that learning is being made possible through inquiry-based learning. The artefacts of the process are a new subject description and a teaching grant application. Peer review is attained through the endorsement of her peers and the funding of their application by the teaching grants committee.

This view of the scholarship of teaching and learning is described by Shulman as follows:

Our work as teachers should meet the highest scholarly standards of groundedness, of openness, of clarity and complexity. But, it is only when we step back and reflect systematically on the teaching we have done ... in a form that can be publicly reviewed and built upon by our peers, that we have moved from scholarly teaching to a scholarship of teaching.

(Shulman 2004, p. 166)

In Case 15.3 (as in the first two cases) and in Shulman's description, no mention has been made of refereed publication as the artefact or outcome, and yet the scholarship of teaching and learning as presented above meets the standards of all scholarly work, as described by the Carnegie Foundation's six standards of scholarship (Table 15.2). Having a focus on student learning rather than external (journal) publication does not mean scholarship is not involved. What the Carnegie Foundation's standards suggest is that the focus on improving learning involves the same high-quality thinking, rigorous processes, critical self-reflection and peer review as are found in approaches to research.

TABLE 15.2 The Carnegie Foundation's six standards of scholarship (Glassick et al. 1997, p. 36. Reproduced with permission of John Wiley & Sons, Inc.)

Carnegie goals	Standards
Clear goals	Does the scholar state the basic purposes of his or her work clearly? Does the scholar define objectives that are realistic and achievable? Does the scholar identify important questions in the field?
Adequate preparation	Does the scholar show an understanding of existing scholarship in the field? Does the scholar bring the necessary skills to his or her work? Does the scholar bring together the resources necessary to move the project forward?
Appropriate methods	Does the scholar use methods appropriate to the goals? Does the scholar apply effectively the methods selected? Does the scholar modify procedures in response to changing circumstances?
Significant results	Does the scholar achieve the goals? Does the scholar's work add consequentially to the field? Does the scholar's work open additional areas for further exploration?
Effective presentation	Does the scholar use a suitable style and effective organisation to present his or her work? Does the scholar use appropriate forums for communicating work to its intended audiences? Does the scholar present her or his message with clarity and integrity?
Reflective critique	Does the scholar critically evaluate his or her own work? Does the scholar bring an appropriate breadth of evidence to his or her critique? Does the scholar use evaluation to improve the quality of future work?

CASE 15.4   LITERATURE REVIEW TO INFORM LARGE-CLASS TEACHING

On returning to work after the summer break, Raphael found that he had been asked to coordinate and teach the large first-year subject in his politics department. As the idea of 'large' in his department means about 1000 students, he decided he needed to explore the consequences for student learning of such a big group. He approached the task through a synthesis of the research literature, seeking an answer to the question: Is class size related to the quality of outcomes of learning? He found that most of the early literature (from around 1960 to 1980) concluded that the consequences for student learning were more dire as the class size increased. However, the recent literature tended towards an 'it depends' conclusion. Large classes can be effective learning environments if they are taught using student-centred approaches. He wrote an overview of the literature, and extracted the information on student-centred teaching that he considered would be useful in teaching his own first-year group. He concluded that if he used a range of approaches described in the literature there did not need to be any significant diminution of learning quality. The literature review and the extracted elements used to inform the changes he made to his teaching were accepted by his colleagues as being a useful departmental teaching resource.

Knowledge outcomes

These four cases of SoTL describe the types of activities many university teachers do as part of their normal practice in attempts to improve their teaching and the learning of their students. In essence they all encapsulate a student-focused approach to teaching (Prosser & Trigwell 1999). The inquiry and peer review elements so familiar to academic staff in their research role is what shifts most of this practice towards SoTL. For some university teachers, the transition from their disciplinary research to SoTL is relatively straightforward, particularly in those cases where social science-type inquiry is their research paradigm. But in most cases, including the four presented here, SoTL is not education research and does not require the use of the educational research methods that would normally be expected of a PhD student in education or an active academic researcher in a department of higher education. But it can be research, and it those cases it does require social science research skills.

A teacher who is interested in improving student learning can investigate their practice in ways that have three quite different knowledge outcomes. They have been previously described by Ashwin and Trigwell as follows:

- An investigation to inform oneself about an aspect of their teaching/learning. This will result in the production of *personal* knowledge.
- An investigation to inform a group within one or more shared contexts (typically department or faculty, institution) about an aspect of their teaching/ learning. This will result in the production of *local* knowledge.
- An investigation to inform a wider (international) audience about an aspect of their teaching/learning. This will result in the production of *public* knowledge.

(2004, p. 121)

These three types of knowledge are similar to Rowland's (2000) distinction between the personal, shared and public contexts of knowledge, which he argues are resources that academics could draw upon in learning about their teaching (p. 61). The three levels of knowledge form an inclusive hierarchy: that is, an investigation to inform a wider audience (normally called research) that results in the production of public knowledge will also lead to the development of personal knowledge and should also lead to the development of local knowledge. The purposes and ways of validating these investigations are summarised in Table 15.3.

TABLE 15.3 Levels of teaching/learning investigations showing relations between the purpose, process and outcomes (adapted from Ashwin & Trigwell 2004)

Level	Purpose of the investigation is ...	Evidence gathering methods and conclusions will be ...	Investigation results in ...
1	To inform oneself	Verified by self	Personal knowledge
2	To inform a group within a shared context	Verified by those within the same context	Local knowledge
3	To inform a wider audience	Verified by those outside of that context	Public knowledge

University teachers could be engaged in all three levels. Level 1 investigations are occurring in most cases much of the time. Examples include the teacher undertaking personal reviews of the literature, monitoring and reflecting on the processes of teaching and learning, and reflecting individually on group discussions. It could be as basic as reflecting on how a class responds to a joke or a request to discuss something with a neighbouring student. If artefacts are produced at all, they include reflective journals, coursework assignments and diary notes, and similar records that reflect the development of personal knowledge. Because they do not involve peer review, Level 1 investigations are usually considered not to be the scholarship of teaching and learning, but they are a part of all good reflective teaching practice.

Level 2 investigations, as in Cases 15.1 through 15.4 above, are undertaken to inform a group (that includes the teacher–investigator) about their shared context, and results in the development of local knowledge. The processes of investigation will have implications for the context in which the teaching is taking place. As the investigator needs to satisfy others (peers) of the validity of their conclusions, this may require more than is needed to satisfy only themselves. The examples in the cases above show that these activities can include literature reviews that examine how a teaching idea might fit within a particular context, the evaluation of a learning activity within a particular context, or an analysis of barriers to learning. Artefacts include documentation of local teaching insights, portfolios produced in development courses, conference papers and reports, departmental minutes, papers, reports and articles in 'in-house' publications.

Level 3 investigations are undertaken to inform a wider audience about some aspect of the teaching/learning context in which the teacher has been involved. The evidence gathered and the meanings drawn, and the ways in which evidence was gathered and meanings drawn, will be verified by people from outside the context, through the peer review process. The outcomes of this research will have implications that go beyond the context in which the investigation was conducted, and the investigator needs to satisfy this wider audience of the validity of their conclusions. The full range of social science research approaches are examples of this research activity. The outcomes are found in research journals in education in the disciplines, such as the *International Journal of Science and Mathematics Education* and *Journal of Architectural Education*, and in some cases the specialist higher education journals such as *Studies in Higher Education* and *Teaching in Higher Education*.

The decisions about which level is relevant in different aspects of a teacher's role are professional decisions, to be made by individual teachers or organisational groups. There is evidence from the poor quality of some SoTL manuscripts submitted by teachers for publication that the decision about which level of investigation is appropriate is one that generally needs to be made prior to the investigation taking place, rather than as an afterthought.

Case 15.5 is an example of a Level 3 investigation. While it was designed to produce new international higher education knowledge (and it eventually yielded three international peer-reviewed journal articles) it was also designed to produce knowledge that was useful in informing a local teaching/learning context (Level 2).

CASE 15.5   THE EXPERIENCE OF LEARNING

Katherine Crawford & colleagues, University of Sydney

Through the 1990s, a group of mathematics academics and educators at the University of Sydney investigated and reported on the learning experience of their students using qualitative (interview) and quantitative (questionnaire) approaches (Crawford et al. 1994, 1998a, 1998b).

They used a 3P student learning model (Figure 15.1, Prosser, Trigwell, Hazel & Gallagher 1994) to inform their investigation. The model suggests that there are relations between the quality of the outcomes of student learning, the ways students conceive of the subject matter they are learning, their perceptions of their learning context and their approach to learning. The investigation focused on the ways first-year mathematics students conceived of the subject of mathematics; whether those conceptions were related to learning approaches and outcomes, and if so, how they were related; and whether there was anything suggested by these relations that might be used to improve the outcomes of learning.

The interviews with first-year students revealed qualitatively different conceptions of what it meant to learn mathematics. For some students the conceptions appeared to be 'fragmented' while for others they were more 'cohesive'. When questionnaires were used to tap the extent of student use of these conceptions, along with their perceptions of workload, assessments, teaching and learning goals and the students' approaches to learning, systematic relations between the elements in the 3P model were found. Students with fragmented conceptions of mathematics were more likely to be adopting a surface approach to learning and have a lower quality learning outcome than those with a cohesive conception. They also experienced a higher workload and less clarity in what was expected of them. These and other results from the study are used by staff in the Mathematics Learning Centre to support the learning of new students in their first semester.

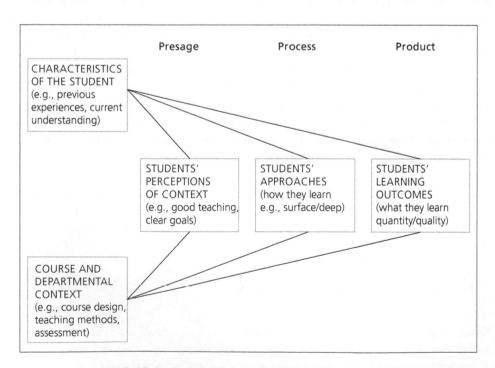

FIGURE 15.1 Presage-Process-Product (3P) model of student learning
(Prosser, Trigwell, Hazel & Gallagher 1994)

Why engage in the scholarship of teaching and learning?

Having now seen five cases illustrating the potential of SoTL to change student learning, you may also be able to see that it is at the core of professional teaching practice. As professionals, the ways teachers think about teaching are at least as important as their knowledge and skills of teaching (Kember 1997; Prosser & Trigwell 1999). It is through the use of processes such as the scholarship of teaching and learning that academics are able to establish the grounds on which to make informed professional judgements in and about teaching. SoTL informs whether the ideas being used with students are ethical, acceptable, effective and transferable to other contexts. Gathering and using evidence in scholarly ways, with peer review, is what provides the validation for those judgements.

This view of SoTL has been presented here through the examples used in the five cases and an emphasis on student learning, rather than through a worded definition. It is a perspective shared by many authors (Boyer 1990; Hutchings & Shulman 1999; Prosser 2008; Rice 1992; Shulman 2000; Trigwell et al. 2000; Trigwell & Shale 2004) but it is not universally accepted. Some authors see different relations between most SoTL and research into teaching and learning, as found in the three publications by Kreber (2001, 2002a, 2002b), by Kreber and Cranton (2000) and by Potter and Kustra (2011). There is continuing debate about the definition of the scholarship of teaching and learning and, for most people, the one they settle upon depends on what they see to be the purpose of SoTL. In this chapter the purpose is the improvement of student learning through the evidence-based practice of student-focused teaching (Prosser & Trigwell 1999), with students being the main beneficiaries.

Teaching is student-focused when it incorporates an awareness of how the learners experience the teaching and subject matter, how they go about learning in the context of that teaching and how the teaching might need to be adjusted in the light of this information. The scholarship of teaching and learning is a sophisticated (professional) way of developing that awareness and using that awareness to make appropriate adjustments.

Getting involved

What do your responses to the questionnaire items in Table 15.1 tell you about your SoTL thinking? What do they suggest you might do to get started or make further progress? Are you already engaged in inquiries similar to those in Cases 15.1 and 15.2?

Preparing the ground for SoTL might involve:
- finding out who in your department is already engaged in SoTL
- contacting your academic development unit to see what they do

- establishing or joining a network of university teachers with whom you can share your thoughts on teaching
- becoming familiar with learning theories (see Chapter 1, Stewart 2012) and teaching ideas and frameworks (see Chapter 2, Hunt et al. 2012)
- attending research conferences that include teaching and learning in your discipline, and conferences about teaching and learning
- listing the questions related to your teaching or your students' learning that you would like to know more about.

Strategically, an important question to ask is whether you see SoTL as a solo pursuit. Some reflective elements and inquiry questions might be best addressed alone, and the skills you have in the type of thinking involved in most research processes should be sufficient to design Level 2 investigations that have the appropriate validity and usefulness. But there are benefits and rewards from sharing and collaborating in SoTL that accompany all communal learning processes.

Doing something similar to Case 15.4, on investigating a question through a literature synthesis, is a good place to start engaging with SoTL. For example, what is known about threshold concepts (see Chapter 3, Land 2012) or approaches to learning (Trigwell & Prosser 1999) in your discipline? If a literature synthesis does not already exist, such a compilation is very likely to be useful to you as well as to colleagues in your discipline. Acceptance and use of the review by your colleagues is a form of peer review.

A very useful starting resource is the guide to informed, reflective teaching entitled *A Tertiary Practitioner's Guide to Collecting Evidence of Learner Benefit* (Alkema 2011). It includes sections on how best to encourage learning, why practitioners need evidence, where to start, and a useful summary overview of evaluative data collection methods. An extract from the guide is shown in Table 15.4.

The focus of most of this chapter up to this point has been on the framework or model used (a) to position and inform the scholarly investigation, and (b) to develop the questions that the data and analytical processes might address (procedural steps 1–3). There are two reasons for this emphasis. First, these elements direct the SoTL activity towards improving student learning, and second, they are the elements most often ignored in SoTL when it is conceived of as research. Having said that, the research elements of SoTL are important, and they are addressed in the rest of this section.

A successful investigation relies on a judicious choice of sources of data and collection methods, and appropriate ways of analysing the data and interpreting the results (step 4). Books on evidence-based educational evaluation (for example, Guba & Lincoln 1985) are a rich source of ideas for investigation questions, sources of data and methodology. Similar, but more contextualised, information can also be found in texts that focus on university teaching development. Light

TABLE 15.4 Example investigation questions and relevant data sources (Alkema 2011, p. 8)

Possible questions	Possible data sources and collection tools
How do I know what my students already know and still need to learn in this course?	• diagnostic assessment (written and oral) • academic records
What progress are my students making? How do I assess the progress of my students? What do my students think of this? How much do my students know about their learning progress?	• formative assessment of course work • pre- and post- tests • observation of learners • data on student engagement in e-learning environments (e.g. electronic tutorials) • questionnaire • interviews • discussion • academic records • student-led reviews

et al. (2009), for example, include a chapter on evaluating teaching and learning which contains ideas on where to find evidence and how to use it. Short, practical guides, such as *Small Scale Research: Pragmatic inquiry in social science and the caring professions* (Knight 2002b), also provide a useful starting point.

However, an approach based on evaluation sources and methods may not be sufficient if you envisage a refereed journal publication as the peer reviewed outcomes of the SoTL process, and you decide to engage in a Level 3 investigation, as in Case 15.5. For most teachers who are not familiar with social science research, the most practical approach to a successful outcome is to be a part of a team of investigators that does include someone familiar with social science research. They might already be a member of your department, a member of an education department or in an academic development unit. They can provide guidance on methodology and interpretation and the key texts on research methods and analytical techniques, such as those by Cohen et al. (2007) and Tight (2003).

A summary of the six procedural steps involved in SoTL are provided below as a further stimulus to getting started.

1. Consider how student learning might be enhanced. What theory or model or framework can be used to ground your thinking?
2. Use the model or theory or framework to identify an intervention designed to enhance learning, or a current practice thought to be doing so, or a collection of information that might lead to enhanced learning.
3. Choose investigation question(s) related to teaching and/or student learning in the chosen context to guide the investigation.

4. Conduct a review or synthesis of the literature to determine what answers to the question(s) already exist.
5. Carry out the investigation to yield a result and some form of public artefact.
6. Have the outcome (artefact) peer reviewed on the clarity and appropriateness of each of the theory, practice, question, method and result elements of the previous five steps of the procedure.

Conclusion: the benefits and rewards of engaging with SoTL

The major rewards and benefits for university teachers in engaging with SoTL are not in research publications, as the major focus of SoTL itself is not on research publication. Publications can be a reward, but some care needs to be taken both in the design of the study and in selecting the quality of the target journal. Many journals that have a focus on research into education in the disciplines are not highly rated by the research community, and the returns in terms of research status and impact are low. For this reason, some scholars of teaching and learning seek intrinsic rewards through the dissemination of their ideas in ways that reach the audiences likely to notice and use them. They find that through SoTL they gain greater satisfaction with the variation in their teaching, the pleasure of seeing enhanced student learning and the stimulation derived from the inquiry process. Engagement with SoTL can accelerate growth as a teacher, provide access to a language and values that lead to more meaningful conversations about teaching and learning, and open doors to higher education networks such as the International Society for the Scholarship of Teaching and Learning (ISSOTL), the Improving Student Learning Symposium (ISL) and the Higher Education Research and Development Society of Australasia (HERDSA).

There are also extrinsic rewards and benefits, for example, through teaching awards, teaching grants, promotion opportunities and money. The University of Sydney distributes additional funds to departments, based on the extent to which teaching staff engage with SoTL activities. This is done through the Scholarship Index, the thinking behind which is described as follows:

> While at Sydney we would want all teachers to 'step back and reflect systematically on their teaching' in ways that are consistent with a commitment to openness and mutual accountability, we do not expect every teacher to be publishing higher education research. Indeed, if the aim is for their peers within the University to build upon this communication, there are far more effective dissemination strategies than journal articles which academics at Sydney might be encouraged

to use to communicate about their teaching ... The scheme is not intended to reward every form of SoTL, rather it seeks to support strategic SoTL activities that deliver the greatest benefit to the University.

(University of Sydney 2012)

Individual university teachers and whole departments accumulate Scholarship Index points annually through any or all of the following (Institute of Teaching and Learning 2012):

- preparing a teaching award application for a local (university level) or national award
- preparing a teaching grant application at a local (university) or national level
- completing a qualification in university teaching, such as a post-graduate certificate in higher education teaching or equivalent
- completing a program on research supervision
- formally mentoring a teaching colleague, for example, a participant in a formal teaching development course
- producing a full length SoTL article for a house journal or equivalent professional university teaching organisation's newsletter or magazine
- running a department-wide SoTL forum, hosted by a department of at least half a day's duration, which engages a significant number of staff in what is evaluated by participants to be a scholarly discussion about teaching and learning.

The points are linked to dollars, with the funding (in total, about AUS$1 million annually) being used differently by departments. Examples include distributing it proportionally to the individual teachers who earned it, or pooling it at the departmental level for teaching development activities including attendance at teaching and learning higher education conferences.

Being aware of and engaging in SoTL is almost certain to be a rewarding experience. It is most likely to be so if it is seen as an integral part of teaching, and engaged in, with others, as questions and issues about teaching and learning arise during practice.

CHAPTER 16

LEADERSHIP IN TEACHING
Paul Blackmore

Keywords
leadership, learning organisations, action learning, action research, change

---

CASE 16.1   RECOGNISING THE NEED FOR LEADERSHIP

'But we can't do this, we're just tutors.'
'Sounds great, but the subject outline is already set and we have to do what it says.'
'Well, my Head of Department isn't interested, because the department is assessed on research output, so innovative teaching isn't even on her radar.'

This dispirited group of postgraduate students were participating in a Foundations of Teaching program specifically geared to early-career university teachers. As the coordinator listened to them, he realised that leadership was an issue that needed to be addressed even at this early stage in their careers. But how is it possible to lead from behind and below – from the position of a part-time tutor's role? How could he help them to promote learning and teaching? Even if they could do little at this stage, these are the academic leaders of the future – how could he facilitate a 'can-do' approach to leadership in teaching?

....

Why pay attention to leadership?

A starting point for developing one's capacities as a leader is to recognise the central importance of leadership in academic work and the opportunities we have to lead, at whatever level in the university we find ourselves. Leadership is a highly relevant topic for academics. Indeed, academic work is inherently an act of leadership because academics should always be at the forefront of what is being thought and done in their domains of knowledge and practice. This is intellectual leadership (Macfarlane 2011) of which teaching forms a part.

Developing an approach to teaching is an important part of growing into an academic role which normally includes teaching, research and administration or service. If we see teaching as being not only about subject content but also about enabling students to develop the capacity to think and write in a rigorous and autonomous way, to develop their own perspectives and their own voices, then not only is teaching an act of leadership but these desired outcomes start to look like aspects of leadership too. Teaching becomes the enabling of intellectual leadership among those who are learning. The teaching role may also be seen as one in which teachers are involved in the improvement of the practice of teaching – both their own practices and those of colleagues – again acts of leadership.

An understanding of leadership matters because change to promote teaching and student learning is very hard to achieve, as Scott, Coates and Anderson (2008, p. 50) noted in an Australian report in which university managers variously described academic leadership as 'Getting butterflies into formation' and 'Trying to drive a nail into a wall of blancmange – little resistance but no result'. Teaching practices in universities remain remarkably similar to those of a century ago, despite major technological developments and immense shifts in the roles of universities. Institutions that try to make major curriculum changes are usually faced with at least five years of intensive work, with little certainty of achieving their desired ends (King's Learning Institute 2010). Much effort has gone into the improvement of individual teachers and teaching new and inexperienced staff the basics of teaching and assessment, and many countries now recognise individual teaching achievement through faculty, university and national awards. There has also been a strong tendency to promote change from beyond the institution, often through targeted funding initiatives. While this may help to bypass local resistance, there is a risk that innovations do not take root in departmental practice. So change led from inside a department has its advantages and may be highly effective, but it has its own challenges. Subject teachers frequently report that the changes they would like to see happen are impossible to bring about, once they return to their home department after taking part in a professional development program. The advantage for people advocating change, sometimes termed 'change agents', within a department is that they have an intimate knowledge of the department and its ways of working. The disadvantage is that they have no external status or support.

Part of the problem was captured by a recent study of subject and program leaders in two universities in the United Kingdom (Blackmore et al. 2008). These are important roles, since they carry responsibility at a practical level for designing, redesigning, delivering, monitoring and reviewing subjects and programs. The difficulties in achieving change were noted by many, often because the sheer weight of work to be done seemed to overwhelm any thoughts about doing it differently.

Those who took up such leadership responsibilities saw the role as being mainly administrative, consisting largely of ensuring that teaching happened and that paperwork was completed satisfactorily. Very rarely did coordinators see it as their responsibility to advance their discipline or its pedagogy through their role. So, those who held some of the most crucial roles in the improvement of teaching did not see it as their job to do so. Further, many had come into the leadership role because it was their turn or because no-one else could be found to do it. These first-level posts of responsibility were not usually seen as places of opportunity; indeed the reverse was often the case, because they could be seen as distracting from the main business of developing research. Johnston and Westwood's (2007) study of 20 UK universities also concluded that there was little formal preparation or support for curriculum leadership roles and that many did not want to take up such roles. This suggests a potentially important outcome from studies of leadership: they encourage early-career academics, who are likely to enter first-rung leadership roles of teaching coordination, to recognise their potential as change agents. Without the ability to lead, academic life can become frustrating because one is driven to accept a sometimes poor working environment that is capable of improvement. This is why a capacity for leadership matters to new university teachers *and* their more experienced colleagues.

This chapter explores attitudes to leadership in academic life and seeks to define leadership in a way that fits the academy. It explores what successful leaders do and how they learn and it suggests practical ways to think about and develop leadership capacities. If you are thinking about your own long-term professional development in academic life, then the growth of your own capacity for leadership will be immensely helpful as you take on roles that require work at a strategic level, such as subject coordinator or associate dean.

Definitions of leadership

Leadership means different things to different people and the term is loaded with ideological baggage. In general, leadership is said to involve vision – a sense of how things might be; seeing the big picture and, therefore, having the ability to be strategic and mobilise others in a desired direction. Leadership is sometimes distinguished from management or administration in that leaders are said to be transformative – that is, they enable people not just to do the same things better, but to do better things, at a different level.

The meaning of the term has fluctuated over time. Middlehurst (1993) identified a number of phases, starting from a 'great man' (sic) view of leadership and moving through behavioural, contingency, power and influence, cultural and symbolic and cognitive theories to a much more situated and embedded view, such as the one that will be taken here. Although a broad sense of movement through these phases over time can be identified, all may be in play at any time. The 'great man' view (van Seters & Field 1990), which is still very much alive, implies that only a few people possess the capacity to lead: most of us therefore are followers who can safely leave leadership to those who have the required traits to do it well. However, this view of leadership does not seem to fit in institutions where there is a great deal of autonomy. Universities have relatively flat hierarchical structures and much decision-making may be at a local level.

Distributed leadership in learning organisations

The literature on learning organisations (Senge 1990) suggests that places of work will be much more flexible and fast-moving if as many people as possible are empowered to think and act. Contemporary views of leadership, then, tend to see it as more widely distributed. A typical example of such a distributive approach is expressed by Ramsden, who claims that leadership is the concern of all who work in universities. He describes it as:

> a practical and everyday process of supporting, managing, developing and inspiring academic colleagues … leadership in universities can and should be exercised by everyone, from the vice-chancellor to the casual car parking attendant.
>
> (Ramsden 1998, p. 4)

Ramsden's definition is helpfully broad and inclusive, but since it applies to everyone the next step is to consider how it might relate specifically to those who undertake academic work. Note, in passing, that the issue of what is and what is not academic work is becoming an increasingly difficult distinction to maintain (Whitchurch 2011).

Leadership is context specific

Leadership has often been seen as a capacity that exists independently of context. However, leadership does imply a domain in which leading takes place. In academic institutions, there has been an equivocal and not always analytical view of leadership, management and administration, signalled by a tendency to use the words interchangeably, sometimes encapsulating them in the term 'managerialism', as if it were much the same thing. This discomfort may stem in part from a traditional belief in academic freedom. Studies of academic staff internationally show that they find the opportunity for autonomy to be one of the most attractive aspects of academic life, but this is in a context in which universities are increasingly centrally managed. Unsurprisingly, this contributes to a sense of suspicion around ideas of leadership and management. There remains a very strong tradition of collegiality in academic life, including a belief in shared decision-making (McNay 1995), which sits uncomfortably with so-called managerial approaches (Deem 1998). Ramsden expressed the problem well by pointing to two 'dangerous myths' in academic life: one of them that academic management restricts freedom and wastes people's time, and the other that academic staff are less productive than they should be and need to be strongly controlled. Ramsden calls these approaches 'unprofessional academic leadership ... excessively lax and responsive or dumbly aggressive and assertive' (1998, p. 4). This tension, coupled with the tendency for staff to be promoted mainly on the basis of research excellence, means that academic staff sometimes have to be persuaded to take up managing or leadership roles, particularly at lower levels. They do so sometimes out of a sense of duty and because it is part of good 'academic citizenship' (Macfarlane 2005), yet studies of university teaching effectiveness show that it is the quality of leadership that distinguishes effective from less effective departments (Martin et al. 2003).

Academic disciplines provide another context for differing attitudes to leadership. It would be difficult to argue that this is a determining feature, but a significant body of research has explored discipline-related attitudes and found varying attitudes to academic and financial risk-taking, to decision-making and conceptions of the role of leadership (Blackmore 2007). These may become particularly significant when promoting teaching across disciplinary boundaries. The importance of context in regard to leadership may be seen through the eyes of those appointed to academic posts from outside the academy. They have worked in very different organisations and are often puzzled at the leadership and management practices of universities, usually feeling that an excessively strong emphasis on collegiality can inhibit needed change (Blackmore et al. 2008). They may find it less clear how to make things happen than in some other organisations. As one interviewee said, 'I no longer have any ideas which levers to pull.'

So, general prescriptions about leadership will take us only so far. In the end, an understanding of how leadership works has to take into account the local circumstances in which it is happening. Knight and Trowler (2001, p. viii) encapsulated this point when they observed that, 'much of the work of leading is contingent ... it involves dealing with the specifics of a time, a place and a set of people' – which, for universities, means a place that is increasingly actively managed, with explicit mission statements. Annual staff appraisals aim to ensure that each member of staff is working in alignment with the institution's mission and objectives. These developments in universities have taken place at the same time as the number of posts that are explicitly designated as 'management' has risen. To borrow a metaphor from Morgan, universities are increasingly managed as if they were machines. In *Images of Organization* (2006), Morgan explores a number of metaphors through which we can see an organisation in different ways. We can see it not only as a machine, but also as an organism, as a political system, and as a psychic prison, attracting to it all those who like to think in a particular way and who find it hard to think otherwise.

The lived experience of those who work in universities suggests that life is not straightforward and therefore that the role of the leader is not simply one of building and tending a predictable machine. Cuthbert (2006) has described universities as 'organised anarchies'. For Cuthbert, universities are characterised by: problematic goals, in that there is no universally shared view of the purpose of a higher education; unclear technology, meaning that we do not know how to make sure that either teaching or research takes place successfully; and fluid participation, referring to the tendency for academic staff not to relate very closely to their 'home' institution, but often to be better networked with colleagues in other institutions. All of these present leadership challenges. They mean that we cannot assume that our colleagues necessarily share our view about the direction in which we should be heading. Even when an institution loudly proclaims its mission, one cannot expect that all colleagues will wish to follow. Any teaching or research problem will have a number of possible solutions and it will not always be clear which of them is likely to lead to the most successful outcome. Finally, we cannot assume loyalty to the 'home' institution. Many staff are what has been termed 'cosmopolitans' – involved with the international professional community – rather than 'locals' – more concerned with their own institution (Merton 1968). One response to such unruliness may of course be to resort to hyper-rationalisation (Mintzberg 1994) – the production of more and more rules to regulate organisational life. However, untidy reality does not disappear, and those who lead in a practical setting need to be able to cope with organisational messiness.

YOUR THOUGHTS

Identify a change to teaching or curriculum that you would like to make and use Morgan's (2006) perspectives as lenses to focus on the different dimensions of the change process.

- What are the structural and procedural changes that would need to take place? (machine or mechanism)
- What incentives need to be built in to encourage people to do what you would like to see done? (organism)
- Who has an interest in the initiative and how can they be brought onside? (politics)
- Are you asking a group of people to change a settled and shared way of thinking? (psychic prison)

What do leaders do?

So, in a world where leadership is distributed and embedded in context, what is it that leaders actually do, when they lead? There are many models of leadership, with varying emphases, although most, in one way or another, focus on the task, team and individual dimensions. That approach is taken here. In addition, it is suggested that leaders enable learning and that key activities include dealing with identifying need, motivation, coordination, and communication or identity awareness.

Task, team and individual

One of the most influential models of leadership was proposed by Adair (1973) who claimed that leaders pay attention to three areas:
1. achieving the task
2. building and maintaining the team
3. developing the individual.

A recent study (Blackmore & Kandiko 2010) offers some practical examples of each of these in higher education, making use of Adair's model to explore the leadership role of those engaged in interdisciplinary work. The findings are relevant here because experienced practitioners were talking about what they had to know and do in order to make things happen when they were often not in a senior position and had no 'line management' authority. Interviewees were faced with considerable challenges, because they were working across conventional disciplinary boundaries, whether as teachers setting up interdisciplinary programs or as researchers pursuing the solution to a problem that crossed disciplines. What became apparent is that Adair's 'task, team and individual' model is highly applicable, when adapted for the context.

Enabling learning

A central and valuable idea that emerged is that leadership involves the facilitation of learning, at individual and group levels. The task of the leader thus becomes one of enabling learning. This seems a simple and obvious point. However, less thought is given to what should be learnt by those concerned in order for different behaviours to happen. Thought of this way, leadership becomes very much like teaching. And just as we now place less emphasis on telling and more on the facilitation of learning when thinking about teaching students, so it may be for leadership. That is to say, working with colleagues to learn different ways of collaborating is likely to be more effective than taking a 'training' approach that assumes their deficiency at the outset. This is especially the case, of course, when in a collegial environment, often with more senior colleagues, where everything has to be achieved by persuasion.

Need, motivation, coordination and communication

What leaders actually do breaks down into four main activities that relate very closely to the focal points of task, team and individual. Firstly, they identified need and opportunity. Rather than simply doing what had always been done, they were alert to the need for change and were able to see when it might be possible to make a change. Secondly, leaders felt they knew about motivation. They had to nurture this, to manage situations in order to encourage colleagues to want to make a change. Thirdly, leaders found they had to coordinate and direct. Bringing together groups of people with differing expertise, all of whom were essential for a successful outcome, was a complex task. Finally, leaders stressed the role of communication. Discussion may sometimes seem long-winded and time-consuming, but it is the only approach in which two-way communication can take place. Interviewees identified the skills of managing communication overall as a key ability and, within that, of managing meetings so that they were productive and reached useful conclusions in reasonable time.

Identity awareness

Working with individuals to achieve change involves having a developed understanding of who they feel themselves to be, professionally speaking, because this makes a major difference to what they feel it is appropriate to do and how they are likely to receive and interpret suggestions for change. Thus Adair's concern for the individual points to a need to understand the sense of identity of those with whom we work. This is an important concern when dealing with an individual colleague; it becomes more so, and more complex, when working with varied groups of individuals. Almost all achievement in organisations comes about as a result of people working together towards an agreed goal. You will inevitably find yourself trying to make things happen by involving people from a range of backgrounds. It may happen because you find yourself leading a subject on which several other staff teach. You may be trying to adapt your teaching to make use of the opportunities of learning technologies and need assistance to do it. In these situations we can think of ourselves as forming teams in order to accomplish a task. Usually we do not think in such a formal way about working alongside colleagues or going to get help to accomplish a task; however, the rules of teamwork do apply – of understanding the perspectives of those involved, ensuring there is a common appreciation of what is to be done and helping the component parts of the team to work effectively together. In the interdisciplinary study (Blackmore &

Kandiko 2010), team issues were magnified because the team members came from different disciplines and professional groups and had to learn to work together.

YOUR THOUGHTS

Identify a small-scale change that would require your own department and another to work together in an interdisciplinary way to develop teaching and assessment.
- What needs to be done to achieve the task?
- Who would need to be involved and how would the team be developed and maintained?
- What sorts of skills and knowledge would you and your colleagues need to develop to effect the change?

How can we learn to lead?

There is a wealth of literature on change leadership in organisations. Trowler et al. (2003) offer a particularly helpful overview of change practices in relation to departments in higher education. The concept of the stakeholder (Mitchell et al. 1997) is a useful one. When contemplating change it is useful to map out all of those who will be affected by the change, and who might have something to gain or lose. Another useful technique is that of force field analysis (Lewin 1951), in which you try to identify the strength and direction of all of the influences around a proposed change. These are simple techniques that you can readily use to get beneath the surface of apparent resistance.

YOUR THOUGHTS

Think of a change that you that you would like to see in your organisation, noting it in the centre of a page.
- Surround it with those individuals or groups whom you think might have a 'stake' in the change, in the sense of being affected by it and being likely to have a view on it.
- Place arrows next to each, pointing towards or away from the change, indicating whether the person or group is likely to be well disposed or not. Greater strength can be denoted by broader arrows.
- Consider how the enthusiasm of those in favour can be harnessed and, secondly, analyse reasons for the lack of support from others and consider ways that this might be changed.

Leadership is a form of professional expertise, which, like so much other expertise, is often tacit (Polanyi 1996), in that it may never have been expressed as words. We often know more than we can say. The great majority of our expertise has never been articulated and may be beyond the capability of an individual to articulate fully, and certainly to account for its development. Expertise is also social in nature – it is learnt unconsciously, by observation of what others do and what happens. We learn vicariously from the experiences of others (Bandura 1977a). In that sense, learning is social. We also know that it is highly situated – we learn things in their context (Lave & Wenger 1991) and transfer from one context to another cannot be assumed. We know, too, that the learning of novices is different in kind from that of experts. Dreyfus and Dreyfus (1986) have claimed that experts think holistically, while the less experienced will often reduce a complex situation to a set of routines.

What are the implications for your own leadership approach, when working with colleagues to achieve a task? A major one is that taking a 'training' approach of formal instruction is not likely to be effective, even if it is available to you. Instead, you and your colleagues will learn from seeing worked examples, by talking to and observing others who have tackled a similar task, and by sharing together the practical difficulties and solutions in a particular field of work. Experienced colleagues may have turned their work into routines that do not require conscious awareness – so asking them to see routine work as problematic and to break it down may need to be approached with care, perhaps with an acknowledgement that the unconsciousness born of experience can sometimes be an impediment to new learning. There is a useful analogy with the training of athletes and sportspeople, who may not be able to progress until they have broken down their performance and practised parts of it; only then can they build it back up again. However, sometimes progress is not made because a task seems too large and ill-defined to be tackled. One of the skills of leadership is to know when to step in and turn a task into a smaller number of manageable steps, so that the threshold of engagement is lower and the chance of success is increased. It is interesting to reflect that much of what students need to learn is of this kind too, so the learning about learning that we engage in to support our leadership may give us some tools to think better about curricula and teaching.

Start with yourself

Learning to lead takes place in a social context and it consists of behaviours. Those wanting to improve their own capabilities therefore need to become aware of their own current behaviours and their effect on others. We have already noted the tacit nature of much expertise so that we do not always know what we know. Equally, we may be less than aware of what we do not know or what we do not do well. This is reflected in the well-known and apocryphal listing of states of understanding: unconscious incompetence; conscious incompetence; conscious competence; and unconscious competence (see, for example, De Phillips et al. 1960, p. 69). In other words, a first step in learning is to become aware of what we are not doing well. We can then consciously try to improve, aiming to arrive at a state where we automatically do things in the right way. This process requires feedback, which, ideally, should come from more than one source. For this reason many leadership development programs include 360-degree appraisal as part of the process, in which participants learn, from a range of others above, below and alongside them in an organisation, about how they are perceived. A coach or mentor can also give feedback – a coach usually has direct experience of the area in question, whereas a mentor may not, but is skilled in asking the right questions.

External support for learning leadership

The UK Higher Education Academy (HEA) and the Carnegie Foundation in the USA provide support to promote university teaching, learning and curriculum change. The Leadership Foundation for Higher Education (LFHE) in the UK and the LH Martin Institute in Australia focus more broadly on university leadership issues. All have been instrumental in enhancing teaching and curriculum leadership, often through action learning sets (Revans 1980), in which those who want to review and develop their professional practice meet to share experiences. The role of the group is to listen to stories and to draw out issues and concerns by asking questions that lead to better understanding and performance. The Change Academy approach fostered by the Higher Education Academy is an example of such initiatives. Change Academy:

> … brings together cross-institutional teams and gives them the time and space to think creatively about and develop a major change initiative … Change Academy is a year-long process that includes specific development opportunities for nominated team leaders, an ongoing support network and a four-day residential. It provides a creative environment in which the whole team can focus on planning and developing strategies for lasting change. Change Academy supports both rapid innovation and capacity-building for longer-term change. This is a unique, high-quality process for professional learning, which provides knowledge and approaches that can be cascaded more widely; access to consultants with national and international experience; and dedicated support from the Higher Education Academy and the Leadership Foundation.
>
> (Huxley 2010, p. 13)

This approach offers groups of people with a shared concern the opportunity to come together and spend dedicated time in exploring the issues and finding solutions. This circumvents the well-known problem of the lone innovator who finds it impossible to make changes when they return to the workplace. Institutions now often use a change academy approach internally as may be seen in Case 16.2, which details Manchester Metropolitan University's (MMU) proposal to the UK Change Academy.

CASE 16.2   UNIVERSITY-BASED CHANGE ACADEMY

Manchester Metropolitan University (Moores 2010, p. 17)

This proposal relates to a project to develop an internal Change Academy at MMU which would provide a supportive 'space' for cross-university teams, made up of staff from all areas of the university and at all levels, as well as students, to work on change projects. The introduction of an internal version of the change academy is also expected to nurture change champions who will help the University to embed positive and inclusive approaches to change and manage projects in a way that ensures success and buy-in. This project has the potential to be transformational for MMU. They see this project as being integral to achieving a higher level of student satisfaction, performance across the University and to the drive for continuous improvement.

A significant feature of the Change Academy model is that it incorporates notions of whole-of-university change in support of teaching and many of the action learning sets comprise both professional and academic staff. It is about learning to lead together.

Build social capital

Social capital – who you know – is immensely important as a way of gaining access to information, sensing key changes in the external environment and working out who might be your ally in a change you would like to make.

You cannot expect always to be trained for new activities. Indeed, if you are leading, you will be ahead of the game. This means that you have to be prepared to go out and look for what you need. You can befriend people in the university who have the skills that you need in order to do what you want to do. They may be in finance, human resources, registry, learning support or other academic departments. Usually they will be only too pleased to offer you advice on how to get things done because their daily life is being made more difficult by people who fail to ask for advice! Extend your network.

Learning from reviews

The adoption of a process for review, even if followed very informally, can help to provide a structure for learning leadership. An action research approach (Stringer 1999) has been widely used in the improvement of teaching. It involves planning a change, implementing it, observing the effects and reflecting on their significance, before moving into a second, similarly structured, round. This may seem rather mechanistic. However, the habit of mind of paying careful attention to what seems to be happening in a particular situation and to consider whether alternatives might be tried is a valuable one, and the questions can be used flexibly, in the midst of day-to-day working. Eraut (1994) used a simple but powerful set of questions that can be used to help think about how we have dealt with a challenging situation and what we might 'take away' from it. They are slightly adapted here to show that they are about both learning and learning about the learning.

- What did I learn?
- How did I learn it?
- How might I have learnt it more effectively?

Learning by doing

Learn about leadership through participation and observation. If you want to know how decisions are made, watch what happens in meetings. Think about what the meetings are ostensibly for and the shape they take. Who says what, and how, and to whom, and with what result? What does the chair of the meeting do and does it produce beneficial results? Who participates effectively in the meeting? Crucially, observe how decisions are arrived at without votes being taken, as is almost always the case in academic meetings. Whose view wins the day, how and why? Often decisions may seem to owe much to the presence of forceful individuals, or may seem quite quixotic. However, usually it is a matter of finding a solution that sits comfortably within a given community of practice and its key reference points, so it is worth making a study of academic decision-making (Lamont 2009).

YOUR THOUGHTS

Explore the minutes of your university or faculty learning and teaching committees.

- Who is on the committee, and to what extent does the committee structure reflect the need for whole-of-university or faculty change to support learning, teaching and curriculum initiatives?
- In the last year, what sort of issues has the committee addressed and how long did it take to get resolution?
- From your experience as a university teacher, what issues do you think should be addressed by this committee and how might you use the committee system to effect change?

Develop an evidence base

Learning to lead effectively in contemporary universities increasingly involves learning to use data. Evidence-informed practice (see Chapter 14, Krause 2012; Chapter 15, Trigwell 2012) is now a major part of organisational life in higher education where there is a strong interest in it as a means of improvement. While this is consistent with the rigorous, discipline-based education of university teachers, it may also be seen as unrealistic, given the kinds of knowledge and expertise that are in question (Thomas & Pring 2004). However, the use of data is important in the move towards greater public accountability for performance. This has major implications for leadership at departmental level. Satisfactory use of evidence is also important when leading from a lower position in an organisation, which requires the ability to manage upwards. Evidence can persuade, especially in a context in which universities must demonstrate successful teaching outcomes through quality assurance audits. This may mean looking at national data such as the UK's National Student Survey scores, or the Course Experience Questionnaire in Australia. Or, it may involve university-generated data such as subject- or program-level student feedback.

Manage upwards

Leading from a lower position in an organisation requires the ability to manage upwards, as you may have the leadership role in advocating an idea or a changed practice but not be in a formal leadership position. There are skills in managing upwards. They include developing an ability to see things from the senior person's perspective. Why do they work the way they do? What constraints do they have on them? What are they having to deliver? How can you make it easy for someone to say yes to you?

Conclusion

In summary, leadership is central to academic work. In universities we need to think about leadership as being distributed widely in a learning organisation. Leadership looks different from one place to another. Those who lead from within a department have some advantages, but often change is hard to do from within and can be assisted with external support. We can get better at analysing situations by thinking of the institution as a mechanism, an organism, a political system or a psychic prison. Each of these sheds light on learning to lead. Effective leaders think about the learning that is needed if change is to happen. They consider need, motivation, coordination and communication. Leadership expertise is tacit, closely related to a situation and learnt often by observing others. We can improve our capacities by getting feedback about our performance, by participating in professional development, by analysing what we do in a structured way, by building networks, understanding decision-making, mastering evidence that supports the changes we want to make, and by analysing change in terms of stakeholders.

An ability to show leadership in teaching will enhance student learning and be helpful to you both in gaining promotion and in performing well. It is easy in these more managed times to feel that there is less space for an individual to take a distinctive path in teaching leadership. However, the reverse can easily be argued. A number of factors, including accountability and the competitive climate in universities, make it necessary to develop leadership and initiative. In many ways there are more opportunities for individuals and groups to participate in leadership than has ever been the case. The conscious development of your own leadership capacities will help you to build a more productive and fulfilling career in academia.

BIBLIOGRAPHY

ABC see Australian Broadcasting Corporation

Acar, BS 2004, 'Analysis of an assessment method for problem-based learning', *European Journal of Engineering Education*, vol. 29, no. 2, pp. 231–40.

Adair, J 1973, *Action-centred leadership*, Gower, Aldershot.

Adams, JT 1929, 'To "be" or to "do"', *Forum*, vol. 81, no. 6.

Akhurst, J 2006, 'Psychology R&T case I: blending research & teaching in the classroom: students researching students' quality of life', Higher Education Academy Psychology Network, York, <http://pnarchive.org/s.php?p=144&db=39>.

Alkema, A 2011, *A tertiary practitioner's guide to collecting evidence of learner benefit*, Ako Aotearoa – The National Centre for Tertiary Teaching Excellence, Wellington, viewed 13 February 2012, <http://akoaotearoa.ac.nz/collecting-evidence>.

Allen, E & Seaman, J 2010, *Class differences: online education in the United States*, The Sloan Consortium, Needham, MA.

ALTC *see* Australian Learning and Teaching Council (now Office of Learning and Teaching)

Amaral, KE & Shank, JD 2010, 'Enhancing student learning and retention with blended learning class guides', *EDUCAUSE Quarterly*, vol. 33, no. 4, viewed 13 February 2012, <http://www.educause.edu/EDUCAUSE+Quarterly/EDUCAUSEQuarterlyMagazineVolum/EnhancingStudentLearningandRet/219137>.

Ambrose, SA, Bridges, M, Di Pietro, M, Lovette, M & Norman, K 2010, *How learning works: seven research-based principles for smart teaching*, Jossey-Bass, San Francisco.

American Council on Education 2010, Tuning USA, American Council on Education, Washington, DC, viewed 13 February 2012, <http://www.acenet.edu/Content/NavigationMenu/OnlineResources/Accountability/Tuning_USA.htm>.

Anderson, G 2006, 'Assuring quality/resisting quality assurance: academics' responses to "quality" in some Australian universities', *Quality in Higher Education*, vol. 12, no. 2, pp. 161–173.

Anderson, J, Perry, J, Blue, C, Browne, A, Henderson, A, Khan, K, Kirkham, S, Lynam, J, Semeniuk, P & Smye, V 2003, 'Rewriting cultural safety within the postcolonial and postnational feminist project: toward new epistemologies of healing', *Advances in Nursing Science*, vol. 26, no. 3, pp. 196–214.

Anderson, T 2008, 'Toward a theory of online learning', in T Anderson (ed.), *Theory and practice of online learning*, 2nd edn, Athabasca University Press, Canada, pp. 45–74, viewed 27 February 2012, <http://www.aupress.ca/index.php/books/120146>.

Anderson, T, Rourke, L, Garrison, DR & Archer, W 2001, 'Assessing teaching presence in a computer conferencing context', *Journal of Asynchronous Learning Networks*, vol. 5, no. 2, viewed 13 February 2012, <http://sloanconsortium.org/publications/jaln_main>.

Andresen, LW 2000, 'A useable, trans-disciplinary conception of scholarship', *Higher Education Research and Development*, vol. 19, pp. 137–153.

Angelo, T 2012, 'Designing subjects for learning: practical research-based principles and guidelines', in L Hunt & D Chalmers (eds), *University teaching in focus: a learning-centred approach*, ACER Press, Melbourne, pp. 93–111.

Angelo, TA & Cross, KP 1993, *Classroom assessment techniques: a handbook for college teachers*, 2nd edn, Jossey-Bass, San Francisco.

Antonio, AL 2001, 'The role of interracial interaction in the development of leadership skills and cultural knowledge and understanding', *Research in Higher Education*, vol. 42, no 5, pp. 593–617.

Arkoudis, S 2006, *Teaching international students: strategies to enhance learning*, Centre for the Study of Higher Education, Melbourne, viewed 13 February 2012, <http://www.cshe.unimelb.edu.au/pdfs/international.pdf>.

Arkoudis, S & Tran, L 2010, 'Writing blah, blah, blah: lecturers' approaches and challenges in supporting international students', *International Journal of Teaching and Learning in Higher Education*, vol. 22, no. 2, pp. 169–178.

Arkoudis, S, Yu, X, Baik, C, Borland, H, Chang, S, Lang, I, Lang, J, Pearce, A & Watty, K 2010, *Finding common ground: enhancing interaction between domestic and international students: guide for academics*, Australian Learning and Teaching Council, Sydney, viewed 13 February 2012, <http://www.cshe.unimelb.edu.au/research/projectsites/enhancing_interact.html>.

Arum, R & Roksa, J 2011, *Academically adrift: limited learning on college campuses*, University of Chicago Press.

Asch, SE 1955, 'Opinions and social pressure', *Scientific American*, vol. 193, pp. 31–35.

Ashwin, P & Trigwell, K 2004, 'Investigating staff and educational development', in D Baume and P Kahn (eds), *Enhancing staff and educational development*, RoutledgeFalmer, London.

Asmar, C 2011a, *Indigenous teaching and learning at Australian universities: developing research-based exemplars for good practice*, Australian Learning and Teaching Council, Sydney, viewed 13 February 2012, <http://www.olt.gov.au/resource-indigenous-teaching-exemplars-melbourne-2011>

Asmar, C 2011b, Indigenous teaching at Australian universities, research conducted as part of an Australian Teaching & Learning Council Fellowship, viewed 13 February 2012, <http://www.indigenousteaching.com>.

Asmar, C 2011c, List of Indigenous centres at Australian universities, Indigenous teaching at Australian universities, viewed 13 February 2012, <http://www.indigenousteaching.com/html/indigenous_centres.html>.

Asmar, C & Page, S 2009, 'Sources of satisfaction and stress among Indigenous academic teachers: findings from a national Australian study', *Asia Pacific Journal of Education*, vol. 29, pp. 387–401.

Asmar, C, Page, S & Radloff, A 2011, *Dispelling myths: Indigenous students' engagement with university*, Australasian Survey of Student Engagement (AUSSE), Research Briefing, Vol. 10 (April), Australian Council for Educational Research (ACER), Melbourne, viewed 13 February 2012, <http://www.acer.edu.au/research/ausse/reports>.

Association for the Advancement of Computing in Education (AACE) 2012, Chesapeake, VA, viewed 13 February 2012, <http://www.aace.org>.

Association of American Colleges and Universities 2012, VALUE: valid Assessment of Learning in Undergraduate Education, Washington, DC, viewed 13 February 2012, http://www.aacu.org/value/rubrics/index.cfm

Association to Advance Collegiate Schools of Business (AACSB) 2011, Business accreditation eligibility prcedures and standards, Tampa, FL, viewed 13 February 2012, <http://www.aacsb.edu/accreditation/standards.asp>.

Australasian Society for Computers in Learning in Tertiary Education 2012, Byron Bay, NSW, viewed 7 February 2012, <http://www.ascilite.org.au/>.

Australian Broadcasting Corporation 2012, NT Intervention, Sydney, viewed 13 February 2012, <http://www.abc.net.au/indigenous/special_topics/the_intervention>.

Australian Education International 2007, *2006 International student survey: higher education summary report*, Australian Government, Canberra.

Australian Government 2011, *Tertiary Education Quality and Standards Agency Draft Provider Standards — Consultation Draft*, Canberra, viewed 13 February 2012, <http://www.deewr.gov.au/HigherEducation/Policy/teqsa/Documents/DraftProviderStandards.pdf>.

Australian Institute for Teaching and School Leadership 2011a, *National professional standards for teachers*, Ministerial Council for Education, Early Childhood Development and Youth Affairs (MCEECDYA), Melbourne, viewed 13 February 2012, <http://www.teacherstandards.aitsl.edu.au>.

Australian Institute for Teaching and School Leadership 2011b, *Accreditation of initial teacher education programs in Australia: standards and procedures*, Ministerial Council for Education, Early Childhood Development and Youth Affairs (MCEECDYA), Melbourne, viewed 13 February 2012, < http://www.aitsl.edu.au/initial-teacher-education-program-accreditation.html>.

Australian Learning and Teaching Council 2010, Discipline groupings, Office for Learning and Teaching, Sydney, viewed 7 February 2012, <http://www.olt.gov.au/standards/disciplines>.

Australian Learning and Teaching Council 2011, Published standards, Office for Learning and Teaching, Sydney, viewed 7 February 2012, <http://www.olt.gov.au/standards/published>.

Australian Qualifications Framework Council 2011, *Australian Qualifications Framework*, Ministerial Council on Tertiary Education and Employment, South Australia, viewed 13 February 2012, <http://www.aqf.edu.au>.

Australian University Teaching Council 2003, *Teaching large classes project 2001: final report*, Teaching and Educational Development Institute, University of Queensland, Brisbane, viewed 27 February 2012, <http://www.olt.gov.au/resource-teaching-large-classes-uq-2003>.

Azer, SA 2005, 'Challenges facing PBL tutors: 12 tips for successful group facilitation', *Medical Teacher*, vol. 27, no. 8, pp. 676–681.

Baddeley, AD 2000, 'The episodic buffer: a new component of working memory?', *Trends in Cognitive Science*, vol. 4, no. 11, pp. 417–423.

Baddeley, AD & Hitch, G 1974, 'Working memory', in GH Bower (ed.) *The psychology of learning and motivation: advances in research and theory*, vol. 8, pp. 47–89, Academic Press, New York.

Bain, J, Ballantyne, R, Lester, N & Mills, C 2002, *Reflecting on practice: student teachers' perspectives*, Post Pressed, Flaxton, Queensland.

Bain, K 2004, *What the best college teachers do*, Harvard University Press, Cambridge, MA.

Ballantyne, R, Bain, J & Packer, J 1997, *Reflecting on university teaching academics' stories*, Australian Government Publishing Service, Canberra.

Ballard, B & Clanchy, J 1991, *Teaching students from overseas: a brief guide for lecturers and supervisors*. Melbourne, Longman Cheshire.

Bandura, A 1977a, *Social learning theory*, General Learning Press, New York.

Bandura, A 1977b, 'Self-efficacy: towards a unifying theory of behavioural change', *Psychological Review*, vol. 84, no. 2, pp. 191–215.

Bandura, A 1995, *Self-efficacy in changing societies*, Cambridge University Press.

Barker P & McLaren, A 2005, 'Teaching first year design by mechanical dissection', Higher Education Academy Engineering Subject Centre, Loughborough University, Loughborough, <http://hdl.handle.net/2134/8644>.

Barker, M 2012, 'Teaching international students', in L Hunt & D Chalmers (eds), *University teaching in focus: a learning-centred approach*, ACER Press, Melbourne, pp. 199–213.

Barnett, R 2000a, 'Supercomplexity and the curriculum', *Studies in Higher Education*, vol. 25, no. 3, pp. 256–265.

Barnett, R 2000b, *Realizing the university in an age of supercomplexity*, Open University Press, Buckingham.

Barnett, R 2007, *A will to learn: being a student in an age of uncertainty*, Society for Research into Higher Education & Open University Press, Maidenhead.

Barraket, J, Payne, A, Scott, G & Cameron, L 2000, *Equity and the use of communications and information technology in higher education (00/7)*, Evaluation and Investigations Programme, Higher education Division, Department of Education, Training and Youth Affairs, Canberra.

Barrie SC 2004, 'A research-based approach to generic graduate attributes policy', *Higher Education Research & Development*, vol. 23, no. 3, pp. 261–275.

Barrie, S 2007, 'A conceptual framework for the teaching and learning of generic graduate attributes', *Studies in Higher Education*, vol. 32, no. 4, pp. 439–458.

Barrie, S, Ginns, P & Symons, R 2008, *Student surveys on teaching and learning*, Australian Learning and Teaching Council, Sydney, viewed 14 February 2012, <http://www.catl.uwa.edu.au/projects/tqi/reports>.

Barrie, S, Hughes, C & Smith, C 2009, *The national graduate attributes project: integration and assessment of graduate attributes in curriculum*, Australian Learning and Teaching Council, Sydney, viewed 14 February 2012, <http://www.olt.gov.au/project-integration-assessment-graduate-sydney-2007>.

Barrows, HS 1984, 'A specific problem-based, self-directed learning method designed to teach medical problem-solving skills, and enhance knowledge retention and recall', in

HG Schmidt & ML DeVolder (eds), *Tutorials in problem-based learning: a new direction in teaching the health professions*, Maastricht, Van Gorcum, pp. 16–32.

Barrows, HS 1988, *The tutorial process*, Southern Illinois University School of Medicine, Springfield, IL.

Barrows, HS 2000, *Problem based learning applied to medical education*, Southern Illinois University Press, Springfield, IL.

Batchelor Institute of Indigenous Tertiary Education c. 2010, Both ways, Batchelor, NT, viewed 14 February 2012, <https://www.batchelor.edu.au/main/both-ways>.

Bath, D, Smith, C, Stein, S & Swann, R 2004, 'Beyond mapping and embedding graduate attributes: bringing together quality assurance and action learning to create a validated and living curriculum', *Higher Education Research & Development*, vol. 23, no. 3, pp. 313–328.

Battiste, M 2000, *Reclaiming Indigenous voice and vision*, University of British Columbia Press, Vancouver.

Baxter Magolda, MB 2006, 'Intellectual development in the college years', *Change*, vol. 38, no. 3, pp. 50–54.

Baxter Magolda, MB 2009, 'Educating students for self-authorship: learning partnerships to achieve complex outcomes', in C Kreber (ed.), *The university and its disciplines: teaching and learning within and beyond disciplinary boundaries*, Routledge, London, pp. 143–156.

Becher, T 1989, *Academic tribes and territories: intellectual enquiry and the cultures of discipline*, Society for Research into Higher Education and the Open University Press, Buckingham.

Becher, T & Trowler, P 2001, *Academic tribes and territories: intellectual enquiry and the cultures of disciplines*, 2nd edn, Society for Research into Higher Education and Open University Press, Buckingham.

Beers, SE 1986, 'Questioning and peer collaboration as techniques for thinking and writing about personality', *Teaching of Psychology*, vol. 13, no. 2, pp. 75–77.

Belbin Associates 2007, Belbin team roles, Belbin Associates, Cambridge, viewed 14 February 2012, <http://www.belbin.com>.

Benz, A 2010, 'Writing a book with students, using Google Docs as shared learning environment: an experience', *International Journal of Innovation in Education*, vol. 1, no. 2, pp. 139–147.

Bernard, RM, Abrami, PC, Lou, Y, Borokhovski, E, Wade, A, Wozney, L, Wallet, PA, Fiset, M & Huang, B 2004, 'How does distance education compare to classroom instruction? A meta-analysis of the empirical literature', *Review of Educational Research*, vol. 74, no. 3, pp. 379–439.

Berthiaume, D 2009, 'Teaching in the disciplines', in H Fry, S Ketteridge & S Marshall (eds), *A handbook for teaching and learning in higher education: enhancing academic practice*, 3rd edn, Routledge, London, pp. 215–225.

Bertola, P & Murphy, E 1994, *Tutoring at university: a beginner's practical guide*, Centre for Educational Advancement, Curtin University of Technology, Perth, WA.

Biggs, J 1996, 'Enhancing teaching through constructive alignment', *Higher Education*, vol. 32, no. 3, pp. 347–364.

Biggs, J 2003, *Teaching for quality learning at university*, 2nd edn, Open University Press, Maidenhead.

Biggs, J & Tang, C 2007, *Teaching for quality learning at university*, 3rd edn, Society for Research into Higher Education and Open University Press, Buckingham.

Billett, S 2011, *Curriculum and pedagogic bases for effectively integrating practice-based experiences*, Australian Learning and Teaching Council, Sydney, viewed 14 February 2012, <http://www.olt.gov.au/resource-integrating-practice-based-experiences-griffith-2011>.

Blackmore, J 2009, 'Academic pedagogies, quality logics and performative universities: evaluating teaching and what students want', *Studies in Higher Education*, vol. 34, no. 8, pp. 857–872.

Blackmore, J & Sachs, J 2007, *Performing and reforming leaders: gender, educational restructuring and organisational change*, State University of New York Press.

Blackmore, P 2007, 'Disciplinary difference in academic leadership and management and its development: a significant factor?', *Research in Post-compulsory Education*, vol. 12, no. 2, pp. 225–239.

Blackmore, P (ed.) 2010, *The King's-Warwick project: creating a 21st century curriculum*, Summary report, King's College Institute, London, viewed 14 February 2012, <http://www.kcl.ac.uk/study/learningteaching/kli/news/kwp.pdf>.

Blackmore, P 2012, 'Leadership in teaching', in L Hunt & D Chalmers (eds), *University teaching in focus: a learning-centred approach*, ACER Press, Melbourne, pp. 268–281.

Blackmore, P & Blackwell, R 2006, 'Strategic leadership in academic development', *Studies in Higher Education*, vol. 31, no. 3, pp. 373–387.

Blackmore, P, Dales, R, Law, S & Yates, P 2008, *Investigating the capabilities of course and module leaders in departments*, Higher Education Academy, York.

Blackmore, P & Kandiko, CB 2010, 'Interdisciplinary leadership and learning', in M Davies, M Devlin & M Tight (eds), *Interdisciplinary higher education: international perspectives on higher education research*, vol. 5, Emerald Group Publishing, Bingley, pp. 55–74.

Blight, J 1995, 'Problem based, small group learning: an idea whose time has come', *British Medical Journal*, vol. 311, pp. 342–343.

Bloom, BS & Krathwohl, DR 1956, *Taxonomy of educational objectives: the classification of educational goals, by a committee of college and university examiners. Handbook I: cognitive domain*, Longmans, New York.

Bloxham, S & Boyd, P 2007, *Developing effective assessment in higher education: a practical guide*, Open University Press, Maidenhead.

Bonk, CJ 2009, *The world is open: how web technology is revolutionizing education*, Jossey-Bass, San Francisco.

Booth, C & Harrington, J 2003, 'Research methods modules and undergraduate business research: an investigation', *International Journal of Management Education*, vol. 3, no. 3, pp. 9–31.

Borland, H & Pearce, A 2002, 'Identifying key dimensions of language and cultural disadvantage at university', *Australian Review of Applied Linguistics*, vol. 25, no. 2, pp. 101–127.

Bouchard, T, Lykken, D, McGue, M, Segal, N & Tellegen, A 1990, 'Sources of human psychological differences: the Minnesota study of twins reared apart', *Science*, vol. 250, pp. 223–229.

Boud, D 1995, *Enhancing learning through self-assessment*, Routledge, London.

Boud, D & Associates 2010, *Assessment 2020: seven propositions for assessment reform in higher education*, Australian Learning and Teaching Council, Sydney, viewed 14 February 2012, <http://www.olt.gov.au/resource-student-assessment-learning-and-after-courses-uts-2010>.

Boud, D & Costley, C 2007, 'From project supervision to advising: new conceptions of the practice', *Innovations in Education and Teaching International*, vol. 44, no. 2, pp. 119–130.

Boud, D, Cressy, P & Docherty, P (eds) 2006, *Productive reflection at work*, Routledge, Abingdon.

Boud, D & Feletti, G 1997, *The challenge of problem-based learning*, 2nd edn, Kogan Page, London.

Boud, D, Solomon N & Symes, C 2001, 'New practices for new times', in D Boud & N Solomon (eds), *Work-based learning: a new higher education?*, Society for Research into Higher Education and Open University Press, Buckingham, pp. 3–17.

Bourn D 2011, 'From internationalisation to global perspectives', *Higher Education Research and Development*, vol. 30, no. 5, pp. 559–571.

Bowden, J, Hart, G, King, B, Trigwell, K & Watts, O 2000, Generic capabilities of ATN university graduates, Australian Technology Network, Adelaide, viewed 14 February 2012, <http://www.clt.uts.edu.au/ATN.grad.cap.project.index.html>.

Bowl, M 2003, *Non-traditional entrants to higher education: 'they talk about people like me'*, Trentham Books, Stoke on Trent.

Boyer Commission on Educating Undergraduates in the Research University 1998, *Reinventing undergraduate education: three years after the Boyer Report*, State University of New York, Stony Brook, viewed 14 February 2012, <http://dspace.sunyconnect.suny.edu/handle/1951/26013>.

Boyer, EL 1990, *Scholarship reconsidered: priorities of the professoriate*, The Carnegie Foundation for the Advancement of Teaching, Princeton, NJ.

Bradley, D 2008, *Review of higher education discussion paper*, Department of Education Employment and Workplace Relations, Canberra, viewed 14 February 2012, <http://www.deewr.gov.au/HigherEducation/Review/Documents/PDF/08_222_Review_AusHEd_Internals_100pp_FINAL_WEB.pdf>.

Bradley, JP, Daniels, LF & Jones, TC (eds) 1969, *The international dictionary of thoughts: an encyclopedia of quotations from every age for every occasion*, JG Ferguson Publishing Co, Chicago.

Bransford, JD, Brown, AL & Cocking, RR (eds) 2000, *How people learn: brain, mind, and experience*, National Academy Press, Washington, DC.

Bremer L & van der Wende, M 1995, *Internationalising the curriculum in higher education: experiences in the Netherlands*, The Netherlands Organisation for International Cooperation in Higher Education, The Hague.

Bressoud, D 1999, 'The one minute paper', in B Gold, S Keith & W Marion (eds), *Assessment practices in undergraduate mathematics*, Mathematical Association of America, viewed 14 February 2012, <http://www.maa.org/saum/maanotes49/87.html>.

Brew, A 2006, *Research and teaching: beyond the divide*, Palgrave Macmillan, London.

Brew, A 2010, *National teaching fellowship final report: enhancing undergraduate engagement through research and inquiry*, viewed 14 February 2012, <http://www.olt.gov.au/resource-enhancing-undergraduate-engagement-research-enquiry-macquarie-2010>.

Brew, A & Boud, D 1995, 'Teaching and research: establishing the vital link with learning', *Higher Education*, vol. 29, pp. 261–273.

Brink, C 2010, 'Quality and standards: clarity, comparability and responsibility', *Quality in Higher Education*, vol. 16, no. 2, pp. 139–152.

British Council 2010, Student decision-making study, British Council, London, viewed 14 February 2012, <http://www.britishcouncil.org/eumd-information-student-decision-making.htm>.

Brodeur, DR, Young, PW & Blair, KB 2002, 'Problem-based learning in aerospace engineering education', *Proceedings of the 2002 American Society for Engineering Education Annual Conference and Exposition*, Massachusetts Institute of Technology, Cambridge.

Brodie, L 2007, 'Reflective writing by distance education students in an engineering problem-based learning course', *Australasian Journal of Engineering Education*, vol. 13, no. 1, pp. 31–40.

Brodie, L 2008, 'Assessment strategy for virtual teams undertaking the EWB Challenge', paper presented to Australasian Association of Engineering Educators, Yeppoon, Qld, 7–10 December.

Brodie, L 2009, Team report 1: getting started, University of Southern Queensland, Toowomba, viewed 13 February 2012, <http://www.usq.edu.au/course/material/eng1101/projects/project1/2009/team_report_1___getting_starteds2.htm>.

Brodie, L 2012, 'Problem-based learning', in L Hunt & D Chalmers (eds), *University teaching in focus: a learning-centred approach*, ACER Press, Melbourne, pp. 145–163.

Brodie, L & Borch, O 2004, 'Choosing PBL paradigms: experience and methods of two universities', in C Snook & D Thorpe (eds), *Australasian Association of Engineering Educators Conference*, University of Southern Queensland, Toowoomba, Australia, pp. 213–223.

Brookfield, SD 1995, *Becoming a critically reflective teacher*, Jossey-Bass, San Francisco.

Brookfield, SD 2006, *The skilful teacher: on technique, trust and responsiveness in the classroom*, 2nd edn, Jossey-Bass, San Francisco.

Brookfield, SD & Preskill, S 2005, *Discussion as a way of teaching: tools and techniques for democratic classrooms*, 2nd edn, Jossey-Bass, San Francisco.

Broome, R 2009, 'Bringing students and community together: Americans in the Gariwerd/Grampians', paper presented at the Forum on Indigenous Teaching and Learning, Melbourne, 11 December, viewed 27 February 2012, <http://www.indigenousteaching.com/html/forum_materials.html>.

Broughan, C & Hunt, L 2012, 'Inclusive teaching', in L Hunt & D Chalmers (eds), *University teaching in focus: a learning-centred approach*, ACER Press, Melbourne, pp. 182–198.

Brown, G 2004, *How students learn*, Supplement to the Key Guides for Effective Teaching in Higher Education Series, RoutledgeFalmer, London, viewed 14 February 2012, <http://www.routledgeeducation.com/resources/pdf/how_to_learn.pdf>.

Brown, JC & Daly, AJ 2005, 'Intercultural contact and competencies of tertiary students', *New Zealand Journal of Educational Studies*, vol. 40, nos. 1 & 2, pp. 85–100.

Brown, R 2010, 'The current brouhaha about standards in England', *Quality in Higher Education*, vol. 16, no. 2, pp. 130–137.

Brown, S & Race, P 2012, 'Using effective assessment to promote learning', in L Hunt & D Chalmers (eds), *University teaching in focus: a learning-centred approach*, ACER Press, Melbourne, pp. 74–91.

Brown, S 2011, 'Retention and the student experience: practice that works to ensure student success', paper presented at the University of the Sunshine Coast, Maroochydore, May 2011.

Brown, S, Rust, C & Gibbs, G 1994, *Strategies for diversifying assessment*, Oxford Centre for Staff Development, Oxford.

Budge, K 2010, 'The diversification of Australian higher education: is the academy prepared for the challenge?', in M Devlin, J Nagy & A Lichtenberg (eds), *Research and development in higher education: reshaping higher education*, vol. 33, refereed papers from the 33rd Higher Education Research and Development Society of Australasia Annual International Conference, Melbourne, pp. 157–166.

Butin, DW (ed.) 2005, *Service learning in higher education: critical issues and directions*, Palgrave, New York.

Byers W 2007, *How mathematicians think: using ambiguity, contradiction and paradox to create mathematics*, Princeton University Press.

Campbell, M & Christie, M 2008, *Indigenous community engagement at Charles Darwin University*, Charles Darwin University, Darwin, viewed 14 February 2012, <http://www.cdu.edu.au/centres/spil/pdf/ICE@CDU_FINAL.pdf>.

Campbell, M & Christie, M 2009, 'Researching a university's engagement with the Indigenous communities it serves', *Learning Communities: International Journal of Learning in Social Contexts*, vol. 1, pp. 2–22.

Carnegie Foundation for the Advancement of Teaching 2011, Carnegie programs, Carnegie Foundation for the Advancement of Teaching, Stanford, CA, viewed 14 February 2012, <http://www.carnegiefoundation.org>.

Carroll, J 2005, 'Strategies for becoming more explicit', in J Carroll & J Ryan, *Teaching international students: improving learning for all*, Routledge, London, pp. 26–34.

Carroll, JB 1968, 'On learning from being told', *Educational Psychologist*, vol. 5, pp. 4–10.

Caruana, V & Ploner, J 2010, *Internationalisation and equality and diversity in higher education: merging identities*, Equity Challenge Unit, London.

Cass, A, Lowell, A, Christie, M, Snelling, PL, Flack, M, Marrnganyin B & Brown, I 2002, 'Sharing the true stories: improving communication between Aboriginal patients and healthcare workers', *Medical Journal of Australia*, vol. 176, no. 10, pp. 466–470.

Center for Instructional Innovation and Assessment at Western Washington University (CIIA) 2007, 'Using clickers in the college classroom', YouTube, 13 December, viewed 14 February 2012, <http://www.youtube.com/watch?v=2G0WzfitDBA>.

Centre for Higher Education, Learning and Teaching 2012, BIOL2121 — plant structure and function, Australian National University, Canberra, viewed 14 February 2012, <http://cedam.anu.edu.au/chelt-cedam-archive/case-studies-and-role-plays>.

Chalmers, D 2007, *A review of Australian and international quality: systems and indicators of learning and teaching*, Australian Learning and Teaching Council, Sydney, viewed 14 February 2012, <http://www.olt.gov.au/resource-review-indicators-teaching-learning-2007>.

Chalmers, D, Barrett-Lennard, S & Longnecker, N 2009, *Good practice guidelines: developing communication skills units and embedding communication skills into the New Courses*, University of Western Australia, Perth, viewed 14 February 2012, <http://www.catl.uwa.edu.au/__data/page/158491/Communication_Skills_Guide.rtf>.

Chalmers, D & Fuller, R 1996, *Teaching for learning at university: theory and practice*, Kogan Page, London.

Chalmers, D & Partridge, L 2012, 'Teaching graduate attributes and academic skills', in L Hunt & D Chalmers (eds), *University teaching in focus: a learning-centred approach*, ACER Press, Melbourne, pp. 56–73.

Chalmers, D & Volet, S 1997, 'Common misconceptions about students from South-east Asia studying in Australia', *Higher Education Research and Development Journal*, vol. 16, no. 1, pp. 87–98.

Chanock, K 2004, 'Autonomy and responsibility: same or different', *Proceedings of the Independent Learning Conference 2003*, Indendent Learning Association, Wellington, New Zealand, viewed 14 February 2012, <http://independentlearning.org/ILA/ila03/ila03_chanock.pdf>.

Chartrand, TL & Bargh, JA 1999, 'The chameleon effect: the perception-behaviour link and social interaction', *Journal of Personality and Social Psychology*, vol. 76, pp. 893–910.

China's University and College Admissions System 2011, General entry requirements, Beijing Chiwest Company, Beijing, viewed 14 February 2012, <http://www.cucas.edu.cn/HomePage/content/content_145.shtml>.

Chomsky, N 1959, 'Review of Skinner's Verbal Behaviour', *Language*, vol. 35, pp. 26–58.

Christie, M 2006, 'Transdisciplinary research and Aboriginal knowledge', *Australian Journal of Indigenous Education*, vol. 35, pp. 1–12.

Christie, M 2008, 'Digital tools and the management of Australian desert Aboriginal knowledge', in P Wilson & M Stewart (eds), *Global Indigenous media: cultures, practices and politics*, Duke University Press, Durham, pp. 270–286.

Christie, M 2010, 'Money matters: payment for the participation of Aboriginal knowledge authorities in academic teaching and research work', *Learning Communities: International Journal of Learning in Social Contexts*, vol. 2, pp. 60–66.

Christie M (ed.) 2011, *Teaching from country*, Charles Darwin University and Australian Learning and Teaching Council, Darwin, viewed 14 February 2012, <http://learnline.cdu.edu.au/inc/tfc>.

Christie, M & Asmar, C 2012, 'Indigenous knowers and knowledge in university teaching', in L Hunt & D Chalmers (eds), *University teaching in focus: a learning-centred approach*, ACER Press, Melbourne, pp. 214–232.

CIIA *see* Center for Instructional Innovation and Assessment at Western Washington University

Citizenship and Immigration Canada 2009, *Facts and figures 2009 — immigration overview: permanent and temporary residents*, Citizenship and Immigration Canada, Toronto, viewed 14 February 2012, <http://www.cic.gc.ca/english/resources/statistics/facts2009/permanent/index.asp>.

Clark, DJ 2002, 'Towards an Aboriginal environmental health pedagogy' in J Cameron, G Shaw & A Arnott (eds), *Tertiary teaching: doing it differently, doing it better*, Northern Territory University Press, Darwin, pp. 83–91.

Clifford, V 2011, 'Internationalising the home student', *Higher Education Research and Development*, vol. 30, no. 5, pp. 555–557.

Clinton, G & Rieber, L 2010, 'The studio experience at the University of Georgia: an example of constructionist learning for adults', *Educational Technology Research and Development*, vol. 58, no. 6, pp. 755–780.

Coate, K, Barnett, R & Williams, G 2001, 'Relationships between teaching and research in higher education in England', *Higher Education Quarterly*, vol. 55, no. 2, pp. 158–174.

Coghlan, D & Brannick, T 2001, *Doing action research in your own organization*, SAGE Publications, London.

Cohen, L, Manion, L & Morrison, K 2007, *Research methods in education*, Routledge, New York.

Colbeck, CL 1998, 'Merging in a seamless blend', *Journal of Higher Education*, vol. 69, no. 6, pp. 647–671.

College of Fine Arts 2011, *Learning to teach online*, University of New South Wales, Sydney, viewed 27 February 2012, <http://online.cofa.unsw.edu.au/learning-to-teach-online/ltto-episodes>.

Colvin, C & Jaffar, F 2007, 'Enhancing the international student experience: the importance of international student groups and peer support at Edith Cowan University', *Proceedings of the 10th Pacific Rim First Year in Higher Education Conference*, Queensland University of Technology, Brisbane, viewed 14 February 2012, <http://www.fyhe.com.au/past_papers/papers07/final_papers/pdfs/2c.pdf>.

Commonwealth of Australia 2011, 'Higher Education Standards Framework (Threshold Standards) 2011', *Tertiary Education Quality and Standards Agency Act 2011*, Department of Education, Employment and Workplace Relations, Canberra, viewed 20 March 2012, <http://www.comlaw.gov.au/Details/F2012L00003>.

Confederation of British Industry 2011, *Building for growth: business priorities for education and skills. Education and skills survey 2011*, Confederation of British Industry, London.

Cook, V 2009, 'Getting off to a Flying Start in HE: an overview of UCLan's summer school programme to aid student transition and retention', in P Jones, J Storan, T Hudson & J Braham (eds), *Towards a new agenda for lifelong learning: access, diversity and participation*, Forum for Access and Continuing Education, London, viewed 27 February 2012, <http://www.f-a-c-e.org.uk/publications.html>.

Cooper, L, Orrell, J & Bowden, M 2010, *Work integrated learning: a guide to effective practice*, Routledge, London.

Cortazzi, M & Jin, L, 1997, 'Communication for learning across cultures', in D McNamara & R Harris (eds), *Overseas students in higher education: issues on teaching and learning*, London, Routledge.

Costley, C, Elliott, G & Gibbs, P 2010, *Doing work based research*, SAGE Publications, London.

Council for Aboriginal Reconciliation 2000, *Documents of reconciliation briefing paper*, Reconciliaton Australia, Canberra, viewed 14 February 2012, <http://www.austlii.edu.au/au/orgs/car/docrec/policy/brief/terran.htm>.

Cousin, G 2008, 'Threshold concepts: old wine in new bottles or new forms of transactional curriculum inquiry?', in R Land, JHF Meyer & J Smith (eds), *Threshold concepts within the disciplines*, Sense Publishing, Rotterdam and Taipei, pp. 261–272.

Cousin, G 2009, *Researching learning in higher education. An introduction to contemporary methods and approaches*, Routledge, New York and London.

Cousin, G 2010, 'Neither teacher-centred nor student-centred: threshold concepts and research', *Journal of Learning Development in Higher Education*, no. 2, pp. 1–9.

Cowan, J 2006, *On becoming an innovative university teacher: reflection in action*, 2nd edn, McGraw-Hill, Maidenhead.

Coyle, R 2008, Community outreach: research project to produce a DVD (Media Studies example 2), The Teaching–Research Nexus: a guide for academics and policy-makers in higher education, viewed 10 February 2012, <http://trnexus.edu.au/index.php?page=arts-and-humanities>.

Craig, N & Zinkiewicz, L 2010, *Inclusive practice within psychology higher education*, Higher Education Academy Psychology Network, University of York.

Crammer, S 2006, 'Enhancing graduate employability: best intentions and mixed outcomes', *Studies in Higher Education*, vol. 31, no. 2, pp. 169–184.

Cranton, P 2006, *Understanding and promoting transformative learning: a guide for educators of adults*, 2nd edn, Jossey-Bass, San Francisco.

Craven, R, d'Arbon, M & Wilson-Miller, J 2011, 'Developing teaching activities' in R Craven (ed.), *Teaching Aboriginal studies: a practical resource for primary and secondary teaching*, 2nd edn, Allen & Unwin, Crows Nest, NSW, pp. 289–314.

Craven, R, Tucker, A, Munns, G, Hinkley, J, Marsh, H & Simpson, K 2005, *Indigenous students' aspirations: dreams, perceptions and realities*, Commonwealth of Australia, Canberra.

Crawford, K, Gordon, S, Nicholas, J & Prosser, M 1994, 'Conceptions of mathematics and how it is learned: the perspectives of students entering university', *Learning and Instruction*, vol. 4, pp. 331–345.

Crawford, K, Gordon, S, Nicholas, J & Prosser, M 1998a, 'Qualitatively different experiences of learning mathematics at university', *Learning and Instruction*, vol. 8, pp. 455–468.

Crawford, K, Gordon, S, Nicholas, J & Prosser, M 1998b, 'University mathematics students conception of mathematics', *Studies in Higher Education*, vol. 23, pp. 87–94.

Crebert, G, Bates, M, Bell, B, Patrick, C-J & Cragnolini, V 2004, 'Developing generic skills at university during work placement and in employment: graduates' perceptions', *Higher Education Research & Development*, vol. 23, no. 2, pp. 147–165.

Crisp, G & Hillier, M 2011, Transforming assessment, Australian Learning and Teaching Council, Sydney, viewed 27 February 2012, <http://www.transformingassessment.com>.

Crisp, G, Sadler, R, Krause, K, Buckridge, M, Wills, S, Brown, C, Mclean, J, Dalton, H, LeLievre, K & Brougham, B 2009, Peer review of teaching for promotion purposes, Australian Teaching and Learning Council, Sydney, viewed 14 February 2012, <www.adelaide.edu.au/clpd/peerreview/peerReviewReport_part1.pdf>.

Cuban, L 2001, Oversold and underused: computers in the classroom, Harvard University Press, Cambridge, MA.

CU-SEI, see University of Colorado Science Education Initiative

Cuthbert, R 2006 Constructive alignment in the world of institutional management, Learning and Teaching Support Network Generic Centre, York.

Davis, BG, 2009, Tools for teaching, 2nd edn, Jossey-Bass, San Francisco.

Davis, BG, Wood, L & Wilson, RC 1983, 'Implement good practices in teaching large lecture courses', in A Berkeley compendium, University of California/Berkeley University, viewed 14 February 2012, <http://teaching.berkeley.edu/compendium/suggestions/file212.html>.

Deal, TE & Kennedy, AA 1982, Corporate cultures: the rites and rituals of corporate life, Penguin Books, Harmondsworth.

Deem, R 1998, '"New managerialism" and higher education: the management of performances and cultures in universities in the United Kingdom', International Studies in Sociology of Education, vol. 8, no. 1, pp. 47–70.

de Graaff, E & Kolmos, A 2002, 'Characteristics of problem-based learning', International Journal of Engineering Education, vol. 19, no. 5, pp. 657–662.

de la Harpe, B, Radloff, A, Scoufis, M, Dalton, H, Thomas, J, Lawson, A, David, C & Girardi, A 2009, The B factor project: understanding academic staff beliefs about graduate attributes, Australian Learning and Teaching Council, Sydney, viewed 14 February 2012, <http://www.olt.gov.au/resource-b-factor-academic-beliefs-graduates-rmit-2009>.

De Phillips, FA, Berliner, WM & Cribbin, JJ 1960, Management of training programs, Irwin, Chicago.

Dempster, FN 1988, 'The spacing effect: a case study in the failure to apply the results of psychological research', American Psychologist, vol. 43, pp. 627–634.

Denham, J 2008, 'HE Speech', paper presented to the Wellcome Collection Conference Centre, London, 29 February, viewed 14 February 2012, <http://webarchive.nationalarchives.gov.uk/+/http://www.dius.gov.uk/speeches/denham_hespeech_290208.html>.

Denzin, N, Lincoln, Y & Smith, L 2008, Handbook of critical and Indigenous methodologies, SAGE Publications, Thousand Oaks, CA.

Department for Education and Skills 2003, The future of higher education, Department for Education and Skills, Norwich, viewed 14 February 2012, <http://www.bis.gov.uk/assets/biscore/corporate/migratedd/publications/f/future_of_he.pdf>.

Department of Education, Science and Training (DEST) 2002, Employability skills for the future, A report by the Australian Chamber of Commerce and Industry and the Business Council of Australia for the Department of Education, Science and Training, Canberra.

Department of Education, Training and Youth Affairs (DETYA) 2000, *The Australian higher education quality assurance framework*, Commonwealth of Australia, Canberra, viewed 14 February 2012, <www.dest.gov.au/highered/occpaper/00g/00g.pdf>.

DiGregorio, K, Farrington, S & Page, S 2000, 'Listening to our students: understanding the factors that affect Aboriginal and Torres Strait Islander students' academic success', *Higher Education Research and Development*, vol. 19, pp. 297–309.

Dochy, F, Segers, M, van den Bossche, P & Gijbels, D 2003, 'Effects of problem-based learning: a meta-analysis', *Learning and Instruction*, vol. 13, pp. 533–568.

Doğru, M & Kalander, S 2007, 'Applying the subject "cell" through constructivist approach during science lessons and the teacher's view', *Journal of Environmental and Science Education*, vol. 2, no. 1, pp. 3–13.

Donald, JG 2009, 'The commons: disciplinary and interdisciplinary encounters', in C Kreber (ed.), *The university and its disciplines: teaching and learning within and beyond university boundaries*, Routledge, New York and London, pp. 35–48.

Douglas, H 2005, 'How Australian law schools endeavour to support Indigenous students', in G Shaw (ed.), *Tertiary teaching and learning: dealing with diversity*, Charles Darwin University Press, Darwin, pp. 177–186.

Doyle, S, Gendall, P, Meyer, L, Hoek, J, Tait, C, McKenzie, L & Loorparg, A 2009, 'An investigation of factors associated with student participation in study abroad', *Journal of Studies in International Education*, vol. 14, no. 5, pp. 471–490.

Dreyfus, HL & Dreyfus, SE 1986, *Mind over machine: the power of human intuition and expertise in the era of computer*, Basil Blackwell, Oxford.

Duckworth, E 1964, 'Piaget rediscovered', in RE Ripple & VN Rockcastle (eds), *Piaget rediscovered*, Cornell University Press, Ithaca, NY.

Dunlap, JC & Lowenthal, PR 2009, 'Tweeting the night away: using Twitter to enhance social presence', *Journal of Information Systems Education*, vol. 20, no. 2, pp. 129–136.

Dunn, L & Wallace, M (eds) 2008, *Teaching in transnational higher education: enhancing learning for offshore international students*, Routledge, New York.

Dunne, C 2009, 'Host students' perspectives of intercultural contact in an Irish university', *Journal of Studies in International Education*, vol. 13, no. 2, pp. 222–239.

Dweck, C 1999, *Self-theories: their role in motivation, personality and development*, Pyschology Press, Taylor and Francis, Philadelphia, PA.

Dwyer, C 2001, 'Linking research and teaching: a staff-student interview project', *Journal of Geography in Higher Education*, vol. 25, no. 3, pp. 357–366.

EDUCAUSE 2012, EDUCAUSE learning initiative, EDUCAUSE, Washington, DC, viewed 14 February 2012, <http://www.educause.edu/eli>.

Edwards, A, Jones, SM, Wapstra, F & Richardson, AMM 2007a, 'Engaging students through authentic research experiences', paper presented at the National UniServe Science Teaching and Learning Research conference, Sydney, 26–28 September, viewed 14 February 2012, <http://eprints.utas.edu.au/8581/1/edwards.pdf> .

Edwards, V, Ran, A & Daguo, L 2007b, 'Uneven playing field or falling standards? Chinese students' competence in English', *Race Ethnicity and Education*, vol. 10, no. 4, pp. 387–400.

Ellison-Loschmann, E 2003, 'Irihapeti Ramsden', *British Medical Journal*, vol. 327, p. 453.

Elton, L 1987, *Teaching in higher education: appraisal and training*, Kogan Page, London.

Elton, L 2006, 'The nature of effective or exemplary teaching in an environment that emphasizes strong research and teaching links', *New Directions for Teaching and Learning*, vol. 107, pp. 35–43.

Engelhard Project 2011, Georgetown University, Washington DC, viewed 14 February 2012, <http://cndls.georgetown.edu/engelhard>.

Engestrom, Y, Engestrom, R & Karkkainen, M 1995, 'Polycontextuality and boundary crossing in expert cognition', *Learning and Instruction*, vol. 5, pp. 319–336.

Engineers Australia 2011, Program accreditation, Engineers Australia, Canberra, viewed 14 February 2012, <http://www.engineersaustralia.org.au/about-us/program-accreditation>.

Entwistle, N, Skinner, D, Entwistle, D, & Orr, S 2000, 'Conceptions and beliefs about "good teaching": an integration of contrasting research areas', *Higher Education Research and Development*, vol. 19, no. 1, pp. 5–26.

Eraut, M 1994, *Developing professional knowledge and competence*, RoutledgeFalmer, Abingdon.

Espasa, A & Meneses, J 2010, 'Analyzing feedback processes in an online teaching and learning environment: an exploratory study', *Higher Education*, vol. 59, no. 3, pp. 277–292.

European Commission 2010, The ERASMUS Programme — studying in Europe and more, European Commission, Brussels, viewed 14 February 2012, <http://ec.europa.eu/education/lifelong-learning-programme/doc80_en.htm>.

Ewell, P 2010, 'Twenty years of quality assurance in higher education: what's happened and what's different?', *Quality in Higher Education*, vol. 16, issue 2, pp. 173–203.

Farrington, S, Digregorio, K & Page, S 1999, 'Yooroang Garang issues in Aboriginal health worker training: listening to students', *Aboriginal and Islander Health Worker Journal*, vol. 23, no. 1, pp. 17–20.

Fenton, E 1967, *The new social studies*, Holt, Rinehart and Winston, New York.

Fialho, M 2012, *Courageous conversations about race*, University of Western Australia, Perth, viewed 14 February 2012, <http://www.osds.uwa.edu.au/about/workshop.asp?workshop_id=121>.

Fielden, J 2007, *Global horizons for UK universities*, Council for Industry and Higher Education (CIHE), London.

Fink, LD 2003, *Creating significant learning experiences: an integrated approach to designing college courses*, Jossey-Bass, San Francisco.

Flanagan, M 2012, *Threshold concepts: undergraduate teaching, postgraduate training and professional development. A short introduction and bibliography*, University College London Department of Electronic and Electrical Engineering, London, viewed 26 February 2012, <http://www.ee.ucl.ac.uk/~mflanaga/thresholds.html>.

Flint, NR & Johnson, B 2011, *Towards fairer university assessment: recognising the concerns of students*, Routledge, Abingdon.

Ford, Payi L 2010, *Aboriginal knowledge narratives and country: marri Kunkimba Putj Putj Marrideyan*, Post Pressed, Mt Gravatt.

Freeman, M 2011, *Learning and teaching academic standards resources for accounting*, Australian Learning and Teaching Council, Sydney, viewed 26 February 2012, <http://www.olt.gov.au/resource-learning-and-teaching-academic-standards-resources-accounting-2011>.

Freire, P 1970, *Pedagogy of the oppressed*, trans Myra Bergman Ramos, Continuum, New York.

Frick, TW, Chadha, R, Watson, C & Zlatkovska, E 2010, 'Improving course evaluations to improve instruction and complex learning in higher education', *Educational Technology Research and Development*, vol. 58, no. 2, pp. 115–136.

Friedman, DB, Crews, TB, Caicedo, JM, Besley, JC, Weinberg, J & Freeman, ML 2010, 'An exploration into inquiry-based learning by a multidisciplinary group of higher education faculty', *Higher Education*, vol. 59, pp. 765–783.

Fry, H, Ketteridge, S & Marshall, S 2009, *A handbook for teaching and learning in higher education: enhancing academic practice*, 3rd edn, Routledge, Abingdon.

Fukuda, K & Vogel, EK 2009, 'Human variation in overriding attentional capture', *The Journal of Neuroscience*, vol. 29, no. 27, pp. 8726–8733.

Gardner, H 1983, *Frames of mind: the theory of multiple intelligences*, Basic Books, New York.

Garnett, J 2007, 'Employers and university partnerships', in S Roodhouse & S Swailes (eds), *Employers, skills and higher education*, Kingsham, Chichester.

Garnett, J 2009a, 'Contributing to the intellectual capital of organisations', in J Garnett, C Costley & B Workman, (eds), *Work based learning: journeys to the core of higher education*, Middlesex University Press, London.

Garnett, J 2009b, 'Developing the work-based learning curriculum to meet the needs of employers: from independent learning to organisational development', in D Young & J Garnett (eds), *Work-based learning futures III*, University Vocational Awards Council, Bolton, pp. 21–28.

Garnett, J 2012, 'Authentic work-integrated learning', in L Hunt & D Chalmers (eds), *University teaching in focus: a learning-centred approach*, ACER Press, Melbourne, pp. 164–179.

Garnett, J, Costley, C & Workman, B (eds) 2009, *Work based learning: journeys to the core of higher education*, Middlesex University Press, London.

Garrison, DR 2007, 'Online community of inquiry review: social, cognitive, and teaching presence issues', *Journal of Asynchronous Learning Networks*, vol. 11, no. 1, pp. 61–72.

Garrison, DR 2011, *E-learning in the 21st century: a framework for research and practice*, 2nd edn, Routledge, New York.

Garrison, DR, Cleveland-Innes, M, Vaughn, N & Akyol, Z 2011, Community of inquiry framework, Social Sciences and Humanities Research Council, Ottawa, viewed 14 February 2012, <http://communitiesofinquiry.com>.

Garrison, DR & Vaughan, ND 2008, *Blended learning in higher education: framework, principles, and guidelines*, Jossey-Bass, San Francisco.

Gibbs, G 1999, 'Improving teaching, learning and assessment', *Journal of Geography in Higher Education*, vol. 23, no. 2, pp. 147–155.

Gibbs, G 2010a, *Dimensions of quality*, Higher Education Academy, York, viewed 26 February 2012, <http://www.heacademy.ac.uk/resources/detail/evidence_informed_practice/Dimensions_of_Quality>.

Gibbs, G 2010b, *Using assessment to support student learning*, Leeds Met Press, Leeds.

Gibbs, G & Dunbar-Goddet, H 2007, *The effects of programme assessment environments on student learning*, Higher Education Academy, York.

Gibbs, P & Garnett, J 2007, 'Work based learning as a field of study', *Journal of Research in Post-Compulsory Education*, vol. 12, no. 6, pp. 409–421.

Gijselaers, W & Schmidt, H 1990, 'Development and evaluation of a causal model of problem-based learning', in A Nooman, H Schmidt & E Ezzat (eds), *Innovation in medical education: an evaluation of its present status*, Springer-Verlag, Berlin, pp. 95–133.

Gillborn, D 2010, 'The colour of numbers: surveys, statistics and deficit-thinking about race and class', *Journal of Education Policy*, vol. 25, no. 2, pp. 253–276.

Glassick, CE, Huber, MT & Maeroff, GI 1997, *Scholarship assessed, evaluation of the professoriate*, Jossey-Bass, San Francisco.

Gould, SJ 1999, 'A critique of Heckhausen and Schulz's (1995) "Life-span theory of control" from a cross-cultural perspective', *Psychological Review*, vol. 106, no. 3, pp. 597–604.

Graduate Skills 2010, Embedding the development and grading of generic skills into the business curriculum (EDGGS), Australian Learning and Teaching Council project, Sydney, viewed 14 February 2012, <http://www.graduateskills.edu.au/project>.

Gravestock, P 2009, *Inclusive curriculum practices*, e-bulletin, University of Gloucestershire, Higher Education Academy, York, viewed 26 February 2012, <http://www.heacademy. ac.uk/assets/documents/subjects/psychology/8-part-Inclusive_Curriculum_ Practicev2.pdf>.

Greening, T 1998, 'Scaffolding for success in PBL', *Medical Education Online*, vol. 3, no. 4.

Grunert O'Brien, J, Mills, BJ, & Cohen, MW 2008, *The course syllabus: a learning-centred approach*, 2nd edn, John Wiley & Sons, New York.

Grust, N 2007, *Studying in Germany: a guide for international students*, 2nd edn, German Academic Exchange Service (Deutscher AkademischerAustausch Dienst), Bonn.

Guba, EG & Lincoln, YS 1985, *Naturalistic inquiry*, SAGE Publications, Thousand Oaks, CA.

Guerin, B 1986, 'Mere presence effects in humans: a review', *Journal of Personality and Social Psychology*, vol. 22, pp. 38–77.

Gurin, PY 1999, Expert report of Patricia Gurin, Gratz et al. v. Bollinger et al., No. 97-75321, Grutier et al. v. Bollinger et al., University of Michigan, viewed 26 February 2012, <http://www.vpcomm.umich.edu/admissions/legal/expert/summ.html>.

Gurin, P & Nagda, B 2006, 'Getting to the what, how and why of diversity on campus', *Educational Researcher*, vol. 35, no. 1, pp. 20–24.

Gurruwiwi, D 2010, 'Teaching students to know themselves', *Learning Communities: International Journal of Learning in Social Contexts*, vol. 2, pp. 23–25.

Gurruwiwi, D & Guyula, Y 2010, 'Intellectual properties', *Learning Communities: International Journal of Learning in Social Contexts*, vol. 2, pp. 50–59.

Hager, P, Holland, S & Beckett, D 2002, *Enhancing the learning and employability of graduates: the role of generic skills*, Business/Higher Education Round Table position paper no. 9. Melbourne, Australia.

Hager, PJ & Holland, S 2006, *Graduate attributes, learning and employability*, Springer, Dordrecht.

Haggis, T 2009, 'What have we been thinking of? A critical overview of 40 years of student learning research in higher education research', *Studies in Higher Education*, vol. 34, no. 4, pp. 377–390.

Halonen, J & Ellenberg, G 2006, 'Teaching evaluation follies: misperception and misbehaviour in student evaluations of teachers', in P Seldin (ed.), *Evaluating faculty performance*, Anker, Bolton, MA, pp. 150–165.

Hamilton, D, Qian, D, & Hinton, L 2007, 'International students: do satisfaction, attendance and results correlate? Challenges for teachers', paper presented to the conference of the International Society for the Scholarship of Teaching and Learning, Sydney, 2–5 July.

Hamilton, IR 2009, 'Automating formative and summative feedback for individualized assignments', *Campus-Wide Information Systems*, vol. 26, no. 5, pp. 355–364.

Harris, K, Farrell, K, Bell, M, Devlin, M & James, R 2008, *Peer review of teaching in Australian higher education: resources to support institutions in developing and embedding effective policies and practices*, Australian Learning and Teaching Council, Sydney, viewed 26 February 2012, <http://www.olt.gov.au/resource-peer-review-of-teaching-melbourne-2009>.

Harrison, N 2011, *Teaching and learning in Aboriginal education*, 2nd edn, Oxford University Press, Melbourne.

Harryba, S, Guilfoyle, A & Knight, S-A 2011, 'Staff perspectives on the role of English proficiency in providing support services', in *Developing student skills for the next decade: proceedings of the 20th Annual Teaching Learning Forum*, Edith Cowan University, Perth, viewed 26 February 2012, <http://lsn.curtin.edu.au/tlf/tlf2011/refereed/harryba.pdf>.

Harvey, L & Bowers-Brown, T 2004, 'Employability cross-country comparison', *Graduate Market Trends*, Winter 2004/5, pp. 3–5.

Harvey, L & Green, D 1993, 'Defining quality', *Assessment and Evaluation in Higher Education*, vol. 18, no. 1, pp. 9–34.

Harvey, L & Williams, J 2010, 'Editorial: fifteen years of quality in higher education', *Quality in Higher Education*, vol. 16, no. 1, pp. 3–36.

Hattie, J 2009, *Visible learning: a synthesis of over 800 meta-analyses related to achievement*, Routledge, New York.

Hattie, J & Marsh, HW 1996, 'The relationship between research and teaching: a meta-analysis', *Review of Educational Research*, vol. 66, no. 4, pp. 507–542.

Hattie, J & Marsh, HW 2004, 'One journey to unravel the relationship between research and teaching', paper presented to Research and teaching: closing the divide? An international colloquium, Winchester, March 18–19, viewed 26 February 2012, <http://www.education.auckland.ac.nz/webdav/site/education/shared/hattie/docs/relationship-between-research-and-teaching-(2004).pdf>.

Healey, M 2005, 'Linking research and teaching exploring disciplinary spaces and the role of inquiry-based learning', in R Barnett (ed.), *Reshaping the university: new relationships between research, scholarship and teaching*, McGraw-Hill and Open University Press, Maidenhead, pp. 30–42.

Healey, M 2011a, 'Rethinking the dissertation', *The Guardian*, 28 June, viewed 26 February 2012, <http://www.guardian.co.uk/higher-education-network/blog/2011/jun/28/flexible-dissertations-for-undergraduates?INTCMP=SRCH>.

Healey, M 2011b, Linking research and teaching: a selected bibliography, viewed 26 February 2012, <http://mickhealey.co.uk/resources>.

Healey, M, Fuller, M, Bradley, A & Hall, T 2006, 'Listening to students: the experiences of disabled students of learning at university', in M Adams & S Brown (eds), *Towards inclusive learning in higher education: developing curricula for disabled students*, RoutledgeFalmer, London, pp. 32–43.

Healey, M & Jenkins, A 2009, *Developing undergraduate research and inquiry*, Higher Education Academy, York, viewed 26 February 2012, <www.heacademy.ac.uk/assets/York/documents/resources/publications/DevelopingUndergraduate_Final.pdf>.

Healy, AF, Havas, DA & Parker, JT 2000, 'Comparing serial position effects in semantic and episodic memory using reconstruction of order tasks', *Journal of Memory and Language*, vol. 42, pp. 147–167.

Heckhausan, J & Schulz, R 1995, 'A life-span theory of control', *Psychological Review*, vol. 102, pp. 284–304.

Henkel, M 2000, *Academic identities and policy change in higher education*, Jessica Kingsley, London and Philadelphia.

Herrington, A & Herrington, J (eds), 2005 *Authentic learning environments in higher education*, Information Science Publishing, Hershey, PA.

Herrington, J, Reeves, TC & Oliver, R 2010, *A guide to authentic e-learning*, Routledge, New York.

Hibbins, R & Barker, M 2011, 'Group work with students of diverse backgrounds', in J Fowler, A Gudmundsson & L Whicker (eds), *Groups work: a guide for working in groups*, 2nd edn, Palmer Higgs, Melbourne.

Higher Education Academy 2011, Teaching international students project, Higher Education Academy, York, viewed 26 February 2012, <http://www.heacademy.ac.uk/international-student-lifecycle>.

Higher Education Academy 2012, *Supporting new academic staff (SNAS) database*, Higher Education Academy, York, viewed 26 February 2012, <http://www.heacademy.ac.uk/snas>.

Higher Education Funding Council for England (HEFCE) 2010, *Student ethnicity: profile and progression of entrants to full-time, first degree study*, HEFCE, Bristol, viewed 26 February 2012, <http://www.hefce.ac.uk/pubs/hefce/2010/10_13>.

Higher Education Funding Council for England (HEFCE) 2011, *Designing learning spaces for effective learning*, JISC, Bristol, viewed 26 February 2012, http://www.jisc.ac.uk/eli_learningspaces.html.

Hills, R, Woods, P, Barker, M., Borbasi, S, Hibbins, R & Arthur, P 2010, Lighting the way: a report on the Local Aussie Mentor Project (LAMP), unpublished internal report, Griffith University, Brisbane.

History wars (2012, January 27), in *Wikipedia, The Free Encyclopedia*. viewed 27 January 2012, <http://en.wikipedia.org/wiki/History_wars>.

Hmelo, C & Evensen, DH 2000, 'Problem-based learning: gaining insights on learning interactions through multiple methods of enquiry', in C Hmelo & DH Evensen (eds), *Problem-based learning*, Lawrence Erlbaum Associates, Mahwah, NJ, pp. 1–16.

Hmelo-Silver, CE & Barrows, HS 2006, 'Goals and strategies of a problem-based learning facilitator', *The Interdisciplinary Journal of Problem-based learning*, vol. 1, no. 1, pp. 21–39.

Hmelo-Silver, CE, Duncan, RG & Chinn, CA 2007, 'Scaffolding and achievement in problem-based and inquiry learning: a response to Kirschner, Sweller, and Clark (2006)', *Educational Psychologist*, vol. 42, no. 2, pp. 99–107.

Ho, ES, Holmes, P & Cooper J 2004, *Review and evaluation of international literature on managing cultural diversity in the classroom*, Ministry of Education and Education New Zealand, Wellington.

Hockings, C 2010, *Inclusive learning and teaching: research synthesis*, Higher Education Academy, York, viewed 26 February 2012, <http://www.heacademy.ac.uk/resources/detail/evidencenet/Inclusive_learning_and_teaching_in_higher_education_synthesis>.

Hogan, C 1999, *Facilitating learning: practical strategies for college and university*, Eruditions Publishing, Melbourne.

Hogan, CF 2007, *Facilitating multicultural groups*, Kogan Page, London.

Hogan, CF 2012, *Facilitating cultural transitions and change*, Practical Action, Rugby.

Holdsworth, A, Watty, K & Davies, M 2009, *Developing capstone experiences*, Centre for the Study of Higher Education, University of Melbourne.

House of Commons 2009, *Students and universities: report of the Innovation, Universities, Science and Skills Committee*, House of Commons, London.

Houston, D 2007, 'Achievements and consequences of two decades of quality assurance in higher education: a personal view from the edge', *Quality in Higher Education*, vol. 16, no. 2, pp. 177–180.

Howard-Jones, PA 2010, *Introducing neuroeducational research: neuroscience, education and the brain from contexts to practice*, Routledge, London.

Howard-Jones, PA & Demetriou, S 2009, 'Uncertainty and engagement with learning games', *Instructional Science*, vol. 37, pp. 519–536.

Hu, S & Kuh, GD 2003, 'Diversity experiences and college student learning and personal development', *Journal of College Student Development*, vol. 44, no. 3, pp. 320–334.

Hughes, H 2009, Come travel: a tourism students' world conference, University of Lincoln, <http://www.heacademy.ac.uk/hlst/projects/detail/ourwork/pedagogic_projects/r10_come_travel_a_tourism_students_virtual_conference>.

Hughes, H & Heitmann, S 2011, Tourism students' virtual conference, University of Lincoln, http://www.tsvc.lincoln.ac.uk

Hughes, J, Jewson, N & Unwin, L 2007, 'Communities of practice: a contested concept in flux', in J Hughes, JN Jewson & L Unwin (eds), *Communities of practice: critical perspectives*, Routledge, London.

Huijser, H, Bedford, T & Bull, D 2008, 'OpenCourseWare, global access and the right to education: real access or marketing ploy?', *International Review of Research in Open and Distance Learning*, vol. 9, no. 1, pp. 1–13.

Hunt, L 2002, Teaching portfolio, unpublished.

Hunt, L, Chalmers, D & Macdonald, R 2012, 'Effective classroom teaching', in L Hunt & D Chalmers (eds), *University teaching in focus: a learning-centred approach*, ACER Press, Melbourne, pp. 21–37.

Hunt, L & Peach, N 2009, 'Planning for a sustainable academic future', in iPED Research Network (eds), *Academic futures: inquiries into higher education and pedagogy*, Cambridge Scholars Publishing, Newcastle upon Tyne.

Hurtado, S, Milem, JE, Clayton-Pedersen, AR & Allen, W 1998, 'Enhancing campus climates for racial/ethnic diversity: educational policy and practice', *Review of Higher Education*, vol. 21, no. 3, pp. 279–302.

Hurtado, S, Milem, JE, Clayton-Pedersen, AR & Allen, W 1999, 'Enacting diverse learning environments: improving the climate for racial/ethnic diversity in higher education', *ASHE–ERIC Higher Education Report*, vol. 26, no. 8, George Washington University, Washington, DC.

Hussin, F 2002, 'Killing off Captain Cook — Indigenous law students at Northern Territory University', in J Cameron, G Shaw & A Arnott (eds), *Tertiary teaching: doing it differently, doing it better*, Northern Territory University Press, Darwin, pp. 118–127.

Hutchings, P & Shulman, L 1999, 'The scholarship of teaching: new elaborations, new developments', *Change*, vol. 31, pp. 10–15.

Huxham, M 2007, 'Fast and effective feedback: are model answers the answer?', *Assessment & Evaluation in Higher Education*, vol. 32, no. 6, pp. 601–611.

Huxley, L 2011, 'Change Academy 2011', *Engage*, no. 24, p. 13.

Immordino-Yang, MH & Damasio, AR 2007, 'We feel, therefore we learn: the relevance of affective and social neuroscience to education', *Mind, Brain and Education*, vol. 1, pp. 3–10.

Ingvarson, L, Elliott, A, Kleinhenz, E & McKenzie, P 2006, *Teacher education accreditation: a review of national and international trends and practices*, Teaching Australia, Canberra, viewed 26 February 2012, <http://research.acer.edu.au/teacher_education/1>.

Inoue, Y 2005, 'Critical thinking and diversity experiences: a connection', paper presented at the American Educational Research Association 2005 Annual Meeting, Montréal, Québec, 11–15 April.

Institute of International Education (IIE) 2011, *Open doors 2011 fast facts*, IIE, Washington, DC, viewed 26 February 2012, <http://www.iie.org/en/Research-and-Publications/~/media/Files/Corporate/Open-Doors/Fast-Facts/Fast Facts 2011.ashx>.

Jackson, ME 2010, 'Plagiarism in literature', Maria talks about avoiding and detecting plagiarism with international students, International Student Lifecycle, Higher Education Academy, York, viewed 26 February 2012, <http://www.heacademy.ac.uk/resources/detail/internationalisation/case_story_staff_maria_jackson_plagiarism>.

Janis, IL 1972, *Victims of groupthink*, Houghton Mifflin, New York.

Jaques, D & Salmon, G 2007, *Learning in groups: a handbook for face-to-face and online environments*, 4th edn, Routledge, Abingdon.

Jarvis, P (ed.) 2006, *The theory and practice of teaching*, 2nd edn, Routledge, Abingdon.

Jarvis, P, Holford, J & Griffin, C 2003, *The theory & practice of learning*, 2nd edn, Kogan Page, London.

Jenkins, A 2004, *A guide to the research evidence on teaching-research relationships*, Higher Education Academy, York, viewed 26 February 2012, <http://www.heacademy.ac.uk/assets/York/documents/ourwork/research/id383_guide_to_research_evidence_on_teaching_research_relations.pdf>.

Jenkins, A & Healey, M 2005, *Institutional strategies to link teaching and research*, Higher Education Academy, York, viewed 26 February 2012, <http://www.heacademy.ac.uk/assets/York/documents/ourwork/research/Institutional_strategies.pdf>.

Jenkins, A & Healey, M 2012, 'Research-led or research-based undergraduate curricula', in L Hunt & D Chalmers (eds), *University teaching in focus: a learning-centred approach*, ACER Press, Melbourne, pp. 128–144.

Jenkins, A, Healey, M & Zetter, R 2007, *Linking teaching and research in departments and disciplines*, Higher Education Academy, York, viewed 26 February 2012, <http://www.heacademy.ac.uk/resources/detail/ourwork/teachingandresearch/LinkingTeachingandResearch_April07>.

Jensen, E 1998, *Teaching with the brain in mind*, Association for Supervision & Curriculum development, Virginia.

JISC 2012, Fieldwork education resources collection, Higher Education Academy, York, viewed 26 February 2012, <http://openfieldwork.org.uk/api/search.php?source=collection&kw=tools%20techniques%20skills>.

Johnson, I 2010, 'Utilising the resource of cultural diversity in the English language classroom', *English Australia Journal*, vol. 26, no. 1, pp. 46–60.

Johnston, V & Westwood, J 2007, *Developing a framework for the professional development of programme leaders*, Higher Education Academy, York.

Jonassen, D 1999, 'Designing constructivist learning environments', in CM Reigeluth (ed.), *Instructional design theories and models, Volume II: a new paradigm of instructional theory*, 2nd edn, Lawrence Erlbaum Associates, Mahwah, NJ, pp. 215–239.

Jonassen, DH & Reeves, TC 1996, 'Learning with technology: using computers as cognitive tools', in DH Jonassen (ed.), *Handbook of research on educational communications and technology*, Macmillan, New York, pp. 693–719.

Joughin, G 2010, *A short guide to oral assessment*, Leeds Met Press, Leeds.

Kelley, CA & Bridges, C 2005, 'Introducing professional and career development skills in the marketing curriculum', *Journal of Marketing Education*, vol. 27, no. 3, pp. 212–219.

Kember, D 1997, 'A reconceptualisation of the research into university academics' conceptions of teaching', *Learning and Instruction*, vol. 7, no. 3, pp. 255–275.

Kember, D, Ho, A & Hong, C 2010, 'Initial motivational orientation of students enrolling in undergraduate degrees', *Studies in Higher Education*, vol. 35, no. 3, pp. 263–276.

Kember, D & McNaught, C 2007, *Enhancing university teaching: lessons from research into award-winning teachers*, Routledge, London.

Kift, S 2009, *Articulating a transition pedagogy to scaffold and to enhance the first year student learning experience in Australian higher education*, Australian Learning and Teaching Council, Sydney, viewed 26 February 2006, <http://www.olt.gov.au/resources/good-practice>.

Kift, S & Israel, M, 2011, *Learning and teaching academic standards for law*, Australian Learning and Teaching Council, Sydney, viewed 26 February 2006, <http://www.olt.gov.au/resource-learning-and-teaching-academic-standards-resources-law-2011>.

Kim, B & Reeves, TC 2007, 'Reframing research on learning with technology: in search of the meaning of cognitive tools', *Instructional Science*, vol. 35, no. 3, pp. 207–256.

Kincheloe, J & Steinberg, S 2008, 'Indigenous knowledges in education: complexities, dangers and profound benefits', in N Denzin, Y Lincoln & L Smith (eds), *Handbook of critical and Indigenous methodologies*, SAGE Publications, Thousand Oaks, CA, pp. 135–156.

Kinchin, IM, Cabot, LB & Hay, DB 2010, 'Visualizing expertise: revealing the nature of a threshold concept in the development of an authentic pedagogy for clinical education', in JHF Meyer, R Land, C Baillie (eds), *Threshold concepts within the disciplines*, Sense Publishers, Rotterdam.

Kinchin, IM & Hay, DB 2000, 'How a qualitative approach to concept map analysis can be used to aid learning by illustrating patterns of conceptual development', *Educational Research*, vol. 42, no. 1, pp. 43–57.

King's Learning Institute 2010, *Creating a 21st century curriculum: the King's-Warwick Project*, King's Learning Institute, King's College, London.

Kingston E & Forland, H 2008, 'Bridging the gap in expectations between international students and academic staff', *Journal of Studies in International Education*, vol. 12, no. 2, pp. 204–221.

Kirschner, PA, Sweller, J & Clark, RE 2006, 'Why minimal guidance during instruction does not work: an analysis of the failure of constructivist, discovery, problem-based, experiential, and inquiry based teaching', *Educational Psychologist*, vol. 41, pp. 75–86.

Knapper, C & Cranton, P (eds) 2001, *Fresh approaches to the evaluation of teaching*, Wiley, New York.

Knight, P & Trowler P 2000, 'Department-level cultures and the improvement of learning and teaching', *Studies in Higher Education*, vol. 25, no. 1, pp. 69–83.

Knight, P & Trowler, P 2001, *Departmental leadership in higher education*, Society for Research into Higher Education and Open University Press, Buckingham.

Knight, P & Yorke, M 2004, 'Self-theories: some implications for teaching & learning in higher education', *Studies in Higher Education*, vol. 29, no. 1, pp. 25–38.

Knight, PT 2002a, *Being a teacher in higher education*, Society for Research into Higher Education and Open University Press, Buckingham.

Knight, PT 2002b, *Small scale research: pragmatic inquiry in social science and the caring professions*, SAGE Publications, London.

Knights, M 2011, *Politics, literature and ideas in Stuart England*, Department of History, University of Warwick, viewed 28 January 2012, <http://www2.warwick.ac.uk/fac/arts/history/undergraduate/modules/stuartengland>.

Knowles, MS, Holton III, EF & Aswansu, R 2005, *The adult learner*, 6th edn, Butterworth Heinemann, London.

Köhler, W 1925, *The mentality of apes*, Harcourt and Brace, New York.

Koizumi, H 2004, 'The concept of developing the brain: a new science for learning and education', *Brain and Development*, vol. 26, pp. 434–441.

Kolb, D 1984, *Experiential learning, experience as the source of learning and development*, Prentice Hall, Englewood Cliffs, NJ.

Kolmos, A 2002, 'Facilitating change to a problem-based model', *International Journal for Academic Development*, vol. 7, no. 1, pp. 63–74.

Koschmann, TD, Myers, AC, Feltovich, PJ & Barrows, HS 1994, 'Using technology to assist in realizing effective learning and instruction: a principled approach to the use of computers in collaborative learning', *Journal of Learning Science*, vol. 3, no. 3, pp. 225–262.

Krause, K 2009, 'Interpreting changing academic roles and identities in higher education', in M Tight (ed.), *International handbook of higher education*, Routledge, London, pp. 413–426.

Krause, K 2011a, 'Transforming the learning experience to engage students', in L Thomas & M Tight (eds), *Institutional transformation to engage a diverse student body*, Emerald, Bingley, pp. 199–212.

Krause, K 2011b, 'Using student survey data to shape academic priorities and approaches', in L Stefani (ed.), *Evaluating the effectiveness of academic development*, Routledge, New York, pp. 59–72.

Krause, K 2012, 'A quality approach to university teaching', in L Hunt & D Chalmers (eds), *University teaching in focus: a learning-centred approach*, ACER Press, Melbourne, pp. 235–252.

Krause, K, Kilsby, E & Grimmer, C 2008, *Documenting evidence of good teaching practice: a good practice guide*, Griffith University, Mt Gravatt, viewed 26 February 2012, <http://www.griffith.edu.au/gihe/resources-support/good-practice-guides>.

Krause, K, Scott, G, Campbell, S, Carroll, M, Deane, E, Pattison, P, Probert, B, Sachs, J, Vaughan, S 2011, *A sector-wide model for assuring final year subject and program achievement standards through inter-university moderation*, Griffith University, Mt Gravatt, viewed 26 February 2012, <http://www.griffith.edu.au/gihe/research>.

Kreber, C (ed.) 2001, *Scholarship revisited: perspectives on the scholarship of teaching*, Jossey-Bass, San Francisco.

Kreber, C 2002a, 'Controversy and consensus on the scholarship of teaching', *Studies in Higher Education*, vol. 27, pp. 151–167.

Kreber, C 2002b, 'Teaching excellence, teaching expertise, and the scholarship of teaching', *Innovative Higher Education*, vol. 27, pp. 5–23.

Kreber, C (ed.) 2009, *The university and its disciplines: teaching and learning within and beyond university boundaries*, Routledge, New York and London.

Kreber, C & Cranton, PA 2000, 'Exploring the scholarship of teaching', *Journal of Higher Education*, vol. 71, pp. 476–495.

Kuh, GD 2003, 'What we're learning about student engagement from NSSE', *Change*, vol. 35, no. 2, pp. 24–32.

Lamont, M 2009, *How professors think*, Harvard University Press, Cambridge.

Land, R 2012, 'Discipline-based teaching', in L Hunt & D Chalmers (eds), *University teaching in focus: a learning-centred approach*, ACER Press, Melbourne, pp 00–00.

Land, R & Gordon, G 2008, *Research teaching linkages: enhancing graduate attributes*, Report of Sector-wide Project, vols 1 and 2, Quality Assurance Agency, Glasgow, viewed 26 February 2012, <http://www.enhancementthemes.ac.uk/resources/publications/research-teaching-linkages>.

Land, R, Meyer, JHF & Smith, J (eds) 2008, *Threshold concepts within the disciplines*, Sense Publishers, Rotterdam and Taipei.

Latané, B 1981, 'The psychology of social impact', *American Psychologist*, vol. 36, pp. 343–356.

Laursen SL, Hunter, A-B, Seymour, E, Thiry, H & Melton, G 2010, *Undergraduate research in the sciences: engaging students in real science*, Jossey-Bass, San Francisco.

Lave, J & Wenger, E 1991, *Situated learning: legitimate peripheral participation*, Cambridge University Press.

Leask, B & Carroll, J 2011, 'Moving beyond "wishing and hoping": internationalisation and student experiences of inclusion and engagement', *Higher Education Research and Development*, vol. 30, no. 5, pp. 647–659.

Lee, MJW & McLoughlin, C (eds) 2010, *Web 2.0-based e-learning: applying social informatics for tertiary teaching*, Information Science Reference: Hershey, PA.

Lee, VS 2004, *Teaching and learning through inquiry: a guidebook for institutions and instructors*, Stylus Publishing, Sterling, VA.

Levy, P 2011, 'Embedding inquiry and research for knowledge-building into mainstream higher education: a UK perspective', *CUR Quarterly* vol. 32, no. 1, pp. 36–42.

Levy, P & Petrulis, R 2012, 'How do first-year university students experience inquiry and research, and what are the implications for the practice of inquiry-based learning?', *Studies in Higher Education*, vol. 37, no. 1, pp. 85–101.

Lewin, K 1951, *Field theory in social science*, Harper and Row, New York.

Light, G, Cox, R & Calkins, S 2009, *Learning and teaching in higher education: the reflective professional*, 2nd edn, SAGE Publications, London.

Liverpool John Moores University (LJMU) 2011, *The forgotten year: tackling the sophomore slump*, LJMU, Liverpool, viewed 27 February 2012, <http://secondyearexperience.ljmu.ac.uk>.

Louie, K 2005, 'Gathering cultural knowledge: useful or use with care', in J Carroll & J Ryan (eds), *Teaching international students*, Staff and Educational Development Association (SEDA), Birmingham, pp. 17–25.

Lutz, J 2009, Microhistory and the internet, University of Victoria, Canada, viewed 27 February 2012, <http://web.uvic.ca/~jlutz/courses/hist481>.

Macfarlane, B 2005, 'The disengaged academic: the retreat from citizenship', *Higher Education Quarterly*, vol. 59, no. 4, pp. 296–312.

Macfarlane, B 2011, *Intellectual leadership in higher education*, Routledge, London.

MacGregor, J, Cooper, JL, Smith, KA & Robinson, P (eds) 2000, *Strategies for energizing large classes: from small groups to learning communities*, New directions for teaching and learning, no. 81, Jossey-Bass, San Francisco.

Macquarie University 2012, Undergraduate research in Australia, Learning and Teaching Centre, Macquarie University, Sydney, viewed 27 February 2012, <www.mq.edu.au/ltc/altc/ug_research>.

Madge, C, Raghuram, P, Noxolo, P 2009, 'Engage pedagogy and responsibility: a postcolonial analysis of international students', *Geoforum*, vol. 40, pp. 34–45.

Maffie, J 2005, 'Ethnoepistemology', in J Fieser & B Dowden, *Internet encyclopedia of philosophy*, ISSN 2161-0002, viewed 27 February 2012, <http://www.iep.utm.edu/ethno-ep>.

Mak, AS, Westwood, MJ & Ishiyama, FI 1994, 'Developing role-based social competencies for career search and development in Hong Kong immigrants', *Journal of Career Development*, vol. 20, no. 3, pp. 171–183.

Mak, AS, Westwood, M, Barker, M & Ishiyama, FI 1998, 'Developing sociocultural competencies for success among international students: the ExcelL programme', *Journal of International Education*, vol. 9, no. 1, pp. 33–38.

Marek, K 2009, 'Learning to teach online: creating a culture of support for faculty', *Journal of Education for Library and Information Science*, vol. 50, no. 4, pp. 275–292.

Marika, R, Ngurruwutthun, D & White, L 1990, *Always together, Yaka Gäna: participatory research at Yirrkala as part of the development of a Yolngu education*, Yirrkala Literature Production Centre, Yirrkala.

Markham, T, Mergendoller, J, Larmer, J & Ravitz, J 2003, *Project based learning handbook*, 2nd edn, Buck Institute for Education, Novato, CA.

Martin, PW 2003, 'Key aspects of teaching and learning in arts, humanities and social sciences', in H Fry, S Ketteridge & S Marshall (eds), *A handbook for teaching & learning in higher education*, 2nd edn, Kogan Page, London and Sterling, VA, pp. 301–323.

Martin, E, Trigwell, K, Prosser, M & Ramsden, P 2003, 'Variation in the experience of leadership of teaching in higher education', *Studies in Higher Education*, vol. 28, no. 3, pp. 247–259.

Marton, F & Säljö, R 1976, 'On qualitative differences in learning: 1. Outcome and process', *British Journal of Educational Psychology*, vol. 46, pp. 4–11.

Marton, F 2009, A threshold concepts focus to curriculum design: supporting student learning through application of variation theory, personal communication to the Steering Committee of the Australian Learning and Teaching Council Project, European Association for Research on Learning and Instruction Conference, Amsterdam, 25 August, cited in JHF Meyer, R Land & C Baillie (eds) 2010, *Threshold concepts and transformational learning*, Sense Publishers, Rotterdam and Taipei, p. xxiii.

Maslow, A 1970, *Motivation and personality*, 2nd edn, Harper & Row, New York.

Matthew, RGS & Pritchard, J 2009, 'Hard and soft — a useful way of thinking about disciplines? Reflections from engineering education on professional identities', in C Kreber (ed.), *The university and its disciplines: teaching and learning within and beyond university boundaries*, Routledge, New York and London, pp. 58–68.

Mayson, S & Schapper, J 2010, 'Talking about research-led teaching: a discourse analysis', in M Devlin, J Nagy & A Lichtenberg (eds.), *Research and development in higher education: reshaping higher education*, vol. 33, refereed papers from the 33rd Higher Education Research and Development Society of Australasia Annual International Conference,

Melbourne, pp. 471–480, viewed 27 February 2012, <http://www.herdsa.org.au/wp-content/uploads/conference/2010/papers/HERDSA2010_Mayson_S.pdf> .

McAlpine, L & Harris, R 2002, 'Evaluating teaching effectiveness and teaching improvement: a language for institutional policies and academic development practices', *International Journal of Academic Development*, vol. 7, no. 1, pp. 7–17.

McBurnie, G & Pollock, A 1998, 'Transnational education: an Australian example', *International Higher Education*, no. 11, pp. 12–14, viewed 27 February 2012, <http://www.bc.edu/content/bc/research/cihe/ihe/issues/1998.html>.

McConaghy, C 2000, *Rethinking Indigenous education: culturalism, colonialism and the politics of knowing*, Post Pressed, Flaxton.

McCune, V & Hounsell, D 2005, 'The development of students' ways of thinking and practising in three final-year biology courses', *Higher Education*, vol. 49 , no. 3, pp. 235–255.

McCutcheon, G 1988, 'Curriculum and work of teachers?' in MW Apple & L Beyer (eds), *The curriculum: problems, politics, and possibilities*, State University of New York Press, New York, pp. 191–203.

McGee, P, Carmean, C & Jafari, A (eds.) 2005, *Course management systems for learning: beyond accidental pedagogy*, Idea Group Publishing, Hershey, PA.

McKee, H 2009, From Amazon to YouTube: the impact of the internet on US cultures and communication, Miami University, Ohio, viewed 27 February 2012, <http://www.users.muohio.edu/mckeeha/h101-09>.

McLeod, A & Dziegiel, A 2011, Five steps to great collaboration, Knowledge Centre, University of Warwick, Coventry, viewed 26 February 2012, <http://www2.warwick.ac.uk/knowledge/themes/01/collaboration>.

McNay, I 1995, 'From the collegial academy to corporate enterprise: the changing cultures of universities', in T Schuller (ed.), *The changing university?*, Society for Research into Higher Education and Open University Press, Buckingham, pp. 105–115.

McWilliam, E 2008, 'Unlearning how to teach', *Innovations in Education and Teaching International*, vol. 45, no. 3, pp. 263–269.

Means, B, Toyama, Y, Murphy, R, Bakia, M & Jones, K 2009, *Evaluation of evidence-based practices in online learning: a meta-analysis and review of online learning studies*, United States Department of Education, Office of Planning, Evaluation, and Policy Development, Washington, DC, viewed 27 February 2012, <http://www2.ed.gov/rschstat/eval/tech/evidence-based-practices/finalreport.pdf>.

Mercier, OR 2007, 'Indigenous knowledge and science: a new representation of the interface between Indigenous and Euro-centric ways of knowing', *He Pukenga Korero: A Journal of Maori Studies*, vol. 8, pp. 20–28.

Mercier, OR 2011, '"Glocalising" Indigenous Knowledges for the classroom', in GJ Sefa Dei (ed.), *Indigenous philosophies and critical education: a reader*, Peter Lang Publishing, New York, pp. 299–311.

Merton, R 1968, *Social theory and social structure*, The Free Press, New York.

Meyer, JHF & Land, R 2003, 'Threshold concepts and troublesome knowledge — linkages to ways of thinking and practising' in C Rust (ed.), *Improving student learning — ten years on*, Oxford Centre for Staff and Learning Development, Oxford, pp. 412–424.

Meyer, JHF & Land, R 2005, 'Threshold concepts and troublesome knowledge: epistemological considerations and a conceptual framework for teaching and learning', *Higher Education*, vol. 49, pp. 373–388.

Meyer, JHF & Land, R (eds) 2006a, *Overcoming barriers to student understanding: threshold concepts and troublesome knowledge*, Routledge, London and New York.

Meyer, JHF & Land, R 2006b, 'Threshold concepts and troublesome knowledge: an introduction', in JHF Meyer & R Land (eds), *Overcoming barriers to student understanding: threshold concepts and troublesome knowledge*, Routledge, London, pp. 3–18.

Meyer, JHF, Land, R & Baillie, C (eds) 2010, *Threshold concepts and transformational learning*, Sense Publishing, Rotterdam and Taipei.

Mezirow, J 1991, *Transformative dimensions of adult learning*, Jossey-Bass, San Francisco.

Middendorf, J & Pace, D 2004, 'Decoding the disciplines: a model for helping students learn disciplinary ways of thinking', *New Directions for Teaching and Learning*, vol. 98, pp. 1–12.

Middlehurst, R 1993, *Leading academics*, Society for Research into Higher Education and Open University Press, Buckingham.

Middlehurst, R 1997, 'Enhancing quality', in F Coffield & B Williamson (eds.), *Repositioning higher education*, Society for Research into Higher Education and Open University Press, Buckingham.

Milgram, S 1963, 'Behavioural study of obedience', *Journal of Abnormal and Social Psychology*, vol. 67, no. 4, pp. 371–378.

Minocha, S 2009, 'Role of social software tools in education: a literature review', *Education and Training*, vol. 51, nos. 5 & 6, pp. 353–369.

Mintzberg, H 1994, *The rise and fall of strategic planning*, Free Press and Prentice-Hall, New York.

Mitchell, RK, Agle, BR & Wood, DJ 1997, 'Toward a theory of stakeholder identification and salience: defining the principle of who and what really counts', *Academy of Management Review*, vol. 22, no. 4, pp. 853–888.

Montgomery, C & McDowell, L 2009, *Assessment for learning environments: two case studies of the experience of international students*, Occasional paper 4, Northumbria Centre for Excellence in Teaching and Learning, Newcastle.

Moore, N, Fournier, E, Hardwick, SW, Healey, M, Maclachlan, J & Seeman, J 2011, 'Mapping the journey towards self-authorship in geography', *Journal of Geography in Higher Education*, vol. 35, no. 3, pp. 351–364.

Moores, J 2010, 'Manchester Metropolitan University', in Change Academy (ed.), *Change Academy Handbook*, Higher Education Academy, York.

Morgan, G 2006, *Images of organization*, 2nd edn, SAGE Publications, Thousand Oaks, CA.

Multimedia educational resource for learning and online teaching (MERLOT) 2012, California State University, Los Angeles, viewed 27 February 2012, <http://www.merlot.org>.

Nakata, M 2007, 'The cultural interface', *Australian Journal of Indigenous Education*, 36S (Supplement), pp. 7–14.

Nakata, M, Nakata, V & Chin, M 2008, 'Approaches to the academic preparation and support of Australian Indigenous students for tertiary studies', *Australian Journal of Indigenous Education*, 37S (Supplement), pp. 137–145.

National public radio (NPR) 2012, NPR RSS news feeds, NPR, Washington, DC, viewed 27 February 2012, <http://www.npr.org/rss>.

Nesdale, AR & Todd, P 1998, 'Intergroup ratio and the contact hypothesis', *Journal of Applied Social Psychology*, vol. 28, no. 13, pp. 1196–1217.

Newman, M 2003, *A pilot systematic review and meta-analysis on the effectiveness of problem based learning*, Learning and Teaching Support Network and University of Newcastle upon Tyne, viewed 27 February 2012, <www.ltsn-01.ac.uk/static/uploads/resources/pbl_report.pdf>.

Newman, M, Ambrose, K, Corner, T, Vernon, L, Quinn, S, Wallis, S & Tymms, P 2001, 'The project on the effectiveness of problem based learning (PEPBL): a field trial in continuing professional education', paper presented at the Third International Interdisciplinary Evidence-Based Policies and Indicator Systems Conference, July 2001, Durham, UK.

Newton, J 2002, 'Views from below: academics coping with quality', *Quality in Higher Education*, vol. 8, no. 1, pp. 39–61.

Newton, J 2010, 'A tale of two "qualitys": reflections on the quality revolution in higher education', *Quality in Higher Education*, vol. 16, no. 1, pp. 51–53.

Ngurruwutthun, D 1991, 'The Garma project', in R Bunbury, W Hastings, J Henry & R McTaggart (eds), *Aboriginal pedagogy: Aboriginal teachers speak out*, Deakin University Press, Melbourne, pp. 107–122.

Nichol, DJ & Macfarlane-Dick, D, 2007, 'Formative assessment and self-regulated learning: a model and seven principles of good feedback practice', *Studies in Higher Education*, vol. 31, no. 2, pp. 199–218.

Nicol, D 2009, *Transforming assessment and feedback: enhancing integration and empowerment in the first year*, The Quality Assurance Agency for Higher Education, Mansfield, UK, viewed 27 February 2012, <http://www.enhancementthemes.ac.uk/docs/publications/transforming-assessment-and-feedback.pdf>.

Nicol, D 2010, *The foundation for graduate attributes: developing self-regulation through self and peer assessment*, The Quality Assurance Agency for Higher Education, Mansfield, UK, viewed 27 February 2012, <http://www.enhancementthemes.ac.uk/docs/publications/the-foundation-for-graduate-attributes-developing-self-regulation-through-self-and-peer-assessment.pdf>.

Norman, GR & Schmidt, HG 1992, 'The psychological basis of problem-based learning: a review of the evidence', *Academic Medicine*, vol. 67, no. 9, pp. 557–565.

Norman, GR & Schmidt, HG 2000, 'Effectiveness of problem-based learning curricula: theory, practice and paper darts', *Medical Education*, vol. 32, no. 9, pp. 721–728.

Northedge, A 2003, 'Enabling participation in academic discourse', *Teaching in Higher Education*, vol. 8, no. 2, pp. 169–180.

Northedge, A 2005, 'Rethinking teaching in the context of diversity: supporting social participation in a knowledge community', in G Shaw (ed.), *Tertiary teaching and learning: dealing with diversity*, Charles Darwin University Press, Darwin.

Nursing and Midwifery Board of Australia 2011, Registration standards, Nursing and Midwifery Board of Australia, Melbourne, viewed 10 August 2011, <http://www.nursingmidwiferyboard.gov.au/Registration-Standards.aspx>.

Oblinger, D & Oblinger, J (eds) 2005, *Educating the net gen*, EDUCAUSE, Washington, DC.

Oh, E 2011, Collaborative group work in an online learning environment: a design research study, dissertation, Department of Educational Psychology and Instructional Technology, University of Georgia, Athens, GA.

Oliver, B 2011, *Assuring graduate outcomes*, Australian Learning and Teaching Council, Sydney, viewed 27 February 2012, <http://www.olt.gov.au/resource-assuring-graduate-outcomes-curtin-2011>.

Oosterhof, A, Conrad, R & Ely, D (eds) 2008, *Assessing learners online*, Prentice Hall, New York.

Orey, M 2002, 'Emerging perspectives on teaching, learning and technology: an e-book', in M Driscoll & TC Reeves (eds), *E-Learn 2002 World Conference on E-Learning in Corporate, Government, Healthcare & Higher Education Proceedings*, Association for the Advancement of Computers in Education, Chesapeake, VA, pp. 2694–2695.

Organisation for Economic Co-operation and Development (OECD) 1999, *Quality and internationalisation in higher education*, OECD, Paris.

Organisation for Economic Co-operation and Development (OECD) 2001, Glossary of statistical terms, OECD, Paris, viewed 27 February 2012, <http://stats.oecd.org/glossary/detail.asp?ID=1052>.

Organisation for Economic Co-operation and Development (OECD) 2007, *Understanding the brain: the birth of a learning science*, Centre for Educational Research and Innovation, OECD, Paris.

Organisation for Economic Co-operation and Development (OECD) 2010a, *Education today 2010*, OECD, Paris, viewed 27 February 2012, http://www.oecd.org/document/10/0,3746,en_2649_35845581_45909898_1_1_1_1,00.html.

Organisation for Economic Co-operation and Development (OECD) 2010b, *International migration outlook*, OECD, Paris, viewed 27 February 2012, <http://www.oecd.org/dataoecd/12/9/45612617.pdf>.

Organisation for Economic Co-operation and Development (OECD) 2011a, *Education at a Glance 2011: OECD Indicators*, OECD, Paris, viewed 27 February 2012, <http://dx.doi.org/10.1787/eag-2011-en>.

Organisation for Economic Co-operation and Development (OECD) 2011b, *Testing student and university performance globally: OECD's AHELO*, OECD, Paris, viewed 27 February 2012, <http://www.oecd.org/document/22/0,3746,en_2649_35961291_40624662_1_1_1_1,00.html>.

Osborne, C, Davies, J & Garnett, J 1998, 'Guiding the student to the centre of the stakeholder curriculum', in J Stephenson & M Yorke (eds), *Capability and quality in higher education*, Kogan Page, London.

Page, S & Asmar, C 2008, 'Beneath the teaching iceberg: exposing the hidden support dimensions of Indigenous academic work', *Australian Journal of Indigenous Education*, 37S (Supplement), pp. 109–117.

Pajares, F 1996, 'Self-efficacy beliefs in academic settings', *Review of Educational Research*, vol. 66, pp. 543–578.

Palloff, RM & Pratt, K 2005, *Collaborating online: learning together in community*, Jossey-Bass, San Francisco.

Palmer, JA 2001, *Fifty major thinkers on education: from Confucius to Dewey*, Routledge, London.

Papert, S 1999, 'Child psychologist Jean Piaget', *Time Magazine*, vol. 153, no. 12, pp. 105–108.

Pascarella, ET & Terenzini, PT 2005, *How college affects students: a third decade of research*, vol. 2, Jossey-Bass, San Francisco.

Pascarella, ET, Palmer, B, Moye, M & Pierson, CT 2001, 'Do diversity experiences influence the development of critical thinking?', *Journal of College Student Development*, vol. 42, no. 3, pp. 257–271.

Pavlov, IP 1927, *Conditioned reflexes*, translated by GV Anrep, Oxford University Press, London.

Perkins, D 2006, 'Constructivism and troublesome knowledge', in JHF Meyer & R Land (eds), *Overcoming barriers to student understanding: threshold concepts and troublesome knowledge*, Routledge, London and New York, pp. 33–47.

Perrenet, JC, Bouhuijs, PA & Smits, JG 2000, 'The suitability of problem-based learning for engineering education: theory and practice', *Teaching in Higher Education*, vol. 5, no. 3, pp. 345–358.

Perry, WG 1970, *Forms of intellectual and ethical development*, Holt Reinhardt and Winston, New York.

Phillips, G 2004, *CDAMS Indigenous Health Curriculum Framework*, Committee of Deans of Australian Medical Schools, LIME Network, Melbourne, viewed 27 February 2012, <http://www.limenetwork.net.au/content/curriculum-framework>.

Piaget, J 1952, *The origins of intelligence in children*, International University Press, New York [originally published 1936].

Piaget, J 1970, 'Piaget's theory', in PH Mussen (ed.), *Carmichael's manual of child psychology*, 3rd edn, vol. 1, Wiley & Sons, New York.

Polanyi, M 1966, *The tacit dimension*, Routledge & Kegan Paul, London.

Polaschek, N 1998, 'Cultural safety: a new concept in nursing people of different ethnicities', *Journal of Advanced Nursing*, vol. 27, pp. 452–457.

Poole, G 2009, 'Academic disciplines: home or barricades?', in C Kreber (ed.), *The university and its disciplines: teaching and learning within and beyond university boundaries*, Routledge, New York and London, pp. 50–57.

Portwood, D 2000, 'An intellectual case for work based learning as a subject', in D Portwood & C Costley, *Work based learning and the university: new perspectives and practices*, paper 109, Staff and Educational Development Association (SEDA), Birmingham.

Potter, MK & Kustra, E 2011, 'The relationship between scholarly teaching and SoTL: models, distinctions and clarifications', *International Journal for the Scholarship of Teaching and Learning*, vol. 5, no. 1, pp. 1–18, viewed 27 February 2012, <http://academics.georgiasouthern.edu/ijsotl/v5n1/essays_about_sotl/PotterKustra/index.html>.

Prensky, M 2010, *Teaching digital natives: partnering for real learning*, Corwin, Thousand Oaks, CA.

Prosser, M 2008, 'The scholarship of teaching and learning: what is it? A personal view', *International Journal for the Scholarship of Teaching and Learning*, vol. 2, no. 2, pp. 1–4, viewed 27 February 2012, <http://academics.georgiasouthern.edu/ijsotl/v2n2/invited_essays/_Prosser/index.htm>.

Prosser, M, Martin, E, Trigwell, K & Ramsden, P 2008, 'University academics' experiences of research and its relationship to their experience of teaching', *Instructional Science*, no. 36, pp. 3–16.

Prosser, M & Trigwell, K 1999, *Understanding learning and teaching: the experience in higher education*, Society for Research into Higher Education and Open University Press, Buckingham.

Prosser M, Trigwell K, Hazel E, & Gallagher P 1994, 'Students' experiences of teaching and learning at the topic level', *Research and development in higher education*, vol. 16, papers from the 16th Higher Education Research and Development Society of Australasia Annual International Conference, pp. 471–480.

Prosser, M, Trigwell, K & Taylor, P 1994, 'A phenomenographic study of academics' conceptions of science learning and teaching', *Learning and Instruction*, vol. 4, pp. 217–231.

Quality Assurance Agency 2011, *Assuring standards and quality*, Quality Assuarance Agency for Higher Education, Gloucester, viewed 27 February 2012, <http://www.qaa.ac.uk/AssuringStandardsAndQuality>.

Quinn, J, 2006, 'Mass participation but no curriculum transformation: the hidden issue in the access to higher education debate', in D Jary & R Jones (eds), *Perspectives and practice in widening participation in the social sciences*, Centre for Sociology, Anthropology and Politics, Birmingham.

Race, P 2006, *The lecturer's toolkit: a resource for developing assessment, learning and teaching*, 3rd edn, Routledge, London.

Race, P 2010, *Making learning happen*, 2nd edn, SAGE Publications, London.

Ramachandran, V 2010, Gender issues in higher education, United Nations Educational, Scientific and Cultural Organization (UNESCO), Bangkok, viewed 27 February 2012, <http://unesdoc.unesco.org/images/0018/001898/189825e.pdf>.

Ramsden, P 1998, *Learning to lead in higher education*, Routledge, London.

Ramsden, P 2003, *Learning to teach in higher education*, 2nd edn, RoutledgeFalmer, London.

Rangachari, PK 2002, 'The TRIPSE: a process-oriented evaluation for problem-based learning courses in basic sciences', *Biochemistry and Molecular Biology Education*, vol. 30, no. 1, pp. 57–60.

Rasmussen, L 2001, *Towards reconciliation in Aboriginal health: initiatives for teaching medical students about Aboriginal issues*, The VicHealth Koori Health Research and Community Development Unit, The University of Melbourne.

Reconciliation Australia 2012, Reconciliation Australia, Canberra, viewed 27 February 2012, <http://www.reconciliation.org.au>.

Reddy, M 1979, 'The conduit metaphor – a case of frame conflict in our language about language', in A Ortony (ed.), *Metaphor and thought*, Cambridge University Press, pp. 284–324.

Reeves, TC 2006, 'How do you know they are learning? The importance of alignment in higher education', *International Journal of Learning Technology*, vol. 2, no. 4, pp. 294–309.

Reeves, TC & Hedberg, JG 2003, *Interactive learning systems evaluation*, Educational Technology Publications, Englewood Cliffs, NJ.

Reeves, TC & Oh, E 2007, 'Generation differences and educational technology research', in JM Spector, MD Merrill, JJD van Merriënboer, & M Driscoll (eds), *Handbook of research on educational communications and technology*, Lawrence Erlbaum Associates, Mahwah, NJ, pp. 295–303.

Reeves, TC & Reeves, PM 2012, 'Designing online and blended learning', in L Hunt & D Chalmers (eds), *University teaching in focus: a learning-centred approach*, ACER Press, Melbourne, pp. 112–127.

Reid, A 2001, 'Variation in the ways that instrumental and vocal students experience learning music', *Music Education Research*, vol. 3, no. 1, pp. 25–40.

Revans, R 1980, *Action learning: new techniques for management*, Blond & Briggs, London.

Ribeiro, LR & Mizukami, MDG 2005, 'Problem-based learning: a student evaluation of an implementation in postgraduate engineering education', *European Journal of Engineering Education*, vol. 30, no. 1, pp. 137–149.

Rice, RE 1992, 'Towards a broader conception of scholarship: the American context', in T Whiston & R Geiger (eds), *Research and higher education: the United Kingdom and the United States*, Society for Research into Higher Education and Open University Press, Buckingham, pp. 117–129.

Rideout, E & Carpio, B 2001, 'The problem-based learning model of nursing education', in E Rideout (ed.), *Transforming nursing education through problem based learning*, Jones and Bartlett, Sudbury, pp. 21–45.

Riding, RJ & Cheema, I 1991, 'Cognitive styles: an overview and integration', *Educational Psychology*, vol. 11, pp. 193–215.

Roberts, ST 2004, *Online collaborative learning: theory and practice*, Information Science, Hershey, PA.

Rochecouste J, Oliver R, Mulligan D & Davies M 2010, *Addressing the ongoing English language growth of international students*, Australian Learning and Teacing Council, Sydney, viewed 27 February 2012, <http://www.olt.gov.au/project-addressing-ongoing-english-monash-2007>.

Rogers, C 1983, *Freedom to learn for the 80s*, CE Merrill, Columbus, Ohio.

Ross, PM, Taylor, CE, Hughes, C, Kofod, M, Whitaker, N, Lutze-Mann, L & Tzioumis, V 2010, 'Threshold concepts: challenging the way we think, teach and learn in biology', in JHF Meyer, R Land & C Baillie (eds), *Threshold concepts and transformational learning*, Sense Publishers, Rotterdam and Taipei.

Rotter, JB 1966, 'Generalized expectancies of internal versus external control of reinforcements', *Psychological Monographs*, vol. 80, pp. 1–28.

Rowland, S 2000, *The enquiring university teacher*, Society for Research into Higher Education and Open University Press, Buckingham.

Ruth, A & Houghton L, 2009, 'The wiki way of learning', *Australasian Journal of Educational Technology*, vol. 25, no. 2, pp. 138–152, viewed 27 February 2012, <http://www.ascilite.org.au/ajet/ajet25/ruth.html>.

Ryan, J 2005, 'Improving teaching and learning practices for international students: implications for curriculum, pedagogy and assessment', in J Carroll & J Ryan (eds), *Teaching international students*, Staff and Educational Development Association (SEDA), Birmingham, pp. 92–100.

Sadler, DR 1989, 'Formative assessment and the design of instructional systems', *Instructional Science*, vol. 18, pp. 119–144.

Sambell, K, McDowell, L & Brown, S 1997, '"But is it fair?" An exploratory study of student perceptions of the consequent validity of assessment', *Studies in Educational Evaluation*, vol. 23, no. 4, pp. 349–371.

Sawyer, RK 2006, *The Cambridge handbook of the learning sciences*, Cambridge University Press.

Schiefele, AK & Winteler, A 1992, 'Interest as a predictor of academic achievement: a meta-analysis of research', in KA Renninger, S Hidi & A Krapp (eds), *The role of interest in learning and development*, Lawrence Erlbaum, New York.

Schmidt, HK, Loyens, SMM, van Gog, T & Paas, F 2007, 'Human cognitive architecture: commentary on Kirschner, Sweller & Clark (2006)', *Educational Psychologist*, vol. 42, no. 2, pp. 91–97.

Schön, D 1983, *The reflective practitioner: how professionals think in action*, Temple Smith, London.

Schön, D 1987, *Educating the reflective practitioner: towards a new design for teaching and learning in the professions*, Jossey-Bass, San Francisco.

Schuell, TJ 1986, 'Cognitive conceptions of learning', *Review of Educational Research*, vol. 56, pp. 411–436.

Scott G, Coates, H & Anderson, M 2008, *Learning leaders in times of change: academic leadership capabilities for Australian higher education*, University of Western Sydney and Australian Council for Educational Research, Melbourne, viewed 27 February 2012, <http://research.acer.edu.au/higher_education/3>.

Scott, G 2005, *Accessing the student voice: using CEQuery to identify what retains students and promotes engagement in productive learning in Australian higher education. Final report*, Department of Education, Science and Training (DEST), viewed 27 February 2012, <http://www.dest.gov.au/sectors/higher_education/publications_resources/profiles/access_student_voice.htm>.

Seaman, J 2008, 'Experience, reflect, critique: the end of the "Learning Cycles" era', *Journal of Experiential Education*, vol. 31, no. 1, pp. 3–18.

Seldin, P 2006, *Evaluating faculty performance*, Anker, Bolton, MA.

Seligman, MEP & Csiksczentmihalyi, M 2000, 'Positive psychology: an introduction', *American Psychologist*, vol. 55, no. 1, pp. 5–14.

Senge, P 1990, *The fifth discipline: the art and practice of the learning organization*, Century Business, London.

Shaw, G 2005, *Tertiary teaching and learning: dealing with diversity*, Charles Darwin University Press, Darwin.

Shea, P, Li, C & Pickett, A 2006, 'A study of teaching presence and student sense of learning community in fully online and web-enhanced college courses', *Internet and Higher Education*, vol. 9, no. 3, pp. 175–190.

Shi, L 2004, 'The successors of Confucianism or a new generation? A questionnaire study on Chinese students' culture if learning English', paper presented at Responding to the Needs of the Chinese Learner conference, 16–18 July, University of Portsmouth, Hampshire.

Shulman, LS 1987, 'Knowledge and teaching: foundations of the new reform', *Harvard Educational Review*, vol. 57, pp. 1–22.

Shulman, LS 2000, 'Inventing the future', in P Hutchings (ed.), *Opening lines: approaches to the scholarship of teaching and learning*, The Carnegie Foundation for the Advancement of Teaching, Menlo Park, CA.

Shulman, LS 2004, *Teaching as community property: essays on higher education*, Jossey-Bass, San Francisco.

Shulman, LS 2005a, 'Pedagogies of uncertainty', *Liberal Education*, no. 91, pp. 18–25.

Shulman, LS 2005b, 'Signature pedagogies in the professions', *Daedalus*, vol. 134, no. 3, the American Academy of Arts and Science, pp. 52–59.

Shute, V, Ventura, M, Bauer, M & Zapata-Rivera, D 2009, 'Melding the power of serious games and embedded assessment to monitor and foster learning: flow and grow', in U Ritterfeld, M Cody & P Vorderer (eds), *Serious games: mechanisms and effects*, Routledge, New York, pp. 293–319.

Sincero, P 2006, *What is inquiry-based learning?*, Inquiry Learn, Canton, MA, viewed 27 February 2012, <http://www.inquirylearn.com/Inquirydef.htm>.

Skinner, BF 1938, *The behavior of organisms: an experimental analysis*, Appleton-Century, Oxford.

Sloan Consortium 2012, Sloan Consortium, Newburyport MA, viewed 27 February 2012, <http://sloanconsortium.org>.

Smart D, Volet S & Ang G, 2000, *Fostering social cohesion in universities: bridging the cultural divide*, Australian Government Publishing Service, Canberra.

Smith P & Rust C 2011, 'The potential of research-based learning for the creation of truly inclusive academic communities of practice', *Innovations in Education & Teaching International*, vol. 48, no. 2, pp. 115–125.

Smith, B 2011, 'Community involvement', in R Craven (ed.), *Teaching Aboriginal studies: a practical resource for primary and secondary teaching*, 2nd edn, Allen & Unwin, Crows Nest, NSW, pp. 194–209.

Smith, L 1999, *Decolonizing methodologies: research and Indigenous peoples*, Zed Books, London.

Spellings, M 2006, *A test of leadership: charting the future of U.S. higher education. A report of the commission appointed by Secretary of Education Margaret Spellings*, US Department of Education, Washington, DC, viewed 27 February 2012, <http://www.web.virginia.edu/iaas/news/spellingsreport.pdf>.

Spronken-Smith, RA & Walker, R 2010, 'Can inquiry-based learning strengthen the links between teaching and disciplinary research?', *Studies in Higher Education*, vol. 35, no. 6, pp. 723–740.

Stafford, R 2010, 'The virtual rocky shore', *Teaching and Learning Essentials Toolkit*, University of Gloucester, viewed 27 February 2012, <http://insight.glos.ac.uk/tli/resources/toolkit/wal/sustainable/Pages/vrs.aspx>.

Steinkuehler, CA, Derry, SJ, Woods, DK & Hmelo-Silver, CE 2002, 'The STEP environment for distributed problem-based learning on the world wide web', in G Stahl (ed.), *Computer support for collaborative learning: foundations for a CSCL community*, Lawrence Erlbaum Associates, Hillsdale, NJ, pp. 217–226.

Sternberg, RJ 1996, *Successful intelligence: how practical and creative intelligence determine success in life*, Simon & Schuster, New York.

Sternberg, RJ, & Grigorenko, EL 2000, *Teaching for successful intelligence: to increase student learning and achievement*, SkyLight Professional Development, Arlington Heights, IL.

Stewart, M 2012, 'Understanding learning: theories and critique', in L Hunt & D Chalmers (eds), *University teaching in focus: a learning-centred approach*, ACER Press, Melbourne, pp. 3–20.

Stokes, A, Magnier, K & Weaver, R 2011, 'What is the use of fieldwork? Conceptions of students and staff in geography and geology', *Journal of Geography in Higher Education*, vol. 35, no. 1, pp. 121–141.

Strathern, M 2008, 'Knowledge identities', in R Barnett & R Di Napoli (eds), *Changing identities in higher education: voicing perspectives*, Routledge, London and New York.

Stringer, ET 1999, *Action research*, SAGE Publications, Thousand Oaks, CA.

Studies in Australia 2010, *International students in Australia*, Hobsons, Melbourne, viewed 27 February 2012, <http://www.studiesinaustralia.com/studying-in-australia/why-study-in-australia/international-students-in-australia>.

Summers, M & Volet, S 2008, 'Students' attitudes towards culturally mixed groups on international campuses: impact of participation in diverse and non-diverse groups', *Studies in Higher Education*, vol. 33, no. 4, pp. 357–370.

Svinicki, M 2004, *Learning and motivation in the postsecondary classroom*, Anker Press, Bolton, MA.

Svinicki, M & McKeachie, WJ 2011, *McKeachie's teaching tips: strategies, research and theory for college and university teachers*, 13th edn, Wadsworth, Belmont, CA.

Swanson, D, Case, S & van der Vleuten, C 1997, 'Strategies for assessment', in D Feletti (ed.), *The challenge of problem-based learning*, St. Martin's Press, New York, pp. 269–282.

Sweller, J 1988, 'Cognitive load during problem solving: effects on learning', *Cognitive Science*, vol. 12, no. 1, pp. 257–285.

Swinglehurst, D, Russell, J & Greenhalgh, T 2008, 'Peer observation of teaching in the online environment: an action research approach', *Journal of Computer Assisted Learning*, vol. 24, issue 5, pp. 383–393.

Tallent-Runnels, MK, Thomas, JA, Lan, WY, Cooper, S, Ahern, TC, Shaw, SM & Xiaoming, L 2006, 'Teaching courses online: a review of the research', *Review of Educational Research*, vol. 76, no. 1, pp. 93–135.

Taylor, PC & Geden, JV 2008, 'Reinvented Labs', in S Bates, M Aliotta, B Sinclair & A Kohnle (eds), *Research-teaching linkages: enhancing graduate attributes: physical sciences*, Quality Assurance Agency for Higher Education, Glasgow, Scotland, pp. 29–33, viewed 10 February 2012, <http://www.enhancementthemes.ac.uk/enhancement-themes/completed-enhancement-themes/research-teaching-linkages>.

Taylor, SF, Stern, ER & Gehring, WJ 2007, 'Neural changes for error monitoring: recent findings and theoretical perspectives', *The Neuroscientist*, vol. 13, no. 2, pp. 160–172.

Teaching–Research Nexus: a guide for academics and policy-makers in higher education 2008, Australian Learning and Teaching Council, Sydney, viewed 7 February 2012, <www.trnexus.edu.au>.

Terenzini, PT, Cabrera, AF, Colbeck, CL, Bjorklund, SA & Parente, JM 2001, 'Racial and ethnic diversity in the classroom: does it promote student learning?', *Journal of Higher Education*, vol. 72, no. 5, pp. 509–531.

Tham, SY 2010, 'Trade in higher education services in Malaysia: key policy challenges', *Higher Education Policy*, vol. 23, pp. 99–122.

Thomas, G & Pring, R (eds) 2004, *Evidence-based practice in education*, Open University Press, Buckingham.

Thomas, J 2000, *A review of research on project-based learning*, The Autodesk Foundation, San Rafael, CA, viewed 27 February 2012, <http://www.bie.org/research/study/review_of_project_based_learning_2000>.

Thomas, M (ed.) 2011, *Digital education: opportunities for social collaboration*, Palgrave Macmillan, New York.

Thomas, T, Petocz, P, Rigby, B, Clark-Murphy, M, Daly, A, Dixon, P, Kavanagh, M, Lees, N, Leveson, L & Wood, LN 2009, 'Embedding generic skills means assessing generic skills', in J Milton, C Hall, J Lang, G Allan & M Nomikoudis (eds), *Assessment in different dimensions: proceedings of the Australian Technology Network Assessment Conference*, RMIT University, Melbourne, pp. 321–330, viewed 27 February 2012, <http://emedia.rmit.edu.au/atnassessment09/sites/emedia.rmit.edu.au.atnassessment09/files/ATNA09_Conference_Proceedings.pdf#page=321>.

Thorndike, EL 1898, *Animal intelligence: an experimental study of the associative processes in animals*, (Monograph supplements no. 8 of *Psychological Review*), Macmillan, New York.

Tight, M 2003, *Researching higher education*, Society for Research into Higher Education and Open University Press, Buckingham.

Toohey, S 1996, cited in Morgan, C, Dunn, L, Parry, S, O'Reilly, M 2004, *The student assessment handbook*, RoutledgeFalmer, London.

Towler, G 1986, 'From zero to one hundred: co-action in a natural setting', *Perceptual and Motor Skills*, vol. 62, pp. 377–378.

Treleaven, L & Voola, R 2008, 'Integrating the development of graduate attributes through constructive alignment', *Journal of Marketing Education*, vol. 30, no. 7, pp. 160–173.

Trigwell, K 2012, 'Scholarship of teaching and learning', in L Hunt & D Chalmers (eds), *University teaching in focus: a learning-centred approach*, ACER Press, Melbourne, pp. 253–261.

Trigwell, K, Martin, E, Benjamin, J & Prosser, M 2000, 'Scholarship of teaching: a model', *Higher Education Research and Development*, vol. 19, pp. 155–168.

Trigwell, K & Shale, S 2004, 'Student learning and the scholarship of university teaching', *Studies in Higher Education*, vol. 29, pp. 523–536.

Tront, JG 2007, 'Facilitating pedagogical practices through a large-scale tablet PC deployment', *Computer*, vol. 40, no. 9, pp. 62–68.

Trowler, P, Saunders, M & Knight, P 2003, *Change thinking, change practices: a guide to change for heads of department, subject centres and others who work middleout.* Report for the Learning and Teaching Support Network Generic Centre, York, viewed 27 February 2012, <http://www.heacademy.ac.uk/assets/documents/resources/database/id262_Change_Thinking_Change_Practices.pdf>.

Trudgett, M 2009, 'Build it and they will come: building the capacity of Indigenous units in universities to provide better support for Indigenous postgraduate students', *Australian Journal of Indigenous Education*, vol. 38, pp. 9–18.

Tufts University 2011, Visual understanding environment, Tufts University, Medford, MA, viewed 27 February 2012, <http://vue.tufts.edu>.

Umbach, PD & Kuh, GD 2006, 'Student experiences with diversity at liberal arts colleges: another claim for distinctiveness', *Journal of Higher Education*, vol. 77, no. 1, pp. 169–192.

United Kingdom Council for Overseas Student Affairs (UKCOSA) 2004, *Broadening our horizons: report of the UKCOSA survey*, UKCOSA, London.

United Kingdom Council for International Student Affairs (UKCISA) 2011, Advice for international students: immigration including visas, UKCISA, London, viewed 27 February 2012, <http://www.ukcisa.org.uk/student/immigration.php>.

United Nations Educational, Scientific and Cultural Organization (UNESCO) 2009, World Conference on Higher Education Communiqué, *The new dynamics of higher education and research for societal change and development*, UNESCO, Paris, viewed 27 February 2012, <http://www.unesco.org/fileadmin/MULTIMEDIA/HQ/ED/ED/pdf/WCHE_2009/FINAL COMMUNIQUE WCHE 2009.pdf>.

United States Geological Survey 2011, *Advanced national seismic system*, United States Department of the Interior, Washington, DC, viewed 27 February 2012, <http://earthquake.usgs.gov/monitoring/anss>.

Universities Scotland 2010, *Race equality toolkit*, Universities Scotland, Edinburgh, viewed 27 February 2012, <http://www.universities-scotland.ac.uk/raceequalitytoolkit/index.htm>.

Universities UK (UUK) 2008, *Quality and standards in UK universities: a guide to how the system works*, UUK, London.

Universities UK (UUK) 2011, External examiners, UUK, London, viewed 27 February 2012, <http://www.universitiesuk.ac.uk/PolicyAndResearch/PolicyAreas/QualityAssurance/HowTheSystemWorks/Pages/ExternalExaminers.aspx>.

University of Central Lancashire (UCLan) 2012, Flying start, UCLan, viewed 27 February 2012, <http://www.uclan.ac.uk/study/flying_start/index.php>.

University of Colorado Science Education Initiative (CU-SEI) 2009 (19 December), 'How to use clickers effectively', YouTube, 19 December, viewed 27 February 2012, <http://www.youtube.com/watch?v=z0q5gQfQmng>.

University of Deusto n.d., Tuning educational structures in Europe, Bilbao, Spain, viewed 27 February 2012, <http://www.unideusto.org/tuningeu>.

University of Gloucestershire 2012, *Rethinking final year projects and dissertations: creative honours and capstone projects*, viewed 27 February 2012, <http://insight.glos.ac.uk/tli/activities/ntf/creativehops/pages/default.aspx>.

University of Melbourne 2010, Attributes of the Melbourne graduate, viewed 27 February 2012, <http://www.unimelb.edu.au/about/attributes.html>.

University of Southern Queensland 2011a, Go Women in Engineering, Science and Technology, Toowoomba, viewed 27 February 2012, <http://www.usq.edu.au/gowest>.

University of Southern Queensland 2011b, USQ graduate qualities and skills: customisation, mapping and alignment template, Toowoomba, viewed 27 February 2012, <http://www.usq.edu.au/learnteach/topics/gradatt>.

University of Southern Queensland 2012, ENG1101 introduction to engineering problem solving, Toowoomba, viewed 10 Feburary 2012, <http://www.usq.edu.au/course/specification/2012/ENG1101-S1-2012-ONC-SPRNG.html>.

University of Southern Queensland n.d., Fleximode policy, unpublished teacher resource.

University of Sydney 2008, *Report of the Learning and Teaching Committee: academic Board meeting agenda appendix G*, 27 August, viewed 27 February 2012, <http://sydney.edu.au/ab/about/2008/2008_Aug.shtml>.

University of Sydney 2009, Scholarship Index 2009 (Reference Year 2008): criteria and evidence requirements, viewed 27 February 2012, <http://sydney.edu.au/learning/quality/si.shtml>.

University of Sydney, Institute for Teaching and Learning 2011, Introduction to mapped universities' statements of graduate attributes, University of Sydney, viewed 26 February 2012, <http://www.itl.usyd.edu.au/projects/nationalgap/resources/gamap/introduction.htm>.

University of Sydney, Institute for Teaching and Learning 2012, The SOTL performance index, University of Sydney, viewed 26 February 2012, <http://www.itl.usyd.edu.au/awards/sotl.htm>.

University of Victoria 2010, Victoria's Victoria, University of Victoria and Malaspina University College, Canada, viewed 27 February 2012, <http://www.victoriasvictoria.ca>.

University of Western Australia 2012, A guide to writing student learning outcome statements, Centre for the Advancement of Teaching and Learning, Perth, viewed 27 February 2012, <http://www.teachingandlearning.uwa.edu.au/staff/policies/outcomes/guide>.

University of Western Sydney (UWS) 2011, *UWS AUQA performance portfolio*, viewed 10 February 2012, <http://www.uws.edu.au/strategy_and_quality/sg/auqa/auqa_cycle_2>.

University of Wollongong 2006, Authentic task design, viewed 13 February 2012, <http://www.authentictasks.uow.edu.au>.

Van Seters, DA & Field, RHG 1990, 'The evolution of leadership theory', *Journal of Organizational Change Management*, vol. 3, no. 3, pp. 29–45.

Veenker, P & Cummins, G 2005, 'Diversity, lifelong learning and the knowledge society', in G Shaw (ed.), *Tertiary teaching and learning: dealing with diversity*, Charles Darwin University Press, Darwin.

Verbik, L & Lasanowski, V 2007, *International student mobility: patterns and* trends, World Education Services, New York, viewed 27 February 2012, <www.wes.org/educators/pdf/StudentMobility.pdf>.

Vernon, D & Blake, R 1993, 'Does problem-based learning work? A meta-analysis of evaluative research', *Academic Medicine*, vol. 68, pp. 550–563.

Victoria University of Wellington 2009, *Treaty of Waitangi Statute*, New Zealand, Viewed 27 February 2012, <http://policy.vuw.ac.nz/Amphora!~~policy.vuw.ac.nz~POLICY~000000000746.pdf>

Victoria University of Wellington 2011, MAOR 317 — Special topic: science and Indigenous Knowledge, New Zealand, viewed 10 February 2012, <http://www.victoria.ac.nz/maori/research/projects/atlas/maor-317>.

Volet, S & Ang, G 1998, 'Culturally mixed groups on international campuses: an opportunity for intercultural learning', *Higher Education Research and Development*, vol. 17, no. 1, pp. 5–23.

von Humboldt, W 1970, 'On the spirit and organisational framework of intellectual institutions in Berlin', *Minerva*, no. 8, pp. 242–267.

Vygotsky, LS 1978, *Mind in society: development of higher psychological processes*, Harvard University Press, Cambridge, MA [originally published in 1930].

Ward C 2001, *The impact of international students on domestic students and host institutions*, New Zealand Ministry of Education, Wellington, viewed 26 March 2012, <http:www.educationcounts.govt.nz/publications/international/the_impact_of_international_students_on_domestic_students_and_host_institutions>.

Ward, C 2006, *International students: interpersonal, institutional and community impacts*, New Zealand Ministry of Education, Wellington.

Ward, C & Kennedy, A 1999, 'The measurement of sociocultural adaptation', *International Journal of Intercultural Relations*, vol. 23, no. 4, pp. 659–677.

Ward, C, Masgoret, A-M, Newton, J & Crabbe, D, 2005, 'New Zealand students' perceptions of and interactions with international students', in C Ward (ed.), *Interactions with international students*, Centre for Applied Cross-Cultural Research, Wellington.

Weiner, A 1974, *Achievement motivation and attribution theory*, General Learning Press, Morristown, NJ.

Wenger, E 1998, *Communities of practice: learning, meaning and identity*, Cambridge University Press.

Wertheimer, M 1959, *Productive thinking*, Harper Brothers, New York.

Westwood, MJ, Mak, AS, Barker, MC & Ishiyama, FI 2000, 'Group procedures and applications for developing sociocultural competencies among immigrants', *International Journal for the Advancement of Counselling*, vol. 22, pp. 317–330.

Whitchurch, C 2011, *The rise of 'third space' professionals*, Routledge, London.

Whitelaw, P, Henderson, F, Jose, P, Defeng, L, Cuiming, G, Wenjie, S & Qinxi, L, 2010, *Investigating the efficacy of culturally specific academic literacy and academic honesty resources for Chinese students*, Victoria University, Melbourne, viewed 27 February 2012, <http://tls.vu.edu.au/altc>.

Wiggins, G & McTighe, J 1998, *Understanding by design*, Association for Supervision and Curriculum Development, Alexandria, VA.

Wiles, A, cited in interview for PBS TV program *Nova*, cited in W Byers 2007, *How mathematicians think: using ambiguity, contradiction and paradox to create mathematics*, Princeton University Press.

Willison, J 2011, *Research skill development for curriculum design and assessment*, University of Adelaide, viewed 27 February 2012, <http://www.adelaide.edu.au/clpd/rsd>.

Willinson, J & O'Reegan, K 2007, 'Commonly known, commonly not known, totally unknown: a framework for students becoming researchers', *Higher Education and Research Development*, vol. 26, no. 4, pp. 393–410.

Wilson, K 2009, *Success in first year: the impact of institutional, programmatic and personal interventions on an effective and sustainable first-year student experience*, paper presented at the First Year in Higher Education Conference, 29 June–1 July, Townsville, viewed 27 February 2012, <http://www.fyhe.com.au/past_papers/papers09/ppts/Keithia_Wilson_paper.pdf>.

Wilson, K & Lizzio, A 2011, *Facilitating commencing students' success with early assessment*, Australian Learning and Teaching Council, Sydney.

Wilson, RS, Gaft, JG, Dienst, ER, Wood, L & Bavry, JL 1975, *College professors and their impact on students*, Wiley, New York.

Woo, Y, Herrington, J, Agostinho, S & Reeves, TC 2007, 'Guidelines for implementing authentic tasks to increase meaningful interaction in web-based learning environments', *EDUCAUSE Quarterly*, vol. 30, no. 3, pp. 36–43.

Woods, DR 1997, *Problem-based learning: how to gain the most from PBL*, 2nd edn, Donald R Woods, Waterdown, Ontario.

Woods, P, Barker, M, Hibbins, R 2011, 'Tapping the benefits of multicultural group-work: an exploratory study of postgraduate management students', *International Journal of Management Education*, vol. 9, no. 2, pp. 59–70.

Worby, G, Rigney, L & Tur, S 2006, 'Where salt and fresh waters meet: reconciliation and change in education', in G Worby & L Rigney (eds), *Sharing spaces: Indigenous and non-Indigenous responses to story, country, and rights*, Australian Public Intellectual Network, pp. 418–447.

Yolngu Advisors to Australian Centre for Indigenous Knowledges in Education 2005, CDU Yolngu Studies, Charles Darwin University, Darwin, viewed 27 February 2012, <http://learnline.cdu.edu.au/yolngustudies>.

Yorke, M 1999, *Leaving early: undergraduate non-completion in higher education*, Taylor and Francis, London.

Yorke, M 2000, 'Developing a quality culture in higher education', *Tertiary Education and Management*, vol. 6, no. 1, pp. 19–36.

Yorke, M & Longden, B (eds) 2004, *Retention and student success in higher education*, Society for Research into Higher Education and Open University Press, Maidenhead.

Yorke, M, Ozga, J, Sukhnandan, L 1997, *Undergraduate non-completion in higher education in England*, Higher Education Funding Council for England (HEFCE), Bristol.

Yothu Yindi Foundation 2006, *What is Garma?*, Garma Festival, Darwin, viewed 27 February 2012, <http://www.garmafestival.com.au/aboutgarma.htm>.

Zamorski, B 2000, *Research-led teaching and learning in higher education*, Centre for Applied Research in Education, University of East Anglia, Norwich.

Zepke, N & Leach, L 2005, 'Integration and adaption: approaches to the student retention and achievement puzzle', *Active Learning in Higher Education*, vol. 6, pp. 46–59.

Zhang, J & Norman, DA 1994, 'Representations in distributed cognitive tasks', *Cognitive Science*, vol. 18, pp. 87–122.

INDEX